James Parkes.
1929

THE GENESIS OF THE SOCIAL GOSPEL

THE GENESIS OF THE SOCIAL GOSPEL

THE MEANING OF THE IDEALS OF JESUS IN THE LIGHT OF THEIR ANTECEDENTS

by

CHESTER CHARLTON McCOWN

Professor of New Testament Literature in Pacific School of Religion

NEW YORK & LONDON

ALFRED · A · KNOPF

1929

TO

H. D. M.

T. D. M.

D. E. M.

D. B. M.

IN RECOGNITION
OF INVALUABLE
ASSISTANCE AND
ENCOURAGEMENT

PREFACE

The value of history is said to lie in its explanations of how things came to be as they are. Usually we can understand what is only when we know how it came to be what it is. One of the most influential factors in modern civilization is Christianity. What it is, and how it came to be what it is, must always be one of the most interesting and important questions of history. The study here presented is an attempt at a partial answer to this often discussed question. It essays to discover the origin and character of the social ideals which, as all will agree, have played a large part in the development of historical Christianity and of modern western civilization. It seeks to do so by applying to the study of Christian origins a method of approach that has been too little used.

The center and soul of Christianity are to be found in the life and teachings of Jesus. The significance of his attitudes on matters of morality and religion is widely acknowledged. In order to learn what the intention of Jesus was with regard to society, and, indeed, in order to discover whether he had a social purpose and outlook, it is necessary to consider, not so much his views on the relations of individuals within their groups, as his conceptions of the economic and political structure of the social organization in general—conceptions not directly stated, but implied in his recorded words and actions. This study has been restricted in the main to conceptions of justice and righteousness in the relations of the social classes, the rich and the poor, the rulers and the ruled. Otherwise the limits of the writer's endurance and the reader's patience would have been sadly exceeded. Ideals on these points, however, may legitimately be regarded as fundamental and characteristic.

In attempting to interpret these basic Christian ideas it is necessary to undertake the survey of a larger field than has usually been included in the historical background of Jesus' life. The fundamental principle of this study, which gives it whatever originality it may possess, is the thesis, now widely accepted, that Judaism in the days of Jesus represented, not the independent evolution of an isolated national group, but a syncretism of all the ancient civilizations which centered about the eastern end of the Mediterranean Sea. In the light of this thesis I have tried to trace the development of the social ideals of the Hebrews and the Jews thruout their history. It has been necessary, therefore, to describe the relevant social ideals of all of the peoples who were neighbors to the Hebrews, especially the Sumerians, Babylonians, Assyrians, Persians, and Egyptians, to whom the Hebrews seem to have owed most, and then to indicate how the peculiar course of Hebrew-Jewish history modified the ideas which the Israelites held in common with their neighbors, and how their varied national experiences prepared them to make their unique contribution to the religious and social thinking of western civilization. Finally, in the light of the new points of view thus won, I have attempted to discover the attitudes and ideals of Jesus. The reason for the exclusion of Greek social thinking is more fully explained in its proper place, in Chapter IV, on "Israel's Spiritual Ancestry." The influence of Hellenism upon the development of nascent Christianity after the death of Jesus was decisive. But that is a different matter, which I hope to discuss in another volume.

So far as is possible for one not professionally trained as such, I have approached the problems here discussed from the standpoint of the sociologist, with the use of all of the "new aids to history." Adding weight to the environmental approach of Taine and the social and evolutionary method of Spencer, the passing years have laid an indispensable emphasis on the functional and genetic study of social institutions and human ideas, while literary and archeological studies have enriched the world with materials almost beyond comprehension. Such a task as that here attempted must, therefore, become a study in the diffusion of cultures and the evolution of society in one particular aspect. The question of method is discussed in Chapter I, Section VI, which presents the scientific *credo* of the work.

Some will object to the application of such a method to the study of the messianic idea. Discussions of Jewish and Christian messianism long moved in a vicious circle. An official theological conception of Jesus' messiahship was used as the touchstone by which to test all related ideas. The unique, divine origin of Christianity was held to require the isolation of the beginnings of Christianity from the rest of history, as if God were practically unrelated to the world which he had made. Jesus was interpreted in the light of medieval and modern dogmatics. The colors for his portrait were taken from the minds of his, often decadent, successors, not of his contemporaries and predecessors. Fortunately this procedure is now generally discredited in theory, if not altogether in practice. The messianic idea is here regarded as an element in a "culture complex" from which it cannot be separated if it is to be appreciated and understood. It is for the reader to decide which is the truer and more rewarding approach to the problem of the interpretation of Jesus' contribution to civilization.

This book is the ultimate outgrowth of the studies made for an earlier volume, *The Promise of his Coming,* which was an attempt at a genetic interpretation of the idea of the Second Coming, and in part it develops views already expressed in that work. However, there were so many points, particularly in connection with the social attitudes of Jesus, on which there was great difference of opinion and prevailing uncertainty that further study seemed necessary in order to determine the basis for the practical application of Christian ideals to the insistent problems of modern civilization. The recrudescence of millennial expectations during and after the war and the later increase of social and political cynicism, the spread of half anti-social mysticism on the one hand, and of thorogoing eschatology on the other, all emphasized the need that the questions here discussed should be subjected to clearer thinking, and that seemed possible only thru wider induction based upon more extensive knowledge of ancient modes of thought. So far as possible, preconceived prejudices and interests have not been allowed consciously to determine the outcome of the investigations. As the evidence was accumulated and interpreted, the writer suffered various fluctuations of opinion. The result is the outcome not of a few months of hasty effort, but of years of study and of repeated discussions of the problems with numerous groups and individuals.

In a study such as this, in which one must use materials from many sources, originally written in various languages, and in which one must touch many fields, errors which will pain the specialist are almost inevitable. The writer can but crave indulgence from those whose peculiar provinces he has invaded, and hope that the mistakes may not be such as to invalidate the argument.

No preface, bibliography, or foot-notes can adequately acknowledge my indebtedness to others. I wish to express my obligation to Professor Wilson D. Wallis of the University of Minnesota, who read a part of the manuscript and has made many helpful suggestions, and to my father, Reverend D. S. McCown, who also read an early draft and assisted me to clearer expression at numerous points.

My gratitude is due various authors and publishers for permission freely granted to quote copyright material: to Professor James Henry Breasted and Charles Scribner's Sons for quotations from the *Development of Religion and Thought in Ancient Egypt;* to Professor Breasted and the University of Chicago Press for material from the *Ancient Records of Egypt;* to the Oxford University Press for the use of various quotations from Professor R. H. Charles' *Apocrypha and Pseudepigrapha of the Old Testament;* to Badger Clark and the Century Company for the use of part of the poem "My Father and I," which appeared originally in the *Century Magazine;* to Professor A. T. Olmstead and Charles Scribner's Sons for quotations from the *History of Assyria;* and to the University of Chicago Press and Professor

S. J. Case, the editor of the *Journal of Religion,* for permission to reprint a large part of my article, "Climate and Religion in Palestine," which appeared in that magazine.

My thanks are likewise due to members of various groups in several churches and of my own classes who at various times have patiently labored thru part of these materials with me. I will be not less grateful to readers whose criticisms may assist toward a more accurate interpretation of the Gospel records and a clearer understanding of the one great Figure whose teachings are the center of this study.

C. C. McCown

Berkeley, California
January, 1929

CONTENTS

THE GENESIS OF THE SOCIAL GOSPEL

THE GENESIS OF THE SOCIAL GOSPEL

CHAPTER I

IS THERE A SOCIAL GOSPEL?

I. WHAT DID JESUS MEAN?

ONE of the fundamental concepts of Jesus was a democratic evaluation of the individual which set personality above all other goods. To the idea of democracy men of all classes, creeds, and religions now do at least lip-service. In a large part of the world it is regarded as the means and end of social endeavor, and to an increasing number of people Jesus is its supreme exponent. But what does democracy mean, and in what sense did Jesus set it forth? On these points there is anything but unanimity of opinion.

In the reported teachings of Jesus there are three other elemental *motifs* which, if genuine, are essential to an understanding of his democracy. Yet they are all but universally ignored, or else are exorcised by exegetical *incantamenta.* They are (1) the praise of poverty and the glorification of the simple life, (2) the denunciation of wealth and autocratic authority, and (3) the hope of a regeneration of mankind, of a social restoration, or revolution, which shall do away with both poverty and wealth, and establish a righteous *régime* in which every individual may fully enjoy the blessings of a democratic life of simple labor and unostentatious happiness. These ideas seem to have been set forth by Jesus quite unequivocally when he said:

"Blessed are you poor, for the kingdom of God is yours."
"Woe to you rich, for you have had your comfort."
"Lay not up for yourselves treasures on earth."

"Seek the Father's kingdom, and these things will be given to you in addition."

"Thy kingdom come, thy will be done on earth as it is done in heaven."

What did Jesus mean by these definite, clear, but revolutionary utterances?

In the ancient and medieval church there were, roughly speaking, three answers to this question. Ecclesiastics who were either rich or dependent on the complacent charity of the rich, all too easily replied: "He meant to approve poverty of spirit, humility; he meant to condemn, not the possession of wealth, but the undue love of riches. The kingdom of God is in the heart or in heaven. If it is to be realized on earth, it can come only after God has created a new heaven and a new earth. Meanwhile, in this mundane existence, one is to make the most of his talents, serving faithfully in the place God has assigned to him. The poor must endure their want without questioning the divine order."

This slave ethic and this preoccupation with heaven to the exclusion of such worldly questions as sufficient wages and sanitary living conditions, have constituted a gospel exactly suited to agricultural Europe with its serf-like peasants and to the modern industrial state with its hordes of wage-earners. So it seemed at least to civil and ecclesiastical authorities who were concerned mainly with maintaining peace and order. It is not surprising that such religion is described as "the opiate of the people."

On the other hand, there have always been those who insisted that Jesus' teachings in regard to wealth and poverty were to be taken literally. Riches were evil; voluntary poverty was a virtue. The true followers of Christ must shun wealth as they would a deadly contagion. Only by the complete abandonment of all worldly possessions could the Christian be sure of obtaining a place in the heavenly mansions. Clement of Alexandria takes the first step toward monasticism when he says:

"It is not the poor simply, but those who have wished to become poor for righteousness' sake that he pronounces blessed—those who have refused the honors of the world in order to attain the good."[1]

So long as Christians were but an infinitesimal minority in a pagan world, without civil rights or political influence, the abandonment of the world and all its goods seemed the only possible way of realizing the true Christian ideal.

Along neither of these lines was a real social gospel possible. At best the preacher of mere servility and otherworldliness might advise paternalistic attention to the conditions under which the multitude lived, but he could say little about democratic opportunity for all and the development of stalwart, independent character as the birthright of every child of God. The gospel of poverty ignores so large an area of the group life of human beings that not even by the farthest stretch of the imagination can it be made to contain any real social elements. It is absolutely antisocial. Accordingly, there are many who deny that there is any social gospel, any salvation for society, and insist that the gospel is purely individualistic, that salvation is purely personal and spiritual.

However, there have never been wanting those who have insisted on applying Jesus' teachings to the practical problems of group life. In the earliest period of the apostolic church there was a partial and voluntary communism of consumption. Under the influence of the apostolic example and of the communistic theories that were rife in the Hellenistic world, the Church Fathers often boasted of the brotherly spirit which led Christians to share their goods. In the Middle Ages, the Reformation period, and modern times there have been numerous radical or revolutionary attempts to establish the kingdom of God on earth. Many find in Jesus' life and words merely inspiration and direction for enterprises intended to reduce the injustices and misfortunes that cloud such a multitude of lives. This type of social gospel has been the foundation of the ideals and methods of social service. Its influence has been felt far beyond the ranks of the professed followers of Jesus. Others read into his mes-

[1] *Strom.*, IV 6 (26).

sage a thorogoing program of social reconstruction. They believe that, if we would put Jesus' principles into practice, we must completely revolutionize our political and economic ideals and methods. Our social aims and institutions alike must be transformed, and, until this is done, real salvation for the individual is impossible. This constitutes a social gospel of the most radical kind.

This summary statement of the chief tendencies in the exposition of Jesus' teachings can do but scant justice to the bewildering variety of interpretations proposed and the complexity of the problems involved. Examples of suggested solutions from modern writers will serve to make the issues plain and will aid to clearer thinking on the subject.

II. SPIRITUALIZING INTERPRETATIONS

For representatives of a spiritualizing interpretation of the teachings of Jesus that touch economics one need not search long in the literature of the past generation. It may be discovered in men to whom no suspicion of ulterior motives can possibly attach. Few have written on Jesus and the Gospels with more charm and insight than Alexander Balmain Bruce. In his *Galilean Gospel* he discusses the Beatitudes at length. Luke's form, he thinks, must be original. Jesus loved striking, sententious modes of speech. Moreover, the poor in spirit, the mourners for sin, were a select band, while the poor, the hungry, the sad were always a large company, embracing probably nine-tenths of the audience to which the Sermon on the Mount was delivered. Can Jesus have had no message for these? Bruce answers that he did. He really is addressing himself to the nine-tenths. He meant to say to them that "the poor man's era was come." "He refers to the kingdom of God as a friend of the poor in our time might refer to Australia or the western prairie lands of America as a sphere in which industry might find for itself ample and hopeful scope."

Jesus, then, assures them that they, the despised and neglected, are to have a part in the kingdom that was supposed to be only for the few who thought themselves righteous. What was their part? He brought them the inspiring and vitalizing benefits of his love and sympathy. Even more than that, Jesus means, "Because ye are poor and hungry and sad, the kingdom of heaven is *nearer* to you than to others." He sought disciples among the ranks of the poor, believing that they were most likely to be found there. The results, moreover, have justified his policy. All spiritual movements find their earliest and most enthusiastic supporters among the same classes, the poor, the sorrowful, the disappointed. Yet what Jesus really offered them, according to Bruce, was only a more spiritual Stoicism. The kingdom that was promised to the poor, the hungry, the sad, is to be found in those "goods of the soul" which enable one to rise above outward circumstance, to be indifferent to privation and bereavement. "The kingdom of heaven is a synonym for the spiritual nature of man."[2] Or, as Bruce puts it elsewhere: "It is as if Jesus were addressing a church meeting and saying, 'Blessed are ye, my brethren, tho poor, . . . for in the kingdom of God, and its blessings, present and prospective, ye have ample compensation.'"[3] In other words, the spiritual blessings of the kingdom of God far outweigh all of the social and economic injustices and the consequent physical woes and moral disabilities under which the poor suffer.

William Sanday, for a long generation perhaps the outstanding English authority on the life of Jesus, presents even more clearly this spiritualizing estimate of Jesus' teaching. To summarize his views:

"The Matthean gloss (on the first Beatitude) is in any case right in sense. . . . The qualities commended ('poor in spirit,' . . . 'meek,' 'merciful,' 'pure in heart,' 'peacemakers') are all of the gentle, submissive, retiring order." This is "the Christian ideal," which "stands out in marked contrast to most other ideals of what is admirable in man." The words are addressed only to the disciples. "The type of character described bears on its face the marks of being intended for the little community of Christians." The "conditions of entrance to the community" are "clearly laid down: 'Except ye turn and become

[2] *The Galilean Gospel,* 4 ed., Cincinnati-New York, 1893, pp. 43-51.

[3] *Expositors Greek Testament,* vol. I, p. 504, on Lk. 6.20; cf. on Mt. 5.3.

as little children, ye shall in no wise enter into the kingdom of heaven.' (Mt. 18.3) . . . The entrance into the kingdom is something more than a deliberate act of the man himself, it is a self-surrender to divine influences." These influences are the kingdom of heaven. "The kingdom of God is not the theocracy of the Old Testament, nor the eschatological kingdom of the apocalypses, nor the Christian Church of the present day, or of the Middle Ages, or of the Fathers. These are phases thru which it passes; but it outgrows one after another." "The βασιλεία τοῦ θεοῦ (kingdom of God) denotes certain divine forces of laws which are at work in the world," and also "the sphere or area" where these forces or laws are operative.[4]

In the same strain Henry Churchill King speaks of the Beatitudes as representing "Jesus' conception of the basic qualities of life." He says:

"The quality, 'poor in spirit' . . . describes 'the man who has a deep sense of his spiritual deficiency and dependence upon God.' Ethically characterized, the poor in spirit are the humble, the teachable, the open-minded, and include as well the trustful. . . . This quality of humble teachableness is fitly placed first in this sketch of the ideal life, for it is the first essential of all growth into better things. It is the door of entrance to the kingdom of science, as well as to the kingdom of heaven."[5]

One may grant that this is true to fact and to the teachings of Jesus. Certainly it is the meaning of the sentence, "Except ye turn and become like children, ye shall not enter into the kingdom of heaven." Jesus bitterly denounced pride; he exalted the spirit of honest humility. But is that what he meant by the first Beatitude?

Orello Cone rightly protests that the current interpretations are not true to Jesus and his times:

"We should be on our guard against substituting our idea of the kingdom for that of Jesus and his contemporaries, and against intruding spiritual and figurative meanings where they are not required or justified by the context." He believes that "in the kingdom of God,

[4] *Outlines of the Life of Christ,* 2 ed., New York, Charles Scribner's Sons, 1912, pp. 84-87.

[5] *Ethics of Jesus,* New York, The Macmillan Company, 1912, pp. 207 f.

which was to be established upon the renewed earth, the 'good things' would not be lacking." But "the Beatitudes were addressed to the 'disciples.' . . . The unqualified 'ye the poor' (οἱ πτωχοί) can mean only the poor in worldly possessions. These are declared to be 'blessed' *as poor* and as disciples—as poor disciples."

Why does Jesus pronounce such a "blessed"? The two reasons given by Cone seem to withdraw all he has said about avoiding figurative meanings. First, Old Testament prophecy has promised the messianic blessedness to the poor and the wretched. Second, Jesus felt a strong sympathy for the poor, based upon a recognition of a special susceptibility on their part to his message. They who are his disciples are blessed in their poverty, in spite of it, and even because of it, for eventually, in the kingdom of the future, full compensation will be made for all they have suffered thru their earthly want.[6]

Is this all that Jesus meant? If so, if in the Beatitudes he had only his little group of disciples in mind, it is difficult to see how he had any message for the great mass of the poor, the sad, the hungry; certainly he had no message that applied to their poverty, their hunger, or their sorrow. He addressed himself only to the small fraction of men who, besides being poor, were sorry for sin, and hungry for righteousness. There is no direct social gospel if this be true.

The same objections may be raised against many interpretations of the term "poor," or "poor in spirit," which are based upon a study of the Old Testament use of the words *'ânî'* and *'ânâw,'* especially as they are found in the Psalms, where they are regarded as a designation of a particular party in Israel. It is described as the party "of the faithful and God-fearing Israelites, who held together, and formed an *ecclesiola in ecclesia,* as opposed to the worldly and indifferent, often also paganizing and persecuting majority."[7]

Almost all recent discussions reflect the study of these terms in their interpretations of the Beatitudes. Clyde Weber Votaw

[6] *Rich and Poor in the New Testament,* pp. 123 f.

[7] Driver, art. "Poor," in Hastings, *DB,* IV, 20.

insists that the teachings of Jesus must be interpreted in the light of the technical sense in which the phrase "the poor" is used in the Old Testament. He says:

"It designated that class, generally in humble circumstances, who lived the higher life, fixing their thought upon God and seeking his spiritual blessings, instead of living in a worldly way to accumulate property and attain social distinction and political power; they were in the world but not of it; they were the faithful and righteous ones whom God could approve and bless."

Votaw believes that, in order to avoid the inevitable misunderstanding of the Greek word for "poor," which had none of the connotations of the Hebrew word, the phrase "in spirit" was added in Matthew:

"The Beatitudes and Woes, as given in Luke, speak only of material want and misery; but that is a perversion of Jesus' teaching as recorded in Matthew. Jesus means, not that spiritual poverty is itself a good thing, but that the man who has a deep sense of his spiritual deficiency and dependence upon God will turn to him and will then receive the spiritual blessings which he needs."[8]

Willoughby C. Allen, likewise, says that the word πτωχός, "poor,"

"compressed a complicated train of Hebrew thought into a Greek word which would be misunderstood if literally interpreted." Therefore Matthew adds "in spirit" to the word "poor" in the Semitic original "the distinction would have been clear. The Lord singled out for his approval both the godly oppressed and the godly humble-minded."[9]

Alfred Plummer, in his commentaries on Matthew and Luke, in this particular, cannot be said to differ from Allen, unless perhaps he shows less of social sympathy. His conclusion is:

"Actual poverty, sorrow, and hunger are declared to be blessed (as being opportunities for the exercise of internal virtues); and this doctrine is emphasized by the corresponding woes pronounced on

[8] Art. "Sermon on the Mount," in Hastings, *DB*, V, pp. 17 f.

[9] ICC, *Matthew*, pp. 39 f.

wealth, jollity, and fulness of bread (as being sources of temptation)."[10]

He quotes, apparently with approval, Augustine's saying: "A rich man who is able to despise in himself whatsoever there is in him by which pride can be puffed up is God's poor man."[11]

Principal A. J. Grieve merely says:

"In Luke Jesus does not qualify the 'poor' (or the hungry); they are, as with the Psalmist, the righteous, and will have their innings in the next life, when the rich (wicked) suffer."

In commenting on the parable of Dives and Lazarus, he almost holds the obvious meaning of the passage. The parable is, he says,

"intended simply to illustrate the contrasted lot of poor and rich in this world and the next. . . . One quality is redressed apart from moral considerations. . . . To the rich man's deprivation is added punishment, so that we have to assume that he was not only rich but wicked."[12]

This seems to mean that the only hope of the poor is in heaven.

The veteran Jewish scholar, C. G. Montefiore, moves in a different direction. Luke, he believes, has the original form, yet,

"the poor are not merely poor in worldly goods, though that is included, but the pious, simple folk who are, more or less, oppressed, unhappy, and disappointed." On the other hand, "as M. Loisy practically admits, Jesus had a bias against the rich, 'l'idée d'un riche humble et détaché se presentait comme contradictoire.' This bias is not a merit, but a limit. It is more difficult for a rich man to be a saint than for a poor man. But it is not impossible."[13]

The same problems and the same varieties of opinion arise with regard to other sayings of Jesus. What, for example, are

[10] ICC, *Luke*, p. 179.

[11] *Exegetical Commentary on the Gospel acc. to Mt.*, New York, 1909, p. 62, from Cornelius à Lapide on Mt. 5.3.

[12] In Peake's one volume *Commentary on the Bible*, p. 729, on Lk. 6. 20-26 and p. 736, on Lk. 16.19-26.

[13] *Synoptic Gospel*, II, p. 477, quoting Loisy, *Évangiles synoptiques*, I, p. 546. The charge of bias is now withdrawn, see below, p. 337.

we to conclude as to Jesus' ideal of life from his advice to the rich and upright young man whom he found so lovable? What does it mean for us today that Jesus said to him, "Go, sell whatever you own and give it to the poor, . . . and come back and follow me"? Was it merely a piece of advice suited to his personal temptations and needs? Or does Jesus make this demand only of the few who are to be his immediate and special followers and the heralds of his gospel? The Gospel of Matthew suggests this interpretation in the phrase, "if you would be perfect." [14] Or is the abandonment of all personal possessions demanded of the Christian? Apparently the earliest disciples of Jesus in the primitive Judean Christian community so understood the spirit of their faith to teach them. Moreover, the Church Fathers long prided themselves on the community spirit which, in principle, if not in detail, exhibited a general disregard of property distinctions. More than one Christian sect has practised communism.

Yet a Protestant clergyman, one of the foremost of American interpreters of the Bible, says:

"Is this a universal call to all Christians? Is the renunciation of wealth a necessary part of the Christian norm of following Christ? This is impossible. No one has ever thought of such an interpretation. It is recognized by the greater part of the Christian world that this is a counsel of perfection, given chiefly for those who undertake the Christian ministry, especially in monastic orders." [15]

Today communism such as the early church attempted is anathema. In America advocacy of it might almost bring one under penalty of anti-syndicalism laws. Jesus' advice to the rich young ruler is not accepted by many Protestants even as a counsel of perfection. It was the necessary antidote to the love of wealth which Jesus discovered in the particular individual he was addressing. Today, however, we have found a better use of wealth than to "sell our possessions and give alms to the poor."

The giving of alms to the poor is to be reinterpreted to include

[14] Mt. 19.21, cf. Mk. 10.21.

[15] Briggs, *Ethical Teaching of Jesus,* New York, Charles Scribner's Sons, 1904, p. 235.

all of that vast multitude of charitable and beneficent enterprises which the complexity of modern society has evolved. Wealth is to be gathered and stored so that it may be used to advance the kingdom of God. This, to be sure, seems to contradict Jesus' saying: "Lay not up for yourselves treasures upon the earth;" but Jesus' teachings are to be explained in the light of the "old Semitic idea of stewardship." Wealth is something given by God to man, to be used as a temporary holding to bless others. It is quite in keeping with Christian principles for a man to get all he can and save all he can, if he also gives all he can. It is the Christian's spirit that counts; the amount of his possessions is not a matter of concern if his affections are set on things that are above, and not on things that are on the earth. Indeed, he who gives a tithe or, better, a still larger proportion of his income, for ecclesiastical purposes is promised the special favor of God himself, who will enlarge a man's possessions in proportion to his generosity. A considerable number of pastors and a still larger proportion of the bureaucratic officials in charge of the various boards which administer the benevolences of the churches are delighted to enlarge upon the duties and rewards of stewardship. It is the Christian's duty to use his possessions so that, when these fail, he shall be received into larger habitations. This obligation, they believe, is to be discharged by munificent gifts to the benevolence they administer. They have the best of exegetical basis for this application of the teachings of Jesus, for the great majority of reputable commentators on the Bible give them just this interpretation.

Adolf Harnack has said:

> "Firm resistance must be offered to all attempts to read into the Gospel any other social ideal than this: 'You are accountable to God for all the gifts you have received, and so for your possessions also; you are bound to use them in the service of your neighbor.' "[16]

For Henry Churchill King the incident of the rich young man

[16] Harnack and Herrmann, *Essays on the Social Gospel,* New York, Oxford University Press, 1907, p. 14.

teaches that Jesus fully recognized the dangers of wealth but set himself to show how they should be overcome:

"For, in his thought, wealth is both a trust and a peril. He does not doubt that wealth is good, but it is good only in its lower relative place, and as mastered by greater ends than itself,—made a servant of self-forgetful love."[17]

It is by no means a new idea. Less than two hundred years after Jesus died, Clement of Alexandria argued that it was quite all right for a convert to retain the riches he had amassed before his conversion or to remain in the wealthy home in which he had been born, for why should God deem a man worthy of temporal comfort but deprive him of eternal life? Wealth in itself could not be evil. He reasoned thus:

"Why need wealth ever have arisen out of the earth at all if it is the provider and agent of death? But if a man can keep within bonds the power that possessions bring and can be modest in mind and self-controlled, seeking God alone, living in a divine atmosphere, as a fellow-citizen of God, such an one stands in relation to the commandments as a poor man, free, unconquered, untouched by the diseases and wounds of wealth."[18]

No one can deny that "the wise administration of wealth as a social trust" is a task requiring both ability and also unselfish devotion of a high order, and that "to discharge one's obligations as a social citizen, far more of the love and power of God is required in the heart of the rich than of the man with moderate means." One gladly acknowledges also that "some of the most faithful followers of Jesus today are men and women who have inherited or amassed large fortunes which they are using devotedly and intelligently for the service of society."[19] Yet did Jesus' ideal of the kingdom of God include the conditions which now prevail when great masses of people are barely able to live, while a few are gathering and using wealth, which is largely the

[17] *Ethics of Jesus,* p. 139.

[18] *Quis Dives Salvetur,* 26.

[19] Kent, *Social Teachings of the Prophets and Jesus,* New York, 1917, p. 230.

creation of others, to bless society, not in the ways which the multitudes who produce it select, but in directions chosen by the wealthy individual according to his peculiar taste and judgment? If "the wise administration of wealth as a social trust . . . contains great potentialities for character development," [20] is it right that the vast majority should be kept forever in the tutelage of the few who have the good fortune or the ability to acquire unusual riches? It is now a question, not of the rich man's duty under our present economic organization, but of the moral character of the organization. Can it be said that our acquisitive society in any measure fulfills the ideal of Jesus?

All of these spiritualizing reinterpretations of the teachings of Jesus constitute a gospel which exactly fits the present organization of society for acquisition. Under prevailing conditions, perhaps the best that can be made of the gospel is to insist that all gifts must be used for the benefit of one's neighbor. The chief objections to this type of interpretation are (1) that it assumes divine approval for the accumulation of wealth and (2) that it regards the inequalities of wealth and poverty that now prevail as divinely ordered and capable of redress only in heaven. The first assumption obscures Jesus' frank condemnation of laying up treasures on earth and being concerned about material things. The second blunts the conscience as to the evils and injustices of society and covers up Jesus' plain sympathy for the poor and disapproval of the rich.

yes

III. SOCIAL INTERPRETATIONS

Quite a different attitude toward the teachings of Jesus is to be discovered in the minds of those who approach them from the standpoint of the nine-tenths who are poor and hungry and sad. The social teachings of Jesus have had a remarkable vogue during the nineteenth and twentieth centuries, and many books have been written on some variation of that theme or on the kingdom of God socially interpreted. For the most part these

true

[20] *Ibid.*, p. 234.

works assumed that the modern category of evolution was to be read back into the mind of Jesus. The kingdom was to be regarded as a body of divine principles, or laws, which were to find their lodgment in the heart and then gradually to work themselves out in human society during the long ages of history.

The profound influence of Jesus' life and teachings is exhibited by the remarkable array of men whose social ideals he has fundamentally affected. There were the early Christian Socialists, among whom Charles Kingsley was an outstanding figure. Frederic Denison Maurice, John Ruskin, Lamennais, Mazzini, and Richard Wagner are but a few of those whose discussions of social problems reflect the spirit of Jesus. In Germany Friedrich Naumann was long an outstanding leader in social thinking, and nearly every German theologian of distinction took part in the deliberations of the "Evangelical Social Congress," and discussed in various publications the social teachings of Jesus. As typical of later interest in England one may name Westcott, Gore, Scott Holland, and Studdert Kennedy. In America there have been successive waves of interest and repeated avalanches of literature. Washington Gladden, Josiah Strong, and Richard T. Ely were the earliest voices crying in the wilderness. They have had able coadjutors and successors in Walter Rauschenbusch, Francis Greenwood Peabody, and Harry F. Ward, not to mention a host of outstanding theologians and clergymen who have written single books on the subject. Sociologists such as Edward A. Ross, Charles A. Ellwood, and Ross L. Finney have made important contributions. Numerous pronouncements by national church conferences and by the Federal Council of Churches in America during the last twenty years have proved the deep concern which Christian men and women feel in regard to questions of social justice. In France there is an active coterie which expresses its high ideals and ardent hopes in the magazine, *Le Christianisme social*. Since the World War the interest of many Christians, especially of the younger generation, has been heightened by the gross reaction toward social conservatism which has affected society at large, and numerous books, pamphlets, and conferences are attempting to apply the principles of Jesus to the solution of current social problems.

The conclusions which all of this thinking and writing about the social teachings of Jesus have produced have ranged all the way from consistent capitalistic conservatism to thorogoing socialism and communism. Perhaps the majority have adopted spiritualizing views as to Jesus' sayings, but they have believed that the kingdom of God is to be regarded as a body of divine principles, or laws, which are to find lodgment in the heart of the believer and then gradually to work themselves out in society during the long ages of history. The fundamental criticism which applies to the major part of these efforts is that they take for granted an understanding of Jesus' principles and make no effort to determine his meaning by the indispensable methods of historical study. Hence their remarkable lack of unanimity is inevitable. Few indeed, however, have failed to point out that radical changes must be made in our present social practice if it is to conform to the ideals of Jesus.

Notwithstanding this pronounced social interest on the Christian side, socialists and communists have usually attacked the "master-class ethics" of the church. They would certainly characterize all of the spiritualizing interpretations quoted above as "master-class" perversions of the meaning of Jesus. In European countries, where the church was a state-supported institution, and, as such, was expected to kiss the hand that fed it, they have attacked not only the church but Jesus himself. Some, however, have tried to use him for purposes of propaganda.

Karl Kautzsky may serve as an illustration of the attitude of the Marxian socialist. He believes that the historical figure of Jesus is irrecoverable, but he insists on the "outspoken proletarian character" of primitive Christianity. At first Christianity was marked by bitter class hatred and by communistic organization. Strangely enough, in a short time it began to attract the rich and, therefore, to alter its character. The "revisionist Gospel" of Matthew reveals this tendency in its astute, re-editing of the Beatitudes and of the tirades against the rich. For example, instead of the terse command to the rich young ruler, "Go, sell whatever you own," Matthew suggests a counsel of perfection. "If you would be perfect, go, sell your possessions." Thus the primitive communism of the proletarian church was reinterpreted and perverted.[21]

English and American socialists and labor leaders have often been sympathetic to religion and even to the church. Many who have attacked ecclesiastical institutions have found in Jesus a teacher to whom they can swear allegiance. Referring to Judaism, many years ago John Spargo wrote of the "ethical teachings of its great prophets, such as Isaiah, Joel, Amos, and Ezekiel," as "the stern rebuke of the oppressors of the poor and downtrodden, the scathing denunciation of the despoilers of the people, the great vision of a unified world in which there should be peace." "So," he continued, "we find in Christianity the same great faith in the coming of universal peace and brotherhood, the same defense of the poor and oppressed, the same scathing rebuke of the oppressor that we find in Judaism."[22]

Coming from the church into Socialism, Bouck White tried to reinterpret the old faith in terms of the new. He prefers the Beatitudes in the "rough but fiery strength" of Luke. He discovers from the Lukan form that

> "The Carpenter's reference to the 'poor in spirit' was in order that they might get over being poor in spirit; he insisted that they were inheritors, in order to arouse them to claim their inheritance. To the hungry he promised a state of society in which they should no longer be on short rations, nor would the sorrowful then be called upon to endure the brutalities which turned their day into night."[23]

According to White, "Jesus planned to make the Jews the nucleus of a federation of the world's proletariat against the world's oppressor." Because of their central geographical position, their immemorial regard for the wrongs of the poor and for the rights of the toilers, their democracy, and their love of liberty, "deliverance was of the Jews."

[21] *The Foundations of Christianity,* New York, 1925, pp. 323-36.

[22] *The Common Sense of Socialism,* Chicago, Charles H. Kerr & Co., 1911, p. 157.

[23] *The Call of the Carpenter,* New York, Doubleday, Page & Co., 1912, p. 108.

"The new state which would be formed when the Deliverer had accomplished his work was looked forward to as the 'Kingdom of God.' It would be characterized by a reign of universal justice. Man's inhumanity to man would be done away. The disinherited classes would be restored to their own. In this reign of economic peace and fruitfulness —an Edenized earth—even the desert would share; it would rejoice and blossom as the rose." [24]

The acme of radicalism, but in a different direction, is to be found in Tolstoy. His version of the Beatitudes is significant of his Christian anarchism:

"Happy are you vagrants, for you are in the power of God: you are happy only when you are vagrants, not simply in appearance, but with your soul."

"Unfortunate are you rich, for you have received everything that you wished for, and shall receive nothing more."

"To work for God and live in the kingdom, that is to submit to him and do his will." [25]

Tolstoy's interpretation of the story of the rich young ruler is characteristic:

"Jesus reminded him that there is a commandment to love others as oneself, and that this is the Father's will. The ruler said he kept this also. Then Jesus said to him: 'That is not true; if you desire to fulfil the Father's will, you would not have property. A man cannot fulfil the will of the Father, if he has a fortune of his own which he does not give away to others. . . . Men think it impossible to live without property, but I tell you, true life is in giving up of one's own to others.'" [26]

To Tolstoy the gospel of Jesus meant anarchy, that is the abolition of war, the renunciation of force, even for the most beneficent ends, the refusal to organize the very agencies of good. Self-abnegation, absolute simplicity of life, thorogoing poverty—

[24] *Ibid.*, pp. 73-83.

[25] Quoted by Weinel and Widgery, *Jesus in the Nineteenth Century and After,* pp. 348 f.; in slightly different form in *The Gospel in Brief,* ch. IV.

[26] "The Gospel in Brief, a Recapitulation," ch. VI, in *My Confession, My Religion,* etc., New York: Crowell, 1899, p. 430; cf. pp. 349 f.

these were the demands of the faith which he preached, but lived only insofar as he could escape the chains which the society he abhorred had placed upon him. Among the common people, in their simple life of laborious toil, he found God, he found life. Thus he escaped the haunting doubts which pictured his life as a stupid and ridiculous joke played upon him by Some One in whom he did not believe. There is no more pathetic figure in history than that of the brilliant and universally respected old man dying in a Russian railway station as he tried to flee from his home to the freedom which civilization denied him.

No less sincere, tho less ruthless, have been numerous attempts of "regular" theologians and economists to discover the basic principles of the social gospel. It is not merely fanatics, dreamers, and socialists who represent Jesus as unconventional, to use the mildest possible word, in his ideas of property. Scholars who have not been unconsciously moved by a desire to save the reputation of Jesus in modern capitalistic society, and who have had a true feeling for the conditions which he faced, have been almost equally radical. White reads history so predominantly with the eyes of the imagination that his conclusions are largely vitiated. Tolstoy read into the Gospels the economic and social experiences of his nation and his class, and the religious turmoil of his own brilliant and highly emotional mind. On the other hand, the views of the veteran Christian socialist, Henry C. Vedder, are based upon careful and considered scholarship. Quoting the Beatitudes from Luke he adds:

> "This is the address of the prophet of the proletariat to toiling and hopeless masses, holding out to them the prospect of an immediate coming of the kingdom of God, in which existing iniquities and injustices will be righted. It was such words as these that gave unpardonable offense to the vested wrongs of his day and led corrupt interests to demand the death of Jesus." In Matthew, on the contrary, "the proletarian element has been spiritualized away, and the promises for this world have been given an other-worldly application."

What did Jesus actually teach? Professor Vedder believes that "critical study has established" the conclusions that "the composer of the First Gospel dealt with his problem in the obvious way, by omitting the inconvenient teachings, . . . rather than the alternative that Luke composed and added the 'Woes.' . . . There can be no reasonable doubt that we have in Luke's version, if not the exact words of Jesus, at least a much closer approximation to them than is given by Matthew." [27]

Jesus "was the great revolutionary of the ages, and he knew it," Professor Vedder maintains in an earlier work. He clearly implied the reconstitution of society as organized under the Roman Empire; and he likewise implied the reorganization of society as it exists today thruout the civilized world. Renan exaggerates little, if at all, when he says, "A great revolution, in which distinctions of rank would be dissolved, in which all authority in the world would be humiliated, was his dream." Jesus was the "great Leveler." [28]

That staunch Modernist, Alfred Loisy, represents the point of view of Jesus as follows:

"It is as impossible for any man to serve God and Mammon as for a slave to serve at the same time two masters. Mammon . . . is wealth in itself, and not merely wealth dishonestly acquired. . . . The incompatibility is absolute between the service of God and the pursuit of riches. It would be arbitrary to hold that one ought not to serve God and Mammon at the same time, although it is permitted to seek and hold wealth on condition of not being enslaved by it. It is exactly the possibility of that supposition which it is intended to exclude. In this sentence, as everywhere else, and particularly in the discourse which follows, Jesus places himself at the ideal point of view of gospel perfection such as ought to be found in those who await the coming of the kingdom of heaven and who are preparing themselves for it. Not only must they be spiritually detached from riches, they must also be actually detached. It is impossible for them to belong entirely to God if they are occupied with earthly goods." [29]

Walter Rauschenbusch says:

"It is hard to get riches with justice, to keep them with equality,

[27] *Fundamentals of Christianity,* New York, The Macmillan Co., 1922, p. 5 ff.

[28] *Socialism and the Ethics of Jesus,* New York, The Macmillan Co., 1912, p. 348.

[29] *Évangiles synoptiques,* I, pp. 614 f.

and to spend them with love. The kingdom of God means normal and wholesome human relations, and it is exceedingly hard for a rich man to be in normal relations to others, as many a man has discovered who has honestly tried. It can be done only by an act of renunciation in some form. . . . The radical teachings of Jesus are not ascetic, but revolutionary, and that distinction is fundamental. What is called Ebionitic is simply the strong democratic and social feeling which pervaded later Judaism. . . . James Russell Lowell said, 'There is dynamite enough in the New Testament, if legitimately applied, to blow all our existing institutions to atoms.'"[30]

IV. ESCHATOLOGICAL INTERPRETATIONS

If this is true, seemingly there can be no doubt that Jesus preached a social gospel of the most revolutionary kind. But behind Loisy's frank recognition of the thorogoing radicalism of Jesus' teachings on economic matters there lurks an idea which seems to sever the connection between Christian social endeavor and the words of the Master. Almost simultaneously with the rise of interest in the social gospel at the end of the last century, there developed in Germany the school of thorogoing eschatology, which has denied that Jesus intended his ethical teachings to accomplish any transformation of society.

This school has grown up thru a comparison of the teachings of Jesus and primitive Christianity with newly discovered or newly interpreted Jewish apocalypses, the revelations of Jewish dreamers who believed that the times were so evil that the present age must have reached its limit, and that God would soon intervene in miraculous power to overthrow the wicked and establish his righteous rule on earth. It cannot be denied that a careful and dispassionate study of the life and words of Jesus in the light of contemporary Jewish history shows that the liberal portrait of the Founder of Christianity, as a mere Jewish prophet or as a social reformer with modern ethical and sociological ideas, is entirely anachronistic. The eschatological school maintains the thesis that Jesus fully shared the views of the apocalyptic writers

[30] *Christianity and the Social Crisis,* New York, The Macmillan Co., pp. 77, 81, 89.

with regard to the imminent end of the present age, and that what he meant by the coming of the kingdom was the catastrophic destruction of the world or the cataclysmic ending of the present age and the supernatural inauguration of a new age in which the will of God could be done, on a reconstituted earth, as it is done in heaven. The instructions he gave to his disciples are an interim morality, merely intended to serve them until the present distress should be overpassed and to prepare them for the sunrise of the miraculous new age of peace, plenty, and righteousness.

Such a view appears to take the ground from under the social gospel as usually understood. If Jesus was merely a Jewish messianist, looking for the immediate supernatural overturning of the existing social and natural order, his ethical ideals can have little meaning for us. Loisy says:

> "Envisaging the imminent end of a social order which he had no cause to wish to save or even ameliorate, Jesus advised his own to endure all of the possible difficulties in the spirit of charity and in the hope of the promised felicity. . . . It is quite superfluous to seek in the gospel a doctrine of social and political economy or even a program of life for individual existences which must unroll themselves, according to the order of nature, in the indefinite continuation of humanity."[31]

Concurrently with the rise of the eschatological school in scientific circles has come a revival of pre-millennialism within the churches. In a different way it cuts the nerve of the Christian's social endeavor. It says, "All human schemes of reconstruction must be subsidiary to the coming of our Lord Jesus Christ."[32] Therefore there is nothing one can do but relieve distress and save souls; for soon all of our efforts to improve society will be rendered abortive by the divine Appearing. A literalistic conception of inspiration and a doctrine of an imminent Second Advent once accepted, there is no escaping this conclusion.

[31] *Évangiles synoptiques,* I, pp. 234 f.

[32] From the pre-millennial manifesto signed by G. Campbell Morgan, R. A. Torrey, and others, and widely published in 1918; see McCown, *Promise of His Coming,* p. 20.

Thorogoing eschatology has not been generally accepted on either side of the Atlantic, yet, with modifications, it is widely acknowledged as much nearer the historical facts than the older evolutionary and post-millennial conceptions of Jesus and his teachings. The pre-millennial interpretation is thoroly unhistorical and misleading. But it cannot reasonably be denied that Jesus fully expected some great and catastrophic change to come upon the world. Various recent writers have emphasized the vividness and certainty of Jesus' faith and have indicated that his ideals could be realized only in a new social order to be achieved by means of a new moral and spiritual dynamic, by a method which should be democratically internal and natural, not magically or autocratically external. The sayings of Jesus, taken at their face value, are permeated with Jewish eschatological ideas. The genuine apocalyptic element is not small. Can they be legitimately reinterpreted so as to retain a social application?

Ernst von Dobschütz has characterized Jesus' belief as "transmuted eschatology," that is, he accepted Jewish ideas as to the end of the age and the coming of the kingdom, but reinterpreted them, transfusing them with the fire of his spiritual vision and making them over into a new faith. The forms of Jewish thinking remain, the content is essentially new. The question immediately arises: What is temporary and what is of permanent validity in Jesus' teaching?

The conclusions of Ernest F. Scott may be taken as representative of the answer of the moderate school to this question. He says:

"The call for renunciation has mainly to be explained from the apocalyptic hope. A day was already near when the existing order and all that belonged to it would be dissolved, and in view of this approaching crisis it was folly for men to entangle themselves with the things of this world. . . . On this side of his thought we can indeed recognize an 'interim' element in the ethic of Jesus. He was influenced not so much by absolute considerations as by the requirements of apocalyptic theory. . . . We have to recognize that the Gospel sayings on the evil of wealth, in so far as they presuppose apocalyptic ideas, are not of permanent validity. They were meant for a definite situation, altogether unique, and are not to be generalized as rules for the Christian life." [83]

The validity and the importance of this conclusion depend upon the truth and the application of the assumed premise, that apocalyptic ideas are necessarily wrong. The particular element in apocalyptic theory to which Scott refers is the expectation of a speedy end of the present age and the immediate inauguration of the kingdom of God on earth. That this apocalyptic idea was wrong, all must admit. No such great change as the Jews and the early Christians expected came to pass. But was Jesus' attitude toward the evils of wealth, his condemnation of Mammon, based merely upon this admittedly mistaken expectation, even granting that he held it in the same form as his contemporaries, which is open to doubt? And are we, therefore, to spiritualize Jesus' sayings as to wealth and poverty *ad libitum?*

We seem to be caught on a three-horned dilemma. If the eschatology of Jesus was thoroly Jewish and thoroly catastrophic, then his teachings regarding social virtues are only an "interim morality." If, however, we accept the theory of a transmuted eschatology, the expectation of a speedy catastrophe still appears to dominate the social thought of Jesus, and we are compelled to reject his seemingly unrestrained condemnation of wealth as an apocalyptic extravagance of no permanent validity. We must, therefore, spiritualize its application. To deny the influence of current eschatology on the thinking of Jesus we must divorce him from his social *milieu* and regard him as timeless and historically unconditioned. Then we are presumably driven back to the spiritualizing method once more. And that method seems to leave us with just so much of a social gospel as accords with the social standards and economic organizations of our groups. Are there no objective criteria to which we can appeal? How can we determine whether Jesus had a social gospel, and, if he had one, what it was?

[83] *Ethical Teaching of Jesus,* New York: Macmillan, 1924, pp. 54, 90.

V. INTERPRETATIONS BASED ON THE HISTORY OF RELIGIONS

During the very period of widespread interest in the social teachings of Jesus a second school of interpreters has arisen to dispute the very existence of a social purpose in the ministry of Jesus. This denial of a direct social gospel comes from the students of the history of religions, the *religionsgeschichtliche Schule*. Nearly a quarter of a century ago, believing that the battle for the scientific, literary, and historical study of the Bible was won, James Hastings declared that the next great attack on Christianity would come from the direction of the comparative study of religions. That has proved true also of the social gospel. Not only have many students of the history of religions denied the finality and superiority of the Christian religion, but some who are sincere and effective defenders of the Christian faith have been led by their studies to deny that Jesus in any true sense was a social reformer or intended to preach a social message. Whatever social implications or effects Christianity may have had are entirely indirect and on his part unintentional. The late Ernst Troeltsch may be taken as an outstanding representative of the religio-historical school of interpreters of Christianity. He approaches the question as to the social import of the teachings of Jesus from a point of view entirely different from any hitherto mentioned. For him religion is an independent force, working in society but not a part of it. The spread and evolution of Christianity were deeply affected by the social conditions prevailing in the Roman Empire.

"But (he says) the dependence (of Christianity) upon social history is nevertheless only indirect. Only he who is able to conceive of all spiritual movements merely as the effects of social movements and particularly of all religions only as the projection of social relations into the transcendental will discover in social conditions a direct cause of the religious transformation (of the Roman Empire). But in truth all unprejudiced investigation of religion shows the relative independence of the religious idea, which possesses its own dialectic and power of development and uses exactly such conditions of the shattering of human hopes and efforts (as existed in the early Empire) to conquer by its ideas and emotions the ground thus rendered free." [34]

True to this principle, Troeltsch finds in Christianity, both as begun by Jesus and as carried forward in the early church, no social program and no direct social teaching. Jesus' teaching on the universal love of God induced a "love communism" in the primitive church and this idea has appeared again and again all thru the subsequent history of Christianity, in practice when there was need, in theoretical schemes when men attempted to formulate the ethical teachings of Jesus. Troeltsch admits:

> "A revolutionary element lay hidden in his words, without, to be sure, any revolutionary intention." Yet "the fundamental idea in Christianity is purely the salvation of the soul." [35]

The social results are only indirect.

Likewise, Christianity was not the result of social movements. Troeltsch insists that the preaching of Jesus and the formation of the new religious community was not the creation of a social movement, that is, it did not spring from a class war nor was it cut to fit a class war; and it was never directly connected with the social upheavals of ancient society. To be sure, Jesus appealed mainly to the oppressed and to the unimportant people. He regarded wealth as dangerous to the soul. He was hostile to the Jewish priestly aristocracy as well as to the ruling theology. It is true that the church in the beginning actually drew its believers mainly from the lower classes of the cities, and that the upper social strata did not begin slowly to flow into it until the second century, and even then not without sharp friction on the part of both education and wealth. But it is equally true, Troeltsch maintains, that the whole of the missionary and edificatory literature of Early Christianity, both within and without the New Testament, knows nothing of a fundamental social problem, that everywhere the problems of the soul's salvation, of monotheism, of life after death, of pure worship, of the proper organization

[34] *Die Soziallehren der christlichen Kirchen,* p. 31.
[35] *Ibid.,* pp. 50 f.

of the community, of the practical testing of believers, of strict rules of holiness, are the center of interest.

Arguing from the ideas and practices of the apostolic and post-apostolic church, Troeltsch has no difficulty in proving that Christianity was neither a class-conscious movement of the proletariat, nor a religious rehabilitation of ancient socialism. It was rather, he insists, a religious movement, and it is to be understood from the point of view, not of social, but of religious history. To be sure, any powerful religious movement must come from the lower classes. The calculating and critical spirit of the upper classes, due both to the wealth and position which they have to lose and to the education which kills enthusiasm and devotion, chains them down. It was inevitable, therefore, that Christianity should spring from the lower classes. The poor are more open and ready. "Poverty and simplicity are the soil of the truth." Granted even that the great religious about-face in antiquity is itself a sequel to its social struggles, still Christianity is not a social movement. The sense of human worthlessness and helplessness due to the failure of the efforts that had been made to create a happy world turned men to other-worldly religion in despair of earthly happiness. Now the heavenly ideal appealed to the poor more than to the rich, for the latter had more to lose, and for that reason the poor flocked into the Christian churches while the rich held aloof. But it was a religious and not a social solution of the problems of ancient society.[36]

Otto Baumgarten aptly summarizes Troeltsch's conclusions, with which he entirely agrees, as follows:

"The attitude toward the state, society, labor, and possessions . . . must be essentially indifferent, seeing in them neither permanent values nor objects of reforming activities. Any program of social renovation, any interest in the improvement of social, political, or legal institutions is wanting. Instead there stands the demand that, within the already existing institutions of the world, in the purely religious fellowship of love and the labor of self-purification, the Christian prepare himself for the coming of God's kingdom, which, however, will bring no new

[36] See Troeltsch's *Soziallehren der christlichen Kirchen,* pp. 15-58.

social order established by God, nor reform of the state, society, or the family, for these, indeed, will no longer exist. The new order is confined to the Christian community itself and is not a program for the social renovation of the people." [37]

From a thoroly scientific point of view, then, there come strong reinforcements to the lines of the pietistic and mystical interpreters of Jesus. The fundamentalistic evangelists who insist that the Christian pulpit should proclaim only the simple gospel of individual salvation without reference to social and economic problems, and all the capitalistic company who resent any application of Jesus' words to the maladjustments and injustices of acquisitive society, have a right to appeal to authority of the highest rank for their rejection of a social gospel.

Troeltsch and Baumgarten have a basis for their denial of a direct social gospel in a fundamental characteristic of Jesus' ministry. His emphasis is always first upon the inner life. He laid down no "law of the kingdom," he proposed no social program. But are there no social principles, no fundamental ethical and spiritual postulates in his thinking which affect group life and which he intended should transform it? And are not these principles and postulates primary and essential in the same degree as his emphasis on the inwardness of religion?

Adolf Harnack discovers three principles in the gospel. The first "essential feature of Christianity" is an "indifference to all earthly affairs which proceeds from the conviction that we possess life eternal." This resulted in "a twofold mental attitude which may be summed up in the words: 'Fear not, be not anxious;' and 'Love not the world, neither the things that are in the world.'" From these two types of precepts arose two tendencies, the tranquil, quietistic, and the radical, or ascetic. But the gospel embraces equally another essential principle: "Love thy neighbour as thyself," and here we have a third tendency or characteristic feature, the social, active tendency, which is as important, as truly fundamental as the other two.[38]

[37] *Bergpredigt und Kultur der Gegenwart,* Tübingen, Mohr, 1921, pp. 18 f.
[38] *Essays on the Social Gospel,* pp. 9 ff.

Troeltsch denies this. Brotherly love, he affirms, does not stand on the same level with the salvation of the soul in the thinking of Jesus and the early church.[39] It is to be noted that this denial of the social gospel is based upon the study of the early church and of the tendencies in first-century Hellenism. It approaches Jesus from the direction of the mystery religions and Hellenistic Christianity, which was already deeply influenced by the mystery cults. Troeltsch makes Jesus only what his early interpreters made him. But, for the understanding of a movement, is it not fully as important to examine its antecedents as its outcome?

Troeltsch's refusal to regard Christianity as a social movement is plainly due in part to a perfectly legitimate reaction against the extravagant claims of the Marxian school. His rejection of the materialistic interpretation of history, which had made Christianity the result of the working of purely economic forces and denied any effect to moral and religious ideas, may account for his separation of religion from society and from social forces and effects. Surely one may admit that religion is only one of the many factors that enter into social life as a whole and that it both acts upon other social forces and is deeply affected by them without denying its fundamental importance or assuming that it is merely derivative and temporary in validity.

VI. HOW SEEK AN ANSWER TO THE QUESTION?

The questions suggested by this long but incomplete summary of recent discussions of the social teachings of Jesus are many. But fundamentally they may be reduced to two: Did Jesus propose to save society as well as the individual, and, if so, from what and to what did he hope to redeem it? In other words, Is there a social gospel and what is its basic meaning?

How shall one enter upon the task of answering this question? In the face of this bewildering variety of opinion, is it possible to understand what Jesus really had in mind? Are there objective criteria by which we may test the innumerable interpreta-

[39] *Soziallehren*, pp. 42 f., note 24.

tions which have been proposed? As it seems to me, it is possible to make progress at least toward a solution of this insistent problem, and the way is to be found in the discovery of objective criteria in the historical background of Jesus' life. Only by conceiving the interpretation of Jesus as a purely historical problem to be approached by the strictest methods of historical investigation can we hope to reach results of permanent value.

The historian has discovered by a long process of trial and error and latterly by experiment and reflection that certain definite principles must guide his investigations. First, he must be critical as to his sources. Tradition need not be haughtily discarded, but, no matter how plausible, it must be thoroly tested by contemporary evidence. Every document used must be carefully scrutinized. No evidence is admissible that has not been adequately verified. Myth and legend cannot be used as statements of fact but only as records of current ideas and beliefs.

Second, the data of history must be genetically and functionally interpreted. Mere unrelated facts mean nothing and have little value. Society is never static; it is always in process of becoming. All its institutions must be studied as functions of the whole, and their functional adaptations must be carefully followed if we would understand them and the society of which they form a part. Only by observing the causes and effects of any given element in the total problem can we hope to discover what is its true nature.

In the third place, as already implied, every historical problem is a social problem. A problem that touches the history of Christianity can be fully understood only in relation to the whole social field. Whatever aids one to understand man in his social relations must be considered as having a possible bearing upon the question. Religion did not arise in a social vacuum, nor can it operate in one. It is a function of society. Separated from the whole the part is unintelligible.

Consequently we must make full use of all the new aids to history in studying Christianity. In recent years almost every science has come forward to claim that it holds the key to the understanding of human life. Once history was a mere chronicle of unrelated events. Then it became biography, and the influence of great men was invoked to interpret human progress. Too often history has been conceived as a study of military strategy. Again the explanation of human progress has been sought in purely political developments, in the history of states and their constitutions. Marx made a real contribution in invoking economics, but he insisted on regarding every element in human life and thinking as the product of economic evolution. Some have made climate, and others geography one of the chief determinants of progress. Darwin's theory of natural selection was inevitably applied to human society. The eugenists would reduce social evolution to a matter of individual physical fitness. Others maintain the thesis that fundamental racial differences have determined the lines which progress has taken in different parts of the world and that, in the long run, the best race survives. Some find in war and others in peaceful social contacts the chief means of social selection and adaptation. Property, the family, law and government, public opinion, education, art, religion, and the growth of ideals, all have been invoked to account for human progress.[40]

Anthropology has made its contributions even to an understanding of the historical period, if in no other way, at least by showing how hasty and unfounded were many accepted generalizations as to the character of highly developed civilizations. Much of the primitive still persists at later stages of culture. The comparative study of religions has cast a flood of light on the development of Christianity. Social psychology, including psychoanalysis, has made important revelations as to the causes and the character of the social movements with which history deals. Archeology has long been recognized as an indispensable aid to historical investigation. But unfortunately too few historians have the opportunity to use the results of archeological discoveries except as they are tardily and imperfectly recorded in books.

[40] Todd, *Theories of Social Progress,* Bristol, *Social Adaptation,* Robinson, *The New History,* Barnes, *The New History and Social Studies.*

Altho the material document which the archeologist discovers is truly more valuable and more easily interpreted than the written document,[41] history has depended largely upon the study of written documents. Particularly is this a fault of biblical scholarship, in which one document, the Bible, holds the centre of the stage and tends to blind the student to all but literary materials.

The study of the New Testament will profit in an unusual degree by the use of the newer aids to history. Since Christianity was, as all admit, a movement among the common people, nonliterary documents are much more valuable than those literary products of a high society which knew nothing of the new religion or of the psychological developments which made it acceptable to the despised multitudes. Philology, paleography, politics, law, constitutional history, the history of ritual, ethics, and theology, to quote a French authority on historical method,

> "do not go beyond superficial and conventional facts, they do not reach the real actions and thoughts of men: in language they deal with written words, not with real pronunciation; in religion with official dogmas and rites, not with the real beliefs of the mass of the people; in morals with avowed precepts, not with the effective ideals; in institutions with official rules, not with real practice. On all these subjects the knowledge of conventional forms must some day be supplemented by a parallel study of real habits."[42]

To understand Jesus and the movement he inaugurated it is essential that we go behind the conventional forms, the avowed precepts, and the official rules. We must attempt to discover the real beliefs, the effective ideals, the real practices and habits of the mass of the people.

How, now, does this demand for reality affect the problem we have undertaken to study? One cannot properly evaluate the expectation of Jesus and his followers with regard to the coming of the kingdom of God without understanding the ethical content which they put into the term. Of the sayings that indicate Jesus' social and ethical ideals, by common confession what he

[41] Langlois and Seignobos, *Introduction to the Study of History*, pp. 65 f.
[42] *Op. cit.*, pp. 268 f.

says about poverty and wealth is still among the most difficult. In this field, if in any, an attempt to discover the effective ideals and the real practices of the mass of the people will aid the interpreter. It stands to reason that we can understand Jesus only as we learn what his contemporaries and predecessors thought on the same subjects. To comprehend what the Gospels say about the poor and the rich, about the kingdom of God and its coming, and about Jesus' messiahship, it is necessary to study what people understood by those terms at that time. Jesus was discussing certain definite social and religious customs and institutions with which his hearers were perfectly familiar. Surely he did not speak in language unintelligible to his audiences, nor use words in senses entirely strange to them. For us, living two thousand years later, the only justifiable method of approach is to study the customs and institutions he discussed and the usage of the terms he employed to describe them as they come to light in his time and the preceding centuries. What later commentators and historians say is of little importance and, indeed, only tends to obscure the issue, except as they attempt to understand the times of Jesus by legitimate historical methods.

Jesus and the people of his day are intelligible only in the light of their social and intellectual inheritance. The genetic and functional methods must come to their rights. That Jesus' words and ideas must be interpreted in the light of the Old Testament has long been an accepted canon of biblical scholarship. Indeed that tradition begins—in perverted fashion, to be sure—with the apostolic quotation of "proof-texts" for supposed messianic prophecy. It must be equally clear that later Jewish literature, particularly that coming from Jesus' era and the centuries immediately preceding it, will be valuable in illuminating his meaning, for it will indicate even more unmistakably than the older Hebrew writings the views and practices which he criticized in his contemporaries as well as those he adopted. A careful study of the apocalypses and other Jewish writings, canonical and non-canonical, which date from the three centuries between 200 B.C. and 100 A.D. becomes, therefore, a *sine qua non* for the understanding of Jesus and primitive Christianity. This is especially important in view of the charge made by the school of thorogoing eschatologists that Jesus had no social message. The charge is based on a comparison of Jesus' ideas with those of the Jewish apocalyptists. Therefore we must determine what they really taught, how great their influence was, and what Jesus actually owed to them.

Jesus, however, held many of his dominant ethical ideas as a direct inheritance from the prophets whose tombs his contemporaries adorned. In the prophetic writings were certain great conceptions of social justice from which Judaism could not altogether escape. These ideals were the reactions of specially gifted, inspired souls to the evils and injustices of society in their days. What did the prophets mean, and what did Jesus owe to them?

We cannot understand the message of Jesus, nor that of the prophets, nor that of the apocalyptists, without a clear conception of the economic, political, and religious conditions which produced the evils against which they protested and of the ideals which caused them to protest. The development of morals and religion among the Hebrews is intelligible only in the light of the political and social conflicts thru which the nation passed. The nature of the conditions under which the prophets and teachers of Israel labored and of the conflicts which made the nation what it was becomes clear only after an investigation of the geographic situation of the land in which they lived. Therefore geography, climate, ethnology, politics, and economics all must have a place in the discussion.

Again, the great civilizations which surrounded Palestine faced in large measure the same social problems which the Hebrews had to meet. Long before the time of the prophets the Babylonian cities had their reformers and lawgivers, and Egypt had her prophetic critics of social injustice. Their language and ideas are often the same as those of the Bible. All the nations of the Levant reached similar solutions of many problems. The biblical ideas on social matters, then, are not entirely new and unique. On the contrary, the Hebrews, developing rather late in the history of Oriental civilization, inherited from their predecessors pattern ideas which were of incalculable influence and value, for the Hebrews were in the closest commercial and diplomatic relations with Egypt, Babylonia, and Assyria thruout their whole history. Thru many centuries they were politically dependent upon one or another of these regions. It is absurd, therefore, to maintain that they were morally and religiously uninfluenced by these older, richer, and more powerful neighbors.

The purpose of this essay is to sketch the devious windings of the path of progress, to outline the conceptions of poverty and wealth, of democracy and social betterment thru the millennia which history can descry before the birth of Jesus and the Christian church, and thus to seek a scientific basis for the interpretation and application of his teachings. If our attempt to interpret him takes us back three thousand years before his time, we can console ourselves with the thought that we are digging into a mound rich in unexpected treasures and are preparing a foundation that is deep and broad.

CHAPTER II

THE PHYSICAL FACTORS IN HEBREW HISTORY

I. PALESTINE AND THE NEW HISTORY

THE new keys to the meaning of history have been tried also upon the records of the Hebrews. The field is unusually inviting because the materials are extensive and familiar. The student may easily go astray because of failure to use the sources critically. Theological prepossessions constantly threaten to becloud his vision. But the attempt is certain eventually to prove fruitful, for there are few lands whose records have been so long, so continuously, and so carefully preserved and so critically sifted as have those that concern the Holy Land. Palestine, therefore, offers an excellent laboratory for the testing of historical theories. Its central situation, moreover, involved the little land in the affairs of all the great nations of antiquity, and thus it introduces one to the complex problems of ancient historiography. Entirely apart, then, from the intrinsic interest of Hebrew history for the student of religion, the land of Palestine makes an especial appeal to the historian. Do the new aids to history make possible a real advance in human wisdom, or are they merely increased mental impedimenta which the historian must carry? Let us test them on the history of the Hebrews. Beginning with the external factors which affect or condition human life, can we understand Hebrew history better by means of a study of Palestinian climate, geography, and economic history?

To put this question is not to espouse the long-lost cause of geographic and economic determinism. Environment does not *determine* the character of a society. Geography does not fix economic and social institutions. Morals and religion are not mere products of external conditions. But *milieu* does decidedly limit social development and it goes far to determine its direction. The earlier students of the history of civilization were inclined to substitute ingenious combination for scientific observation. Generalizations that appeared perfectly obvious overlooked equally obvious difficulties. When Renan suggested that the monotheism which developed among the Semites—the Israelites and the Mohammedans—was due to the monotonous expanses of their desert home, he overlooked the important fact that the Semite of the Arabian steppe has always accepted the rankest polytheism.[1] Miss Semple faces the same fatal fact when she proposes to derive "Semitic monotheism" from the simplicity of life, the leisure for contemplation, the wide-ranging travel, and the big horizons which the nomad enjoys.[2] S. Passarge is equally unfortunate in making monotheism the natural consequence of living in a *Narilandschaft,* a landscape of deficient moisture and low natural resources which, in consequence, exposed its inhabitants to repeated conquests and long subjection to other and stronger nations.[3] The fact that various peoples who, like the Hebrews, lived in a *Narilandschaft* and developed a subject mentality did not achieve a belief in monotheism, should have been enough to save him from the error. It could hardly have been such a combination of landscape and history which suggested monotheism to the Greek thinkers. And what was it that turned the thoughts of the writers of the Upanishads toward the essential unity of the universe?

Sir George Adam Smith seems to make the genial suggestion that the eruptive and revolutionary character of the Galilean Jews in Jesus' day was in some way connected with the volcanic origin of the soil in that region.[4] Surely he does not mean to imply that

[1] See Sir George Adam Smith, *Historical Geography of the Holy Land,* p. 29.

[2] *Influences of Geographic Environment,* New York, 1911, p. 1; cf. p. 27.

[3] *Grundzüge der gesetzmässigen Charakterentwickelung der Völker auf relig. und naturwiss. Grundlagen und in Abhängigkeit von der Landschaft,* Berlin, 1925, pp. 105 f.

[4] *Historical Geography,* pp. 421 f.

long extinct volcanoes, or, for that matter, active ones, could have any such effect on human character? The Hawaiians are not noted for their volcanic temperament or their revolutionary activities. Yet physical conditions act as limiting factors to prevent the growth of social institutions and intellectual concepts, while certain environments are favorable to the development of certain ideas just as truly as the date palm produces its fruit only in a frostless clime. The conditions under which the Hebrews lived had a large part in determining their contribution to morals and religion.

In assessing the value of the physical factors in Hebrew history there is no lack of materials to use. Among the many works on the historical geography of various lands admittedly one of the most brilliant books that has ever been written is Sir George Adam Smith's *Historical Geography of the Holy Land.* An instructive book on the relation of Palestine's climate to its history comes from the pen of the foremost representative of the climatic interpretation of history, Ellsworth Huntington's *Palestine and its Transformation.* These are but two of a great number of books and articles which discuss the subject. The economic history of Palestine remains to be written, but the subject has been frequently discussed and for Jerusalem it has received extensive treatment in Sir George Adam Smith's two volumes on *Jerusalem* and in the first part of a work now being published by Joachim Jeremias, *Jerusalem zur Zeit Jesu.* In spite of the tendency of biblical scholars to confine themselves too largely to literary studies, even the most skeptical will concede that the aids which these investigators offer cannot be safely neglected, particularly by those interested in the social history and ideals of the Hebrew nation.

Certain characteristics of the promised land must always be borne in mind by the student of Hebrew social and religious history. It was a very small land, measuring only about one hundred and fifty miles in length and averaging but forty miles in width on the west of the Jordan River. It lies between 31° and 34° north latitude, that is, roughly in the latitude of San Diego, Fort Worth, Savannah, Tripoli, Lahore, and Shanghai, and belongs, therefore, to the southern side of the Temperate Zone. Except to the desert nomad or the purblind fanatic it can hardly be a beautiful country. There are strange and picturesque scenes innumerable; there are prospects of magnificent desolation.[5] There are few quiet landscapes where the eye delights to dwell and the soul is invited to rest and repose. In Palestine proper there are no magnificent rivers, no wide-sweeping plains, but everywhere stony heaths and desolate moors, rough rocks and rugged gorges, interspersed with occasional orchards, meadows, and fields. Forests are now entirely wanting in western Palestine. During the greater part of the year the country is a drab combination of gray and brown. Only in late winter and early spring is there an outburst of flowers and green foliage that charms the Easter tourist into ecstasies.

A thousand years before the Hebrews entered Canaan an Egyptian sketched a clever characterization of the land and people as they appeared to the dweller on the Nile:

> "Behold the wretched Aamu (Syrian), toilsome is the land wherein he is, (a land) troubled with (?) water, (made) difficult by many trees, its ways (made) toilsome by reason of the mountains. He dwells not in a single place, but his legs are (ever) driven wandering (?). He is fighting (ever) since the time of Horus. He conquers not, nor yet is he conquered."[6]

Palestine is no longer made difficult by many trees, though it is not many years since scrubby forest in some parts of the country sheltered dangerous robber bands. It has always suffered for want of water, rather than because of it, but the Egyptian, accustomed to a rainless sky, would necessarily find traveling in Palestine during the rainy season most unpleasant. The description of the inhabitants is accurate for the greater part of the period with which we are concerned. Internal unity was rarely achieved.

II. PALESTINIAN TOPOGRAPHY

As will appear again and again in the course of this discussion, the peculiar topography of Palestine, which the Egyptian had

[5] See Sir George Adam Smith's charming descriptions, *Historical Geography*, pp. 90-104. It is all true but stresses one side of the story.

[6] "Admonitions (of Akhthoi) to Merikere," translated by Gardiner, *JEA*, I (1914), p. 30.

noted, has played a prominent *rôle* in its history. Relief has gone far to determine the moods of its climate, the nature of its economic activities, and the character of its economic and political relations with the rest of the world. Within the little land there are innumerable varieties of relief which are most important from the standpoint of health and which, as will be more easily shown at a later time, have played a decisive part in shaping its history. Only its main features may here be set down. Its long and fascinating topographical life story we cannot undertake to follow, but the chief results must be constantly borne in mind.

The eastern coast of the Mediterranean may be best conceived as a great arch of rocks, the axis of which runs north and south, while the sea washes its western flank and the desert borders it on the east. A great fault runs the full length of the arch along its axis, making place for the valleys of the Orontes and the Jordan between the two mountain ranges thus formed. Innumerable other faults and flexures have arisen. Taking advantage of these, erosion has worked out a bewildering pattern of valleys and gorges. Both flanks of the western range are cut deep by the rushing rains of winter into countless wadis, or stream beds which are dry except after rains. The eastern range is much less rugged and broken. Its western edge is of much the same character as the western range, but in the region of Palestine it rises so little above the level of the steppe and the rains which fall are so light that its eastern side blends almost imperceptibly with the plain. Indeed, if Syria and the Lebanons be left out of account, Palestine might be likened to the edge of a table which had cracked off along the Jordan rift and then been whittled into numberless depressions and heights.

The great Jordan depression, the Ghôr, as the Arabs call it, was formed by parallel faults between which a narrow ribbon of rock has dropped down. It begins far up in the Lebanons in the rocks of Mt. Hermon, which is 9,300 feet above sea level, and reaches its greatest depth in the Dead Sea, the bottom of which is 2,600 feet below the sea. Then it rises again as it passes through Edom, cutting off any possible inflow from the ocean, to fall once more to sea level at the Gulf of Akabah on the eastern side of the Sinaitic Peninsula. The western mountains, better called the Central Mountain Range because they are central to western Palestine, the area which chiefly occupies the attention of the biblical student, fall from Mt. Lebanon, 6,000 feet above sea level, to Upper and then Lower Galilee. After the break of the Plain of Esdraelon and the Valley of Jezreel, which almost connect the Mediterranean and the Jordan, rising only to 200 feet above the sea at the highest point, the mountains rise again thru Samaria and Judea to heights of more than 3,000 feet. They fall away again west of the southern end of the Dead Sea, rise once more into the mountains of Edom, and, after another dip downwards, reach 8,500 feet in the Sinaitic Mountains at the southern tip of the Peninsula.

Geologically, by far the largest part of Palestine belongs to the Upper Cretaceous epoch. South of Mt. Hermon and east of the Sea of Galilee is a great area where once there was tremendous volcanic activity. Most of the Haurân is a great lava bed, and there are extensive extrusions into the upper Jordan Valley and into Lower Galilee southwest of the lake. Basalt appears in patches on both sides of the Sea of Galilee and about the Plain of Esdraelon, and again in the mountains east of the Dead Sea. A part of the cliffs which form the eastern wall of the Dead Sea is Nubian sandstone. But in the main the mountains of Palestine are limestone. Its permeability and ease of erosion have been decisive factors in determining the relief and controlling the water supply of the land.

The mountains of Samaria and Judea are bordered on the west by the narrow seacoast plain of more recent geological formation. It is the richest, most easily cultivated, and most accessible section of the land. The seacoast itself is unbroken. There are no islands, no land-locked bays, no river estuaries, no indentations of any kind to form natural harbors or to be easily transformed into artificial ones. Unlike the coast of Phoenicia, it had neither a rich and well watered hinterland to send forth its products nor satisfactory shelters even for the little ships of antiquity. Wherefore Palestine was not intended to be the home of a great maritime nation.

III. THE CLIMATE OF PALESTINE

The climate of Palestine, so different from that of Egypt on the one hand, and from that of more northerly regions on the other, was the fundamental cause of the peculiar character of the Holy Land and a decisive factor in the social, moral, and religious development of Israel. Climate affects the individual and the group directly because it conditions physical and mental vigor and spiritual outlook. It affects human life indirectly, for it is a basic element in economic evolution, which, in turn, sets definite limits to social organization and ideals and to cultural development. This is not to adopt a climatic determinism. It does not at all exclude the influence of other essential factors. But it does mean that climate cannot be ignored in an investigation into the social evolution of a people, for "climate is the most important of all the geographic factors." [7]

Man's cultural advance has consisted largely in achieving independence of environment. Primitive man was at the mercy of external conditions. The earliest great civilizations developed where nature was not too difficult to master. It is equally true that civilization does not seem to have originated where life was so easy as to furnish no compelling incentives to labor and where climate bred lassitude and lethargy. Therefore the earliest civilizations arose, not in the fertile and luxuriant tropics, but in the sheltered river valleys on the southern side of the Temperate Zone. On the banks of the Indus, the Euphrates, and the Nile man escaped the stupid cold and the drowsy heat and the deadly caprice of uncertain drought and flood. But other climatic and economic conditions were necessary to the development of still higher culture.

Climate and religion are much more intimately connected than we are accustomed to acknowledge. Primitive man joined nature and religion in a fashion that the most fanatical of modern pan-

[7] Huntington and Cushing, *Principles of Human Geography,* p. 205; cf. Sauer, *Morphology of Landscape,* pp. 41 f. This section appeared in part in *JR, VI* (1927), from which it is reprinted by permission of the editor.

theists has outgrown. Natural phenomena were directly connected with the deities of the ancients. They were the immediate manifestations of the character and moods of the gods. Indeed, they were the gods. When a tribe migrated, it usually changed its gods, for, especially among agricultural populations, the gods belonged to the land and not to the people. In Egypt the life-giving Nile was one of the earliest and greatest gods. In lands of storms and marked seasonal changes, meteorological phenomena, so strange and inexplicable to the primitive mind, were the direct revelation of the spiritual beings who were thought to cause them. Climate and religion, therefore, were bound together into a conception that is entirely foreign to our thinking.

There are, then, three principles to be followed in estimating the effects of climate. Their detailed application must be made with all circumspection, but their importance cannot be denied. Consideration must be given, first, to the direct effect of climate upon physical and mental vigor and upon the capacity for thought and invention; second, to the influence of climate upon the fertility of the soil and the productivity of human labor. Human capacity and material resources determine the character of the civilization which arises in any region, and this, again, reacts upon the character of the people and of their social institutions and ideals. Lastly, there must be an attempt to reckon with the intellectual and emotional impressions made upon the mind of primitive man by the meteorological phenomena which he witnessed and projected into the transcendental, for the notions which he read into the character of his deities went to form his religious ideas and his moral-social standards.

The influence of climate upon the face of the land itself and upon plants, animals, and men must, therefore, be taken into consideration. Unfortunately, we still have much to learn on many points. The medical profession is only beginning to study scientifically the effects of climate and of meteorological phenomena. In the less complex problems of agriculture more progress has been made, but in many matters uncertainty still prevails. Least of all can one speak of definite and final conclusions in the field of social and religious studies. In such abstruse and complicated problems the danger of oversimplification is at its greatest. Does a sunny climate breed a sunny disposition, and a hot climate hot emotions? Do sexual crimes depend upon temperature?[8] Then the drawing of isotherms ought to divide the earth into zones of crime and virtue. Such a *reductio ad absurdum* should be sufficient to indicate the dangers of hasty generalization. The boundaries beyond which one may not pass in stating conclusions are difficult to determine. It is better to err on the side of safety. Recognizing the dangers and difficulties of the attempt, one must, nevertheless, use also this key to the gate of ancient Hebrew history, for it leads to regions where there is more than fools' gold.

As to the climate of Palestine in ancient times there is difference of opinion. Archeologists and climatologists are not in accord as to the extent and the effects of the changes which climate has undergone in historic times. While it is now almost unanimously agreed that the earth has not suffered from progressive desiccation since the beginnings of civilization, there can be no doubt that there have been and still are secular variations in both temperature and humidity. Uncertainty still exists as to the periodicity and the range of these pulsations, and their consequent effect upon human society. Were the successive oscillations in the cultural level of Palestine due to fluctuations in its productivity caused by pulsatory changes in its climate? Were the Amorite conquest of Babylonia, the Hebrew invasion of Palestine, and the rise of Islam due to periods of desiccation which drove the thriving nomad tribes of the Arabian Steppe into the cultivated lands for food? Did the pueblos of Arizona and New Mexico and the Maya cities of Yucatan rise and fall because of changes in climate? These larger problems of historical climatology must be passed by until further archeological and historical research as well as longer and more widespread meteorological observations have provided less ambiguous data. To justify my later treatment I can only state a reasoned opinion based upon the

[8] See Febvre, *Geographical Introduction to History,* pp. 110 f.

available meteorological and archeological evidence but subject to correction, that minor climatic oscillations have at times coincided with historical changes of a political and economic nature and have intensified effects which would have manifested themselves even if climate had remained absolutely uniform.

Fortunately we know that in its general features the climate of Palestine has been the same since the earliest records. By combining the experiences of modern travelers and the somewhat fragmentary observations of meteorological stations in Palestine during the last seventy years with the chance remarks found in the Bible, the Talmud, and other ancient literature, we can discover with sufficient definiteness what this climate was and can make progress toward determining how it affected the development of Hebrew society. A brief summary of the climatic characteristics of Palestine will prepare for an appreciation of the part climate has played in its social history.

Palestine lies in the subtropical zone at the southern edge of the belt of prevailing westerly winds. Situated as it is at the east of a great body of water, it enjoys a climate similar to that of southern California, Italy, and Greece, with two seasons, a cool, rainy winter and a hot, dry summer. Its two seasons are due to the fact that in winter its climate is under the cyclonic control which prevails in the temperate zone, while in summer the high-pressure zone of tropical calms, the zone of the great deserts, moves slightly northward with the sun, and tho not affecting its westerly winds, for five months effectually overcomes any cyclonic movements or any local tendencies to rain. The mean annual isotherm of 68° F. (20° C.) passes over it, marking the line between the subtropical and temperate zones. For the historical relations and influence of Palestine it is significant that it is a very small land lying on the border line between various zones and between contrasting types of geographical landscape, between the sea on the west and the Syrian Desert and Arabian Steppe on the east, between the abundantly watered heights of the Lebanons on the north and the almost rainless areas of high pressure and tropical calms, the great desert belt of the Sahara,

Sinai, and southern Arabia on the south. Since Palestine is placed by the sea, it should enjoy an oceanic climate, but its mountains are so close to the shore and the eastern end of the Mediterranean is so enclosed by land masses that the moderating effect of the ocean is felt but a few miles inland. For the same reason the winds from the ocean carry their moisture only a short distance beyond the coast. The winds blow at times from the desert, more often, fortunately, from the sea. In spring and autumn the east or southeast wind brings lassitude and desiccation because of its high temperature and low humidity, in winter it brings invigoration and clear skies. The west winds always bring coolness and moisture. They are the great saving factor in the meteorology of Palestine. But the desert is never far away.

The remarkable variation of altitude within the land itself adds to the bewildering confusion of its climates and the resulting variety of its fauna and flora. The tremendous rift of the Jordan Valley, descending below sea-level at Lake Huleh and dropping to 1,300 feet below the sea at the surface of the Dead Sea, the lowest spot on the earth's surface, provides a practically tropical climate where, as in the region of Gaza also, the date palm can flourish. Yet it is only a little over 100 miles to the eternal snows on the peak of Mount Hermon. This meteorological microcosm includes nearly all the earth's climatic zones and belts of vegetation. On the banks of the lower Jordan is the tropical jungle; the savannah grass lands are on the eastern plateau; and the desert with its xerophilous plants not only lies on the east and south, but, in the Judean Wilderness, penetrates into the heart of the land. The main part of the country belongs to the belt of tropical dry forest with its non-deciduous trees such as the olive and the live-oak, but the little country reaches into the next vegetation province also and has deciduous oaks and other trees of colder climates in abundance up to the great conifers of the Lebanons, where a sub-Alpine flora is found. The coastal region forms a distinct floral zone, similar to that of the other Mediterranean lands. There is a similar variety of fauna. Thus, the meteorological phenomena and the plants and animals of all the zones from the tropics to the Arctic Circle are found within the compass of a little more than one hundred miles, a fact which materially contributed to making the literature which arose in this insignificant country intelligible to all the nations of the world.

Did the climate of Palestine contribute to vigor of body and mind? Measured by the requirements of modern industrial civilization Palestine is ranked low in health value. In five "zones of climatic energy" Huntington places it next to the last.[9] Yet it has many advantages. The cold is never extreme and the heat of the dry summer is far from being markedly dangerous or unpleasant. Only during the relatively brief periods in May and October when the Sirocco blows does the heat entail great lassitude. Otherwise the nights are almost always cool. During the long summer the daily sea breeze brings humidity and coolness with great regularity. In the mountains of Judea the mean monthly temperatures range from 44° F. in January to 73° in August, with an annual mean of 61°; on the coast from 53° in January to 78° in August, with a mean of 67° for the year. The Jordan Valley is warmer, ranging from 55° F. to 87°, with a mean of 75° in the region of the Sea of Galilee. The temperature has been known to fall as low as 19° F. at Hebron and 21° at Jerusalem, but such occasions are extremely rare. In the greater part of Palestine it never freezes. The maxima are 108° F. for Jerusalem, 110° for Nazareth, and 114° for Tiberias, but such heat also is not common. The means in the mountains at least are but a little above Huntington's optima of 40°-64° with the mean of 51°. When one takes into account the character of that ancient civilization with which we are concerned, its less strenuous competition, its lack of provision against cold, particularly in Palestine where coal and peat are unknown and wood has usually been scarce, the conclusion is justified that, so far as temperature is concerned, conditions were more favorable there for the development of health and vigor than they would have been in a colder region.

The chief disadvantage of Palestine's climate is that its long,

[9] Huntington and Cushing, *Principles of Human Geography*, p. 255.

dry summer lacks that variability due to frequent storms which is regarded as one of the outstanding advantages of more northerly temperate regions. The summer from May to October is a monotonous round of sunny days and brilliant nights, broken occasionally by great cumulus clouds, but almost never by rain or thunder storm. Yet even so there is a very considerable daily range of temperature. Except during the brief Sirocco periods there is never a coincidence of extreme heat and aridity, nor is there ever extreme heat combined with excessive humidity. Indeed, the mean humidity of the Palestinian atmosphere ranges close to the optimum of 75 or 80 per cent. While at Jerusalem the annual mean falls to 62 per cent., and in the Jordan Valley (at Tiberias) to 58 per cent., even at the worst it is rarely below 50 per cent. Its range would appear to suit the prevailing temperatures so as to provide almost the maximum of comfort and energy. In this extremely important health factor, as in the matter of variability, Palestine is far superior to Egypt, Babylonia, and India. Such a climate makes for a maximum of outdoor life. Its variability may not be sufficiently stimulating to meet the demands of modern industry for energy and speed, yet it escapes deadening extremes of both heat and cold, and its moods have sufficient variety to develop no small degree of vigor and adaptability.

The variety of climates wrought by its diversified topography did not a little to compensate for lack of variety in any one locality. Whereas the people of the great central valley of North America may have to travel a thousand miles to effect a real change of climate, the inhabitant of Jerusalem has only to drop down ten or twenty miles into the Jordan Valley, the Wilderness of Judea, or the Maritime Plain to escape from his bleak and wind-swept mountain top into an entirely different world. The ordinary peasant of the highlands, as he cultivates his fields, some of them in the mountains, others in the plain or the valley, as he follows his flocks in search of pasture, as he carries his goods to market, is constantly subjecting himself to differences of barometric pressure, of humidity, and of temperature. Pilgrimages and occasional visits to more distant regions for pleasure or business add a still greater variety to his climatic experiences. So far as health is concerned, the mountain-dwelling Hebrews were much more fortunately situated than either the Egyptians or the Babylonians; they were but little behind the Greeks and the Romans. Given the conditions under which men lived in ancient times, it must be agreed that Palestine presented the climatic factors for a vigorous physical and mental life. It bred, indeed, an energy for which its material resources offered an insufficient outlet. But the adaptability which it necessarily produced made its children successful colonists in every part of the world. The climate of Palestine has played no small part in aiding the dispersion and so the world-wide mission of the Jews.

Along with healthfulness, productivity is an essential element in the habitat value of a land. Temperature and humidity with variability are the important factors in healthfulness. The other essential element is rainfall, which has little direct influence upon human health and character, but, in combination with temperature, determines the nature of the soil and its fertility. This in turn sets definite limits to the civilization which any land may develop and fixes its economic institutions, thus indirectly but powerfully affecting every feature of society.

As to rainfall Palestine is again in a zone of transition. Along the coast and in the mountains from a little south of Hebron and Jaffa to Phoenicia and northern Galilee the mean annual rainfall runs from twenty-five to twenty-seven inches. The region of the Sea of Galilee has a mean of about twenty inches. The southern end of the Jordan Valley about the Dea Sea probably has much less, but there are no series of regular observations for this region. Sufficient data are lacking also for the sections east of the Jordan. Probably the rainfall in all the Ḥaurân, in Gilead, and in Moab averages from twelve inches down, growing less as one goes south. Gaza has an annual mean rainfall of about sixteen inches, Beersheba, probably from ten to fifteen inches. Still farther south, in the mountains of Edom, where torrential rains fall in winter, successful agriculture is almost impossible because of the brief period during which the rains occur. At Nahkl in the center of the Sinaitic Peninsula and at Suez an inch or less falls each year. Thus, from a precipitation of over thirty-five inches annually at Beirut and of sixty inches or more in the Lebanons (el-Kereiyeh) the amount gradually diminishes as one goes southward until it reaches the vanishing point. West of the central watershed and north of Beersheba Palestine has an abundant rainfall. East of the Central Mountain Range desert conditions appear sporadically, as in the Wilderness of Judea, and are more and more intensified the farther east one goes. The southern portion of the land also projects into the desert.

Since Palestine lies thus on the very edge of the desert, slight fluctuations of climate may easily introduce most untoward conditions. Every summer, indeed, puts the land partially under the meteorological controls of the great desert belt. Every year, especially in May and October, the Sirocco brings the desert, with its hot, dry air and its flying sand, into the heart of the land. Not infrequently a partial failure of the winter rains or a deficiency of the "former rains" of October and November or of the "latter rains" of March and April causes partial or total failure of crops and a dearth of water for man and beast. The uncertainty of rain as to both amount and distribution has been one of the prime hindrances to the economic development of Palestine.

How great this uncertainty is may be seen from the observations which were made with great regularity at Jerusalem from 1861 until the beginning of the World War and with less regularity for considerable periods at other stations. From these it appears that there has been a certain periodicity in the succession of wet and dry seasons. Between 1861 and 1880 fifteen winters were below the mean, some of them fifty per cent. below. In the next two decades fourteen seasons were above the mean. The four seasons from 1898 to 1902 were deficient in rainfall. In the next eleven years four were deficient at Jerusalem, a dry year alternating with two wet ones. During and since the War dry years seem to have preponderated; at Nazareth seven out of the last ten years have been below its twenty-seven year mean.

A single dry year is not usually fatal to the farmer, but a succession of them such as is repeatedly recorded at Jerusalem and other Palestinian stations inevitably brings destitution and debt from which succeeding moist years are hardly sufficient to effect a rescue. The occasional year with a large surplus may do something to raise the level of the ground water in the plains and valleys, but, tho it also raises the means which the meteorologist calculates, it does the farmer little good, for it runs away from the hills and leaves the land no better off than in a year of moderate rainfall.

Likewise, the failure of the "former" and "latter rains" is a serious matter. As numerous allusions in the Bible and the Talmud and the reports of modern observers agree in indicating, these autumn and spring rains play a part quite out of proportion to their bulk. A small rain in October softens the soil, which in many places cannot otherwise be brought into tilth after the baking heat of summer, and allows the timely sowing and sprouting of winter cereals. These will not fill out after the cold rains of the winter unless there be rains in the latter part of March and in early April before the heat ripens them. Likewise the entire growth of the summer crops, such as millet, and the abundance of the vintage and fruit harvest depend upon the "latter rains." The observational data now available are not sufficient to determine how low the autumn and spring rains may fall without serious injury to crops, but a very brief study of the monthly rainfall for any considerable number of years shows how irregular it is. In one year there may be no rainfall until late in November (Nov. 29, 1915, Nazareth). In another there may be a notable, but useless rain in September. October may range from zero to four or five inches, April from zero to seven or eight inches (Hebron, 1907). May is almost as uncertain as September. The length of the rainy season may vary from one hundred twenty-five to two hundred seventy-five days, and the succeeding dry period from one hundred to two hundred days.

The average for the rainy period is about one hundred ninety, for the dry, about one hundred and seventy days.

So rapid is evaporation in Palestine that it is estimated that a vessel left open to rain, sunshine, and air would, in a normal year, show practically no water until the end of November. At the end of March at Jerusalem it would contain about fourteen inches (356 mm.) of water, but early in July this would disappear and the vessel remain dry till November came again.[10] The injury wrought, therefore, by a short rainy season is easily realized, especially since the earth does not retain the winter stores of water as a vessel does.

Again, the number of days during the season when rain falls is an important factor in Palestinian agriculture. If, during the winter, there are a few days of heavy rainfall and many of sunshine, it follows that, while human beings may rejoice, the crops suffer, for the surplus water the more quickly runs off and the ground dries in the intervening periods of sunshine. If, on the contrary, there are many days of rain, there is little evaporation and less rapid drainage, and the soil becomes thoroly saturated. In this matter also there is the greatest diversity between seasons. The number of rainy days within the rainy season may vary from thirty-three (Sarona, 1916-17) to eighty (Karmel, 1906-07). The average for the mountains and seacoast plain in the sections where the mean annual rainfall is twenty-five inches or more is from fifty to sixty days each rainy season. The average for the Sea of Galilee is fifty days. East of the Jordan and south of Jaffa and Hebron the number falls rapidly. Unfortunately an average, 'normal' year rarely comes. Two or more years with few rainy days are usually succeeded by two or three with a number above the average. But, fortunately, the years with deficient rainfall are not always those with few rainy days. When both combine, the situation is serious. In 1924-25 the German station at Jerusalem reported less than twelve inches of rain and only thirty-eight rainy days. At Nazareth forty-one days brought less than seventeen inches.

[10] Exner, *ZDPV*, 33 (1910), 139.

The chief weather hazards which the Palestinian peasant faces are drought and hot winds. Storms are infrequent. In the sense of heavy winds they come on the average during from eight to twenty days in the year, growing less from north to south. Thunder storms may be expected on from six to twelve days. Fortunately for the harvesting they are practically unknown after April. It is a miracle if one comes in summer.[11] Snow and frost are practically unknown except in the mountains, and even there they are light. Frost may come at Jerusalem from November to February, usually in January and on less than four days in the average year. Snow falls there nearly every year, often to a height of six inches; occasionally it reaches two or three feet, but it rarely remains on the ground more than a day or two. Hail may fall two or three days in the year, most commonly in February, March, and December. Very rarely is the cold or snow sufficient to do serious damage to crops. An occasional wet year may cause mildew. Other crop hazards are from insects, especially the locust, which in both ancient and modern times periodically works dire havoc. Probably climate has much to do with the dangerous multiplication of such pests.

These facts regarding the Palestinian climate I have set down in some detail because the problems and difficulties of a society under such conditions must be fully appreciated before one attempt to trace the development of its institutions and ideals. So far as concerns health and vigor of body and mind, the climate of Palestine must be ranked close to those of Greece and Rome; due regard being paid to conditions of living in ancient times, it was a good climate. But the uncertainties of rainfall were such that, irrigation being impossible, it was but a step in Palestine from prosperity to adversity. Babylonia and Egypt did not enjoy so healthful a climate, but in those lands, so long as society remained fairly stable and consequently irrigation could be properly carried on, the staple crops were sure. Disaster came rather from the hand of man, from revolutions and invasions. We can well understand that such disturbances of the social order were the

[11] I Sam. 12.17 f.

great terror of the dwellers on the Nile. In Palestine, on the contrary, all depended upon the very capricious smile of nature. While man also might interfere with the orderly processes of nature, the danger from his hand was as nothing to the frown of the God who commanded the clouds. Remembering that many factors entered into the making of Hebrew religion, one cannot but conjecture, nevertheless, that the Old Testament conception of Providence was in part at least the product of a capricious climate.[12]

Upon the social structure of the Hebrew people, in the course of its long development, the vagaries of their climate exercised a far-reaching influence. It was its climate which set Palestine upon the edge of the desert. To the consequences of the Hebrews' familiarity with the desert and with pastoral life we shall frequently return. Climate also set the economic problems to the solution of which the great Hebrew prophets gave their best thought. In such a climate no man was assured wealth in perpetuity. Where there was abundance today there might be dire want tomorrow. The evil effects of successive years of drought following years of good rainfall have been apparent in many lands, in Kansas, Nebraska, and the Dakotas in the United States, in western Canada, in Australia, in central and northern India. The dangers are especially great in lands that lie on the edge of the dry-farming zone, where irregularity of precipitation is the rule, not the exception. Good years lead to overexpansion and to careless methods of farming. Bad years that follow are fatal. How easily a failure of rain may make an agricultural population slaves of an unscrupulous or grasping financial aristocracy has been too often demonstrated. Some of the stirring crises of Hebrew history center around this kind of economic maladjustment.

From such uncertainties and difficulties two ways of escape lie open. One is to discover other resources in the land or other means of earning a livelihood beside agriculture. The other is emigration. Palestine had a healthful climate that produced a vigorous, prolific, and adaptable people. Under the conditions there

[12] See Sir George Adam Smith, *Historical Geography,* pp. 73-76, 88 ff.

was an inevitable and unceasing overflow into neighboring lands. The Bible records such an emigration in the story of Joseph and his brethren. A similar movement, or possibly the same, is to be seen in the Hyksos invasion of Egypt. Egyptian documents are full of fear of inroads by the bedouins. The Hebrew Dispersion, beginning certainly as early as the seventh century B.C., is in part due to other causes, but its mainspring was the poverty of a land which could not support its energetic and prolific inhabitants. A climate that is favorable to human health and fecundity but not to food production is certain to be the source of endless strife and eventually to produce strange results. What possible sources of wealth did Palestine possess?

IV. NATURAL RESOURCES

In the case of Palestine other geographic factors combined to intensify the deficiencies of her climate. The natural resources of Palestine did not counterbalance the handicaps placed upon her inhabitants by a semi-arid and capricious climate and the means, therefore, by which the Hebrews might earn a livelihood were strictly limited.

The basic factor is the ground. All wealth begins there. That being the case, Palestine was never intended to be the home of wealth and luxury. What to the wanderer in the desert may have seemed a "land flowing with milk and honey" [13] seems to the European or American a gray, barren waste of rocky hills and gorges. The annual miracle of the blossoming of the Wilderness astonishes the eye for a brief period following the rains of winter, but May, or April if the "latter rains" be scant, sees the grass wither and the flower fade. The long drought of summer presents only hot, gray hillsides to the glare of the sun.[14] To be sure,

[13] It is possible that even the Hebrew was not thinking of fertility in the concrete when he used these terms, for "milk and honey" may be *Götterspeise;* see Gressmann, *Ursprung der israel.-jüd. Eschatologie,* pp. 210-216, but also Hölscher, *Die Propheten,* p. 171.

[14] In March flowers are everywhere in the mountains of Judea, cyclamen, anemones, poppies, and a dozen other brilliant blossoms. In December (1920) the writer found Galilee still brown and bare, and in April, because of a failure of the spring rains, it was already dusty again and the flowers gone.

the westerner may allow himself to be deceived by unfamiliar appearances. Limestone hills have a wonderful way of fertilizing themselves. In spite of lack of humus, the soil of Palestine is rich. In any climate such that, during a considerable portion of the year, evaporation far exceeds precipitation, vegetable matter does not rot upon the ground to form humus, but the salts in the ground are brought to the surface by the capillary rise of moisture toward the air instead of being washed away as they are in equatorial and temperate regions of heavy rainfall. In such a climate rotation of crops and bare fallowing will maintain the fertility of the soil at a fairly high level. In large sections of Palestine, moreover, the soil is quite retentive of moisture in spite of its underlying strata of porous limestone. In this soil, antiquated tho his methods were, the persistent labor of the modern fellah, even under Turkish rule, accomplished wonders. One never ceases to be astonished at the terraced wadis and hillsides, at the fig and olive orchards planted in holes dug in the rock. Yet, when all is done, the soil of Palestine can never produce such wealth as one easily takes from the valley of the Mississippi, the Ganges, the Euphrates, or the Nile.

There is little land to till. The total area of the Palestine of the British Mandate, which almost coincides with the land of the Hebrews west of the Jordan, is 5,845 square miles, or 3,740,000 acres.[15] It is a little larger than Connecticut, a little smaller than Wales, and about one-third the San Joaquin Valley in California. But relief sharply restricts the agricultural possibilities within this small area. The Department of Agriculture of the present government estimates the amount of land which is uncultivable, including forest, pasture, and swamp land, at 1,740,800 acres,[16] or nearly 47 per cent. of the whole. Of the total arable land the districts of Beersheba and Gaza, both of which, as we have seen, have a decidedly low rainfall, include 40 per cent. Of arable land within the zone that has more than twenty inches of rainfall there remain probably not more than 1,200,000 acres, or 1,870 square

[15] 1,514,038 hectares, Sawyer, *Agric. Situation,* Pt. IV, App., p. 1.

[16] That is 704,488 hectares, Sawyer, *loc. cit.*

miles. Not a little of this can be successfully used only by building terraces or employing other expensive processes of intensive cultivation. Eastern Palestine is estimated at 4,000 square miles. When one counts out the large amount of pasture and waste land, there can remain at best only some hundreds of thousands of acres that are worth cultivating, and that only by dry-farming methods, for the rainfall is everywhere less than fifteen inches.

Soils in semi-arid countries are extremely rich if they can be brought under irrigation. But in Palestine the possibilities of irrigation are relatively small. Deuteronomy describes Canaan as a "good land, a land of brooks of water, of springs and pools, flowing forth in valley and in mountain." [17] But again it is an ideal picture painted by the patriotic imagination. Palestinian villages depend largely on rain-filled pools and cisterns to meet their domestic requirements; very few have their water from springs. Beisân, Nazareth, Ḳaṣṭal Ṣaffûriyeh, el-Fendaḳûmîyeh, Nâbulus, and 'Ain Kârim are among the bright exceptions to the rule.[18] And every tourist knows how small the flow at Nazareth is. It may well serve as an example of what most of them are. The springs south of Solomon's Pools have not proved sufficient to supply Jerusalem even with drinking water. Cistern water is the only recourse. There are practically no flowing brooks. Nearly all the water courses are wadis, waterless except after a rain. In two or three regions, notably the Jericho Plain, with water from its own 'Ain es-Sultân and from Wâdî Kelt, the wonderfully watered valley about Beisân from Jebel Fuḳû'a eastward, and the Plain of Esdraelon along the River Kishon, there are possibilities of easy irrigation. Parts of the Maritime Plain and the Plain of Esdraelon may be irrigated from wells, as is much valley land in the semi-arid west. But all told, such possibilities are meager. Both relief and lack of water forbid. The Jordan Valley, aside from one region south of the Sea of Galilee and another around Jericho, is out of the question. The valley at best is narrow, and

[17] Chap. 8.7.

[18] See the list in Sir George Adam Smith, *Historical Geography,* note 3, pp. 77 ff. One of the great disappointments I suffered in Palestine was the lack of good drinking water when traveling.

the little river has worn itself a channel too deep to allow bringing its waters out upon the terraces of the ancient inland lake. It was never attempted in ancient times. There are no vast supplies of snows, as in the Sierra and Rocky Mountains, to furnish the life-giving moisture. Damascus shows what might be accomplished in the Ḥaurân if a river were available, but the Yarmûk, like the Jordan, is small and thru much of its course inaccessible. While much more can be done thru the use of the smaller tributaries, and much more was done in the most prosperous ancient periods than under Turkish rule, there is no place for such enterprises as have enriched arid America and India. Palestine could not compete with the valleys of the Euphrates and the Nile.[19]

Its climate and relief being what they are, Palestine must always have been largely a pastoral country. While the scarcity of rain renders agriculture impossible in many sections, the constitution of its soil fits it for cattle raising and sheep breeding. Still today large numbers of its people, who cultivate fields and live during the winter in permanent villages, leave their stone houses in March and spend the remainder of the year until October following their flocks from place to place in search of pasture, turning aside at the proper seasons to reap their fields, thresh their grain, and care for their vineyards. Thus, even the settled agriculturalist leads a semi-nomadic life, while over large areas both east and west of the Jordan the bedouin roams at will with his flocks of sheep and goats.[20]

Agriculture and animal husbandry are the only significant internal sources of wealth in Palestine. Deuteronomy to the contrary notwithstanding, the stones of Canaan were not iron, nor did men dig copper from its hills, unless Sinai and the Lebanons were included within it, and this the Hebrews were never able permanently to accomplish. There is evidence, to be sure, that the ancients had copper or iron mines in the mountains of Edom near Fênân, thirty miles south of the Dead Sea, and iron

[19] See Sawyer, *op. cit.*, p. 7, and Pt. II, pp. 1-6.

[20] See the writer's article, *Journal of Geography*, 23 (1924), 341-345.

mines in the ridge between Wâdî Râjib and Wâdî ez-Zerkâ (the Jabbok). There are numerous small deposits of iron. But, so far as is now known, there are none that would have contributed appreciably to the wealth of the land. The Dead Sea deposits have always provided salt and bitumen. Judean pitch was famous in antiquity. Modern methods can make use of the phosphates in which the land is rich, can turn its limestones into Portland cement, and may find valuable supplies of petroleum. But ancient Palestine had no notable mines or other sources of mineral wealth. It produced no precious stones. Even its abundance of building stone boasts little or no fine marble. Much of its limestone is soft when quarried and thus lends itself to an easy-going and not too fastidious artistry. Palestine possessed no substantial sources of subterranean wealth.[21]

The products of the land were, therefore, strictly limited. Aside from flocks and herds, which must always have represented a considerable proportion of its wealth, Palestine produced grain on the rolling plains east of the Jordan and on the western mountains wonderful grapes, olives, and figs. Grain, no doubt, was always grown in the plains and even the terraced wadis of western Palestine, but probably never in sufficient quantities to supply the local demand. Vineyards and olive orchards, especially the latter, have ever been the principal sources of wealth in the mountains of western Palestine. The export of wine and oil has been the chief means of preserving Palestine's balance of trade.

Lack of sources of material wealth has been one of the important factors in determining what Palestine's contribution to world culture should be. Her gifts to civilization could never lie in the realms of invention, industry, and art. Life was too hard and too serious. At the same time there could be little temptation for her people to lose themselves in industrial pursuits. The thorns of worldly cares and deceitful riches did not grow luxuriantly in Palestinian soil. It never offered an economic basis for the

[21] H. C. Luke and E. Keith-Poach, *Handbook of Palestine*, London, 1922, pp. 238-41; Klausner, *Jesus of Nazareth*, pp. 176 f.; Driver in *ICC* on Dt. 8.9; Dalman in *PJB*, IX (1913), 68.

growth of a world empire and its resulting brutal temper and ruthless pride. There was merely enough material wealth to nourish a vigorous, abstemious farming population marked by plain living and high thinking.

V. GEOGRAPHIC RELATIONSHIPS

From every point of view, economic, political, cultural, and religious, the geographic relationships of Palestine with the rest of the world have been of supreme importance. Her unique central situation was the most significant factor in her history. Much has been made of the isolation of the Israelites. On one side they were hemmed in by the sea, on the other by the desert. Their one river is hardly more than a mountain torrent, at no point navigable for more than a few miles; it flows thru a hot, narrow, and unattractive valley and ends in a desolate cul-de-sac, a "sea of death" that is without parallel on the face of the earth. The Jordan is as useless for defense as it is for navigation. It divides without separating. The Sea of Galilee is too small to contribute largely to the prosperity of the neighboring regions. The tideless Mediterranean shore offers no attractive harbors to encourage shipping. The arid steppe on the east sheltered only sturdy nomadic tribes which constantly threatened their more civilized neighbors and formed a barrier to commerce and expansion. Neither river nor seas made any effective contribution to the economic history of Israel.

Yet in ancient times Palestine was not isolated. Today, but for its sacred places, the currents of civilization would leave it untouched. But in antiquity, when world culture centered around the eastern Mediterranean and communication by sea was relatively undeveloped and dangerous, Canaan was the bridge between the principal nations, the common meeting place of civilizations. Lying between the desert and the sea, at the southwestern tip of that fertile crescent in which lay Babylonia, Assyria, Mitanni, and Syria, and almost touching the delta of the Nile, Palestine was always a great commercial highway. It was the connecting link between Africa and Asia. The oldest road in the world runs from Ḳantârah on the Isthmus of Suez to Raphia and Gaza. Across the land ran the great trade routes from the Hittites of Asia Minor, the Aryans of Mitanni, the Sumerians and the Semites of Nineveh, Babylon, and Damascus to Egypt. Across it also passed the caravans from southern and central Arabia to the Mediterranean. To the roadsteads on the coast came the ships of the sea-lords of Crete and other centers of old Aegean civilization, and from these poor havens Canaanite ships sailed to the most distant ports of the Mediterranean. From Elath on the Red Sea there was a bond by water with eastern Africa and southern Asia. Palestine was a causeway of the nations.

Accordingly it has always been a battle-ground between competing nations and cultures. Primarily a land of settled, agricultural life, it has again and again become the prize of conquest by the nomads of the desert. It was one of those rich, civilized lands which were ever a bone of contention between the vigorous tribes of the northern mountains and the energetic and prolific Semites of the Arabian plateau.[22] It is, in fact, a frontier between settled and nomadic civilization. Likewise, Palestine is a frontier between Egypt and Asia. Any military power from Asia must pass thru it to the rich valley of the Nile. Here lay the only land route by which Egypt could reach out toward the other civilizations of the world. The people on the Nile could never well defend themselves and could never make conquests in Asia without holding Palestine. From the beginning of history its plains have shaken with the tread of armies and its towns have welcomed traveling bands of foreign merchants and roving nomads. So many battles have been fought on its soil and especially upon the Plain of Esdraelon, where Carmel thrusts a natural barrier across the path from north to south, that one can well understand how the Seer of Patmos, remembering his native land, located the last great battle at Har-Magedon, the mountain of Megiddo.

As a consequence of this relation to trade, commerce, and military strategy, the land of the Hebrews was always a storm cen-

[22] Cf. Eduard Meyer, *Geschichte des Altertums,* I, 2, pp. 347 ff.

ter of international politics. Her cities were conquered and reconquered. They revolted and were captured and razed, only to spring up again and engage in new intrigues and insurrections. Because of its central position among the civilizations of antiquity, Palestine was from age to age the focus upon which shone the rays of the new cultures which sprang up round about. Every fresh wind that blew in any part of the ancient world soon breathed new life into Palestine. Stratum upon stratum in the excavated ruins of its cities bears witness to the contacts between its peoples and the rest of the world. Far from being isolated, Palestine was what Christian sentiment for another reason has long called it, the center of the world.

In view of these relationships it was inevitable that Palestine should depend upon commerce for surplus wealth. We have noted the relative poverty of the land itself. Fields, vineyards, olive orchards, flocks, and herds could maintain a hardy, abstemious peasant population. Wealth and luxury could come only from service as a carrier of trade. It is significant that all of the great cities of Palestine, with the exception of Jerusalem, were on important trade routes. Some were at the confluence of roads, like Gaza and Ludd, others guarded a mountain pass, like Megiddo, Bethshean, and Shechem, or the entrance to a section of the mountains, like Gezer, others lay at precarious havens, like Jaffa and Ptolemais. Their wealth came from the tolls they were able to levy upon passing caravans, both directly, and indirectly for food and fodder.

For another reason, therefore, it cannot be counted strange that Palestine never made any contribution to the material culture of the world. She was a carrier, but not a creator of cultural values of the material kind. Without great physical resources, dependent upon passing trade for all that raised her above the subsistence level, harried by conflicting civilizations that were always battling across her plains, she received what the world had to offer of material and artistic goods, but she never gave back anything in kind. "The Semitic natives (of Palestine)," says Macalister, "never invented anything; they assimilated all the elements of their civilization from without."[23] In these regards Palestine was always overshadowed by her richer neighbors. From a frontier region contributions to culture can hardly be expected!

Neither is it strange that Palestine never became the center of world-wide empire. Centers of civilization may develop at points of contact where important routes converge or cross, but other factors must not be overlooked. Mesopotamia offered both a rich river valley and such a cross roads. Her people were, therefore, both agricultural and commercial. But the protection from attack which a land like Egypt enjoyed is also a momentous factor, in some cases the deciding factor in the beginnings of a state. Flowers do not grow in trodden paths nor gardens on causeways. States do not develop in the highways of armies and migrations. Buffer states rarely become anything more. The Hittite Empire began in the barren uplands of Asia Minor. Athens and Sparta, not Corinth on its Isthmus, were the great states of Greece. Russia was born, not in the rich black lands of the south over which the migrating hordes of Asia swarmed at will, but in the little *polia,* or *poliany,* the clearings in the less fertile, but also less accessible wooded zones. The British Empire began on an island. Palestine had neither protection nor unusual resources. Her cities were always in danger of invasion by the swarming tribes of the desert, the hardy mountaineers of the north, and the trained soldiery of "civilized" lands. The land was ravaged and laid under tribute by the Egyptians, Hittites, Babylonians, Assyrians, Persians, Greeks, Romans, and Parthians. Between raids and invasions her little nations never had breathing space. It was a situation that favored the growth of imperial ambitions but never allowed them opportunity for realization.[24]

Yet the central situation which gave Palestine a place of importance in diplomacy, military strategy, and commerce was another factor of inestimable value in preparing the Hebrews to make a contribution to the moral and religious side of human

[23] *History of Civilization in Palestine,* p. 31.

[24] See Febvre, *Geog. Intro. to Hist.,* pp. 175 ff., Teggart, *The Processes of History,* pp. 45-53. The latter emphasizes the importance of conflict in nation building, but has isolated one factor at the expense of others.

culture. Sitting on their rough mountains that overlooked the sea and the desert, the people of Israel could not be ignorant of what the rest of the world was thinking and doing. They watched Egypt, Phoenicia, and Babylon struggle with the problems of life, and from their seat of semi-detachment they meditated on the passing show of history, in which at times they became involuntary or voluntary actors. Gradually they worked out certain principles to govern human conduct. They discovered no new glazes for pottery; they evolved no new principles of sculpture; they invented no new styles of architecture; they made no contribution to the arts of war; they gave no fresh impulses to physical science, no ideas to metaphysics. But in the realm of literary expression they surpassed every ancient race but the Greeks. The best that ancient Egypt and Babylonia produced is turgid, confused, and repetitious. The Hebrews thought clearly and expressed themselves with a simplicity and directness that has become a model for the modern world. In the realm of morals and religion their clear thinking enabled them to see thru the confusions of human life, to isolate the essential factors, and to enunciate the fundamental principles that make social progress possible. The literatures of the ancient world, the best thinking of its greatest peoples, came into their hands. With unerring keenness, with a supernatural instinct for the finest and purest, they borrowed and reshaped the choicest that came to them and with true originality they turned lead into gold; they created the sublimest moral and religious literature the world knows.

VI. INTERIOR DIVERSITIES

In the foregoing I have, in the main, spoken of Palestine as a whole. But the little land is far from being geographically, and therefore economically and culturally, a unit. Diversities of relief and consequently of climate within the land have had a profound influence upon its history. The geological processes that produced the strange jumble of mountain, plain, and gorge which makes the Holy Land different from any other divided it into little sections by frontiers which the limited cultures of the tribes and city states of antiquity could not surmount. The deep cleft of the Ghôr, or gorge of the Jordan, cut off eastern from western Palestine. The Plain of Esdraelon and the Valley of Jezreel separated Galilee from Samaria and Judea.

Even more important was the fact that diversity of terraine created diversity of economic life. In spite of Esdraelon, southern Galilee is more like Samaria than Samaria is like its neighbor, Judah. In spite of the Ghôr, Gilead was more nearly related to Samaria than Judea was to the Maritime Plain. In lower Galilee and in Samaria are mountains with level valleys and plains between, quite in contrast to the rocky tableland and narrow gorges of Judea. They offer more land for cultivation at less expense of labor. One sees proportionately many more cattle in the north than in Judea, more sheep and goats in the south.[25] In the south the land is too broken and precipitous and too barren to provide suitable ranges for cattle. Samaria and Galilee are not only much richer, they are more easily entered and crossed and much less easily defended. In consequence the northern kingdom of Israel developed power, comfort, and luxury much more easily and quickly than the south, and was much more deeply permeated by foreign influences. For the same reason Galilee was a "circle of the nations" in both Old and New Testament times, being far less thoroly and strictly Jewish in the times of Jesus than was Judea.[26]

In like manner the Maritime Plain was differentiated from the mountain regions. There are minor differences; its agriculture was of another type; its products were dissimilar. Whereas one finds great grain fields and, in modern times, orchards of citrus fruits on the seacoast plain, the olive is confined largely to the mountains and the Shephelah. Flocks of sheep and goats are not wanting but they are proportionately and actually smaller than in Judea. But the decisive difference is in accessibility to commerce. The great transcontinental trunk lines of traffic ran across

[25] A government census in 1920-21 confirms a traveler's impression; Sawyer, *Agricultural Situation,* Part IV, Appendix, pp. 1, 27.

[26] Is. 9.1; Mt. 4.15.

the Plain, and its seaports, tho almost negligible for modern steamer traffic, were not impossible havens for the little merchant vessels of antiquity. In both war and peace the Maritime Plain was the scene of great activity. No army would try to cross or even to enter the mountains of Palestine, except under dire necessity. Even the peaceful caravan would, if possible, avoid their hot, toilsome defiles, where attacks from robbers were easily made and with difficulty repelled. Accordingly, the Maritime Plain was always a center of foreign influences, where bloomed a culture compounded of all the exotic elements that found their way to the center of the world. It is not without significance that the Philistines found their seat here, and that later Gaza and Askalon were commercially important and architecturally beautiful Greek cities. All that I have said of the centrality of Palestine applies with double force to the land of the Philistines.

Between the Maritime Plain and Judea lay the Shephelah, a region with a character all of its own. Cut off by a long valley like a shallow foss from the mountains of Judea, which rise quickly to an elevation of between two thousand and three thousand feet behind it, and showing distinctly higher than the plain to the west of it, it lies like a sloping shelf between the land of the Philistines and Greeks on the one hand and the homeland of the Jews on the other. The great wadis that cut so deep into the edge of the Judean tableland are here broad valleys where are springs, brooks with pebbly beds, and great grain fields. On the hillsides are olive groves finer, thinks Sir George Adam Smith, than those of either lowland or mountain.[27] It is a land of limestone buttes and subterranean caverns,

"a rough, happy land, with its glens and moors, its mingled brushwood and barley fields; frequently under cultivation, but for the most part broken and thirsty, with few wells and many hiding-places; just the home for strong border-men like Samson, and just the theater for that guerilla warfare, varied occasionally by pitched battles, which Israel

[27] So he remarks in *Historical Geography,* p. 208, but in *Jerusalem,* I, p. 300, he says: "Round Jerusalem . . . the Palestine olive reaches its best."

and Philistia, the Maccabees and the Syrians, Saladin and Richard waged with each other." [28]

By the same token it was the battle-ground of civilizations, a frontier between warring cultures, between the semi-nomadism and difficult tillage of the hills and the rewarding agriculture and blooming commercialism of the plain.

The southerly border of Palestine is the Negeb, where the Central Range lets itself down by broad undulations, thru which the great Wâdî Khalîl winds as far as Beersheba and then as Wâdî es-Seba' turns sharply westward to the sea. The Negeb is the *South,* the 'dry,' or 'parched land.' South of Beersheba and Wâdî es-Seba' lie sixty miles of wild, bare mountain country, almost impassable and inhabited by the most untamed of Ishmaelites. North of Beersheba the land is green and fertile compared with the desert mountains to the south, and forms an open and attractive frontier to anyone who holds the mountains and the roads which skirt them. This could not well be a path for "civilized" armies, but it has been no barrier to the sons of the desert. It is to them an open frontier. Beyond the mountains of the Negeb, in the days before the Hebrew Conquest, dwelt the Kenites. Here at some sacred well, Kadesh-barnea, the wandering tribes that later constituted the Hebrew people, or a dominant part of them, gathered. From this region possibly some of them made their way directly northward into the "land of promise." North of this range, in the most easterly part of the Negeb, at the southern edge of the Wilderness of Judea, lay the region which the Kenites, after their entry, chose as their own. Next to them dwelt the Jerahmeelites, Judah, and then Caleb, all of them semi-nomadic tribes in or bordering on the Negeb.[29] The Negeb was the Edomite frontier and thru it the children of Esau pressed in the days of Judah's weakness, during the Exile, to seize Hebron and the adjacent territory.

The Wilderness of Judea represents the eastern frontier of the Southern Kingdom, as the Shephelah does the western. Shelv-

[28] *Historical Geography,* p. 209. To Sir George Adam Smith belongs the distinction of first making clear the limits and character of the Shephelah.

[29] 1 Sam. 27.10; 30.14.

ing off by successive steps from the mountains of Judah to the tremendous depression of the Ghôr, cut by winding wadis that are dug deep by the torrents from winter rains on the mountains, but arid and treeless, it is a true desert. It has almost no streams and few springs. Occasionally there are wells in the wadi beds or cisterns to store the surface water of winter. In the winter and spring of a normal year vegetation shoots up for a little while and the wandering tribes who inhabit the region sow grain and reap a scant harvest from the few broad valleys and undulating hills. Within it no settled, agricultural life can ever have existed, except at ʻAin Jidî, without a change of climate for which the evidence is not as yet conclusive. Remains of ancient cities, aside from En-gedi, are found only on its borders.[30]

It is a geographical fact of the utmost historical importance that a desert region measuring rather uniformly from twelve to fifteen miles across ran the full length of the eastern border of Judea. It was in itself a sufficient bulwark against the "civilized" armies of ancient times. But it was a frontier which, like the Negeb, the nomad loved and which it was impossible to fortify against him. While Moab and the Ghôr saved Judea from being repeatedly wasted by hordes from the desert, the Wilderness lay like an open door on her eastern border, connecting with the Negeb at the south to allow the slow infiltration of nomad clans and likewise to permit the settled inhabitants of her cities and villages to escape to freedom and solitude whenever danger threatened or inclination beckoned.

Within the boundaries we have described, Judea occupies a unique position. The isolation ascribed to Palestine as a whole can be truly predicated of the mountains of Judea. While her northern frontier was uncertain and difficult to defend, she was easily protected on her other borders against the attacks of superior civilizations. She lay between the sown and the unsown, partaking of the character of both. Her own territory was small, some fifteen to twenty miles wide and forty long. It was rough

[30] See my article, "The Wilderness of Judea and the Nomadic Ideal," *Journal of Geography*, 23 (1924), p. 347.

and unattractive, offering within itself no high peaks, no magnificent and overwhelming outlooks, and few beautiful, quiet landscapes. The bare, rocky moorland plateau is cut deep on its eastern and western borders by steep and narrow wadis that carry off the winter rains. Only here and there, as in the neighborhood of the "Shepherds' Fields" east of Bethlehem, in the Valley of the Rephaim, or near Abu Ghosh, does one see broad, fertile fields or quiet country scenes. Judea, even more than other parts of Palestine, has no wealth of products. She cannot now and never could raise her own grain supplies. Only in figs, wine, and olive oil, possibly also in wool or woolen cloth, did she produce enough for export.[31] This little, barren hill country could never be attractive either to commerce or conquest. She had too little to offer. And it was this, coupled with her difficult approaches, that saved her again and again during the troubled centuries that followed David's adoption of Jerusalem as his capital. She was not worth the strenuous efforts necessary to capture her and she rarely had the military strength to menace the armies which she could so often watch marching along the seacoast plain.

The people of the Southern Kingdom were for the most part confined to their mountains. Only during rare eras of special strength, in the age of Solomon, of Asa, of Uzziah, and of the Maccabees, were they able to hold seaports. During much of their history they did not control the cities of the plain thru which the caravan trade of the world had to pass. Therefore, they were dependent upon the scant products of their rocky hillsides. Theirs was a home by the side of the road, from which they watched the races of men go by without being able to mingle effectively, as a nation, in the throng. They were in the world, but not of it. Wherefore the shepherds and peasants of Judea watched their flocks and tilled their vineyards and olive orchards, in happiness and comfort when their rulers succeeded in wresting tribute from their neighbors, in levying tolls upon passing caravans, and in gathering profits from their commerce; in weakness and misfortune when they in turn were mulcted for tribute and lost their

[31] See Smith, *Jerusalem,* I, pp. 297-376; Jeremias, *Jerusalem,* Pt. I.

precarious sources of surplus income. At length Jerusalem became more and more a shrine of pilgrimage and began to reap the profits of religion. Then the Holy City entered upon a new era in her history and became what she was in New Testament times and is today, a religious mendicant, living on the tourists and pilgrims who come to visit her sacred places. When David chose Jerusalem as his capital and Solomon built the Temple there, they determined the whole future history of their people. A worse center could hardly have been found for a great empire. Indeed, an empire was impossible with such a capital. The choice of Jerusalem involved the division of the kingdom. It set the scene for the center of Hebrew worship and religious development in a poverty-stricken land where luxury was the exception, where industry, simplicity, and hardihood were common virtues. The social ideals which are the subject of the present study are, in a very true sense, the outcome of the geographical situation of Jerusalem.

The peculiar diversities just sketched are, then, responsible for much that is unique in Palestinian history. They produced difficult problems of internal politics and international diplomacy. In the fields of economics and social relationships they forced the Hebrews into experiences which were peculiarly broad and representative. They were largely responsible for the failure of the Israelites ever to achieve permanent unity such as is necessary for a strong and conquering nation. But in struggling with the problems caused by these diversities, the prophets of Israel evolved the religious truth which has won their nation more honor than if they had gained the whole world.

VII. SUMMARY AND CONCLUSIONS

How now shall we summarize the part which the physical factors—geographical relief, geographical relationships, climate, and natural resources—have played in the development of the economic and social thinking of the Hebrews? At first glance Palestine does not seem to have been blessed with the physical basis for making any contribution to human culture. Her mountains do not provide the awe-inspiring scenery which Buckle, no doubt wrongly, thought to be directly stimulating to the human mind. Her capricious climate may have contributed to the Hebrews' conception of God and his providence, but other nations had the same climate without ever achieving such religious ideas. It might be suggested that the vividness and concreteness of the Hebrew imagination and the incisive clarity of Hebrew thought and speech are due in part to the simple yet clearly drawn and sharply contrasting pictures which the seasons painted, the vivid green and flowery brightness of spring, the glaring white of summer, the dull gray of winter. A like contribution might be found in the wonderful transparency of the fogless atmosphere, the brilliancy of the sky, the sharply chiseled lines of the mountain ranges, the silver ribbon of surf between the staring white of the sand dunes and the radiant blue of the sea. The luxuriant and unbridled imagination which could produce the complicated impossibilities of Indian art and legend, the puerile inconsistencies of Egyptian theology, and the gay exuberance of Greek mythology does not seem at home in such an environment, but rather a mind well balanced and far seeing, given to common sense and a realistic appreciation of the hard facts of life. But Egypt and Greece have much the same atmosphere. Such direct effects of landscape and climate are not to be sought. Rather, it is the indirect effects of all the physical factors working thru historical experience and social contacts which are not to be overlooked.

The history of the Hebrews in Palestine does not entirely bear out Miss Semple when she says:

"Mountain regions discourage the budding of genius because they are areas of isolation, confinement, remote from the great currents of men and ideas that move along the river valleys. They are regions of much labor and little leisure, of poverty today and anxiety for the morrow, of toil-cramped hands and toil-dulled brains. In the fertile alluvial plains are wealth, leisure, contact with many minds, large urban centers where commodities and ideas are exchanged. The two contrasted environments produce directly certain economic and social results, which, in turn, become the causes of secondary intellectual and artistic effects."[32]

This is true insofar as Judea, the most isloated of the districts of Palestine, was also the least progressive. Jerusalem produced the great prophets, but she also murdered them. Galilee reared Jesus to die at Jerusalem. What Palestine offered the Hebrews was an inimitable combination of mountain and plain. The rough, forbidding, and unproductive mountains in a healthful, variable climate produced a race blessed with bodily and mental vigor, a love for manual labor, and boundless adaptability. Tho they protected, they did not fully isolate, nor did hard labor dull the minds of all. In the fertile plains below, the hardy mountaineers made contacts with the whole of the ancient world. They were at once isolated and centrally situated. Mentally and religiously they belonged both to the desert and to the sown. They knew both mountain and plain, both sea and land. They were acquainted with the wild, free life of the uncultivated wilderness, the joyful harvests and the gay vintages as well as the vexing hardships and the fatal failures of agriculture, the grinding toil of industry, the rich rewards and the bitter losses of commerce. In the indirect effects of a remarkable combination of upland and lowland, of sterility and fruitfulness, of remoteness and worldwide intercourse, we find the origin of the unique social ideals of the Hebrews.

In spite, then, of apparent disadvantages, Palestine's climate and geographical situation were such as to prepare the Hebrews for an intelligent and original contribution to international civilization, not in the fields of economics and politics, not in imaginative literature nor in art, not in science nor speculative philosophy, but in practical morality and religion. Directly, but indirectly far more, the unique geographical conditions of Palestine played a large part in the development of Hebrew life and thought. Much must be conceded to the geographical interpretation of history.

Under ancient conditions of travel and intercourse the variety

[32] *Influences of Geographic Environment,* New York, Henry Holt & Co., p. 20, quoted by Bristol, *Social Adaptation,* pp. 112 f.

of climate and contour within the country gave to its different sections their own idiosyncrasies of outlook and, therefore, caused each to play its own peculiar part in the drama of history: Judea the self-sufficient and sometimes fanatical Puritan, Samaria the liberal-minded, open-hearted spendthrift, Galilee the enterprising, forward-looking pioneer. The Israelites' conception of God and his providence was the product partly of the difficulties with which they wrestled on a rough and rocky soil under a capricious climate, and partly of the tragic drama of world history in which their location forced them to be subordinate and unwilling actors. Their pattern ideas in social matters, tho transformed in passing thru their minds, were in good part inherited from older nations with whom their geographical location forced them to live as allies or subjects. Their democracy was due partly to their close proximity to the Arabian steppe, from which they had come and from which they received repeated infusions of nomadic blood and ideals, and partly to the fact that, in their geographical situation, overflowing luxury and highly complex social and economic organization were impossible. Proximity to the desert kept the blood of frugal, hardy, liberty-loving nomadism ever fresh in the veins of the Hebrews. Nearness to lands where wealth, luxury, and international intercourse were common prepared them for participation in world affairs and for sharing with the world the products of their vigorous thinking. The social ideals of their great prophets were in good part at least the product of the long conflict between nomadic, agricultural, and urban-commercial ideals, a conflict forced upon them by their exceptional location between the desert and the sown and on the highways of international commerce. And finally their unique contribution as missioners of their ideals to all the world was due again to the toughness and adaptability bred in them by their environment and to the central location in which their land was placed. To the elaboration and proof of these statements and to the interpretation of these effects as seen in Hebrew history, the succeeding chapters are given.

CHAPTER III

THE FATHERS ACCORDING TO THE FLESH

I. THE IMPORTANCE OF ETHNOLOGICAL AND POLITICAL FACTORS

For the understanding of the social and economic ideals of the Hebrews certain facts in their racial and political history are of decisive importance. The influence of racial peculiarities on the progress of a group and the part which racial differences play in history are matters of dispute. There is disagreement as to the elements and even the fact of racial superiority. Now, it cannot be denied that in the course of time environment and natural or artificial selection come to mark each race with its own peculiar characteristics which play their part in its history. The physical *differentiæ* are easily determined. Height, weight, size and shape of bones, and especially the measurements of the face and head, clearly distinguish one race from another. But what is their historical and social value? A large brain does not always mark the genius. The psychological *differentiæ* are measured with much greater difficulty and there is complete disagreement as to their origin. Are they handed down by physical inheritance and are they then responsible for the social organization and cultural progress of each race? Or is it the social inheritance, that which each generation learns from its predecessor, that counts?

It is not possible nor would it be highly profitable to attempt to answer these questions with regard to the Hebrews. Yet in view of widespread misconceptions it is necessary to consider briefly their racial history and inheritance. It will tend to conciseness if, at the same time, we trace Palestine's international political relationships, another important factor in the development of its social institutions and its culture. The course of Israel's racial history is to no small degree also the course of its political and its religious history. Given its central position, it was inevitable that Palestine should become the stage of a most complicated struggle between races and nations of very diverse kinds. Its situation gave it a part, however modest, in the greatest political movements of history. The racial and political forces which used the natural resources and the geographical conditions of Palestine are, therefore, of fascinating interest. A proper estimate of the racial characteristics of the people who came to inherit the unique land we have described and of the long process of experience thru which they developed their social institutions is essential to an understanding of the ultimate outcome.

As to race, the fundamental fact is that the Hebrews came from an extraordinary mixture of stocks. There is no small justification for the contention that there is no Semitic race. There are numerous peoples who speak related languages which, for want of a better term, may be called Semitic. But it is far from true that the nations which speak these languages were originally of one blood or, if they had been, that they were all alike in character or institutions.[1] The Hebrews were not only a mixture of various Semitic-speaking peoples, they also assimilated important elements from entirely non-Semitic races. Palestine's central location at the bridge-head between Asia and Africa brought into it peoples from the north and the south, the east and the west. Aegean and Egyptian, Semite and Aryan, possibly Mongolian, with others of less clearly defined affinities, have made their contribution to its racial and political history. Briefly to canvass the evidence for this most important fact will throw light on Hebrew social ideals.

II. PRE-HEBREW PALESTINE

The inhabitants of Palestine before the entrance of the Hebrew tribes were of various stocks. The age of the Neanderthal man,

[1] H. G. Richardson, "The Semites," *AJSL,* 41 (1924), 1-10.

whose bones were recently discovered by the Sea of Galilee, lies too far back to affect the historical problems which are here to be discussed. Besides a paleolithic race of which slight traces have been found, abundant evidence in caves, megalithic monuments, stone implements, and skeletons, in surviving non-Semitic place and race names, and in literary allusions proves the existence of at least one cave-dwelling race of short stature and thick, long-headed skulls, a people of the highland breed. Myres says:

> "Their implements, pottery, and other equipment are in strong contrast both with everything Egyptian, and with the grassland [Arabian] influences which predominate later. Arabian man has occupied the 'good land' again and again; but the moist air seems to be fatal to him, and many of the peasantry of south Palestine are hardly to be distinguished from their neolithic predecessors."[2]

Whether the Anakim, Rephaim, and Nephelim are to be identified with a tall pre-Semitic race is questionable, for no skeletons of such a people have been found. Likewise we are still in darkness as to who the Emim, Zamzummim, and Zuzim were, tho it is not unreasonable to regard them as aboriginal peoples whose non-Semitic languages seemed to their Semitic conquerors a succession of unintelligible hissing sounds. The biblical Horites have been supposed to be aboriginal cave-dwellers, but they may well be offshoots of the Hurrites of northern Mesopotamia, of whom considerable remains have been discovered.[3]

These peoples were succeeded by a Semitic-speaking race which partly destroyed, partly assimilated them. Whether these Semites are to be called Amorites or Canaanites, whether they came in one wave or two, does not concern us. The fact of importance for the present discussion is that "grass-land" people from central Arabia made their appearance in Palestine before its history begins and that the population remained predominantly Semitic until the

[2] *CAH,* I, p. 39. Cf. Macalister, *Hist. of Civilization in Palestine,* pp. 8-26; *Gezer,* I, pp. 58 f., 75-152; Barton, *Arch. and the Bible,* pp. 118-22, 157 f.; H. Vincent, *Jérusalem sous terre,* pp. 27 f.; Meinhold in *Baudissin Festschrift,* pp. 331-53.

[3] See Chiera and Speiser in *Annual ASOR,* VI (1926), 75-90.

beginning of the second millennium. From the mountains of Elam to the Mediterranean there seems to have been a fairly uniform culture. Both Egypt and Babylonia began to interest themselves in Syria and Palestine at least early in the third millennium, as their records and the archeological discoveries at Byblus (Gebal) prove.

Shortly after 2000 B.C. the Semitic world in the west and the east was rudely disturbed by the intrusion of northern races, the Kassites in Babylonia, the Hittites in Asia Minor, and Mitannians on the upper Euphrates. The Aryan-speaking Kassites, or Cosseans, killed the germs of progress in Babylonia for over half a millennium, during which time Assyria was founded and gradually developed. The Aryan-speaking Mitannians, so far as certain evidence is discoverable, never succeeded in wielding influence or making settlements so far south as Palestine. The Hittites established a much more enduring and far-reaching empire, including at the height of their power, in the fourteenth century, northern Syria and nearly all of Asia Minor. Their racial affinities will remain doubtless for some time a matter of dispute. The discovered hieroglyphic and cuneiform documents indicate that they spoke several languages, but indubitably one of them was Aryan. Doubtless the armies of both the Hittites and the Mitannians were largely recruited from people of native stock. There is no indisputable evidence that the Hittites ever came in large numbers so far south as Palestine. Yet Abraham is said to have bought the cave of Macpelah at Hebron from the children of Heth. Abdi-Khiba, or Abdi-Hepa, king of Jerusalem in the Amarna age, was either a Hittite or Mitannian, and the unfortunate Uriah the Hittite, who was married to Bathsheba, later the mother of Solomon, may be taken as guarantee for the presence of many of his countrymen among the Israelites.

The Hyksos kings of Egypt are an unsolved ethnological problem. Concurrently with a general restlessness of the nations they passed thru Palestine and conquered Egypt, probably about 1700 B.C. It is impossible to label them as to race, but, whatever the name Hyksos may mean, they are properly called shepherd kings and in social institutions were much more like the grass-land Semites than the Egyptians. The names of some of them, such as Jacob-el, show the presence of Semites, but it seems hardly probable that they were homogeneous. From all the data available it is reasonable to conclude that they were a mixed host of Mitannians, Hittites, and other northern peoples, perhaps from central Asian grass-lands, and gathered to themselves many Semites as they passed southward. With them, possibly, the Jacob tribes entered Egypt.

If these are matters of uncertainty, the events following the expulsion of the Hyksos kings from Egypt, which were of immense importance to Palestine, are well known. Egypt had long maintained commercial relations with Palestine and had occasionally made raids in that direction. Semites had repeatedly entered Egypt, as traders, as temporary or permanent immigrants, and as conquerors during the "First Interregnum"[4] and during the Hyksos period. The Eighteenth Dynasty, in developing the military spirit and prowess necessary to drive out the foreign conquerors, produced in their self-sufficient land by the Nile, for the first time, a far-reaching militaristic and imperialistic ambition. The result was a great Asiatic empire that endured in Palestine, with much loss of prestige in the Amarna age, from the reign of Thutmose I, about 1500 B.C., until the irruption of the sea-peoples in the reign of Ramses III, early in the twelfth century. Even then, as archeological remains and occasional allusions in the Bible prove, Egypt did not cease to cherish ambitions and to wield influence in Palestine. And there is evidence to show that in the Negeb, in the neighborhood of Gerar (Umm Jerâr, some eight miles south of Gaza), there was an Egyptian outpost or dependency, perhaps defended by Nubian mercenaries, down to the time of Hezekiah.[5] The extent of negro and Egyptian influence in southern Palestine today may be taken as an index of what it

[4] H. Frankfort, "Egypt and Syria in the First Intermediate Period," *JEA*, 12 (1926), 80-99.

[5] The evidence is presented by W. F. Albright, *JPOS*, IV (1924), 131-61, who would substitute Gerar for Gezer in 1 Kg. 9.15 ff. See now the work of Flinders Petrie, *QSPEF*, July, 1927, pp. 129-40.

has always been. The oldest road in the world was well trodden many millennia before the railroad was laid along its route. The influence of the Egyptians upon the Israelites was much greater than we have been accustomed to recognize.

It was, therefore, a variegated population that held the land into which the Hebrews entered. Descendants of the cave-dwellers were still to be found. Various immigrations of grass-land Semites had passed over it. Invaders of Aryan tongue, Hittites and Mitannians, and possibly some of other stocks, had come. The anatomical evidence points to a larger infusion of these peoples, especially the Hittites, than would be suspected from the historical evidence at present available. Babylonians, Sumerian and Semitic, had not been wanting and there had been constant intercourse with Egypt. The predominant stock was, no doubt, Amorite-Canaanite, but the others must not be forgotten.

III. HEBREW PALESTINE

A discussion of the many questions that remain unanswered in regard to the Exodus and the Hebrew settlement of Palestine need not delay us. Whether the Hebrews and Habiru are identical or not, whether they were Aramean in language or Amorite-Canaanite, whether all the tribes were in bondage in Egypt or not, whether some entered from the Negeb or all from across the Jordan, these questions do not materially affect the problems with which we are concerned. The facts of importance for the present argument are widely accepted. It is agreed that at least some of the Hebrew tribes, including that from which the priestly families of Israel were thought to be derived, were for some generations in Egypt, probably living in the eastern Delta, where they could continue their inherited semi-nomadic type of life. All of the entering tribes were nomads and they brought with them a tradition of dealings with Yahweh, the god of the nomadic Kenites whose home had been the regions south of the Negeb. The process of settlement in Canaan was long and gradual. It involved constant conflicts with unconquered Canaanite cities and with other nomadic peoples, but only in rare instances their destruction under the *ḥerem,* or ban. Only in the rougher, mountainous sections was Hebrew dominance achieved. Here the Hebrews reduced the conquered population to servitude. The Maritime Plain was never Hebrew in population. Jerusalem was a Jebusite enclave until David's time. The gradual assimilation of the agricultural population and the transition from nomadic to settled life were accomplished more rapidly and thoroly in some parts of the country than in others. In the north the Canaanite element was considerable; in the south the Hebrew, or nomadic, stock was predominant, and culture was more slowly achieved. The physiography of Palestine and the diverse character of the incoming tribes as well as of the subjugated populations gave rise to ethnological and cultural variations.

The weak and scattered Hebrew tribes, not yet fully at home in their new environment and divided by the Jebusite kingdom at Jerusalem, were finally driven together by the threat of annihilation at the hands of the Philistines. Unfortunately we know too little about this race, but certain facts are clear. The fourteenth, thirteenth, and twelfth centuries were times of extraordinary restlessness among the peoples of the Aegean as they were also among the bedouin tribes and the little nations of Palestine and Syria. Put in motion by the pressure of the Hellenic tribes which were moving down from the north, they set out to find new homes. In the *débâcle,* the remarkable Aegean civilization was practically destroyed. In the latter part of the thirteenth century some of these peoples started southward with their wives and children, in ships by sea and in wagons by land, destroying the Hittite kingdoms of northern Syria as they came. Ramses III met them somewhere on the Palestinian or Syrian coast and administered such a defeat that they abandoned their intention of entering Egypt, but they were still strong enough to occupy the fairest part of the land of Palestine, the fertile Maritime Plain, from Carmel south to the desert. Settling in the coast cities of Palestine about the time when the last of the Hebrews were arriving in the mountains, they soon began to expand over the Shephelah. The struggle with this foreign race drove the racially related Canaanites and Hebrews together and forced them in self-defense to give up their tribal independence and to unite under a king.

The names which the Egyptians gave these "sea-peoples" are differently interpreted, but some of them were probably of the same tribes as those which later conquered and gave their names to Sardinia and Sicily. The *Sherden,* or *Shardina,* may have come from Sardes. The *Denyen,* or *Daanau,* may be the Δαναοί, Greeks. The *Akaiwasha* may have been the Achaeans. The *Pulesati* are without doubt the Philistines. They at least are said by the biblical writers to come from Crete, but the Egyptian accounts and their armor and dress ally them with the Lycians and Carians. It seems probable, therefore, that their home was originally the southwestern corner of Asia Minor and that they had made a temporary home in Crete, perhaps destroying the kingdom of Knossus.

It was a mixed multitude that seized the fairest plain in the land of Canaan. Some of them were of the new invaders who had caused their migration. The greater part belonged to the Anatolian branch of the Aegean civilization. Yet Crete had made its impress upon them. The dress and armor of the Philistines as depicted on the Egyptian monuments and their armor as described by the biblical writers, in Goliath's case for example, are not those of the Cretans, yet there are many features of their architecture and art, especially their pottery, which link them closely with Crete. Apparently they knew the use of iron and were, therefore, a formidable enemy to the bronze-using peoples of Canaan. Tho uncircumcized northerners, they apparently coalesced with the Semitic population who already occupied the plain. They adopted Semitic deities, Dagon of Gaza and Ashdod, Derceto, or Atargatis, of Askalon, Astarte of Beth-shean, Baal-zebub of Ekron, and Baal of Gaza, altho they did not forget religious traditions that bound them to their former homes. They brought with them Cretan pottery and apparently the theater, or theatral area, of the Cretan palace along with the games that were played in it, such as boxing and bull-baiting.

The importance of this non-Semitic element in the population of Palestine has often been overlooked. Traditional biblical interpretation regards them simply as a menace to the Israelites. They were much more. Since they belonged to a distinctly higher type of civilization, contact with them gave a decided upward swing to Hebrew culture, while their attacks were forcing the formation of the Hebrew monarchy. Tho their coming did not inaugurate the age of iron,[5a] they introduced many other features of Aegean culture. The persistence of their influence is notable. Not only did the name of their most important tribe attach itself permanently to the land they had conquered; they themselves maintained until classical times a tradition of their overseas origin and so a claim to superiority over the Semitic population among whom they lived. Beginning probably as subjects of the Pharaohs, a century later the newcomers could mock at his envoys, as did the *Zakkal* (Sicilians) of Dor at Wenamon. Adad-nirari records the receipt of tribute from Tyre, Sidon, the "land of Omri," Edom, and *Palashtu* (Philistia), but Judea is not worth mentioning (802 B.C.). In Hezekiah's time they are still a force to be reckoned with. It is the presence of the Philistines, rather than racial antipathy to the sea or the poor character of the harbors on the coast, that was ultimately responsible for the failure of the Israelites ever to become a seafaring people.

This is another ethnological element in the inheritance of the Hebrews. The stories of Samson and of David's outlaw years are enough to show that even the greatest Israelite heroes could have the closest relations with the uncircumcized Philistine. Carites, Cherethites, and Pelethites, for generation after generation royal mercenaries at Jerusalem, are Carians, Cretans, and Philistines, for these peoples were as famous as mercenaries at that time as the Swiss formerly were in Europe. In so small a land as Palestine it is impossible that there should not have been constant intermixture between the various races, for up to the time of the Exile there appears to have been no attempt among the Hebrews to prevent marriage outside the race.

[5a] See Flinders Petrie on his excavations at Gerar, *QSPEF,* July, 1927, pp. 137, 142.

The proportion of Hebrew, Canaanite, Philistine, and other elements in the population after the Hebrew settlement in Canaan cannot be estimated. The original invading Hebrews were, no doubt, thoro Semites, with straight noses, large, straight mouths, and narrow, high, and sloping foreheads. It is now a widely accepted theory that the profile which is supposed to be distinctly Jewish and which differentiates the race from the Arabs and other Semites as well as from the Nordic races was an heirloom from a non-Semitic, Armenoid strain in the Canaanite population due to the Hittites and Mitannians. It is also suggested that the Pseudo-Gentile type, characterized often by fair color and a Greek profile, is due to the Philistines.[6] Since, after the Exile, the Jews set up a wall between themselves and their neighbors, and Christian hate has until recently built it higher, the hypothesis seems possible that the racial mixture which gave rise to the divergent Jewish types took place in the period we are studying. In any case, all the circumstances point to a large amount of intermixture. The proportion of non-Semitic blood must all together be great. Another inference is comparatively certain: the Hebrew type would be purest in the ruling classes and in the more nomadic clans; the Canaanite and Amorite elements would be largest in the peasant, agricultural population. The conquered always fall to the lowest and most abused stratum. Thus racial differences would tend to develop social distinctions. However, the whole period down to the Exile must have been marked by a growing intermixture of the Hebrews with the various types that had been in Canaan before them and by the gradual disappearance of racial peculiarities.

The brief blossoming of Hebrew civilization under David and Solomon was made possible by the temporary weakness of all the great nations of antiquity. Their conquest of the Philistines had developed coherence in the Israelite group of tribes. The Hittite Empire had been weakened or destroyed by the sea-peoples. Mitanni disappeared at about the same time. Assyria and Baby-

[6] Dr. R. N. Salaman, "What Has Become of the Philistines?" *QSPEF*, 1925, pp. 37-45, 68-79, who denies the claim of Fishberg that the Jewish type is assimilated to that of the surrounding non-Jewish population.

lonia were just awakening from their long sleep under the Kassites. Egypt was decadent under sacerdotal rule. The Philistine menace gone, the Israelites fell apart again. The exactions of Solomon, his levies, taxes, and other interferences with the freedom to which they had been accustomed, could not be endured. The chief reason for the division of the kingdom was probably economic. The southern tribes, among which Judah is given the highest rank, were far less advanced in civilization than the northern. The nomadic element was much more prominent in the south. Indeed, the conquests of David were really the victory of the stalwart and ruthless sons of the desert over kinsmen who had begun to be weakened by the arts of peace. But once the prestige of their leader and the war-cry of Philistine oppression were lost, the southerners were too weak to hold their suzerainty. The richer northern clans would no longer submit to their ruder brethren of the south. The southern clans were held to the Davidic dynasty partly by the loyalty of kinship, partly by the fortress at Jerusalem and its mercenaries. Probably they had been favored by David and Solomon and had not felt the burdens of the monarchy as had the northern tribes, while they had profited from the growth of Jerusalem.

After the division of the kingdom the diverse circumstances of the two sections of the nation tended to separate them more and more. Their interests ran in opposite directions. For the greater part of the two centuries following the death of Solomon the kingdom of Judah was under the suzerainty of its larger and more powerful northern neighbor. The latter suffered severely from the constant attacks of the Aramean kingdom of Damascus and from frequent revolutions and dynastic changes, which testify to lack of internal unity. Civil strife which was due to a combination of economic, social, and religious elements played an important part in preventing the steady growth of the Israelite kingdoms. The struggles of which we hear the echoes in the Elijah-Elisha stories indicate a new infusion of nomadic blood and ideals. They mark the beginning of a bitter conflict between pastoral-agricultural and commercial customs and standards of morality. The contest was the fiercer because the prophets of Yahweh espoused the one side, the priests and prophets of Baal the other, and political and dynastic intrigues of a far-reaching character, even international in their scope, played their part in the bloody drama. The importance of the economic elements in the troubles which called forth the matchless eloquence of the prophets of Israel has long been recognized. The momentous part of their nomadic inheritance in the social development of the Israelites has only recently been given adequate attention. To this we shall return at a later time.[7]

Neither northern nor southern kingdom was able to achieve real prosperity until the advances of Assyria westward drew off the forces of Damascus. Then, for a long generation, Israel under Jeroboam II and Judah under Uzziah enjoyed a warm Indian summer of foreign conquests and commercial expansion, with resulting wealth, poverty, and social disturbances, before they fell under the power of the mailed fist of Nineveh. The two centuries beginning with this period of prosperity were the great creative period in Hebrew thinking and writing, but they were far from constituting a period of uniform political success and economic prosperity. Assyria's policy of deportation removed a large portion of the northern Israelites and substituted foreigners in their places. Assyrian annals mention the significant fact which the Bible omits that the new colonists were tribes of Tamud, Ibadid, Marsiman, Khayapa, and the "distant Arabs" of the desert.[8] The Assyrians frequently mention difficulties with Arabian and desert tribes during this era. Evidently they were restless and seeking to expand. The settlement in the territories of fallen Samaria indicates a new infusion of nomad blood into Palestine.

After the fall of Samaria Judah continued a precarious existence as a little mountain state for a century and a half. Oppressed and drained of tribute by the ruthless Assyrian, the tiny subject nation was distracted by antagonistic religious ideals and competing political parties, divided between a group loyal to Yahweh and condemning foreign alliances, another desiring conformity to Assyrian culture and religion, and a third that continually intrigued with

[7] See below, chap. V, pp. 124 f., 140, 150 f.

[8] *CAH,* III, pp. 57 f., 383, Olmstead, *History of Assyria,* p. 210.

Egypt, tempted also by Babylon and neighboring states which were restless under the burdens of Assyrian suzerainty. During the reign of Manasseh Assyrian influence was at its height. The religious and moral ideas of Nineveh and the culture of the Tigris-Euphrates valley must have made a very considerable impression upon the Israelites, and there was no doubt a tendency toward racial intermixture.

The Deuteronomic reform, the outstanding event of the whole period from David's capture of Jerusalem to its fall before Nebuchadrezzar's armies, put a temporary end to the policy of cultural assimilation. It crystallized the prophetic principles into a political creed, and, in so doing, it choked the life out of them and petrified them into a legal code. Thus it provided definite and visible means of resistance against further efforts at denationalization while it also introduced clear-cut lines of cleavage into the social group. But it did more than that. It tended to sap the vitality of religion and to tie the hands of moral and spiritual progress. It elevated the vicious sentiment of racial superiority into a lofty virtue with the highest religious sanctions. Wrapped up in it were the germs of Pharisaic particularism and Gentile anti-Semitism, from the Samaritan schism to the Ku Klux Klan. It made Jerusalem eventually the greatest center of superstitious veneration in the world. The return from the Exile, the Crucifixion, the Crusades, Allenby's campaign, all center about Jerusalem because for a decade the priestly-prophetic party under King Josiah held the field. Both politically and religiously the Deuteronomic reform was an event with unique results for world history.

Josiah's untimely death caused a reversal of policy. The recently discovered Babylonian account of the fall of Nineveh is interpreted as indicating that Egypt was at least nominally allied with Assyria and that Josiah lost his life because he was pursuing an anti-Assyrian policy.[9] In any case the reform came to an end and the kings whom the Egyptian and Babylonian overlords allowed to remain on the throne were outwardly friendly to their foreign

[9] C. J. Gadd, "The Fall of Nineveh," *Proceedings of the British Academy*, vol. X, 1921-23. *The Fall of Nineveh*, British Museum, 1923; cf. *ZAW*, 42 (1924), 157 ff.; J. M. P. Smith, *The Prophets and Their Times*, pp. 122 f.

suzerains. But they were constantly intriguing against their liege lords, and the weak and vicious policies of these sons of Josiah led to repeated deportations and finally to the destruction of the city. One is not to suppose that the land of Judea was left desolate and uninhabited, as the prophets proclaim. But for the subsequent racial history of the Jews as well as for the political and economic history of the period it is important to bear in mind that the deportation of the nobility and the skilled workmen took away those sections of the group in which the purer Semitic strain may be supposed to have persisted. The poorest people of the land who remained as vine-dressers and plowmen must have represented the lowest racial as well as the most meager social inheritance. Economic poverty would carry with it mental and cultural impoverishment. The land was in the hands of ignorant peasants who were farthest from representing true Hebrew blood and tradition.

The racial and religious situation was complicated further by a new infusion of nomad blood. The same restless movements of the tribes of the steppe which had already peopled Ephraim with Arameans and Arabians now affected Judah. While the country was unprotected and half denuded of inhabitants, the untamed nomad tribes from the south pressed in and occupied it almost up to Jerusalem itself. Edom had taken the mountains of Israel to be its own, to prey upon its pastures.[10] Probably they had been dispossessed by other tribes crowding in from the steppe behind in those migrations and economic readjustments which eventually gave rise to the Nabatean kingdom and made Petra a great city.[11] The newcomers were of the same race as the original Hebrews. Their customs and manner of life would differ from those of the poor inhabitants of Judah only by insensible gradations. In the course of a few years the sense of difference would largely disappear and the two groups would become practically one.

IV. THE PERSIANS AND GREEKS IN PALESTINE

Under the milder rule of the Persians the little Hebrew state revived again, thanks to the self-sacrificing religious and patriotic

[10] Ez. 36.5.
[11] Cook in *CAH,* III, pp. 405 f.

zeal of a few of the exiles who were willing to return and to the gifts of others who preferred the richer life of the Euphrates valley to the barren hills of their native land. The various attitudes of modern Judaism toward Zionism assist one to a reconstruction of the ancient return from exile. The contemporary prophetic documents, Zechariah 1-8 and Haggai, prove that the Chronicler's story in Ezra-Nehemiah has confused situations of different dates. If there was a return immediately after the accession of Cyrus, the number of those who came must have been small indeed and the resources of the little province extremely limited, for the community was scarcely able to rebuild the Temple after twenty years, and then only in a form which contrasted pitiably with the glory of Solomon's building.[12] The major part of the population consisted of the poor and backward vine-dressers and plowmen who had been left in the land at the time of the Exile and of the semi-nomadic intruders who had forced themselves into it.

Down to this time there is no evidence that the Hebrews as a group had exercised unusual care to keep their race pure. Deuteronomy, the only law code which had received official recognition, allowed them to make alliance with conquered cities, at least at a distance, and to take unto themselves the wives and children of their slain foes. While it prohibited them from intermarrying with the peoples of Canaan, or admitting them into their community, no such interdict stood between them and the Edomites or the Egyptians, nor indeed the Babylonians, Assyrians, Persians, and Greeks.[13] The proselyte from other nations was welcomed; the "stranger" was given special protection. That the ruthless warfare and uncompromising exclusiveness which Deuteronomy advocated with regard to the Hittites, the Amorites, the Canaanites, the Moabites, and all the rest of the original inhabitants had never been practised either in the days of the Conquest or at any subsequent period until the time of Nehemiah is abundantly evident. Deuteronomy, as noted above, was enforced only for a brief decade.

[12] Cook's discussion in *CAH,* III, pp. 408-15, may be taken as the best that can now be done toward a reconstruction of this dark period.

[13] Dt. 7.1 ff.; 20.17; 23.3-8. The Philistine, strangely enough, is not mentioned.

Innumerable statements in the historical books show that the Deuteronomic laws of exclusion were unknown. The very complaints of Ezra and Nehemiah indicate not only that the earlier "returns" under Cyrus or Darius had exercised little effect upon conditions in Judah, but also that there were still the closest relations between the Judean population and their neighbors, the Edomites, Moabites, Ammonites, Samaritans, and the peoples of the Maritime Plain, such as the Ashdodites. Intermarriage had gone so far that Jewish children were growing up in ignorance of their own language, and spoke half in the speech of Ashdod, or Ammon, or Moab. Even a grandson of the high priest had married the daughter of a Samaritan grandee with an Assyrian name. The extent of non-Jewish elements in the Jewish population is evidenced also by the genealogical lists in First Chronicles 2 and 4 and the semi-Edomite names which the Chronicler elsewhere uses.[14] We have already noted the renewed infusion of nomadic elements at this time.

The vicissitudes of the Zionist movement may serve to illustrate what took place at this time. Before the World War there had been a not inconsiderable return of Jews to Palestine. There were many European Jews in Jerusalem and several flourishing agricultural colonies had been founded. In spite of their sharp religious differences Jews and Moslems were living together in peace. Jewish agriculturalists were employing their Moslem neighbors as laborers and teaching them better methods of farming, without, to be sure, close social relationships. If these Palestinian Jews had been cut off for generations from contacts with their co-religionists in other lands, even the inherited exclusiveness of centuries could hardly have availed to prevent a mutual assimilation to a common type such as is occurring in the United States. After the War the same change occurred as when Nehemiah arrived in Jerusalem. Militant Zionism, backed by a supposedly omnipotent overlord, returned to Palestine with the avowed intention of possessing the land. The result has been open war with the non-Jewish inhabitants and sharp conflicts with many of the prewar immigrants.

[14] Cook in *CAH,* III, pp. 405, 478 ff.

The chauvinistic nationalism and bitter exclusiveness which Nehemiah manifested had long been developing. Its origin must be traced to the prophetic conflict with Baal worship. To be sure, the prophets exhibit very little one-hundred-per-cent patriotism. We turn to them for one of the earliest and finest manifestations of broad-minded humanitarianism and genuine internationalism. Yet the nomadic strain in their social and religious standards stood in sharp contrast with the customs of neighboring nations that were farther advanced in material culture. Their uncompromising moral earnestness made it impossible for them to regard with any degree of allowance the practices which they disapproved. The danger of contamination to Israel's religion which they saw in intercourse with their neighbors led naturally to a demand for separation. In the smaller minds that adopted these prophetic ideals and tried to reduce them to rules of conduct the inevitable outcome was a narrow and anti-prophetic exclusiveness.

This anti-foreign spirit comes to expression in Deuteronomy, as well as in other passages which are regarded as Deuteronomic in their origin.[15] In the prophets of the exilic period it is greatly intensified. Against Edom, which is not mentioned in the Deuteronomic condemnations, they wax especially bitter because Edom took advantage of their weakness to seize their native land.[16] All of the surrounding peoples come under the same condemnation, for they all rejoiced in Judah's downfall.[17]

The date of many of the passages which express these feelings of hatred is difficult to determine. This attitude of nationalistic narrowness first comes to practical expression, if we may take Nehemiah and Ezra as essentially trustworthy, in the middle of the fifth century. Certainly Haggai and Zechariah offer no evidence for its existence at the time of the rebuilding of the Temple. Rather they expect all nations to come to Jerusalem to worship Yahweh. But the returning exiles of the next century, nurtured in Babylon on the ancient literature of their nation and unac-

[15] Dt. 7.3; Ex. 34.16; Jos. 23.12; Dt. 20.17; Ex. 23.23 f.

[16] Ez. 25.12; 35; 36.5; Jer. 49.7; Is. 34.5, 6; Ob. 1-21. Am. 1.11 f. is commonly regarded as an interpolation of this period.

[17] Jer. 46-50; Ez. 25-28.

quainted with the conditions under which the poverty-stricken community was living in Judea, came back with national ideals and patriotic hatreds that were shocked into vigorous action.

The messianic hopes which had centered around Zerubbabel had been terribly disappointed. Unfortunately no record has been preserved to explain the process. The new elements which were introduced by Ezra or Nehemiah or which, at any rate, come to view in their time are various. The accepted form of government in the infinitesimal province becomes eventually that of a city-state with a priestly ruler; it is a sacerdotal state, piously called a theocracy. The returned exiles probably formed an aristocracy within which the priestly families gradually developed into a special ruling caste, self-centered and self-sufficient. Quite distinct from them was the poor but numerous agricultural population. To save the nation from complete assimilation to the standards of its neighbors, the conscientious priestly scribe, Ezra, and the pious and patriotic layman, Nehemiah, inaugurate and enforce the laws which demand complete separation from all non-Jews. It is interesting to note that the speaking of the Hebrew language [18] receives special attention, just as in modern Zionism, since this stands as an impressive symbol of the national culture which the return then, as now, aimed to develop. The result then, as in modern Palestine, was to arouse the bitterest interracial conflicts. It is the culmination of the process begun in Deuteronomy. It marks the foundation of the Judaism of New Testament times.

From that time on it may be supposed that the Hebrew stock was kept measurably pure, at least among some of the stricter families. The little community, restricted by the Edomite settlement at Hebron to a few square miles around Jerusalem, set itself off more and more from the peoples living in the other sections of the country. Yet it would be a mistake to suppose this separation to have been so complete as in later times. Indeed, there never has been complete uniformity in Judaism. At the period when what we have called the "prophetic hatred" of foreigners was receiving its sharpest expression, other prophets, Second Isaiah,

[18] Dalman thinks Hebrew is meant, though the returned exiles must have spoken both Hebrew and Aramaic, *Jesus-Jeschua*, Leipzig, 1922, p. 8.

Zechariah, and Malachi, were proclaiming the mission of Israel to bring the knowledge of Yahweh to all the nations, and were praising the pagan nations for worshiping him more truly than the Jews themselves.[19] Likewise, there were protests against the new exclusiveness voiced by some of the finer spirits of the nation, as we see in Jonah and Ruth. The Psalms, of which a large number are post-exilic, reveal the same division of sentiment. In some there is bitter hatred for their nearest neighbors, Edom, Moab, Philistia, but in others the faith that all the ends of the earth should turn unto Yahweh.[20] The fact that so much of the magnanimous internationalism of the earlier writers is preserved is in itself proof that it had not entirely disappeared in the age when the ancient writings were being re-edited and accepted as the divine word. That the spirit of exclusiveness was far from universal is evident also from the events of the next period, when Hellenism came to tempt the people away from the Law.

With the fall of Persia and the conquest of the east by Macedon a new situation was created. For a century Palestine returned to its old allegiance to Egypt, and a combination of Egyptian and Hellenistic influences began to flow in upon the Jews. Unfortunately literature which can be definitely dated and even historical traditions from this period are extremely meager. Stories such as those which Josephus tells of the Tobiadae, Joseph and Hyrcanus, show how far men of families related to the high priests could go in accommodation to the customs of their foreign rulers.[21] And the remarkable ruins of the palace at 'Arâḳ el-Emîr which Josephus describes and upon which the name Ṭobîyah is found shows the wealth and luxury to which leading Jews could aspire as well as the fact that they were not confined to the territories of Jerusalem.[22] During this period there was no direct attempt to attack the ideals of the Jews.

Their conquest, however, by the Macedonian dynasty in Syria was succeeded by an energetic effort at Hellenization. It took

[19] Is. 42.4-7; Zech. 8.20-23; Mal. 1.11.
[20] Ps. 2.9; 22.27 f.; 33.12-15; 106.34 ff.
[21] *Ant.*, XII 4.
[22] See G. A. Smith, *Jerusalem,* II, pp. 424 ff., and Plates XII-XV.

various forms. The founding of Greek colonies such as that of the Sidonians who carved out and decorated the peculiar painted tombs at Marisa, the introduction of Greek institutions such as the gymnasium, the theater, and the stadium, efforts to influence the leading Jewish families directly, these were followed at length by the attempt of Antiochus Epiphanes to blot out Jewish social and religious non-conformity by the hand of force. The direct and indirect means used to allure the Jews toward Hellenism might have succeeded; indeed, they had prospered so well that Antiochus thought merely to hasten the process by wiping out the small recalcitrant minority. He reckoned without an understanding of the psychology of the people with whom he had to deal. Coercion produced rebellion. Rebellion, which seemed hopeless, succeeded for several reasons. The danger united the hostile factions in Judaism which were responsible for her weakness. The difficult character of the approaches to Jerusalem, the ease with which the defeated patriots could conceal themselves in the caves of the Shephelah or the fastnesses of the Wilderness, all this made their complete overthrow almost impossible. Most of all, the death of Antiochus and the rivalries of the various candidates for his throne established the Maccabees in a kingdom which came to be larger and more powerful than that of David.

The psychological result of the ill-advised attempt of Antiochus to force Hellenism upon the Jews was to embitter the nation and to fix in the Jewish consciousness an ineradicable anti-foreign complex. Perhaps it would be more accurate to call it an anti-Greek complex. For oriental ideas there was no special hatred, since no oriental monarch had attempted to force his civilization upon them. The anti-Greek feeling was fed by the rapid influx of Greeks into Palestine and by the constant friction which contacts between them and their Jewish neighbors produced. Outside Palestine the case was quite different, tho Jewish social exclusiveness and commercial success combined to produce a decided anti-Semitism. In the Greek-speaking world the Jews forgot their Hebrew and Aramaic, studied Greek literature and philosophy, and accommodated themselves in many ways to their environment without abandoning either their ancestral religion or morality. Palestinian Judaism also had groups that were inclined to break down the wall that separated them from the Gentiles. Apparently the Hasmoneans and many of the Sadducees were of this mind. Doubtless wealth and social position as well as their political duties entailed temptations that were too strong to be borne. But the ruling tendency was anti-foreign.

A very similar division of sentiment can be discovered today in the United States or any other country where a foreign immigration of any magnitude has taken place. The wealthier, commercial classes are in general inclined to be friendly to the foreigner, not merely because they have a broader education and wider outlook, but because their own interests are served by the larger contacts that result from his presence. The working classes and the farmers, with whom the immigrant comes into competition, are of quite another mind. So it must have been in Palestine in the New Testament period. One does not realize the extent of Hellenistic influence until one begins to list the cities which may be called centers of Greek culture. On the east of the Jordan, from Damascus south to Macherus, there are as many as eighteen, in Galilee five or six, in Samaria some five, in southern Judea three, and on the Maritime Plain eight or more. Only in the immediate neighborhood of Jerusalem, that is within fifteen or twenty miles, none can be certainly located. Jews were living in the majority of the Hellenistic cities and Greeks, no doubt, in a large proportion of the Jewish towns and villages. In Jerusalem there were not only enough returned Greek-speaking Jews to make at least one and possibly five synagogs necessary for their worship,[23] but there were also large numbers of Greeks and other foreigners resident for purposes of trade. No village could be so remote that its people would not constantly come in contact with Greeks. That constant contacts would always result in personal animosity between individuals one cannot for a moment suppose, but that the prevailing atmosphere was one of mutual suspicion and enmity is

[23] Ac. 6.9; note the recently discovered Greek inscription from a Jerusalem synagog, Barton, *Archaeology*, p. 513 and fig. 311.

abundantly evidenced by the readiness with which Jews and Greeks flew at one another's throats when occasion offered.[24]

The psychological effects of the Maccabean victories and the subsequent rapid deterioration of the dynasty were equally unfortunate. The desperate victories of the little bands of Jews introduced new factors into the political situation. The minor priestly family of the Hasmoneans, in spite of jealousies and opposition on the part of older claimants and of Pharisaic sticklers for legal technicalities, secured the high-priesthood and finally the kingship. They were the nucleus of a group with strong nationalistic feelings. Other priestly families of great influence had come to form the party of the Sadducees, the ruling aristocracy. They were concerned to maintain the priestly ascendancy and seem to have cared little for national independence or religious exclusiveness. The Hasidim of the period of the Maccabean revolt were a party that avoided politics. They aided the Hasmonean brothers when their religion was threatened and basely deserted them when religious liberty was promised in return for political submission. The Pharisees who, half a century later, are found as the opponents of the Sadducees, had much the same attitude. Their concern was for the Law and its observance. They much preferred direct Roman rule to that of Archelaus because they believed that he would make more vigorous efforts to Hellenize the country in order to please his overlords than would a Roman himself.[25] All that they wished was to be left in peace to carry out their religious observances. Religious separateness was the one and only aim of their politics. When the Hasmonean dynasty failed, the dominant antiforeign feeling made the Pharisees the nation's popular leaders.

The successes of the Maccabees had so impressed many of their partisans that they had been hailed as the fulfilment of the promise of the messiah.[26] When the mad exploits and ungoverned passions of Alexander Janneus had brought his brilliant qualities into con-

[24] Cf. Josephus, *War,* II, 18, 1 ff.

[25] See Josephus, *Ant.,* XVII, 11, 2, where one of the chief accusations brought against Herod was his fondness for Greek cities.

[26] Test. Reub. 6.7-12, Test. Levi 8.10, etc.; see Charles, *Test. Twelve Patriarchs,* p. xcvii.

tempt and aroused his countrymen to revolt, and when the weakness of the half-imbecile Hyrcanus II and the rival ambitions of his brother Aristobulus had brought the nation under the yoke of Rome and the goad of the Idumean Herod, the idea of a Levitic messiah became detestable. The national hopes which had risen to the skies suffered a complete overthrow. Is it not legitimate to regard the racial pride and exclusiveness which marked the Jews as due in good part to the deep sense of disappointment and frustration produced by their long history of national calamities and failures to achieve the destiny they believed marked out for them?

V. SUMMARY

The political situation with which Jesus had to deal can be discussed more successfully at a later point, for other elements entered into it beside those that have thus far been mentioned. Here it is sufficient to state summarily the conclusions that are to be drawn from this brief sketch of the mutual relations of the racial and political history of the Hebrew-Jewish people.

First it is to be said with all emphasis that the Jews had anything but a simple pedigree. Like all of the races which have made notable contributions to civilization, they are of mixed ancestry. It seems probable that the narrow exclusiveness which finds expression in some of their legal codes was never practised on any considerable scale until the threat of Hellenization drove them into racial isolation. Down through all the greater part of their history, therefore, they had been accustomed to mingle with other races with no more hesitation than was common in antiquity, perhaps rather with less, for their literature, along with manifestations of narrow exclusiveness, reveals also a fine strain of broad-mindedness, humanitarianism, and internationalism. The Hebrews seem to have taken to themselves anatomical characteristics from the Hittites and the Philistines. There is, therefore, a distinct highland element of more than one type which marks them off from the Semites to whom they owe their language.

Beside the grass-land Semite, they included the Amorite and the Aramean among their ancestors, their own prophets being witness.[27] Babylonians as well as Egyptians and Nubians belong to the list, not to mention the pre-Semitic cave-dwellers. Such a combination of stocks makes for hardihood and adaptability. It constituted an excellent physical basis for a great nation. It provided them with a great variety of mental traits, which the Hebrew race in ancient and modern times has used to the great advantage of civilization.

Tho the pure Semitic type of head is not found to predominate in the modern Jew,[28] and probably did not in his ancestors, the historical evidence indicates that the largest single strain in the Hebrew inheritance was that from the grass-land Semites. It was the dominant element in the original Hebrew invaders of Canaan, and it was repeatedly reinforced by constant infiltration and by new infusions from the steppe at important crises in the nation's history, in the time of David, in the age of Elijah and Jehu, at the fall of Samaria, and during the Exile, perhaps also thru the Idumeans during the Maccabean empire.

Interbreeding is particularly favorable to variation, for its result is plastic. Upon the numerous elements that entered into the Hebrew race the course of history worked to select certain types. After the time of David the Hebrews, particularly those of Judah, never had opportunity to engage in far-reaching military exploits nor to deal with large problems of statesmanship, as Hebrews. That type of ability the race no doubt possessed and could have developed, but to exercise it the Hebrew had to go to other lands; in his own country there was no scope for it because of the material limitations set by geography and climate. The same was true of scientific and artistic ability. The life of the steppe from which the Hebrews had come develops individual leadership, self-reliance, and initiative rather than docility and blind obedience. It produces loyalty to a small group rather than subservience within a large one. Conditions in Palestine continued to develop this in-

[27] Ez. 16.3; Dt. 26.5.

[28] Salaman, *QSPEF,* 1925, p. 41.

heritance, and thus the Hebrews thruout their few square miles of territory could never unite permanently under one government. Mixture with the Canaanites and long experience in pastoral-agricultural Palestine modified, tho it did not eradicate, the fortitude and the capacity for strenuous effort which life in the desert demands. But it did develop habits of industry and a capacity for passive endurance with which the nomad is less acquainted.

Most important of all, the course of natural selection in the history of the Jews tended to produce a religious temperament. Jerusalem was a sacred site long before the time of Solomon. Indeed, its shrine may have determined its selection as capital by David. After the building of the Temple, its sanctity constantly increased. Deuteronomy set the divine seal upon it and attempted the elimination of all rivals. There was little but its reputed sanctity to attract men to Jerusalem. Those who were interested in other matters migrated if they could. Those of northern Israel and of the Dispersion who were especially religious returned to it. Thus the poverty of the land tended to drive away the venturesome and ambitious, all those with initiative and varied abilities. Those who remained were the individuals to whom religion and patriotism made their appeal or who were too weak to make their escape, the timid and docile.

The Exile worked in the same directions. The Assyrian and Babylonian deportations removed the best of the people, religious and irreligious. To the remnant in the land, as poor in mental and physical ability as they were in culture and worldly goods, there came back a group whose dominant ideas were religion and patriotism, the two being inextricably intertwined. They were thus of a very different sort from the modern Zionist to whom race and culture are the great values. For the Jew of the post-exilic period, race and nation were swallowed up in religion, but, nevertheless, constituted a large part of it. The exclusiveness which rapidly developed, especially during the Graeco-Roman period, operated to reinforce the selective process. The more deeply religious were those who could withstand the seductions of Hellenism and the persecutions of the nation's enemies. They were the ones who would be most scrupulous in observing all the rules which kept them free from Gentile contact and contamination. The non-religious were lost to the race. Beside those of strong religious temperament was another group, the culls in the selective process, the poor of the land, the weak and spiritless, who submitted readily to the leadership of their stronger brethren and received their ideas from them. They were the people of the land, strong in the passive virtues and deeply influenced by the religiousness of the scribes and Pharisees.

Finally it is to be noted that, while the sense of racial superiority which the nomad always feels towards farmers and townspeople may have contributed, in a sense, to the intense exclusiveness of the Jew, it was rather the political, social, and religious experiences thru which the centuries led him that developed it into a dominant factor in Jewish history. In all that may be said about the influence of race it must be continually borne in mind that there are other more important factors. The advantages or disadvantages which the climate, the geographical situation, and the natural resources of a country have to offer seem to affect the outcome more than the innate aptitudes or disabilities of the race which inhabits it. Whatever abilities and tendencies the race may possess, given such large capacity and adaptability as the Hebrews possessed, the race's contribution to civilization will depend far more upon its customs and ideals than upon innate physical or psychical factors. Race is, in the last analysis, largely a matter of psychology, not in the sense that a particular group of psychical traits is inherited, but that "races persist because the majority of men believe in them heartily, passionately, desperately." [29] Race is "a unity which finds its origin in intellectual phenomena such as language, religion, custom, law, and culture." [30]

The "fathers according to the flesh" were not the children of Abraham. They never were a race until their religious *differentiæ* set them off from their neighbors. The traveler in 800 B.C. could have seen little difference between Tyre and Jerusalem except that

[29] Todd, *Theories of Social Progress,* p. 280 f.

[30] Todd, *op. cit.,* p. 283, quoting Gumplovicz, *Rassenkampf,* p. 193.

one was rich and the other poor. It was the prophets who contributed the distinctive religious characteristics to the culture of their race. They tried to teach their countrymen that they were a peculiar people. It required the Exile and the conflict with Hellenism to convince them. Thus they became a race, a religious race, not because of innate characteristics, not because selection had bred a religious temperament—other city-states were equally religious—but because of the kind of ideas they associated with their religion. To the spiritual inheritance of the Hebrew people, those more important factors which really constitute the racial characteristics of the nation, the customs, laws, and religious beliefs which differentiate them from others, we now turn.

CHAPTER IV

ISRAEL'S SPIRITUAL ANCESTRY

THE ideals of the great religious leaders of Israel cannot be studied in isolation. One of the commonest fallacies is to suppose that an idea can be studied *in vacuo,* so to speak, and properly appreciated. The precise connotation of a word can be discovered only in the sentence. The meaning of a sentence—a biblical text, for example—is to be determined only from its context. So the religious beliefs, the social standards, and the moral ideals of the Hebrews can be properly understood only as a part of the total civilization of the world to which they belonged. As we have already noted, the Hebrews, far from being isolated, were in the very center of the ancient world, with all the currents of civilization flowing thru their little land. Politics, economics, and material culture were profoundly affected by the nations with which they came in contact. How far were their social customs and their moral and religious ideas and ideals modified by the same influences? To what nations did they owe most?

I. NON-SEMITIC INFLUENCES

As yet we are not in a position to estimate the Hebrews' debt to the ancient races of highland breed. If we knew certainly who the Hittites and the Hyksos were, we know too little of their culture to be able to trace any connection between them and the Hebrews in matters intellectual, moral, and religious.[1] The genial suggestion that Jesus was of Aryan ancestry has no shred of

[1] See the Hittite laws in Barton, *Arch. and the Bible,* 4 ed., pp. 369-88, and now the further discussion in the 5 ed. (1927), pp. 547 f.

evidence on which to stand, except in the sense that the Mitannians and Hittites may have contributed elements to the Hebrew race. When enough documents of the Mitannians are discovered and deciphered, when the languages of the Hittites have fully yielded to the attack of modern scholarship, as have the hieroglyphs of Egypt and the wedges of Babylonia, one may have material with which to fill the blank. Exactly the same may be said of the indebtedness of the Hebrews to the Aegean civilization. Archeological evidence proves that Palestine owed not a little of impulse, suggestion, and progress to the invasion of the Philistines, as well as to the influences brought to its shores by means of commerce with Crete and similar centers. But no lines of spiritual ancestry can as yet be traced to the blooming civilization of the Mediterranean lands, for its earliest script still eludes decipherment.

II. TIGRIS-EUPHRATES CIVILIZATION

Concerning Israel's debt to the great civilization of the Tigris-Euphrates valley there is no question. It is hardly necessary to marshal the evidence which, since George Smith discovered the Babylonian account of the Flood in December, 1872, has grown to overwhelming proportions. Volumes too numerous to mention have catalogued the cuneiform parallels to the Old Testament. Yet it is necessary to recall the points which affect the present investigation.

At the beginning of the third millennium before Christ is to be placed the first recorded raid from Babylonia upon Syria under Lugalzaggisi, the Sumerian ruler of Umma and Erech. His successors, Sargon, Naram-Sin, and Shar-Gali-Sharri of the Semitic line of Agade, again laid the west under contribution and may have gone as far as Cyprus. When the Amorite dynasty whose most famous king was Hammurapi made Babylon the capital of western Asia, they succeeded to a highly developed civilization from which they borrowed their script and a large part of their laws, their social institutions, their morals, and their religion.

Hammurapi succeeded in establishing Babylon in a position so high that, whether the political center of western Asia or not, she remained its commercial and cultural capital down to the rise of Greece and Rome. In the time of Egypt's greatest glory under the eighteenth dynasty, the age of the Amenhoteps, Ikhnaton, and Tutenkhamon, the Pharaohs corresponded with their vassals in Palestine in the language and script of Babylonia. When the powerful monarchs of the Hittites and the kings of Mitanni wrote to the Pharaohs they used, not their own language or the hieroglyphs of Egypt, but the language of Hammurapi. And fifteen hundred years after his time the Persian conquerors of Babylon made use of its script when they reduced their language to writing. The knowledge of a language carries with it to no small extent the spiritual goods of a people. How far Babylonian ethics and law, so highly developed under Hammurapi, affected the lands about the Mediterranean and particularly the Hebrews is a moot question. But the difference of opinion touches only details. All agree that according to the evidence the influence was considerable.

The secret of Babylon's influence was her commercial importance. She was situated at a spot thru which the commerce of East and West most naturally passed. To her came the traders and travelers of all the world. Her merchants went out into all the world. The extent of her commerce and the complexity of her business and social life demanded a written language, and this she inherited from the inventiveness of the conquered Sumerians. Her social and commercial progress demanded the elaboration and refinement of her laws and customs. She must exhibit a high degree of moral insight if her social structure was to endure. It was entirely natural, therefore, that she should establish rules of business and conceptions of justice that became models for the whole world. Hammurapi's code, if not itself widely published, represents ideals of business honesty and social righteousness which Babylonia propagated even where the code as such was not known.

Down to the sixth century B.C., Babylonia as a civilizing force had no rival in all western Asia. The irruption of the Kassites, the Mitannians, and the Hittites disturbed the orderly progress of her development, but in the end the interlopers became the vassals of her culture, if not of her kings. Egypt likewise intervened in force for but a brief period. When Nineveh became the official representative of Tigris-Euphrates civilization, her policy of deportation, ruthless as it was, contributed to the further spread of Babylonian influence. When Aramaic became the language of commerce and diplomacy in all western Asia and was adopted by the Jews, the possibility of direct influence was increased and the large Jewish Dispersion in Babylon kept up the connection between Judea and the East even when the Greek and Roman conquests forcibly turned the faces of the Hebrews westward. For the communication of the older pattern ideas of Babylonian civilization to the Jews, it is not unimportant that they were on the banks of the Euphrates when the archaizing tendencies of Nabonidus unearthed so much of ancient lore. We have every reason, therefore, to consider the social standards and moral ideals of Babylonia in an attempt to discover the meaning which the Hebrews attached to theirs. In the absence of any extensive literature from other Semitic countries, the mass of materials which excavation has recovered in Babylonia serves admirably to indicate what the Hebrews had in common with the other branches of the Semitic family of nations.

III. EGYPT

With regard to Egypt the case on the surface is not perfectly clear. It becomes necessary, therefore, to canvass the facts somewhat at length. The dwellers on the Nile were so self-satisfied and self-sufficient that they were slow to colonize other countries. They were normally so well protected by sea and desert against attack that they never developed great military prowess, except under the twelfth and eighteenth dynasties, after they had suffered invasion. The Egyptian hieroglyphic system of writing was too difficult for other nations to master and adapt to their own uses as they did the cuneiform. The language itself also, in spite of Semitic elements, could not be learned by the Asiatic Semites as they could learn a sister tongue. Accordingly, while numerous objects have been discovered in Palestine that bear the stamp of Egypt and while the land on the Nile must have contributed constantly to Palestine's material progress, we find no permanent Egyptian colonies in Canaan except possibly in the south, and no widely accepted theories of Egyptian influence upon the thinking of the Hebrews. Yet there are not wanting those who would trace the beginnings of civilization to the Nile and not to the Euphrates. Dr. G. Elliot Smith says: "If borrowing took place, it was Sumer that learned from Egypt and not the reverse."[2] Close connections between the two with mutual borrowing is acknowledged by many. Syria must be the common meeting place. While Pan-Egyptianism must not be allowed to become the successor of Pan-Babylonianism, the extensive propagation of Egyptian culture in other lands cannot be denied.

When all the evidence is weighed, it is impossible to believe that Palestine and the Hebrews could have escaped being influenced by the original and deeply productive thought of the wise men who lived on the Nile. There had always been commercial intercourse and travel back and forth. The sand-dwellers, the Aamu, or Syrians, and the Shasu, or bedouins, were constantly entering Egypt. That oldest road in the world, from Egypt to Palestine, has carried the products of both hand and brain between them from time immemorial. Connection by ship was also made from early times. The documentary evidence for it begins in the reign of Snefru, who is as ancient as, or more so than, Lugalzaggisi. This presupposes, and archeological evidence proves, long previous intercourse. Egyptian inscriptions, scarabs, and ornaments discovered in Palestine and Syria indicate closer and closer relations as time passes. Then the Hyksos invasion, which set its capitals at the eastern edge of the Delta to facilitate communication with Palestine, whence the conquerors had come, established new bonds between Egypt and Asia. They were not

[2] *The Ancient Egyptians,* new ed., London-New York: Harper, 1923, p. 158.

severed but strengthened by the Asiatic conquests of the eighteenth dynasty. Even the Habiru did not end Egyptian domination in Palestine. The recent excavations by the University of Pennsylvania Museum at Beisân have added new evidence. Even when Ramses II lost Syria to the Hittites, he still held Palestine. The coming of the Philistines limited, but did not end, Egytian influence.

Thruout the monarchy the attempts of Egypt to interfere in Syrian affairs were continued. The connections of Solomon and Jeroboam with the Pharaonic court must have meant a large influx of Egyptian ideas. Archeological materials, indeed, seem to point to the period from the tenth to the seventh century as one of most active Egyptian influence in Palestine.[3] The presence of an Egyptian party in the Judean court of Hezekiah could not but mean a considerable acquaintance with things Egyptian as well as the presence of Egyptians to carry on their propaganda. In other words, just at the time when Hebrew prophecy was taking shape, Egyptian influence was at its height. The flight of the Judean remnant to Egypt after the fall of Jerusalem tells a story that has been wonderfully illuminated by the Elephantine papyri. The large Jewish Diaspora in Alexandria, the translation of the Septuagint in Egypt, and the composition there of numerous other documents of importance in the history of later Judaism—not forgetting Philo—all point to constant intercourse and marked friendliness between the two countries. Traces of Egyptian influence on the art of the Sidonian tombs at Marisa and the correspondence of Tubias and others in the Zeno archives are subsidiary evidence.[4] How lightly the journey between Palestine and Egypt was esteemed is indicated again and again in the literature of both nations, by the "Romance of Sinuhe" (ca. 2000 B.C.), the stories of Joseph and his brothers, of Absolom, Hadad, and

[3] D. G. Hogarth in *JEA,* I (1914), 13 ff.

[4] Peters-Thiersch-Cook, *The Painted Tombs at Marissa,* London: Pal. Expl. Fund., 1905; Deissmann, *Licht vom Osten,* pp. 128 f., *Light from the Ancient East,* new ed., 1927, pp. 162 ff., C. C. Edgar, *Zeno Papyri* (Cat. gén. des ant. égypt. du musée du Caire), vol. I, 1925, nos. 59003-5, 59007-10, 59075 f.

Jeroboam in the time of the monarchy, and of the Flight into Egypt.

Perhaps the strongest indirect evidence of Egyptian influence upon the Hebrews is to be found in the traditions of the latter. Abraham, to be sure, came from Ur of the Chaldees; the Hebrew acknowledged a wandering Aramean as his father.[5] But if the original ancestors in the days of their nomadic solitariness came from Mesopotamia, the whole nation was thought to have grown to its maturity in Egypt. The "wandering Aramean" went to Egypt with his entire household and generations later went out a multitudinous people. According to a late tradition the founder of their nation and their religion, a member of the priestly clan, was versed in all the learning of the Egyptians. Another tradition connects Joseph with the high priest of Heliopolis, a most important center of Aton worship. At the very founding, then, of the Hebrew nation and the first formulation of its laws and its primary religious ideas, Egyptian influence should have been at its greatest. These Hebrew traditions may be due to the same reverence for antiquity that led the Greeks to trace their religion back to Egypt, yet, if their details cannot be fully trusted, they must rest upon a substantial substratum of fact. Constant intercourse with Egypt thruout the whole millennium from the founding of the monarchy to the beginnings of Christianity could not have been without marked influence upon the Hebrews.[6]

This being the case, one ought to discover hieroglyphic parallels to the Old Testament. Considering the difference of outlook and language which tended to prevent direct borrowing and to obscure the evidence of it, they are to be found in no inconsiderable measure. Some of the most striking are in the story of Joseph, into which have been incorporated features from the account of the trials of a virtuous youth in the Egyptian "Tale of the Two Brothers." Its local color, like that of the accounts of

[5] Dt. 26.5.

[6] For further details and bibliography see the writer's article, "Hebrew and Egyptian Apocalyptic Literature," *HTR*, 18 (1925), pp. 359-62.

the Sojourn and Exodus, points unmistakably to the period of the Hebrew monarchy, when the historical traditions and social ideals of the Israelites were taking shape. The resemblances between many verses of Psalm 104 and certain sections of the Amarna hymns to Aton are still more notable. When one places them side by side, remembering that Aton is the sun conceived as the great God of the universe, he can hardly escape the conclusion that the Hebrew psalmist knew some form of the hymns of Aton. In the two documents the descriptions of the night, of what happens by day, of the sailing of the ships, and of the relation of the whole to the divine Creator are cast in the same forms of thought, often in the same phrases. A single example may be quoted. One section of the Aton hymn runs:

> "How manifold are thy works!
> They are hidden from before (us),
> O sole God, whose powers no other possesseth.
> Thou didst create the earth according to thy heart
> When thou wast alone:
> Men, all cattle, large and small,
> All that are upon the earth;
> (All) that are on high,
> That fly with their wings."

Remembering that the Egyptian word for "heart" may mean either "desire," "understanding," or "wisdom," one notes the similarity of the following verse from the Psalm:

> "O Yahweh, how manifold are thy works!
> In wisdom thou hast made them all;
> The earth is full of thy creatures."[7]

The parallels between the two hymns seem too close for them to be entirely independent. If so, since the Aton hymn was inscribed on the Amarna tombs about 1370 B.C., years before the earliest

[7] Ps. 104.24; "creatures," ARV mg.: text, "riches." There can be little doubt that the margin is right.

possible date for the Exodus, there can be no question as to the side upon which dependence lies.[8]

If the objection be made that this remarkable parallel can be explained as due merely to analogous development of thought under similar circumstances, such an interpretation is not possible of the recently discovered likeness between passages in Proverbs (22.17-24.22) and the Egyptian "Admonitions of Amenophis." As several scholars have pointed out, the passage in Proverbs follows its Egyptian prototype almost word for word, and certain hitherto unexplained difficulties in the Hebrew text are easily resolved by reference to the Egyptian original. In this case there can be no question that the Hebrew writer borrowed, using a direct translation. The only question is as to the period when it took place, whether it is before or after the Exile.[9]

The question as to the date of the passage in Proverbs may not easily or quickly receive a decisive answer. But in any case the Hebrews were in the closest relations with the Egyptians during both of these periods, as archeological and historical evidence unequivocally proves. The thought world of the two nations, despite marked differences in some directions, was much the same. Jeremiah, for example, uses a figure of two trees, one planted in the desert and the other "by the waters," to illustrate the opposite fates of those who trust in God and those who do not. Amenophis uses the figure of a tree in the forest that is cut down and burned and a

[8] Breasted's version of the hymn, quoted above, may be found in *RTAE,* p. 326, *CAH,* II, pp. 117 ff., as well as in others of his works. The hymn and the corresponding passages from Ps. 104 are printed in parallel columns in Breasted, *Hist. of the Anc. Egyptians,* pp. 273-77; *Hist. of Egypt,* pp. 371-76, and Weigall, *Life and Times of Akhnaton,* New York, 1923, pp. 134 ff.

[9] See Erman, "Eine ägyptische Quelle der Sprüche Salomos," *SBA,* Phil.-hist. Klasse, 1924, pp. 86-93; Gressmann, "Die neugefundene Lehre des Amen-em-ope," *ZAW,* 42 (N.F. 1, 1924), 272-96; M. H. Dunsmore, "An Egyptian Contribution to the Book of Proverbs," *JR,* 5 (1925), 300-308. The document was published by Budge, *Facsimiles of Egyptian Hieratic Papyri in the British Museum,* Series II, and with new translation in *The Teaching of Amen-em-apt.* See now the translation by Griffith in *JEA,* XII (1928), 191-231, with discussion by Simpson, *ibid.,* 232-39.

well watered and fruitful tree in a garden to contrast the "hot-headed man in the temple" and "the true silent one."[10] Many such illustrations of the similarity of Hebrew and Egyptian processes of thought might be adduced. The parallel between Ikhnaton's hymn and Psalm 104 is at least that, if nothing more. Egyptian love-poetry and the Song of Songs, the "Dialog of the Man-weary-of-life with his Soul" and Job are other examples. Considering all of these, one can hardly deny that the Egyptians and the Hebrews thought alike on a large number of social and religious subjects.

Even more significant for the present investigation are the similarities between Egypt's social prophets and those of the Hebrews. Numerous Egyptian documents give evidence of the high moral standards which had developed already in the third millennium B.C.[11] Following the two periods of invasion from Palestine with the consequent disorders and sufferings which ended the Old Kingdom and the Feudal Age, or Middle Kingdom, Egypt developed two eras of social questioning and criticism which find expression in many documents describing the evils of the times. The "Admonitions of Amenemhet" may express merely the disillusionment and disappointment of wearied old age, but the "Complaint of the Eloquent Peasant," the "Musings of Khekheperresonbu," and the "Dialog of the Man-weary-of-life with his Soul" are keen and often bitter arraignments of economic evils and social injustices. These documents, composed, some just before the twelfth, others before the eighteenth dynasty, are truly prophetic

[10] Jer. 17.5-8; Amenophis in Gressmann, *ZAW*, 42, p. 280; Budge, *Teaching of Amen-em-apt*, p. 148; cf. McCown, *HTR*, 18, p. 364.

[11] Evidence for this and the following discussion in Breasted, *Development of Religion and Thought in Ancient Egypt*, pp. 165-256; Peet, *CAH*, I, pp. 346-50; and the writer's article, "Hebrew and Egyptian Apocalyptic Literature," *HTR*, 18 (1925), 357-411, which was written as a study preliminary to this for the purpose of exhibiting the close relation between the social thinking of the Egyptians and the Hebrews. This thesis is not universally accepted but is receiving wider and wider approval. Gressmann, who has long advocated close connections between Hebrew and foreign prophecy, presented his views in *JTS*, 27 (1926), 241-54, see especially pp. 242-49. See also Meek in *JR*, VII (1927), 251 ff.

in the larger sense that they criticize social conditions from a moral point of view. Some of them urge the abolition of the evils they portray and the establishment of justice and righteousness.

Two other writings are not merely prophetic but predictive, or pseudo-predictive, in form. The "Admonitions of Ipuwer" and the "Vision of Neferrohu," both dating from about the twentieth century B.C., expose the evils of the time in which they are supposed to be written and look forward to a better age in the future. The prediction may be *ex eventu;* it may reflect the happier period of the twelfth dynasty, as well as the disorders of the interregnum which had preceded. But it testifies to the presence of the hope of a new age, or it would have no meaning.[12] This type of prophecy did not disappear with the social disturbances which first occasioned it. The various documents we have mentioned must have been copied over and over again. Of some of them, the "Vision of Neferrohu," for instance, which is in tone the most distinctly apocalyptic of all, numerous fragments on stone and papyrus are known—a strong testimony to its popularity.

The old prophecies continued to be copied and read and new ones were written. Slightly earlier than the Book of Daniel is the so-called "Demotic Chronicle," which is in reality a series of proverbial or paradoxical oracles which are interpreted as applying to the history of Egypt. It pretends to be composed under Tachos, the Teos of Manetho (362-61 B.C.?), and mentions the names of the previous rulers for half a century. After Tachos no names are mentioned, but several kings are so distinctly described that they can be easily identified. Then the predictions run out into glittering generalities, as does Daniel after the Maccabean revolt. In one section a day equals a year. The whole work is thoroly nationalistic, like most of the Jewish apocalypses. Like Daniel it employs the *motif* of darkness before dawn, terrible evils to be followed

[12] See the documents translated in Breasted, *RTAE,* pp. 205-10, and by Gardiner in *JEA,* I (1914), 20-36, 100-06, and summarized in *HTR,* 18 (1925), 369-400. Cf. Erman's interpretation in *SBA,* 1919, pp. 804-15, see *HTR,* 18, p. 381. Their messianic implications will be discussed below, pp. 220-25.

by a glorious salvation for the nation. As in Daniel there are two series of oracles covering the same period.[13]

In view of the entire unlikeness of the historical materials, these similarities in form, striking as they are, cannot be held to indicate borrowing on the part of the author of Daniel or any other of the Jewish apocalyptists. But there surely must be some literary connection, a documentary link or series of links, between the two types of writing. Still later apocalyptic, or eschatological, documents come to us from Egypt in both Demotic and Greek, showing that this kind of writing continued long to be popular. As Meyer well says of the "Admonitions of Ipuwer,"

> "The scheme is exactly the same as . . . with the Hebrew prophets, first the fearful catastrophe, then the messianic kingdom. Among both peoples it is thoroly traditional and fixed from of old. In each case what is different is only the application to a given historical situation. Of the development and deepening which it underwent at the hands of the great Hebrew prophets there is no trace in Egypt. Creative individuality was lacking also in this province (in Egypt)."[14]

Another remarkable likeness must not be overlooked in comparing the social thought of Egypt and Israel. The Hebrews and the Egyptians passed thru very similar stages in the course of their religious development. In Egypt there is the great blossoming of social thinking under the twelfth and again under the eighteenth dynasty. There follows the strange reformation of Ikhnaton in the direction of monotheism. But after these two magnificent creative periods, there comes a time of decline marked by strong archaistic tendencies. Reverence for the past and for its laws and customs was so overwhelming that farther progress was rendered impossible. Ancient law, mainly of a ritualistic character, supposed to be divinely given and upheld, was the norm by which all actions were judged, and all that happened to a man was divine reward or punishment for his obedience or disobedience to this law. In the midst of the reaction from Ikhnaton's reforms to this reign of law, there developed a strange religion of the poor, marked by

[13] See *HTR*, 18, 387-92, and the literature there cited.

[14] *Geschichte des Altertums*, I, 2, p. 274.

deep devotion and mystical piety. Only a few monuments of it have been found. That the better type of Egyptian social and religious thinking never produced abiding fruit may be due to the magical ideas which eventually gained complete ascendancy. Combined with the other unfortunate tendencies within Egyptian religion, they completely throttled the vitality of Egyptian thinking. All these tendencies, both good and bad, were present among the Hebrews also and made their appearance in due time. This gives to a comparison between the social and religious ideas of the two nations added interest and value. On the one hand, one must be prepared for analogous developments; on the other it must be acknowledged that the similarity of conditions made borrowing on the part of the Hebrews easier. Finally, one wishes to ask why the Hebrews escaped the fate of the Egyptians. Why have they survived and why have their social ideals become a most precious element in the heritage of modern civilization?

yes

The evidence presented is at least sufficient to prove that Egypt as well as Babylonia must be considered as a probable source of the pattern ideas which the Hebrews used in preparing their unique contribution to human thinking. We must carefully note what Egypt felt and thought upon the themes with which we are concerned.

IV. PERSIAN AND GREEK INFLUENCE

Two other great peoples in their time affected Hebrew thinking, the Persians and the Greeks, but neither of them contributed to the development of Hebrew social ideals in such significant measure as did the Babylonians and the Egyptians. From the time of Cyrus' conquest of Babylon, the Hebrews in Babylonia, Palestine, and Egypt were for generations under Persian influence. Yet it is extremely difficult to determine how extensive were the effects of the long ages of contact between Mazdaism and Judaism. We are first of all confronted with the fact that the Mazdian scriptures in their present form are comparatively recent, for according to the accepted tradition, the collection was made between the first and the fourth century of our era. Since that time, it is calculated, as much as two thirds of the Avesta have been lost. The problem of determining how much of the remainder is the work of Magian priests, of reconstructing what was originally Zarathushtra's out of the fragments preserved in later writings, and, indeed, of discovering what Mazdaism was in the Persian Empire, is a difficult one. It is certain from the few contemporary notices that the religion of the Persian monarchs of the sixth, fifth, and fourth centuries was very different from that of Zarathushtra, but it is not easy to discover just what it was when the chief sources are sacred scriptures written during the first three centuries of the Christian era, by people who had long been in contact with Judaism and Christianity. The problem of the relations of Judaism and Mazdaism, therefore, tho it has long been debated, is still far from solution.[15]

Here it is possible to register only certain tentative conclusions which at least, it is hoped, do not go too far. Tendencies toward dualism, hypostatization, demonology, and angelology, and many of the wilder elements in Jewish eschatology, ideas of heaven and hell and possibly of fixed cycles and a millennial reign of a supernatural messiah on earth, Judaism may have borrowed from Magianized Zoroastrianism, or, if it did not borrow outright, yet it developed them along lines suggested by the Persians. For the evolution of Jewish eschatology, then, Mazdaism was of the greatest significance. Many of the most startling *motifs* of the apocalypses were due to Persian imagination. But to the social significance of apocalyptic thinking Zoroastrianism seems to have made no considerable contribution. The best that one can say for it is that it sharpened the antithesis between good and evil as no other religion, not even the Hebrew, had done; the worst, that it provided a basis for a pessimism and an other-worldliness that has sometimes completely erased the sense of social wrong and the hope of social progress.

[15] See Moulton, *Early Religious Poetry of Persia,* pp. 10-27, *Early Zoroastrianism,* pp. 1-37; Eduard Meyer, *Ursprung und Anfänge des Christentums,* II, pp. 58-120; L. Patterson, *Mithraism and Christianity,* Cambridge, 1921, R. Reitzenstein, *Das iranische Erlösungsmysterium,* Bonn, 1921; Meek in *JR,* VII (1927), 259 f.

Jesus and the social ideals he proclaimed owe little or nothing to Hellenism. The Sermon on the Mount and other parts of the teaching of Jesus show an almost Greek joy in life, an appreciation of the world as a happy place for man's existence which is quite Hellenic. There is no anti-feminine complex in Jesus, no asceticism. But the utterances which exhibit this healthy-minded spirit show no marks of Greek origin. With Stephen and Paul the Christian community stepped out into another world. The religious faith of Jesus himself was of such simple and fundamental character that it would have been at home among any people not blinded by creedal or ritualistic prepossessions. But his social ideals as well as his eschatology were largely foreign to the Greek view of life. To be sure, there were revolutionary social doctrines rife in the Hellenistic world. There were certain expectations of the end of the world and the return of the Golden Age which prepared for the acceptance of Christianity. Yet, in the main the history of Christianity in the Graeco-Roman world was the story of its departure from the ideals of Jesus. It is a story with which we are not now concerned, but it indicates that original Christianity as it came from Jesus was not of the same stuff as Greek morality, philosophy, and religion.

That Hellenism had deeply affected Judaism, had indeed all but swallowed it up, we have noted. No doubt Greek philosophical thought may be credited with having assisted the more intellectual circles in Judaism to slough off the cruder anthropomorphism of their national tradition. The Jews in Palestine were familiar with the Greek world, adopted Greek words and ideas into their Aramaic, and were not by any means an isolated people. But their anti-Greek complex, due to Antiochus Epiphanes and the Maccabean revolt, prevented them from consciously adopting any considerable elements of Hellenistic thinking. The reaction against the scheme of forcible Hellenization attempted by Antiochus had resulted in turning the nation as a whole into personified hatred of all things Greek. That may well account for the fact that, with Greeks all around them, the Jews of Palestine and Jesus himself show almost no clear traces of Greek influence.

V. THE NEAR EAST AS ONE CULTURE AREA

It is no purpose of this study to attempt to weigh the influence of this or that nation upon Israel, but only to insist that the thinking of the Hebrews can be understood only as part of a complex cultural system. In spite of political and economic changes, the rise and fall of empires, the shifting of trade routes, and all the multifarious developments of history, in spite of marked differences between the Hittites, the Aegean peoples, the Babylonians, the Egyptians, the Persians, the Greeks, and the Hebrews, the region about the eastern end of the Mediterranean was linked together into a cultural unity much as is Europe today. Neither the Arabs of the steppe nor the Greeks in their cities differed absolutely, but only by degrees, from the peoples living nearer the center of this culture area. By the time the Hebrews had come upon the stage of action, these peoples had been living together for thousands of years. They had a common heritage of religious and mythological ideas, varying indeed from nation to nation, but at bottom alike. Into their religious and mythological notions were woven their ideas of science, of politics, and of morality, their recollections of the past, their norms for the present, and their hopes of the future. Each nation worked out its own organization of the common heritage according to the possibilities which its environment offered and the stimuli which its political, economic, and social history afforded. The psychical substratum was much the same in all of these nations. There were in all the same reactions to the phenomena of nature, the same attitudes toward society, the same superstitions, the same bondage to custom, and fundamentally similar customs, ideals, and aspirations. The higher classes, especially the thinkers who have left us the literatures of these peoples, were those among whom differentiation was most likely to appear. But they operated with the materials inherited from the past of their nations. The inventor uses old tools and materials, and in the Levant these old tools and materials were essentially the same for all, just as the same plow is used in all that region.

The thought inventions of the Hebrew prophets and seers are

our present concern. We cannot understand the products of their inspired imaginations nor what they meant to the rank and file of the nation unless we consider the common stock of psychological tools and materials, the common pattern ideals, that they shared with the rest of their world. Harry Elmer Barnes has well said:

"Anthropologists and cultural historians have long recognized the fact that far the most potent force in breaking down stagnation, provincialism, and complacent self-satisfaction in culture is the contact of different civilizations." [16]

The Hebrews did not lack in contacts with different civilizations. That which they all had in common bound them together and made them intelligible one to another. Their differences offered the stimuli necessary to progress.

We shall consider the significance of the foreign contributions and analogies to Israel's thinking as we take up one and another of the primary elements in her social ideals. The basis of the Hebrew nation was the group of nomadic clans which invaded Palestine between the fourteenth and the twelfth centuries before Christ. They lived in a world that spoke Semitic languages and was dominated by the civilization that centered in Babylon. In various ways they repeatedly, almost continually, fell under the influence of Egypt. The Persians and the Greeks made their contributions for good and ill. But there were certain heritages that came directly from the nomadic life which they had once lived and which beckoned to them from the neighboring Negeb and Wilderness. To this inheritance from the desert we shall turn in the next chapter and attempt to trace the fascinating history of its development and transformation thru the strange fluctuations of Hebrew national life.

[16] *The New History and Social Studies,* p. 574.

CHAPTER V

THE DAWN OF DEMOCRACY

I. THE ORIGIN AND MEANING OF DEMOCRACY

THE origins of democracy have been sought in many different directions. According to some they are to be found in the proto-Aryan village communities, from which are thought to be descended the ideals of democracy that developed among the Greeks and the Teutonic peoples of Europe, ideals and customs still to be found, to a considerable extent unimpaired, among the simple villagers of India in the *panchayat* government. Others have derived modern democracy from the Teutonic folk-mote, in which, it is supposed, all the men of the tribe had an opportunity to express their will as to community life. When, however, one looks carefully into these ancient institutions, he discovers that their democracy is largely a product of the historian's imagination. As they actually existed, these bodies were far from embodying modern ideals of political democracy. Nearly all peoples show evidences of having at some period practiced communism in the holding of tribal lands. Government by elders or by councils, large or small, has been common at some stage in the political development of nearly every race. But it is not some strain of primeval communism in the blood which is responsible for modern political theories.

In the West we have been taught to look back to the Greek and Roman republics as the original homes of democracy and to think of the struggles of the citizens of those ancient states against tyrants, oligarchies, and aristocracies as the first great efforts of the human race to throw off the shackles of despotism. We are prone to forget that in the ancient city-states of the Mediterranean world only a small proportion even of the free residents had a right to vote and that the glory that was Greece and the splendor that was Rome were built upon the labor of a multitude of slaves that made up a considerable percentage of the total population. The *demos* that ruled was a small minority. Classical antiquity bequeathed to us the language of liberty without ever having known its reality. Stoic philosophy may be credited with a much larger share in fashioning modern political ideals. Its frequent references to one universal Father and to human brotherhood, its emphasis on the value of personal character entirely apart from accidental attributes such as wealth and birth, as embalmed in Greek and Latin literature, had much to do with preserving the best in Greek thinking thru the medieval period into the modern age of revolutions. Combined with this tradition the vigor, virility, and love of individual liberty which characterized the forefathers of western Europe have played a considerable part in the development of those free political institutions which have long been the boast of many western nations.

Yet the one ideal which has been most continuously and effectively present in the mind of occidental nations has been that which is summarized in the life of Jesus. There can be no dispute that, of the three nations which have united to make the beginnings of modern western civilization, the Greeks, the Romans, and the Jews, the most democratic was the last. Still less can it be questioned that the social idealism of modern times which would fill the concept of democracy with a richness of content that was utterly foreign to the greatest of Greek philosophers and moralists is largely an inheritance from the great social prophets of the Hebrews and from their successors, Jesus and his humble followers. It is the fascinating story of the development of these ideals thru thirty centuries of history that I am seeking to outline.

Democracy is a much abused word. It has as various meanings as the groups that use it and the sections of human activity to which it is applied. Its first and obvious meaning is government of the people, by the people and for the people. In this sense, if "people" be taken to mean all the inhabitants of both sexes, it cannot be maintained that real democracy has ever existed. Certainly none of the great modern nations can claim to have discovered the machinery by which the will of great masses of individuals can be effectively exerted in their own government. Just as little can one claim that the Hebrews, the Greeks, or the Romans enjoyed real political democracy. Only in a somewhat figurative sense can the Hebrew monarchy be said to have been limited.[1] Industrial democracy is just as surely an airy figment of the imagination. In a purely agricultural society, such as the later Hebrew historians supposed their nation to have been at the time of their first settlement in the Promised Land, equal economic conditions for all free men and the participation of each in the determination of the conditions under which he should labor were as near realization as they ever have been. But one may seriously doubt whether such a purely agricultural society actually existed even then. There were certainly some of the Hebrews who were richer than others and thus possessed decided advantages. Nabal, the foolish sheep owner who angered David, may serve as an example of a numerous class. After the settlement in Canaan democracy of opportunity was not long maintained. Even so far as there was democracy among the Hebrews, it was a democracy of deep poverty. There were rich cities in the Maritime Plain; there were the lordly Philistines. Palestine was never a land of either political or industrial democracy.

There is another sense in which the word democracy is used, that of simplicity of tastes and of mode of living. It usually keeps company also with social democracy, that is, the absence of social distinctions, of the caste spirit. That all of the Hebrews approved such economic and social democracy one cannot claim. But it will become evident as we study Hebrew and Jewish social life that this type of democracy was an ideal that was held before the eyes of the Israelites by many of their greatest moral leaders. It is possible to observe certain *motifs* entering into the thinking of the Hebrews which combined to lay emphasis on the worth of the individual as such. It eventually came about that, with the Jews as with the Stoics, the dominant moral ideal valued the individual, not for the accidents of wealth or birth or position, but for himself

[1] See Edward Day, "Was the Hebrew Monarchy Limited?" *AJSL,* 40 (Jan., 1924), 98-110.

as a person. With political democracy, then, the Hebrews had little concern. They thought of industrial democracy only in the sense that their ideal was that each Hebrew should possess his own patrimony and live in agricultural independence. Social democracy, the recognition of the worth of every individual Israelite and eventually of every man who accepted their religious and moral standards, came to be one of their outstanding ideas. The concept of economic democracy, that is the ideal of the simple life, the belief in the right of every man to a minimum of material well-being and in the wrong of undue wealth, dominates much of Hebrew and Jewish literature. The "dawn of democracy" is to be discovered among the Hebrews, not in the invention of political machinery, but in the elaboration of democratic ideals of living.

II. PROGRESS BY CONFLICT

For the Hebrews the story of democracy begins in the desert. Their fundamental social ideals were formed during the uncounted centuries of the nomadic stage of their existence long before they entered the land of Canaan. It was with nomadic customs as a basis that they evolved the social institutions and ideals of the period of the monarchy. In Canaan their geographical situation was such as to throw them immediately into contact with agricultural and commercial types of society, each with its own peculiar customs, standards of morality, and religious beliefs. The whole history of the Israelites from the time of their entrance into Canaan is a series of conflicts between differing social standards. If higher morality is the product of a conflict of social ideals,[2] the Israelites had ample opportunity for the comparisons and decisions necessary to the development of consciously chosen, intelligent standards of conduct. It was the process of struggle between competing groups, the choice between incompatible standards and customs, that brought about the ethical development of the Hebrews.

The history of Israel is marked by seven periods of storm and stress when these character-forming conflicts come especially to

[2] MacDougall, *Intro. to Social Psychology*, pp. 215-33; Bristol, *Social Adaptation*, p. 310.

the surface of the onward-flowing social process. The first was during the period of settlement, when the nomad was becoming a farmer. The second was the reigns of David and Solomon, when the loose confederacy of clans became a nation and began to embark on commercial enterprises. The next was the era of struggle between Baalism and Yahwism, between a reaction to the nomadism of the steppe and the attractions of agricultural life in the mountains and commercial civilization on the seacoast. Elijah and Elisha stand on the one side, the house of Ahab and its court on the other. The fourth period is that of the great pre-exilic prophets whose writings have come down to us. This long period of struggle with the civilization of the Tigris-Euphrates valley, extending from 785 B.C. to 540 B.C., may be subdivided into three: (a) the period of Assyrian advance, 785-700 B.C., when Amos, Hosea, Micah, and Isaiah prophesied; (b) the period of Assyrian ascendancy, 700-625 B.C., during which the Deuteronomic Code was probably elaborated in opposition to the current Assyrianizing policy of the court; and (c) the period of Assyrian decline and Babylonian hegemony, 625-540 B.C., signalized by another group of brilliant prophets, Zephaniah, Habbakuk, Nahum, Jeremiah, and Ezekiel, and by the inauguration of the Deuteronomic Reform under Josiah and its failure under his successors. The fifth main period was that of Persian domination, 540-332 B.C., when undoubtedly certain Zoroastrian or Magian elements entered into Jewish thinking, but when Hebrew separatism began to produce that defensive armament which saved the national culture from annihilation during the two subsequent periods. The sixth, or Greek, period was that of the deadly struggle with Hellenism, which culminated in the Maccabean revolt against Syria in 168 B.C. It was this revolt which saved Judaism from being swallowed up by Hellenism. The seventh and last period of the history which is now under review, that of the struggle against Rome, was, like the preceding, a struggle with Hellenistic culture. It culminated in two disasters to Judaism, the Christian schism and the destruction of Jerusalem. The first resulted in the temporary eclipse of the prophetic element in Judaism, the second in the permanent disappearance of Judaism as a political entity. Unfortunately also the exclusion of the Christians by the Jews threw the movement Jesus had inaugurated into full alliance with Hellenistic mysticism. In the resulting syncretistic mixture the essential elements of the religion of Jesus were almost lost. Today liberal Judaism on the one hand and progressive Christianity on the other are trying to recover what both were in danger of losing, those fundamental elements of true religion which Jesus combined more successfully and more powerfully than any other religious teacher. It is the task of this book and especially of this chapter to sketch the history of this series of bitter conflicts down to the schism in Judaism which gave rise to Christianity. By such a sketch one may make progress toward discovering what the character of the final outcome was in moral standards and ideals.[3]

During the long and complicated historical process which produced Judaism there were three crucial periods when nomadic tribes with their characteristic customs and ideals of life pressed into Palestine and left their impress upon the life and literature of the Israelites. The first was that of the Hebrew conquest of Canaan, the one period which the biblical writers recognize as a time of nomadic intrusion. The second was that of the struggle of Elijah and Elisha against Phoenician Baalism, the third that of the Exile and the immediately succeeding post-exilic period. The earliest historical traditions of the Hebrews were receiving their shape during the second period, and the great prophets, who were deeply affected by nomadic ideals, immediately follow. During the third period and shortly thereafter the laws of Israel were worked over into the Five Books of Moses, the early historical traditions were edited into the Former Prophets, and all the other important books of the Old Testament were written or re-edited.

[3] See Dewey and Tufts, *Ethics,* chaps. V and VI. One must take issue with the conclusion reached at the close of chap. VI, p. 108 f., regarding "the social ideal of justice, love, and peace;" it is an excellent example of the fallacies that arise when all the factors are not taken into consideration. For an excellent discussion of the theme see Wallis, *The Sociological Study of the Bible.*

There can be little doubt that conditions prevailing in these later periods have left their mark on the editorial activities which have given us the Old Testament as we have it. To the second and third, as well as to the first, incursion of nomadic tribes we owe some of the pronounced evidence of the effects of nomadic ideals upon Hebrew thinking. Nor must it be forgotten that Palestine was on the edge of the desert and that the values and the disadvantages of nomadism were continually before the eyes of her inhabitants. Infiltration from the desert must have been going on at all times, and not merely during the periods of special invasion. The fact that all the nomadic elements have been transferred by the later editors of Hebrew literature to the beginning of their national history should not obscure the importance of the nomadic point of view and its effects upon the ideals with which we are here concerned.[4]

What were the social customs and standards of Semitic nomadism with which the Hebrews entered Palestine and which later comers repeatedly reintroduced in subsequent periods? Such tribes were essentially homogeneous, with a customary morality of low type in which the virtues of courage in war and faithfulness to one's clan along with hospitality, generosity, and a strong but elementary sense of justice outweigh all others. Religion was simple and unostentatious, and the social pleasures of the group were restricted to certain fixed family and religious festivals which custom prescribed and regulated and to which it gave a divine sanction. There were almost no poor, for every individual belonged to a family and every family to a clan. The larger unit cared for the smaller with scrupulous solicitude. There was community of feeling within the group such that the property was practically held in common. Every individual could achieve all of which he was capable. There was room for all. It may well be that the earliest form of capital is to be seen in flocks and herds, for under the conditions of nomadism any group with enterprise and ability could easily acquire such possessions, yet it was not capital in the strict modern sense, nor was it a

[4] See above, pp 85 f., 88 f., and below, pp. 140, 150 f.; S. A. Cook in *CAH*, III, pp. 370 ff., 383 ff., 405 ff., 478 ff.

purely individual possession. As there was no private ownership of land there could be no considerable number of homeless dependents. Men who could not maintain an independent life perished or became the slaves or clients of the strong. Useless defectives perished; the women with their children belonged as wives, concubines, or slaves to some man. Tho woman was a chattel, yet by personal ability and force of character she could rise to a place of commanding importance, as Deborah did. Family life might be marked by real affection as in the case of Jacob and Rachel. There was no social question, for there were no questioners, nor, indeed, were there many who, because of superior position or wealth, might oppress, except as one group enslaved another, and that rarely happened till attachment to the soil prevented the conquered group from escaping. The struggles were between tribal groups, not between individuals or classes within them. In the wandering life of the steppe and even during such a period as that of the settlement in Canaan, group conflicts tended to solidify each society and to subordinate the individual so completely that the question of individual rights could not arise.

The Semites have been variously described because there are so many varieties of them. As to the real grass-land breed, however, there is closer agreement. It has been said, to be sure, that the nomad is naturally democratic, but that the Semite was aristocratic.[5] Both are true. He was democratic in the simplicity of his life, in the relative uniformity of social standards and achievements for all members of each group, and in the readiness of each to sacrifice himself for certain accepted group *mores.* In spite of the dominating social solidarity he was an individualist insofar as his mode of life demanded action in limited groups where each individual counted large, and where each was often required to act for himself. He was an aristocrat because the family was the basic unit in society, and family honor and glory necessarily were the highest goods of life. In other words, nomadic democracy is not a matter of political institutions. It means rather simplicity in the accepted standards of living and in the organization of society. It stands in marked contrast to the lux-

[5] S. A. Cook, in *CAH,* I, p. 195.

ury and complexity that arise in an agricultural-commercial society.

The entrance into Canaan changed the outward environment of the Hebrew clans. The next two centuries were marked by a conflict of nomadic and agricultural standards. We can surmise that confederation between the various tribes raised questionings in the minds of some on matters moral and religious. We have abundant evidence that contact with the relatively rich civilization of Canaan began at once to develop serious problems. The story of Achan pictures a man who attempted to outstrip his neighbors. We cannot doubt that many another succeeded where he was detected. The story of Nabal of Carmel and the characterization of David's outlaw followers as the distressed, the discontented, and those in debt,[6] if historical, are sufficient evidence of developing difficulties. The absorption of such groups as the Gibeonites (Josh. 9) created a subject class. Plainly, also, idolatrous practices of the Canaanites, which were closely bound up with agricultural customs, became prevalent among the Hebrews and led to an intemperance in the use of wine and to a sexual license in connection with religious worship to which the nomadic Hebrews were entirely unaccustomed. J. M. Powis Smith aptly characterizes the change of environment from the simple life of the desert to the rich and complex society of agricultural and commercial Canaan. He says:

> "The Hebrews coming in from the simple life of the nomad in the desert were confronted by all the limitations and trials that a rich and highly developed culture presents to primitive people. They were like the country boy coming to earn his living in the big city; it will either make or break him."[7]

Smith mentions another factor in Hebrew ethical development which is of great importance in understanding its progress: the mental and moral fluidity of the tribes during the long period of perhaps two centuries while they were slowly drifting in from

[6] I Sam. 25; 22.2.

[7] *Moral Life of the Hebrews,* University of Chicago Press, p. 5, see also pp. 323 f.

the desert and conquering the land of Canaan.[8] They were continually observing the new standards of the Canaanites among whom they lived while they were "kept in closest contact with the life fresh from the desert." It was a lack of social unity, a mental and moral fluidity, which made it possible for every man to do that which was right in his own eyes. There was thus a conflict of moral standards in which whatever in nomadism was crude and unsuited to a more complex social organization had to meet the test of trial in a new set of conditions. At the same time the *mores* of the Canaanites were scrutinized by eyes with the long vision of the desert. The majority of the Hebrews seem to have accepted the new ways without question, but there were those with sufficient insight and independence to reject much of the new.

This mental fluidity and conflict of standards continued thruout the monarchy, partly by reason of attacks from the great culture nations, partly by reason of renewed nomadic intrusions, partly on account of conditions which were continually present. In a land where every farmer is also a shepherd, where a large number of the families spend a considerable portion of the year "under the black tent," where people living a life that is more nomadic than settled are always only a few miles away, and where every child is familiar from earliest infancy with the freedom of the wilderness, where "everyone who is in difficulties, everyone who is in debt, everyone who has a grievance" [9] has only a few miles to walk to escape entirely from his burdens, in such a land there cannot be the same servile submission to injustice, exploitation, and autocracy that often arises under other circumstances.[10] The customs of nomad life could not be forgotten by the Hebrews. Its freedom and its joys could not but be frequently before their minds in bright contrast to the labors, the taxes, the *corvée,* and the other evils and exactions consequent upon the

[8] *Op. cit.,* p. 4.

[9] 1 Sam. 22.2 (Moffatt).

[10] See P. Baldensperger, *The Immovable East,* London, 1913, pp. 218-46, for a modern illustration; see also the writer's article, "The Wilderness of Judea and the Nomadic Ideal," *Journal of Geography,* 23 (1924), 338-49.

adoption of a more civilized life and a more or less autocratic government.

Hebrew literature often opens the window upon these domestic difficulties. The traditions of J and E, and the books of Judges, Samuel, and Kings all alike disclose an ideal of life which closely combines an acceptance of agriculture with a love for nomadism. Abraham is pictured as a pure nomad. The patriarchs after him are semi-nomadic, cultivating fields and occupying certain spots for indefinite periods, and yet relying principally on their flocks and herds for their wealth. For forty years Moses was a shepherd. David, most popular of Hebrew heroes, was a shepherd boy. Yet the accepted ideal is that every Hebrew shall possess his own inheritance and dwell under his own vine and fig tree. The nomad hated wine, but in the "Blessing of Jacob" Judah is to "wash his garments in wine and his vesture in the blood of the grape. His eyes shall be red (*or,* heavy) with wine." Asher is to have his fill of bread and royal dainties and Joseph is to be a fruitful bough by a fountain.[11] The same joy in agriculture appears in the Deuteronomic "Blessing of Moses," which probably dates from the time of Jeroboam II. Joseph is to enjoy "wealth of crops from the sunlight . . . with choice fruit from the ancient hills." Asher is to dip his foot in olive oil and Israel is to dwell in a land of grain and wine.[12] In contrast to the hopefulness of the priestly and Deuteronomic writers, the Yahwist represents agriculture, wine growing, and indeed all civilization as under a curse.[13] In truth, the active conflict between pastoral and agricultural ideals of life continues during the entire existence of the monarchy down to the destruction of Jerusalem by Nebuchadrezzar. It is reflected in Jewish literature down to the New Testament period.

It was not merely a dual, but a triangular, conflict in which the Israelites were involved. Palestine, especially Judea, is a frontier between three types of civilization, nomadic, agricultural, and commercial. The Hebrews had no sooner adapted themselves to

[11] Gen. 49.11 f., 20, 22.

[12] Dt. 33.13-17 (see Moffat), 24, 28; see Driver in *ICC.*

[13] See below, p. 136.

agricultural conditions in Canaan than they were thrown into a new conflict with the active commercial life of the coast and the transcontinental trade routes. The development of commerce and of intercourse with other nations under Solomon introduced a still more extended knowledge of alien and strange customs. The tremendous significance and the danger of Palestine's central position now becomes plain. The comparison of their nomadic customs with the moral and cultural standards of the whole world was at once inevitable. The consolidation of the separate clans into the United Kingdom was a long step in their conscious adaptation to their social *milieu*. It resulted in the eventual abandonment of tribal political organization and the loss of the independence of the clan unit. It involved the subserviency of all to the larger national group and to the concrete representative of the larger whole, the king and his court.

Now the monarchy needed large funds, and, along with the tribute from conquered nations, tolls from traffic, and contributions levied on groups or rich individuals, commerce appeared an easy road to wealth. Like many other ancient monarchs, David, Solomon, and their successors were merchants, reserving at least a part of the foreign trade to themselves as a royal monopoly.[14] Enlarged boundaries with their increased contacts with other lands and the wealth which resulted from successful wars provided natural opportunities and incentives to commerce, which the demands of the royal exchequer artificially increased and sharpened.

It was providential that the presence of the hostile Philistines on the coast and then the revolt of the northern tribes put serious obstacles in the way of this development in its infancy. Otherwise the commercial spirit and the seductions of superior civilizations might have deflected the line of evolution and the Hebrews might have become another nation of Phoenicians. As it was, from the time of Solomon until that of Uzziah, Judah held to her semi-agricultural, semi-nomadic mode of living. Her circumscribed and unproductive territory with its forbidding mountains prevented her engaging extensively in foreign trade. In the reigns of Omri

[14] G. A. Smith, *Jerusalem,* I, p. 340.

and Ahab the northern kingdom made decided strides in the direction of commerce, even to the establishment of trading quarters in Damascus.[15] But the revolt of Jehu with its recrudescence of nomadic influence cut short for the time being her cultural advance. The constant wars of this century and a half (ca. 925-775) must have hindered development even in agriculture. The people could never get far away from their pastoral life, nor become completely and successfully agricultural. Thus further internal conflicts of social ideals were for the time postponed.

The Indian summer which the two little Israelite kingdoms enjoyed in the eighth century brought on a crisis in the *Kulturkampf*. Once more successful wars, with their concomitants of reparations in the way of plunder and tribute, were the basis for a wave of prosperity, accompanied by ambitious commercial enterprises. They were followed also by those other inevitable concomitants of war and commercial progress, a vast increase of extravagance, luxury, and licentiousness on the one hand, and of poverty, suffering, and social injustice on the other. Each type of economic organization has its advantages and its disadvantages. Nomadic society with its simplicity, its mobility, its freedom from continuous laborious toil, its independence of political control, its alternation of quiet and excitement, and its opportunities for individual initiative and advancement, has also its long periods of severe exertion and bitter exposure, its seasons of want and privation, and its general barrenness, absence of comfort, and lack of large rewards for the strenuous life it involves. Agriculture, with its greater regularity and security, its larger certainty of food, clothing, and shelter, and its opportunities for gradual advancement in comfort and well-being, has also its dull, monotonous toil, wearying to body and deadening to mind, its uncertainties as to markets, its dangers of loss beyond recovery in periods of drought and war, and its exposure to the exactions of tax-collectors and to the manipulations of buyers and creditors. Commerce builds cities and supplies them with pleasures, comforts, and excitements of which the country does not dream. But it builds

[15] 1 Kg. 20.34.

them with dishonesty and injustice. It balances its theaters with slums, its gymnasia with gaming houses, its temples with brothels. All the disadvantages as well as the advantages of the more highly organized life of agriculture and commerce flooded over Palestine as a result of the Israelites' sudden accession to wealth and power.

The prophetic indictment of current morality is evidence as to the nature of the conflict. As to religion, they criticize the cultus as it was carried on in the local high places and the national shrines, not the high places and shrines in themselves, but the manner of worship, the drinking and sexual license sanctioned by religion.[16] Agriculture came under the ban insofar as wine was one of its chief products and the feasts which the prophets despised were agricultural feasts. The innumerable references to neglect of the poor and the repeated enactments intended to protect and care for them show how individualism had developed in an agricultural society where "only the hard and patient worker gets a reward and he does not like to share it with the lazy, or even with the weaker."[17] Still more bitterly did the prophets inveigh against abuses and injustices which had arisen as a result of the prosperity of the land. The men who had become wealthy in the successful wars of Jeroboam II and Uzziah, the princes and warriors whom the king favored, had made good use of their special privileges to increase their holdings by taking advantage of the less fortunate. What the prophets most indignantly denounced was the exploitation of the poor by loans, pledges, and the taking of interest, with the further result of finally seizing their lands and selling the owners and their families for debt. Added to heartless exploitation was the misuse of the courts for carrying out these oppressions. The evils of eighth-century Hebrew society were exactly those which every country faces sooner or later, when the land is fully occupied and commercial development allows the more clever to take advantage of the underprivileged. Great estates took the place of the numerous small holdings which were

[16] Am. 2.7 f.

[17] Dewey and Tufts, *Ethics,* p. 77.

the Hebrew ideal. Landlords took the place of peasant proprietors, and the peasants became unskilled laborers or slaves. Property, not personality, became the standard by which worth was weighed. Luxury, extravagance, the miscarriage of justice, and special privilege took the place of industry, honesty, and brotherliness.

The Hebrew people had been struggling to decide between two sets of standards, each based purely on custom. Elijah had boldly set before them the religious alternatives involved: "How long are you wavering between the two sides? If Yahweh be the God, follow him; if Baal, follow him."[18] The great eighth-century prophets do not consider this alternative. Jehu had settled it. They put another more difficult choice before the two little nations, the alternative of two types of morality. For the prophets it is no longer a blind choice, an unconscious conflict. It is not possible for them, as it was for the recorders of Israel's ancient traditions, to combine and harmonize inconsistent points of view. Looking back upon the history of four centuries of conflict, they had passed from custom to conscience, from group morality to personal morality.[19] But in this case it was not the old standards, so far as they applied to economic evils and social injustice, that needed to be abandoned, in the judgment of the prophets. Rich and selfish individualists were breaking up the social group, were destroying the nation by their base abandonment of the old paths. The higher level of morality among the Hebrews was reached by a conscious choice of what the prophets believed to be the ancient morality and religion of the nation and by the rejection of the *mores* of the culturally more advanced nations which were trying to absorb them and whom the king and his court were imitating. The prophets chose the patriarchal, or nomadic, ideal.

III. THE NOMADIC IDEAL

Renan made much of the patriarchal ideal in his *History of the People of Israel*. He refers to the work of Amos as "this great

[18] 1 Kg. 18.21.

[19] Dewey and Tufts, *Ethics*, p. 73. The process and the results among the Hebrews, however, were not as described on pp. 74 ff.

struggle against the progress of civilization in the name of patriarchal ideas."[20] Again he says:

"We have already pointed out that whenever a prospect of material civilization opened before Israel, the conscience of this curious people reverted to a past ideal of a nomad life and monotheism."[21]

Recently his fellow countryman, Antonin Causse, of the Protestant Theological Faculty in the University of Strassburg, has developed the theme, especially in his volume, *Les "pauvres" d'Israël*.[22] The struggle, as he sees it, is *"les prophètes contre la civilization royale."* The patriarchal ideal is to be seen in the combination of Elijah, Elisha, the prophetic schools, and the Rechabites against civilization and syncretism; it is to be discovered as a thread running thru the "sacred history," especially in the Yahwist editor, *"un grand historien religieux,"* in the eighth-century prophets, and in the social legislation of the Torah.

Thirty years ago Budde canvassed the ground with much the same result. Taking Jehonadab ben Rechab as its symbol and representative he followed the nomadic ideal thru all Hebrew history. He discovered its origin in the choice of a nomad deity by Moses and the Israelites. At Sinai they adopted Yahweh, originally god of the nomadic Kenites. Their covenant with Yahweh involved his promise to aid and protect a people who were not previously his worshipers on condition that they should do his will. Thus instead of a relation based on kinship or other primitive conceptions of the bond between a god and his people, a moral element was introduced into Israel's religion, the germ of all its future development. Because the Israelites had covenanted to worship Yahweh, they were bound to adhere to the ancient and primitive nomadic customs of the tribe from which he had been borrowed. To this conception Jonadab ben Rechab was true when he commanded his children:

"You shall drink no wine, neither you nor your sons forever. Neither shall you build house, nor sow seed, nor plant vineyard, nor possess

[20] Vol. II, p. 366 f.

[21] Vol. II, p. 240. Similar references are numerous.

[22] See pp. 1-80.

any; but all your days you shall dwell in tents, that you may live many days in the land where you are sojourning."[23]

As a Kenite he was bound to remain true to the ancient deity "of the steppe and of the roaming nomads, to whom agriculture, fixed to the soil, cannot be an acceptable honor."[24]

The Kenite hypothesis is not a necessary factor in the consideration of the nomadic ideal. Whether one accept this origin for Israel's religion or suppose it to have come from some other Hebrew tribe, the facts as to the nomadic elements in Israel's life and thought are too numerous and patent to gainsay.[25] In the foregoing I have sought to point out how the conditions made for the perpetuation of the nomadic ideal. Let me briefly indicate its bearing upon the question of Hebrew democracy.

First, it is to be noted that the Hebrews came into Palestine as nomads. On this point there is no difference of opinion. Second, they long maintained many of the *mores* of nomadism after they had adopted a settled mode of life; for example, clan, or tribal organization, the rule of elders, or sheikhs, the nomad's conception of the family and family relationships, and his food, clothing, and amusements. The old phrase, "to your tents, O Israel," shows how the language of the desert still lingered on their tongues when they have been living in the stone hovels of

[23] Jer. 35.6 f.

[24] The Kenite Hypothesis, proposed by Tiele (*Histoire comp. des anc. relig.*, 1882, p. 350) and Stade (*Gesch. d. Volkes Isr.*, pp. 131 f., 358-518), is set forth by Budde in his article "The Nomadic Ideal in the Old Testament," in *The New World,* IV (Boston, 1895), 726-45 (*Preussische Jahrbücher,* 1896), and his *Religion of Israel to the Exile,* New York, 1899, pp. 1-38. For criticism of the Kenite hypothesis see J. M. P. Smith, *Moral Life of the Hebrews,* pp. 63 ff., and Montefiore, *Ancient Hebrews* (Hibbert Lectures), pp. 50 ff.

[25] They have recently been set forth *in extenso* by John W. Flight, "The Nomadic Idea and Ideal in the Old Testament," *JBL,* 42 (1923), 158-226. The geographical factors are emphasized in the writer's article, "The Wilderness of Judea and the Nomadic Ideal. A Study of the Social and Religious Effects of Geographic Environment," *Journal of Geography,* 23 (1924), 333-49.

mountain villages.[26] Furthermore, as we have noted already, the Hebrews in Palestine were constantly under necessity of living as nomads and were being leavened by the infiltration of nomadic families or clans who pressed in to share the riches of Canaan.

Again, there were many in Israel who were never reconciled to settled society. They believed the nomadic life the only kind really blessed by Yahweh. The earliest written documents of the Hebrews, J and E in the Hexateuch, reflect this attitude.[27] The offerings of Cain the farmer were rejected by Yahweh, those of the shepherd Abel accepted. The patriarchs are represented as nomads or half-nomads, and the writers of Israel's traditions loved to dwell on this Golden Age of their forefathers. Some of the ancient documents go farther than a mere dreamy idealization of nomadic life. Settled civilization is thought to be abhorred of Yahweh. There is a curse upon the tiller of the soil. The first farmer is the first murderer. Descendants of the accursed Cain build the first city and invent the instruments and arts of civilization. The city culture of Babylon built the *ziggurat* which led to God's curse and the dispersion of mankind. The story of the Flood is motivated by the wickedness of the civilization founded by the descendants of Cain. They and their works must be destroyed in order that man may begin over again a simple life of trust in Yahweh.[28] The cities of the plain also were destroyed, and Lot, the nomad led astray by their glamor, escapes only with his life.

The story of the Creation and Fall bears unconscious marks of the conflict between nomadism and civilization.[29] To the priestly writer all that God has created is good. Man, both male and female, is created in God's image and given dominion over a rich and bountiful earth with the command to be fruitful and multiply. In Psalm 104 and Job 38-39 there is the same joy in the good world which God has made. A like hopefulness appears in the blessing of Noah:

[26] See Flight, *JBL,* 42, pp. 158-96.

[27] Luther in Meyer, *Die Israeliten,* pp. 129 ff.

[28] Flight, *op. cit.,* 213 f.

[29] See above, pp. 129 f.

"So long as the earth remains, seedtime and harvest, cold and heat, summer and winter, day and night, shall not cease. . . . Be fruitful and multiply, and replenish the earth. . . . And the bow shall be in the cloud; and I will look upon it, that I may remember the covenant between God and every living creature of all flesh that is upon the earth." [30]

The multiplication of families and nations, the rise of the first warrior, Nimrod, and the founding of city states are related as steps in the progress of mankind "before the Lord."

It is argued with great plausibility that the Yahwist writer, on the other hand, conceives of human history as a long series of catastrophes. In the beginning God made a world in which there reigned universal peace and happiness. Nature was not "red in tooth and claw," but all animals ate the fruits of the ground. The wolf dwelt with the lamb and the leopard with the kid, the lion ate straw like the ox. But in this happy world there was a sinister imperfection: God could not find a companion for man. The woman created to make good the deficiency caused the great catastrophe of the Fall, and upon this followed enmity between man and the animal world, the cursing of the ground, murder, the fall of the angels, and the Flood. Agriculture, the building of cities, the rise of warriors and men of renown, the development of civilization again after the Flood, and the dispersion of mankind by God's curse, all of these are parallel, progressive steps in the development of civilization and the deterioration of mankind.[31] Progress in culture is progress in evil.

This love of nomadism and hatred of civilization might be thought a mere literary survival from an earlier stage of tradition or perhaps an affectation, like the Hellenistic and Roman praise of the simple life, were it not for more direct evidence. The monarchy was not received whole-heartedly in Israel. Driven to imitate their

[30] Gen. 8.22; 9.1, 16.

[31] A. Menes, "Die sozialpolitische Analyse der Urgeschichte," *ZAW*, N. F. 2 (1925), 33-62. Note the J passages, Gen. 9.18-27; 10.8-19, 21-30; 11.1-9. If this catastrophic view is, as it seems, that of J, he is already an apocalyptist. Menes' interpretation of the Cain legend seems to me to raise more questions than it answers.

neighbors for their self-preservation, the Hebrews, even down to the time of the Exile, show the old nomadic impatience of governmental restraint. In particular the great prophets were the opposition party, the critics who point out the mistakes and shortcomings of the government, as Nathan did to David. Many of them are confidants and counselors of their monarchs. Some so-called prophets are mere sycophants.[32] But at every important break in the dynastic succession, the prophets are the leaders in revolt. It was Ahijah who encouraged Jeroboam to lead the northern tribes away from Solomon and the new civilization he was introducing. Elijah headed the opposition to Jezebel and Ahab and the same kind of civilization. Elisha engineered the revolt of Jehu. Both of them, and especially Elijah, were representatives of the old, wild nomadic opposition to the luxury of civilization and the royalty which furthered it. With biting irony Isaiah denounces "the scoffers that rule this people that is in Jerusalem." [33] "Children," he says, "are their oppressors, and women rule over them." [34] Micah complains:

> "Ye heads of the house of Jacob, and rulers of the house of Israel, that abhor justice, and pervert all equity. They build up Zion with blood, and Jerusalem with iniquity." [35]

The prophets attack the culture of the courts and the capitals, Samaria and Jerusalem. It was, to use the phrase of Causse, *"les prophètes contre la civilization royale."*[36] Amos denounces the "cows of Bashan, the women of high Samaria," and cries:

> "Woe to the careless citizens,
> so confident in high Samaria,
> leaders of this most ancient race,
> who are like gods in Israel!" [37]

[32] The patriotism of the prophets will be discussed in the next chapter.
[33] Chap. 28.14.
[34] Chap. 3.12.
[35] Mic. 3.9 f.
[36] *Les "pauvres,"* p. 9.
[37] Chap. 4.1; 6.1 (Moffatt).

Isaiah pours his scorn upon the "daughters of Zion" and all their finery. He pronounces woes upon Samaria:

"Woe to the proud crown of the drunkards of Ephraim,
to the fading flowers of his glorious adornment
Which is at the head of the fertile valleys
of men who are overcome with wine."

And likewise upon Jerusalem:

"Woe to you, God's own hearth and altar,
O City where David encamped!"
"How unfaithful she has turned,
the city once so true and trusty!
Sion once so full of justice,
once the seat of right
and now a haunt of murderers!
Your silver, it has turned to dross,
your wine is spoiled with water.
Your rulers are unruly men,
hand in hand with thieves,
every one fond of his bribe,
keen upon fees,
but careless of the orphan's rights,
and of the widow's cause."[38]

Bitterest of all in his denunciation of the city is Micah, the peasant prophet from the country village of Mareshah in south-western Judea. He says:

"What is Jacob's transgression? Is it not Samaria?
And what is Judah's sin? Is it not Jerusalem?"
"Therefore . . . shall Sion be ploughed up like a field,
Jerusalem shall become a heap of ruins."[39]

Judah's cities and strongholds are classed with her chariots and horses, her witchcrafts and her soothsayers, her graven images, her pillars, and her Asherim among the evils which Yahweh in the day of his appearing will utterly destroy.[40] To the eyes of

[38] Chap. 3.16; 28.1 (H. Schmidt); 29.1 (Moffatt); 1.21 ff. (Moffatt).
[39] Chap. 1.5; 3.12 (Cf. Moffatt).
[40] Chap. 5.10-14 (9-13).

the man of the country the destruction of the cities was an essential step in the restoration of morality.

Not only have we the literary evidence to be found in the prophetic criticism of contemporary civilization. There is ample concrete historical evidence. The first purely objective indication of a rejection of settled life and an insistence upon nomadism as the ideal is to be found in the Rechabites. What that ideal was we learn from Jeremiah. They had been bound by their forefather, Jonadab ben Rechab, thruout all their generations not to drink wine, build houses, sow seed, plant vineyards, or even to own houses or fields, but to dwell in tents.[41] By a strange chance, as it seems, Jonadab ben Rechab had appeared on the scene to play a part in one of the most tragic incidents in all Israel's history, the revolt of Jehu against the house of Omri. As Jehu was on his way from the murder of Jezebel and her court to wreak his terrible, ironic vengeance on the worshipers of Baal in Samaria, he met Jonadab, or Jehonadab, ben Rechab near "Betheked (the dwelling place) of the shepherds," a fitting place in which to find a nomad. The son of the Wilderness assures the sanguinary reformer that his heart is with him. They clasp hands and in the chariot of the new king the Kenite sheikh rides into Samaria to have his share in the annihilation of Ahab's house and the worshipers of Baal.[42]

It cannot be merely fortuitous that we find the founder of the semi-religious, nomadic order of the Rechabites and the king whom the prophets had chosen here together. It was probably the time of a new influx of tribes from the steppe and nomadism was an influence to be reckoned with in all the land.[43] It had become evident to many in Israel that the conflict between Yahweh and Baal was not merely a matter of religion. The civilization which Jezebel and Ahab had promoted was inimical, so they believed, to the old Hebrew virtues. Religion and the economic organization of society seemed to be bound up together. Jonadab ben Rechab ap-

[41] Jer. 35.6; see above, p. 134 f.

[42] 2 Kg. 10.12 (see the Hebrew text), 15 ff., 23; 1 Chr. 2.55.

[43] See above, p. 124 f.

proved the destruction of Baal worship, and he was willing to take the still more radical step which he thought necessary to save his clan from the contamination of commerce and agriculture in order that they might live many days in the land where they were merely passing travelers.[44] The nazirites are a similar evidence of the feeling that the worship of Yahweh required abstention from the indulgences, particularly in wine, which Canaanite civilization was promoting.[45]

Some of the prophets seem to have been prepared to take a farther step, the logical outcome of Rechabite reasoning. The evils of agricultural and commercial life had gone so far that only an intervention as drastic as the Flood could save the nation. As the early historical documents, J and E, love to dwell on the patriarchal period as the Golden Age of Hebrew history, so these prophets turned back to the time of the wandering in the Wilderness as the period when Israel really knew and truly worshiped Yahweh. Hosea thinks of God as looking back upon the infancy of Israel with the yearning tenderness that a father feels for the childhood of sons who have grown up to disappoint or disobey him. Yahweh says to Hosea:

> "I loved Israel when he was a child,
> and called my son out of Egypt."
> "It was I who shepherded thee in the desert,
> in the land of scorching heat."[46]

Even Isaiah, the prophet of the capital city and the court, appears at times to anticipate the destruction of the monarchy, for just after a fierce arraignment of the city and its rulers, he says:

> "This therefore is the sentence of the Lord,
> the Lord of hosts, Hero of Israel:
> 'Ha! I will have the comfort of vengeance on my foes,
> on folk who dare to resist me!

[44] Jer. 35.7.
[45] See Harper, *ICC, Amos and Hosea,* p. 56 f.
[46] Chap. 11.1; 13.5; cf. Am. 2.10 f.

I will turn my hand against you,
smelt your dross out in a furnace,
and clear out all your alloy;
I will give you judges as at the first,
and councillors as at the beginning,
and then a "citadel of justice" shall you be,
a true and trusty City.' "[47]

Others go back another stage and believe that in the Golden Age to come nomadic conditions are to be fully restored. Hosea insists that in Canaan Israel had become too prosperous. He makes Yahweh say:

"They fed and filled themselves,
then their heart was lifted up
and they forgot me."[48]

Jeremiah expresses the same idea. Israel was like a well-fed horse roaming at large.[49] The thought is common in Deuteronomy. The Song of Moses complains:

"Jacob ate their fill,
Jeshurun fattened and grew restive—
ay, you fattened, gross and gorged!
They forsook God who had made them,
scorned the Steadfast One, their succor."[50]

Hosea puts the whole conception of the evils of commercial life in Canaan as contrasted with the delights of the pure and beautiful simplicity of nomadism into two vivid verses:

"Canaan!
In his hand are false balances, he loves to defraud.
And does Ephraim say, 'Yes, I have become rich,
I have gained for myself wealth'?

[47] Chap. 1.24 ff., following Moffatt in the main; but the reference to *shopheṭîm* seems to me an allusion to the "judges" of pre-monarchical times, who were really sheikhs such as nomads have.

[48] Chap. 13.6.

[49] Chap. 5.7 f.

[50] Dt. 32.15 (Mof., cf. LXX); cf. 8.12 f.

Not all his gains will compensate for the guilt of his sin.
For I, Yahweh, have been your God ever since you left the land of
Egypt,
And I will again make you to dwell in tents as in days of old." [51]

Whether the last verse is a threat or a promise is not clear from the context.[52] But if chapter 2.14 may be taken as authentic, it is clearly a promise. In chapter 2 Israel's life in Canaan is represented as one continual round of harlotry with the Baalim. Her vines and her fig trees, which she has taken as the hire of her lovers, Yahweh will utterly destroy. And because she has bedecked herself with the ornaments of her wealth and luxury and, forgetting Yahweh, has gone after her lovers, the Baalim, "therefore," says Yahweh, "behold, I will allure her and bring her into the wilderness and speak comfort to her heart." [53] Aside from the theory that denies the possibility that the eighth-century prophets ever had a message of comfort, there can be no reason for trying to twist this verse into a threat or denying it to Hosea. That the prophets of Egypt twelve centuries before Hosea had combined both threat and promise removes from the field one of the strongest arguments of those who would eliminate the promises of the eighth-century Hebrew prophets as later interpolations.[54] It was an essential element in the prophetic style thus to alternate threat and promise. Therefore, taking the words "allure" and "speak (comfort, or love) to the heart" in their natural sense, we find

[51] Chap. 12.7-9 (8-10), a difficult passage; cf. Harper, *ICC, Amos and Hosea,* pp. 384 ff., Moffatt's translation, and Gressmann, *Die Schriften des Alten Testaments,* II, 1, pp. 394 f.

[52] Harper determines for the former and lists the authorities on both sides. Gressmann takes the view that it is a promise.

[53] Hos. 2.14 f.; cf. Harper and Gressmann, and the excellent article by Paul Humbert, "La logique de la perspective nomade chez Osée," *Vom Alten Testament,* Beiheft z. *ZAW* 41, pp. 158-66.

[54] See the argument in *The Promise of His Coming,* pp. 57, 81 f., and "Hebrew and Egyptian Apocalyptic Literature," *HTR,* 18 (1925), 378 f., 407 f. I do not mean to say that none of the "hopeful passages" are interpolations, but that objective philological and historical evidence, not the subjective argument of inconsistency, must be the basis for the conclusion that they are such.

Does it mean wealth of settled. Agri + Ind civ will destroy its civ, in war + revert again to nomad?

Hosea representing the future Golden Age as one when Yahweh himself will lead Israel in love and tenderness back to a wilderness life. The very difficult passage, chapter 12.7-9, is clear as to two things: the trafficking of Canaan is thoroly evil and the remedy is a return to nomadic life. Only by a return to nomadism can Israel escape from her present evil plight and become truly the people of Yahweh. After such a purification she can again enter upon the enjoyment of the riches which Yahweh, not the Baalim, will give her in the promised land.

Isaiah (7.21-25) is equally certain that "in that day," the day of Yahweh's self-revelation, the land of Canaan itself will no more be digged or plowed but will produce an abundance of milk and honey. In other words, there is to be a return to completely pastoral conditions. Isaiah's pictures of the age of peace and plenty are so highly colored that one cannot be certain that they were intended to include nomadic ideals of life, and, therefore, it is uncertain whether this little section is to be taken as a promise of the age of blessedness or as a threat of the punishment that must precede it. But in either case the desert must be crossed before the promised land, the Garden of Eden, can be reached, where the wolf will dwell with the lamb.[55]

The same attitude towards the nomadic period in Israel's history appears a century later in Jeremiah and Zephaniah. Jeremiah hears Yahweh say to his people:

> "I remember the devotion of your childhood,
> the love of your bridal days,
> how you followed me in the Wilderness,
> in a land not sown.
> Israel was set apart for Yahweh,
> holy like the first fruits of his harvest."[56]

[55] The meaning of the passages where the phrase "milk and honey" seems to stand for the highest condition of happiness and prosperity is most uncertain. Does *debash* equal Arabic *dibs,* a sweet concoction from grapes or dates, (see Hastings, *DB,* II, 30a, 37b, G. A. Smith, *Jerusalem,* I, p. 303, *HGHL,* additional note to p. 83 on p. 673), or is it honey from bees? In either case is the phrase one borrowed from Semitic mythology and meaning "Götterspeise"? See H. Gressmann, *Ursprung der israelitisch-jüdischen Eschatologie,* pp. 209-15.

[56] Chap. 2.2 f.

But when Yahweh brought them into "a garden land, to eat the fruit and the good things of it," they defiled it by disobeying Yahweh and serving the Baalim. Jeremiah's approval of the descendants of Jonadab ben Rechab does not necessarily apply to their nomadic life, but rather to their faithfulness.[57] In other words, he does not advocate abandoning houses for tents, but he does approve the simpler pastoral life of Israel's earlier history. When he pictures the conditions in the restored land after its punishment, he has cities and habitations of shepherds in friendly contiguity. They shall again plant vines on Samaria's slopes; the bounty of Yahweh includes grain, oil, and wine as well as yearlings of sheep and of cattle. But the clearest evidence of the restoration of the land is that everywhere, in the highlands, in the lowlands, in the south, in the district of Benjamin and about Jerusalem itself the flocks shall pass by to be counted.[58] In the new age of happiness Palestine shall be a pastoral country.

Zephaniah, Jeremiah's more ruthless contemporary, is a thorogoing exponent of the nomadic ideal. The cities of the Maritime Plain shall be utterly destroyed and the whole land become a habitation of shepherds. Yahweh's decree is this:

"I will destroy you, O land of the Philistines,
till not an inhabitant is left,
till you are turned into huts for shepherds,
into folds for flocks,
that couch by night in the houses of Askelon,
and pasture beside Ekron."

From Jerusalem pride and luxury will disappear. Yahweh says:

"I will clear out of your midst
the arrogant and haughty men—
no more vaunting on my sacred hill!
And I will leave within you
a lowly, little people."[59]

[57] Chap. 35.12-19.

[58] Chaps. 31.5, 12, 24, 27, 38 ff.; 33.12 f. In 6.3 is to be seen a threat and not promise, but the "shepherds" are perhaps foreign armies.

[59] Zeph. 2.5 ff.; 3.11 f. (Moffatt).

IV. PRE-EXILIC INFLUENCE OF THE NOMADIC IDEAL

As to the meaning of the nomadic ideal and its influence upon the moral and social progress of the Hebrews, the conclusion must be that they were not by any means uniform. No one inaugurated a concerted movement for the abandonment of agriculture and city life and a return to the desert as a means of securing the favor of Yahweh. Even Jonadab did not insist that all Israel should follow his example. With the characteristic detachment and independence of the nomad he took his way and let others take theirs. He did not even condemn the monarchy. Elijah and Elisha never counseled the overthrow of the monarchy nor the abandonment of agriculture. Elisha certainly and Elijah probably came of farmer stock.[60] Elijah's hairy mantel and nomadic habits were a symbolical protest against the luxuries of civilization, but he would have been the last to demand that everyone adopt them. It was not expected that all Israelites should separate themselves in the fashion of the Rechabites and the nazirites, but these two peculiar institutions stood as a perpetual protest against the debaucheries of which the prophets complained.

It cannot be maintained that the prophets desired a return to a completely nomadic mode of life. Some of them, Hosea and Micah for example, seem to have looked upon the city as an unmixed evil. Others, like Isaiah, with all their invective against city dwellers and their ways, still saw that cities must continue and looked upon Jerusalem as inviolable.[61] Even Hosea promises that, after Israel has once more gone thru the Wilderness, her vineyards shall be restored and she shall rejoice in grain, new wine, and oil.[62] For some the return to nomadism was a punishment, for

[60] Flight, *JBL,* 42, p. 213, n. 326, is wrong in thinking that birth in Gilead points to nomadic ancestry or even unusual nomadic influence. Causse, *Les "Pauvres,"* p. 41, puts the matter more satisfactorily, but still too strongly.

[61] The historicity of Is. 36-39 is often denied, but it seems to me unnecessarily. With all Isaiah's greatness he was human and Jerusalem must have been dear to him. (I do not refer to the miraculous elements.)

[62] Chap. 2.14 f., 21 f.

others a blessing. Some adopted the nomadic ideal as meaning a real return to pastoral life, for others it had a symbolical value. Even for those who believed in it as the only way of escape from the injustices and debaucheries of Canaanite civilization, it was a part of an eschatological scheme and not a social or political program. God would bring it about by his supernatural power. Meantime the faithful Hebrew could only keep himself free from pollution.

Yet the nomadic ideal, visionary though it might be, played no small part in the ethical development of Israel. Upon certain matters the moral leaders of Israel were agreed. The negative and positive content which the prophets put into their conception of morality as a result of the conflict of nomadic with agricultural-commercial ideals is the point of moment for the present study. To consider first the negative result, we discover that they dropped some features of nomadic life. The *jus talionis,* while recognized, is limited. The autonomy of the clan and the independence of the individual are to some extent limited by obligations to a larger unit, the nation. In the main, however, the nomadic ideal leads to the criticism of civilization. As a result of their comparisons of the customs of agricultural and city life with those of nomadism there were certain features of culture which the prophets unhesitatingly and unsparingly condemned. They saw its luxury and consequent effeminacy and debauchery as unmixed evils to be scorned, despised, and feared. The tendency to centralization and the exercise of autocratic royal authority, the rise of a class of rich nobility with the consequent depression and oppression of the ordinary peasant they saw as the crying evils of their times. The individualism which enriched the few at the expense of the many they could not brook.

On the positive side what the prophets adopted from the nomadic ideal may be briefly stated, tho its ultimate richness of implication will not easily nor quickly be realized. In the most concise terms it was simplicity of life and equal rights for all. They were perfectly aware that, when some live in luxury, others must live in want; that when certain groups rise too high in their standard of living, others must fall too low. Therefore, they demanded economic justice, economic democracy, that is, democracy in the distribution of the good things with which God has blessed the earth. Of political democracy they knew nothing. Applied to their ideal, indeed, the word democracy as usually employed is a misnomer, for they were not concerned with questions of rulership or management as such, but thought only of giving every man an opportunity to make the most of life in industrious and independent simplicity. Every man living under his own vine and fig tree with no proud aristocracy to molest him, no rich neighbor to make him afraid, this was the ideal which Israel developed out of her nomadic inheritance. If this ideal is not hostile to civilization as such, it is bitterly inimical to certain accepted institutions of culture societies, to aristocracy and servitude, to riches and poverty.

One of the great services of Israel's prophets was the development they gave to religion. However we may estimate the various attempts to explain the origin of the ethical element in Hebrew religion, the fact of it and the part the prophets played in fixing and clarifying the relationship of ethics to religion is not in doubt. It cannot be denied, moreover, that the great factor in this process was the conflict between Baal and Yahweh conceived as the representatives of two systems of *mores*. In the conflict *mores* became morals. The nomadic ideal as Hosea, Micah, and Zephaniah espouse it is no mere blind allegiance to the customs and moral judgments of the group, but a conscious choice of certain manners of life as the only righteous social order. It may be short-sighted. It may rest upon a naïve philosophy of society and of ethics. But it is not mere customary morality. And the religion that goes with it is no mere form, no mere observance of tabus and magical rites. The prophets made the difficult ascent to a higher level of morality and a higher level of religion at the same time. It was an ascent which established the prophets in a position that, from the standpoint of both ethics and religion, was hostile to society and to culture as they usually exist.

V. THE NOMADIC IDEAL IN JUDAISM

What of the situation in post-exilic and New Testament times? Had the nomadic ideal ceased to play a part in the thinking of Judaism and did it have no influence upon Jesus? What relation does it have to the democracy which we associate so insistently with his life and teachings?

The situation in Judaism is illustrated by contrast with that to be found in the religion of the prophet of Iran. Mazdaism and Hebrew religion had much in common, but in one respect they are diametrically opposed. When Zarathushtra began his reforms, he and his people were fully committed to agriculture. Nomadism was a long forgotten stage in their history, if they had ever passed thru it. Nomads were their enemies. Agriculture was the only righteous method of earning a livelihood. It is possible that veneration for the cow in both India and Iran is a survival of the days when the Aryan-speaking peoples were nomads of the plains, but that origin had long been forgotten in Zarathushtra's day and the ox, or cow, was for him and his contemporaries a symbol of agriculture.[63]

Students of the Gathas agree that for Zarathushtra, as for his people, the life of agriculture was the highest ideal. Thus a part of *Yasna* 45 runs as follows:

> "I will speak of that is best in this life—from Right the Wise One knoweth it, who created the same, even the father of active Good Thought (i.e. the doctrine of Agriculture); and the daughter of the same is Aramaiti of goodly deeds."

Moulton explains that "the true faith of Agriculture is apparently the 'father' of Good Thought, which is here really collective, the pious workers in the field."[64] Next to offerings, obedience to the laws, and worship, Ahura Mazda is most pleased by a believer who builds a house, has a wife and children, dogs and cattle, and cultivates the soil. The growing of grain frightens the *daevas*,

[63] Moulton, *Early Religious Poetry of Persia*, pp. 44, 88.

[64] *Op. cit.*, pp. 104 f.

grinding it crushes them. Industrious labor was highly regarded, poverty due to laziness was one of the greatest of disgraces. The possession of wealth was a chief good, as also in the eyes of the Hebrews, but it was the wealth neither of the nomad nor the merchant and manufacturer.[65]

In *Yasna* 31. 9, 10, we are told that the creator of the Cow ordered her path so that she chose rightly between the tiller of the soil and him who was never a tiller.

> "Of the two she chose the husbandman, the trifty tiller of the fields, as a holy master endowed with the Good Mind's wealth. Never, Mazda! shall the thieving nomad share the good creed." [66]

This is enough to show how much farther away from nomadism were the beginnings of Mazdaism than was even the Judaism of Jesus' day. The contemporaries of Zarathushtra looked upon the nomad as the Egyptian did; he was always an enemy, always a thief. Such an attitude was practically impossible to Judaism. The nomadic traditions of its literature were too many. But it could and did agree as to the righteousness of agriculture and the suspicious character of commerce.

The nomadic ideal as such may be said to disappear with the Jewish exiles in Babylon and Egypt while their poorer brethren left behind in Palestine were practicing it. After the Restoration, Judaism was too much an affair of the Holy City for a social ideal that was hostile to city life to continue to exist. The religion, the very salvation, of the nation and the world was bound up with the little city. There could be no thought of a return to the desert. Yet tho, after the Exile, the nomadic ideal does not meet one in new Jewish literature, still its influence is not lost. Its essential elements, opposition to luxury and approval of the simple life, are not forgotten. The large influx of nomadic blood into Palestine during the Exile and the very simple economic conditions which prevailed for generations later left their lasting impress upon the national ideals and literature. The editors of

[65] Edward Lehmann, in Bertholet-Lehmann, *Lehrbuch der Religionsgeschichte,* 4 ed., Tübingen, 1925, vol. II, pp. 241 f., 263 f.

[66] L. H. Mills, *Zend Avesta,* III, *SBE,* 31, pp. 45 f.

Old Testament literature in post-exilic times show their sympathy for the pastoral-agricultural point of view by their inclusion of so much that speaks for it.[67] Works composed during this period reflect it.

Tho Jesus ben Sira much prefers the study of the Torah, he nevertheless approves husbandry and dislikes commerce. He says:

> "Hate not laborious work,
> Nor husbandry, which the Most High hath ordained."
> "He that tilleth his land shall raise high his heap."
> "A merchant shall hardly keep himself from wrong doing
> And a shop keeper shall not save himself from sin." [68]

In Ethiopic Enoch it is the fallen angels who teach men arts, crafts, and the enjoyment of luxuries, including the use of cosmetics and ornaments.[69] The collection of psalms ascribed to Solomon says: "If a man abound overmuch, he sinneth. Sufficient are moderate means with righteousness." [70] In the Testaments of the Twelve Patriarchs we read:

> "And now, hearken to me, my children,
> And walk in singleness of your heart,
> For I have seen in it all that is well-pleasing to the Lord.
> The single-minded man coveteth not gold,
> He overreacheth not his neighbor,
> He longeth not after manifold dainties,
> He delighteth not in varied apparel.
> He doth not desire to live a long life,
> But only waiteth for the will of God.
>
> . . . .
>
> Keep, therefore, my children, the law of God,
> And get singleness,
> And walk in guilelessness,
> Not playing the busybody with the business of your neighbors,
> But love the Lord and your neighbor,

[67] See above, p. 124 f.
[68] Eccls. 7.15; 20.28; 26.29.
[69] 1 En. 8.1.
[70] Ps. Sol. 5.19 f.

Have compassion on the poor and weak,
Bow down your back unto husbandry,
And toil in labors in all manner of husbandry,
Offering gifts to the Lord with thanksgiving."[71]

The author of I Maccabees indicates his ideal of life in the sympathetic picture he draws of the happy rule of Simon:

"They tilled their land in peace, and the land gave her increase, and the trees of the plains their fruit. The ancient men sat in the streets, they communed all of them together of good things, and the young men put on glorious and warlike apparel. He provided victuals for the cities, and furnished them with all manner of munition, until the name of his glory was named unto the end of the earth. He made peace in the land, and Israel rejoiced with great joy: and they sat each man under his vine and fig tree, and there was none to make them afraid."[72]

Two centuries later Josephus, tho far from being a farmer himself, represents agriculture as the proper occupation for his countrymen. He says:

"We, therefore, neither dwell in a maritime country, nor do we enjoy commerce nor the mingling with others caused by these things, but our cities are built in the mountains far from the sea, and, as we occupy a good country, we work it thoroughly."[73]

Josephus goes on to explain that they had, therefore, had no occasion to enter into commercial relations with the Greeks as the Greeks had with the Egyptians—as if Egypt were not a fertile land—for the sake of imports and exports, nor as the Greeks had with the Phoenicians on account of the greed of the latter and their love of trade and commerce. Josephus is not describing the actual facts, for by his time thousands upon thousands of his people were living by retail trade and commerce in the great cities of the Roman Empire. He was stating the official ideal, like the conventional English notion of the landed gentry, or the American notion of a home-owning citizenry. Josephus may also have

[71] Test. Iss. 4.1-5.3.
[72] I Mac. 14.8-12; cf. Ps. 115.12-15.
[73] *C. Ap.* I, 12 (60).

in mind the bucolic ideal that so fruitlessly permeated Roman society. But tho we may feel compelled to make allowances for Josephus, the fact still remains that the simple country life was the ideal of the Jew.

In the attitude of Judaism toward labor we have a valuable precipitate from the older ideals of the nomadic and agricultural periods of the nation's history. The Jews never despised labor with the hands as did the more aristocratic Greeks and Romans. Unlike Greece and Italy, Palestine had not yet passed into the semi-industrial stage of economic life in which hired and slave labor, often assembled in groups comparable to those in our modern factories, did the hard work of the world, while the educated and aristocratic lived by the nimbleness of their wits and the power of their purses, exploiting the muscles of the less fortunate. The industries of Palestine were still to a large extent probably carried on in the home. But there were also large numbers of free Jewish artisans. Tho a scribe like Jesus ben Sira despised all manual labor as compared with the study of the Torah,[74] every Jewish boy, even a rabbi himself, was expected to have some trade. No profession, not even that of the study and teaching of the Law, was thought so honorable that it could excuse one from labor with the hands. Shemaiah, one of the pair, or two leading rabbis, of the time of Herod the Great said: "Love work and hate mastery, and make not thyself known to the government."[75] Three hundred years later Rabban Gameliel, son of Rabbi Jehudah the Prince (the editor of the Mishnah) said:

> "Study of Torah along with worldly occupation is seemly; for labor in the two of them makes sin forgotten. And all Torah without work ends in failure and occasions sin." [76]

Thus labor with the hands was familiar among the Jews and stood high in social approval. The professions of war and politics and the practise of commerce had not absorbed the attention of

[74] Eccls. 38.24-39.11.
[75] *Pirkê 'Abôth,* I, 10.
[76] *Ibid.,* II, 2.

any considerable number of Palestinian Jews, partly because of lack of opportunity. The scorn of labor with the hands that contributed so largely to the failure of Greek and Roman society never infected ancient Judaism.

It might be supposed that a direct effect of the old nomadic ideal is to be seen in New Testament times in the life and teaching of John the Baptist and in the organization of the Essenes. Yet such is not the case. John the Baptist came in the garb of Elijah. His food was that of the wanderer in the wilds. He summoned the people to him in the Wilderness. Yet, so far as we have record, he did not ask others to follow his example as to food and clothing. If we may trust the brief account in Luke, who alone gives concrete examples of his ethical demands, "fruits worthy of repentance" did not mean a return to nomadism but only that the tax-gatherer should be honest, the soldier just, and everyone generous and kindly.[77]

The Essenes are the sole example of any considerable unmistakable attempt to put into practice ideals of life different from those which society customarily approves. Some of the brotherhood actually fled from civilization into the wilderness. They all lived lives of extreme simplicity, as far as possible from contact with the bartering and bickering, the luxury and licentiousness of the city. But it was not the nomadic ideal nor even the old Hebrew agricultural ideal which they were trying to practice. Most of them seem to have had their communities in towns or villages. They were farmers, rather than shepherds. They lived in monasteries, not in tents, and for the most part they were celibates. In most particulars, therefore, they went exactly counter to the old ideals of their nation. It was foreign theosophy of a Buddhistic or Pythagorean type which taught them to avoid animal food and animal sacrifice and to follow their extraordinary methods of maintaining ritual purity. It was some ascetic and anti-social philosophy of a type that was utterly abhorrent to the Jewish love of family life and the Jewish tendency to social solidarity

[77] Lk. 3.10-14. See Mk. 1.1-6; Mt. 3.1-12; Lk. 3.1-9; Josephus, *Ant.* XVIII, 5, 2.

which suggested the celibate and monastic *régime* for which they were famous.[78] The Essenes, then, embody the essential elements of the nomadic ideal but combine it with much that is non-Jewish. Neither in John the Baptist, the Essenes, nor in any one else can we discover a conscious and organized effort to reintroduce the nomadic ideal, but we do find a wide acceptance of its basic attitudes toward life running thru all of Jewish thinking.

In the life and teachings of Jesus still less than in the Essenes and in John is any direct echo or explicit approval of the nomadic ideal to be discovered. Yet in view of the evidence submitted as to the views of the Hebrew prophets, the scribes, the rabbis, and the apocalyptists of Judaism, and indeed of the whole nation, is it too much to insist that in all probability Jesus adopted the essential elements of the old and still persistent conception of life? Tho in Jesus there is a healthy joy in living and in human society which proves him to be no slavish follower of John and to have been no disciple of the Essenes, there is an equally healthy disdain of the softness of kings' houses. The Nazareth Carpenter and his following of Galilean fishermen and peasants were men to whom the Hebrew agricultural ideal, as set forth in the Old Testament read to them sabbath by sabbath in the snyagog, must have made a strong appeal. Jesus was reared in a working man's home to a life of industrious labor. He took delight and saw deep meanings in all the homely routine tasks of seed-time and harvest, of caring for the ox and the ass, and following the flocks. He believed thoroly in the simple life. The laying up of treasures and the anxiety for food and clothing which mark the life of the rich on the one hand and the poor on the other were not the paths to the kingdom of God he came to inaugurate. If men were to be ready for the society where God's will is done as it is in heaven, they must live lives of simplicity and unaffected kindliness, sharing whatever they had with their neighbors in a truly nomadic spirit of hospitality and brotherliness. They must live naturally and honestly, trusting in God, facing the real issues of life, but

[78] Josephus, *Ant.* XVIII, 1, 5; *War,* II, 8, 2-13; Philo., *Quod omnis probus liber,* 12; Pliny, *Natural History,* V, 17; see below, p. 315.

unconcerned for earthly treasures and for the preferments and applause of men. There must be none of the artificial distinctions due to wealth, birth, and power.

As the true successor of the ancient prophets of Yahweh, Jesus was driven by these ideals into a position of hostility toward the social institutions of his people and his age. Men could not live the kind of life God approved while conditions were such as Jesus found them. The struggle of the nomadic ideal against the agricultural and urban-commercial society of Canaan had been the means by which Israel's conceptions of ethics in social relationships had been developed. The very geography of Palestine had providentially conspired to prevent the blood of the Hebrews from ever becoming completely poisoned by the virus of a greedy, agricultural-commercial conception of life. If the wealth and luxury of these types of social organization ever threatened to blind them, there was always present before their eyes the corrective of the nomadic ideal which men were living at their very doors. With such an inheritance of pattern ideas, it was inevitable that Jesus should find himself forced to a similar prophetic hostility against accepted social and religious customs and standards which he found inconsistent with the fundamental ideals of his people.

Was Jesus then a revolutionary? From the ancient nomadic ideal he inherited his hatred of wealth and luxury, his love for simplicity of living and for democratic brotherliness in economic and social relationships. As the successor of the prophets and the fulfilment of their hopes, he was necessarily in revolt against a social and economic order which was in diametrical contradiction to his basic principles of living. May we also expect to find him in revolt against political and ecclesiastical authority?

One of the most important factors in the development of social morality is the conception of the relation of God, that is of religion, to priest and politician, to society as organized in church and state. This is one of the problems with which Israel's leaders from Amos to Jesus had to struggle. What was God's relation to the nation, that is, the social group politically organized? What had he the right to expect of them as a people and they of him? What was God's relation to ritual and to the sacerdotal organization that promoted it?

The complaint is often made that religion is conservative, and, applied to religion in its organized expressions, it is no doubt justified. Priesthoods, hierarchies, and religious orders have more often than not stood in the way of progress. It is true of the priestly caste and the scribal profession in Israel. But it is most emphatically not true of the Hebrew prophets. On the whole, political institutions are fully as conservative as religious ones. Political and religious fundamentalism are equally dangerous. The Hebrew prophets had to meet the opposition of both the priests and the princes of their nation. With few exceptions their political leaders were fully as hostile as were the priests to the ethical demands of a dynamic religious conscience. As we have seen, the prophets were often revolutionaries; the princes and the priests were often allied against them. The problem of the relation of religion to the state was, therefore, a most complicated one. In the attempt to solve this problem, the pre-exilic prophets made astonishing progress in the development of both morality and religion. To a survey of their attacks upon it we must now turn.

CHAPTER VI

POLITICS AND RELIGION

I. THE PROPHETIC DILEMMA

THE problem of the relationship of religion to other institutions and interests of the social group is by no means purely academic. What has the state of today the right to demand of the church? Is the church, like the newspaper, the telegraph, the railroad, only one of the social institutions which, in case of danger, the state has the right to commandeer for its own uses? If, in the next war, the state is to conscript wealth as it conscripts man-power, will it openly and unashamed conscript also the forces of religion, as it always has implicitly and furtively in the past, and insist that one pray no prayers for the enemy?

The protest of religion and morality against such conscription is well expressed in a poem of the recent war. Charles Badger Clark describes the difference between himself, a soldier in the World War, and his father, a veteran of the Civil War, thus:

"And now what about
Me in my own day of battle?
Could I put my prayers behind a slim Springfield bullet?
Hardly, except to mutter: 'Jesus, we part here.
My country calls for my body, and takes my soul also.
Do you see those humans herded and driven against me?
Turn away, Jesus, for I've got to kill them.
Why? Oh, well, it's the way of my fathers,
And such evils bring some vast, vague good to my country.
I don't know why, but today my business is killing,
And my gods must be luck and the devil till this thing is over.
Leave me now, Lord. Your eyes make me slack in my duty.'

My father could mix his prayers and his shooting,
And he was a rare true man in his generation.
Now, I'm fairly decent in mine, I reckon;
Yet if I should pray like him, I'd spoil it by laughing.
What is the matter?"[1]

The matter with Mr. Clark and many more who have the same hatred of war is that they have come to see something in the teachings of Jesus about love for one's enemies which few in previous generations saw. They have come to believe that truly moral religion in some mighty fashion transcends patriotism. They have come to put Jesus above Caesar. In this they are far from original. One hundred and fifty years after the crucifixion of Jesus some obscure Christians from the little town of Scilli in North Africa stood before the Roman tribunal in Carthage. The proconsul, P. Vigellius Saturninus, urged them to buy their freedom by swearing "by the *genius* of our Lord the Emperor." The spokesman, Speratus, replied, "I know no empire (*imperium*) of this age. . . . I know my Lord, the King of kings and Emperor of all peoples." Donata, one of the women of the party, declared that one may give "honor to Caesar as Caesar, but fear to God," and that, therefore, they could not worship the *genius* of Caesar.[2]

Donata was echoing the words of her Master, "Give to Caesar what belongs to Caesar, and to God what belongs to God." Is the modern Christian right who believes that God stands before the state, that the right does not "belong to Caesar" to conscript the conscience? What did Jesus teach and how did he comport himself in his relations to the powers that be? No one who seriously attempts, with as little theological bias as possible, to study the ministry and the death of Jesus as historical problems can avoid the conclusion that politics entered largely into the difficulties of his people for which Jesus tried to find a solution. The recent essay by Simkhovitch, an economist's attempt to assist *Toward the Understanding of Jesus,* finds the problem a purely political

[1] "My Father and I," from Martha Foote Crow, *Christ in the Poetry of Today,* New York: The Womans Press, 1917, p. 182.

[2] R. Knopf, *Ausgewählte Märtyrerakten,* Tübingen, 1901, p. 34 f.

one and practically ignores economic issues. One cannot deny that Jesus' crucifixion was due, in large part at least, to resentment against his political activities. The authorities, both Roman and Jewish, misunderstood and rejected the solution which he proposed for the political *impasse* in which they were caught, and therefore united in putting him to death. There is room for difference of opinion as to the nature of Jesus' remedy. The facts can be discovered only by a careful survey of what Jesus' predecessors taught and did with regard to the problem of patriotism.

We are justified the more in turning to the prophets for light because the dilemma in which they found themselves was not essentially different. It was a problem of religion against patriotism, of loyalty to God against loyalty to the king, of adherence to the moral imperative of conscience against subserviency to the accepted customs and beliefs of the social group. It was also a question of progress against reaction.

II. THE NATURE OF PROPHECY

The difficulty of the dilemma in which the prophets and the people of ancient Israel found themselves was greatly enhanced by the ecstatic origin of prophecy and the resulting popular misconception as to its nature. The prophet was supposed to speak in an ecstasy, losing all control of his own mind and speech under the power of the divine spirit which possessed him. This primitive conception of the method of the deity in communicating with his chosen spokesmen is apparently as old as religion, certainly much older than the Hebrews. We find it illustrated at the court of the prince of Byblus when Wenamon visited him in the eleventh century. The account runs.

"When the king of Byblus sacrificed to his gods, . . . the god seized one of his noble youths making him frenzied so that he said, 'Bring (the god) hither! Bring the messenger of Amon who hath him. . . . Send him, and let him go.'"[3]

[3] Found conveniently in Barton, *Arch. and the Bible,* p. 411; Breasted, *AR,* II, 570.

This timely intervention on the part of the gods of Byblus saved the success of Wenamon's mission. The frenzied youth continued in his ecstatic condition during the night, and Wenamon, who was to have been sent away empty-handed, was summoned to the king's presence and eventually discharged his mission, securing the necessary timber for the barge of Amon-Re.

At almost the same time in the hills of Canaan at Gibeah of God a youth of the tribe of Benjamin

"met a band of prophets (dervishes) coming down from the high place with lutes, drums, flutes, and lyres playing in front of them while they prophesied. . . . And the spirit of God came upon him and he prophesied among them."[4]

In another account Samuel, the "father of his country," the instigator and leader of revolt against the Philistine overlordship, stands at the head of a band of dervishes who are prophesying and the frenzy seizes the messengers of Saul and eventually Saul himself, so that "he prophesied before Samuel and lay down naked all that day and all that night."[5] Evidently the kings of Israel kept ecstatic prophets of this kind at their courts and depended upon their ravings for direction when some undertaking was proposed. Such also we may suppose to have been the "sons of the prophets" to whom Elisha seems to have been leader.[6]

Modern psychology suggests what must necessarily be the product of the mind of a person speaking in ecstasy. There may be no conscious control of the utterance, but the subconscious mind is in full activity. The speaker may himself be astonished at what he says, just as our dreams often surprise us. In dreams, however, the mental activity is lowered rather than heightened. Since in ecstasy, on the contrary, the whole emotional nature is deeply stirred and the ordinary inhibitions are removed, the product of the mind may be far richer and more elevated than anything of which the individual ordinarily seems capable. The prophet himself, therefore, may easily be persuaded that he is under the control

[4] 1 Sam. 10.5-13.
[5] 1 Sam. 19.20-24.
[6] 2 Kg. 2.5, 7, 15; 4.1, 38; 6.1; 9.1.

of higher, supernatural powers. But, whether its product is good or bad, the mind under such circumstances is actually working under the control and at the suggestion of the ideas which are deposited in it during conscious activity. If patriotism or desire for royal favor or any other motive has fixed itself deeply upon the prophet's conscious thought, he will produce in his ecstatic frenzy, perhaps quite unconsciously, a prophecy that suits the situation and embodies the ideas in which the mind has set itself, just as truly and definitely as the hypnotist determines by his suggestions the actions and words of his patient. No doubt many of the popular prophets were mere charlatans and simulated ecstasy with success. But it was entirely possible for many of them to be sincere, but self-hypnotized and self-deceived.

The great prophets of Yahweh, on the contrary, being antimonarchical, would prophesy, as surely in ecstasy as in their sober senses, against the king and against the national customs and policies which they believed to be incompatible with the will of the God whom they were serving and whose spirit, as they believed, filled them with a burning hatred and an uncontrollable wrath against the evil doings of the king and the people. That some of the true prophets of Yahweh spoke at times in an ecstatic, dervishlike frenzy is entirely probable, but they early began to break away from this type of prophecy. Micaiah ben Imlah suggests that the spirit of ecstasy is a lying spirit.[7] Amos denies that he is a prophet in the popular sense or belongs to one of the prophetic guilds.[8] Probably he and his successors spoke under the conscious control of their intelligence, and, if this be so, they thus escaped a vast amount of puerile nonsense in their utterances. Yet the chief distinction between them and those whom they branded as false prophets was the fact that they gave their allegiance to God and not to the king or to the voice of the people.

Now, one of the most striking things about these ecstatic prophets is that, in two periods of Israel's history when they make their appearance, the nation is menaced with destruction at the

[7] 1 Kg. 22.20-23.

[8] Chap. 7. 14.

ayez

hands of external enemies, the Philistines in the earlier time, and later the Arameans. Apparently the prophets were the leaders in a national movement, in a revival of patriotism. The worship of Yahweh and fidelity to the national ideal, religion and love of country, were closely associated. For Elijah and Elisha the problem was ostensibly one of holding to the old paths. They could claim that allegiance to Yahweh, tho it might involve rebellion against the king, was loyalty to the nation and the national religion. They must save the people from the insidious invasion of Phoenician Baalism under the leadership of Jezebel. In this they must oppose the king and his court. But they could not allow the nation to be overwhelmed by the armies of Damascus. On this issue they were thoroly at one with the royal government.

III. THE NATIONAL HOPES OF THE HEBREWS

To appreciate the problem of the prophets one must bear in mind the political, economic, and religious situation which confronted them. The fundamental element in their problem was the fact that, in their day, no one dreamed of trying to separate two factors in the social process which God had indissolubly joined together, religion and politics. Yahweh was the God, not of the universe or the individual, but of the nation as such. They were his only worshipers. If the nation suffered disaster, he would suffer loss of the tribute of sacrifices and offerings which, in times of prosperity, they would naturally bring him. He was their leader in war, as the gods of other nations were of their peoples. Their glory was his glory; their success was his success. Their defeat was his also. The god of the strong battalions was the strong God.

To be sure, it was admitted that a nation might suffer serious reverses in punishment for neglect of its god or transgression of his laws. National misfortune could be explained on no other basis if faith in the deity was to be maintained. Mesa, king of Moab, in his famous inscription explains Moab's servitude to Israel on this principle: "Omri, king of Israel—he oppressed Moab many days, because Chemosh was angry with his land, . . . but Chemosh restored it in my day."[9] So, when repeated defeats came to Israel, when the nation suffered year after year and generation after generation under the oppression of foreign suzerains, as it did almost uninterruptedly after the brief and overestimated glories of David and Solomon, the people would have been driven to unbelief, despair, and apostasy but for their expectation of the "day of Yahweh."

By a combination of their confidence in Yahweh as the God of the nation with certain elements in their mythology, a part of their racial inheritance as Semites, the Hebrews had come to believe that, as in the beginning the world was created by a divine Savior-hero who overthrew the evil dragon of the abyss with her myriad minions, so, in the end, Yahweh would come to their rescue and overthrow all the enemies from whom they suffered and would establish them as the one ruling nation of the world.[10] Thus religion and patriotism were inextricably intertwined in current theology. It was believed that he who in any way offended Yahweh, either by breaking some tabu, as in the case of Achan and the Jericho booty or Saul and his captive, Agag, or by neglecting his worship as did Solomon when he married foreign wives and Ahab when he allowed Jezebel to introduce the priests and cult of the Tyrian Baal, injured the nation by angering its God. He who was irreligious was unpatriotic, and, by the same token, he who was unpatriotic was irreligious. He who suggested that any incurable disaster or permanent disability could befall the nation was suggesting the incompetence of Yahweh to care for his worshipers. Even a temporary reverse was proof of Yahweh's anger, and he who predicted or proclaimed the divine displeasure was a "troubler of Israel."

In the days of the Judges and the earlier kings apparently there had been little consciousness of the incompatibility of the worship of Yahweh and that of the Baals whose high places the Canaanites had scattered over the land, just as today the Moslem *fellaḥ* prays to his local *weli* without consciousness of wrong.

[9] See Barton, *Arch. and the Bible*, p. 422.

[10] See *The Promise of His Coming*, pp. 46-53.

But as time went on, the transition from the nomadic to the agricultural mode of living began to make itself felt in the body politic by serious disturbances. The Baals with their "high places" were singled out as the symbols of the new type of civilization and, therefore, as the causes of the disturbances and evils which the transition caused, while Yahweh stood for the old simplicity and democracy of nomad life. The issue came to be clearly drawn when Jezebel tried to introduce the worship of the Baal of Tyre, a cult more highly organized and possibly more licentious and luxurious than those of the less civilized cities of Canaan. The new cult was introduced concurrently with the expansion of commerce and the growth of Samaria into a metropolis and, therefore, with the rise of new disturbances and conflicts. The new religion, the tyranny of Ahab and Jezebel, and the economic evils from which the common people suffered, all came under the same condemnation. Elijah and Elisha were the champions of Yahweh against the unfaithful or temporizing house of Omri. The struggle went on with varying fortunes. The bloody measures of Jehu who, with the approval of Elisha and Jonadab ben Rechab, the representatives of primitive simplicity, blotted out the house of Ahab and massacred hundreds of the followers of Baal did not put an end to the cult. Hosea makes it one of his chief criticisms. Even the thoro measures of Josiah did not eradicate the rivals of Yahweh. The exiles who carried Jeremiah off to Egypt were far from having turned whole-heartedly to their national deity. The religion of the majority was as little affected by the fulminations of the prophets as were the evils of the civilization they abhorred.

Nevertheless, if one may judge from the words of the eighth-century prophets, the nation was at least officially giving lip-service to Yahweh during all this period. Both the northern and the southern kingdoms were nominally Yahwistic thruout nearly all their history, even as the United States, England, and Germany are officially Christian, tho worshiping other gods. The northern kings insisted that the calves of Bethel and Dan were representations of Yahweh. Apparently all the four hundred prophets who performed for the delectation of Ahab and Jehoshaphat claimed to speak in his name. With few exceptions the southern kings kept up the worship of Yahweh in the temple which Solomon had built at Jerusalem. The grave danger of apostasy to Baal worship seems to have been over before the beginning of the eighth century, tho many of its evils still persisted among the populace. Amos, Isaiah, and Micah do not criticize the nation for not worshiping Yahweh, but for the manner in which they thought to please him. The folk are satisfied that they are the people of Yahweh, a chosen people. He has made an indissoluble covenant with them, and must eventually save them in his great day, tho meantime, on account of their sins and for reasons which they cannot understand, they must suffer temporary subjection to other nations.

IV. THE TASK OF THE PROPHETS

The prophets found their task rendered doubly difficult by the inherited union between prophecy and patriotism and by the national faith that Yahweh was bound by covenant to Israel. If I were to suggest a modern text for the prophets, I should choose two lines from *Macbeth,* in which Hekate tells her witches,

> "And you all know security
> Is mortals' chiefest enemy."

The great mission of the prophets was to proclaim the ideal. But to gain men's attention to the ideal future they envisaged, they must often criticize the unideal present which enthralled the vision of the multitude. They were at their best when leading the party of the opposition. It was because they were so frequently called upon to shake the nation free from false security, to waken it from suicidal lethargy in the presence of internal wrongs and external dangers, that they have been called Israel's storm-petrels.

A vivid narrative well illustrates how apt that designation is. Ahab and Jehoshaphat are about to undertake a campaign against Ramoth-Gilead. which is in the hands of the Arameans. Jehoshaphat insists that they first seek an oracle from Yahweh, for then, instead of declaring war and afterward praying God's blessing upon the undertaking, it was regarded as proper first to inquire as to the divine will, whether God would bless the enterprise or not. Four hundred prophets whom Ahab supports gather before the two kings, as they sit in their royal robes on thrones placed near the monumental gateway to the city of Samaria, and they all with one accord commend the royal intention. They say, "Go up to Ramoth-Gilead, for the Lord will deliver it into the king's hand." One of them goes so far as to make horns of iron, fasten them on his head, and pretend to drive away the others, saying, "Thus saith Yahweh, With these you shall push the Syrians, until they perish." But Jehoshaphat for some reason is not satisfied. Apparently these men do not impress him as having the true marks of prophets of Yahweh, and he insists that another be summoned, one Micaiah ben Imlah, whom Ahab hated because he had prophesied not good but evil on a former occasion. The messenger sent to call him, wise in the ways of the court, tells the prophet what he ought to say in order to please the king. But Micaiah answers, "As Yahweh lives, whatever Yahweh tells me I will say." Let the remainder of the brief account be given in the words of the Hebrew story-teller:

"And when he came to the king, the king asked him, 'Micaiah, shall we go to attack Ramoth-Gilead, or shall we refrain?' And he answered, 'Go and prosper, for Yahweh will give it into the hand of the king.' The king said to him, 'How often must I adjure you to tell me nothing but truth in the name of Yahweh?' Micaiah said, 'I had a vision of Israel all scattered upon the mountains like sheep without a shepherd; and Yahweh said, "They have no master; let each of them go home in peace."' So the king of Israel said to Jehoshaphat, 'Did I not tell you he would not prophesy good of me, but evil?' And Micaiah said: 'Therefore hear the word of Yahweh. I saw Yahweh sitting on his throne, and all the host of heaven standing by him on his right hand and on his left. And Yahweh said: "Who will deceive Ahab into going up and falling at Ramoth-Gilead?" And one said this and another that. Then one spirit came forward and stood up before Yahweh and said: "I will deceive him." And Yahweh said to him,

"How?" And he said: "I will go forth and become a lying spirit in the mouth of all his prophets." And Yahweh said: "You will certainly succeed in deceiving him. Go forth and do so." See now, Yahweh has sent a lying spirit into the mouth of all these prophets of yours, and Yahweh has decreed evil against you.' "[11]

Here we have a clearly marked distinction between two classes of prophets that form a significant feature of Israelite history, the prophets of good and the prophets of evil, prophets of prosperity and prophets of misfortune. After the reformation of Jehu, both groups alike claim to be the representatives of Yahweh. How then could the people know which to believe? The one group promised what the king and the people wanted to hear and, consequently, they had the government and public opinion with them. The others brought an unpalatable message, they were "calamity howlers." Often they were imprisoned, as was Micaiah in this case. Sometimes they suffered martyrdom. Usually, as in Micaiah's case, they were in the minority. Yet it is significant that the great messages of Israel which we cherish, the prophecies preserved in the Bible, with but one or two unimportant exceptions, came from the derided, hated, persecuted few who prophesied misfortune. History has decided that the "one-hundred-per-cent patriots" were false prophets, that the unpatriotic critics of the national sins were true spokesmen of God.

All the "writing prophets" of the next two centuries know these lying prophets who lulled princes and people into false security. Micah says of Jerusalem:

> "Her chiefs give verdicts for a bribe and her priests give oracles for pay and her prophets divine for money; yet they lean upon Yahweh and say, 'Is not Yahweh in the midst of us? No evil can befall us.' "[12]

Isaiah says that his people refuse the oracles of the seers and reject true revelations from the prophets, insisting that the prophets speak pleasant messages and give revelations that are illusions; they take refuge in lies and seek safety in falsehoods.[13]

[11] 1 Kg 22.15-23.

[12] Chap. 3.11.

[13] Chap. 30.10; 28.15. The opposite passage, 3.12, looks like an interpolation.

But it is in the case of Jeremiah, two hundred and fifty years after the time of Micaiah and Ahab, that we find the closest parallel to that earlier conflict of opinion. In an account of a colloquy between the prophet and Yahweh, the latter says of the prophets of peace and prosperity:

"It is lies that the prophets are prophesying in my name. I have not sent them, I have not given them orders, I have not spoken to them. It is a false revelation, worthless divination, an illusion of their own minds that they are prophesying to you."[14]

Jeremiah's difficulty is dramatically set forth in an altercation he had with Hananiah, another prophet. The emissaries of some of the little Syrian principalities were in Jerusalem seeking to secure the aid of the Hebrews in a revolt they were planning against Nebuchadrezzar. Convinced of the futility of their puny resistance to the mighty power of Babylon, Jeremiah, under divine inspiration, sent them a message to carry home to their kings to the effect that God had willed the sovereignty to the Babylonian monarch. As a visible symbol of the truth revealed to him the prophet appeared before the people wearing a yoke upon his neck and proclaiming to the king and the nation: "Put your necks under the yoke of the king of Babylon, serve him and his people and live."[15]

Then Hananiah, a prophet of Gibeon, filled with the spirit of patriotism, which he mistook for the spirit of Yahweh, meeting Jeremiah in the Temple, proclaimed in the presence of the priests and all the people the heartening message from Yahweh, "I have broken the yoke of the king of Babylon." Within two full years Jerusalem would see her exiles and her treasures fully restored. In an ecstasy of optimistic zeal Hananiah snatched the yoke from Jeremiah's neck and broke it in pieces. Jeremiah met this outburst with steadfastness and dignity. He said:

"Amen, may Yahweh do so. Nevertheless . . . the prophets of old who were before you and me prophesied war and disaster and plague

[14] Chap. 14.14, cf. 11-18; see also 23.9-32; 6.13 ff.

[15] Jer. 27.

against many lands and against great kingdoms. The prophet that prophesies peace shall be known as one whom Yahweh has truly sent when that prophet's word comes true." [16]

Events proved that Jeremiah was right. In two months Hananiah was dead. In eight years Jerusalem was a heap of ruins because, in blind patriotism, Zedekiah had revolted against Nebuchadrezzar.

In the interval, while events were taking their inevitable course, the position of the prophet was a difficult one. How would a Boer preacher have been regarded who in 1899 advised submission to the British? How were the few Southerners treated who stood by the North in 1861? Jeremiah's compatriots thought him to be in the pay of Babylon. He was a traitor to his people and a false representative of Yahweh. He was mobbed, imprisoned, thrown into a cistern, and he finally died in Egypt among apostate and idolatrous exiles who had taken him against his will away from the land he loved, and all of this because he insisted that it was the will of Yahweh that they should submit to Babylon.[17] Patriotism in the ordinary sense and religion as the prophets understood it seem to be diametrically opposed.

V. THE EFFECTS OF PROSPERITY

The history of Israel during the two centuries before Jeremiah's time explains why his point of view was unintelligible to the majority of the people. Popular faith in Yahweh received a great accession of confidence during the eighth century in the prosperous reigns of Jeroboam II and Uzziah. To the Israelites the sudden development of the power and wealth of the two allied kingdoms

[16] Jer. 28. This passage with 5.12 seems to indicate that the prophets always had a message of gloom. The passages cited above concerning lying prophets prove that there were those with a more encouraging message. It is difficult to determine which were the more numerous, yet it seems reasonable to suppose that the latter must have been many. (But see Duhm, *Kurzer Handkommentar, Jer.*, p. 225.) It is to be noted that Jeremiah does not say that predictions of good never came to pass.

[17] Chap. 44.

seemed indisputable proof of Yahweh's favor and approval of their conduct. The prophetic compiler of the Book of Kings, altho he considered Jeroboam II a sinner because he had not destroyed the calves of Bethel and Dan, nevertheless deemed the king's successes the fulfilment of a favorable prophecy spoken by Jonah the son of Amittai, and he adds:

> "Yahweh saw how bitter was Israel's suffering, . . . and Yahweh had not said that he would blot out the name of Israel from under heaven, but he rescued them by the hand of Jeroboam the son of Joash."[18]

If such a view could be taken a hundred and fifty years later, when history had shown how short was this Indian summer of Israel's life, the people who enjoyed its brief warmth and color may well be pardoned for believing that they stood at the dawn of a new era of prosperity.

Yahweh had blessed them with grain and wine and oil and had heaped upon them silver and gold.[19] Their land was full of riches, neither was there any end of their treasures; their land was full of horses, neither was there any end to their chariots.[20] The wanton and haughty daughters of Zion, mincing thru the streets of Jerusalem with their tinkling anklets and pendants and bracelets, their perfume boxes and amulets and rings and nose-jewels, their gay robes and mantles and turbans and veils, were occular evidence of progress and prosperity.[21] How impossible for the prophets to convince the people that behind all this gaiety and plenty, underneath the surface of success, lurked the evils that were preparing the nation for destruction!

true

The people regarded their religious zeal as a guarantee of the continuance of the good fortune they were enjoying. Were they not crowding the sacred precincts at Bethel, Gilgal, and Jerusalem, bringing their sacrifices every morning and their tithes every three days? Faithfully they observed their new moons and their sabbaths,

18 2 Kg 14.26 f.
19 Hos. 2.8.
20 Is. 2.7.
21 Is. 3.16-24.

their sacred assemblies and their appointed festivals. They were keeping their part of the covenant;[22] Yahweh would surely perform his. Their victories in war, their prosperity in peace, the weakness of their rivals, Damascus, Assyria, and Egypt, proved him greater than the gods of those nations. Little wonder that the nobles were at ease in Zion and secure on the mountain of Samaria!

One feature of primitive thinking proved both an advantage and a disadvantage to the prophets. In common with all social groups at the level of customary morality, the Israelites regarded the laws of the group, the practices of which society approved, as the laws of the national deity. This accepted belief had been one of the chief causes of the conflict between nomadic and agricultural religion in Canaan.

In the mind of the ordinary uncritical Israelite, the argument unconsciously took some such form perhaps as this: "This field is under the protection of the Baal who dwells in the high place which overlooks it. He gives it its fertility. If I do not follow his laws—which were the customs of Canaanite society—he will give me no crops." Accordingly, he thought it necessary to visit the *qedêshâh,* the sacred prostitute, to celebrate the vintage festival with drunkenness, and to make the customary offerings at the local shrine, just as it was necessary to plow the ground and sow the seed. To the primitive mind, innocent of the conception of natural laws of cause and effect, the magical and sometimes, to our mind, licentious rites connected with the spring and autumn festivals were fully as important and efficacious in insuring a good crop as the actual tilling of the soil. When the Hebrew went into trade and commerce, the problem was the same. The ancient Phoenician made his vows and sacrifices to his Baal before he undertook a journey, just as the modern Palestinian Christian or Moslem peasant makes his vows to el-Khadr before he sets out to make his fortune in America. Naturally, the Hebrew thought he must imitate the Phoenician in this as in other methods of business, if he would succeed in trade and commerce. The strict devotees

[22] Am 4.4; 5.4, 21.

of Yahweh wished to substitute him for Baal in all these transactions. The difficulty they had in convincing the people that Yahweh was the source of the fertility of the field is well illustrated by Hosea's sarcastic references to the hire of Israel's lovers and her ignorance of the fact that Yahweh had given it all to her.[23] Isaiah represents Yahweh as teaching the farmer what things to plant and what to sow and how to apply different methods of harvesting and threshing to spices and to grain.[24] Doubtless that conviction represents a long advance over the common point of view in the times of the early monarchy.

Now all the customs of the people were regarded as belonging to the same category. They were an intricately interwoven cultural complex. If the customary routine of agriculture, the plowing, the breaking of clods, the broadcasting of one kind of seed, the sowing of another in rows, the use of various methods of harvesting and threshing, was all from Yahweh, how much more were the civil, moral, and ritual laws and customs of the community from the hand of its deity! When Hammurapi codified the laws of Babylon, many of which were a direct inheritance from the Sumerians and others from the Semites who were before him, he represented them as given directly to him by the hand of Shamash. They were really the precipitate of custom created by the judgments of sheikhs, or elders, whose wise decisions had become precedents. But all were regarded as divine laws, just as all Hebrew law was represented as given to Moses on Sinai.

Therefore, when the Hebrews entered Palestine, the *mores* of nomadism were the laws of Yahweh and the *mores* of Canaanite society were the laws of the Baalim. Fortunately, neither code was so sharply defined at the beginning that it could not be modified. Hebrew society was fluid. It was possible for Yahweh to become the patron of agriculture before the great conflict of the ninth century set the nomadic ideal in opposition to the agricultural. The "Book of the Covenant," [25] the work of an unknown author

[23] Chap. 2.8, 12.

[24] Chap. 28.25-29.

[25] Ex. 20.22-23.33.

of the early monarchy, represents part of the customary law then in force, a law that was already fully adapted to agricultural society, as was the Decalog. As a result of the struggles and sufferings of Micaiah, Elijah, Elisha, and many another who is nameless, Yahweh was the God of an agricultural nation in the land of Palestine, not merely of nomad clans on the steppe; but in countless shrines the rites and the moral standards were those of Baalism, tho worship was celebrated in Yahweh's name. If the era of prosperity had continued, it is difficult to see how the Hebrews could have risen to a higher scale of morality than they then had. Rather, they would have sunk to the level of their neighbors. If the mountain home of the Hebrews had possessed the capacity of maintaining a rich farming community, the simplicity and austerity of nomadism might easily have been forgotten and the prostitution and drunkenness of Canaanite shrines might at length have become fully accepted Yahwist rites, as they were temporarily in the days of Amos and Hosea. If the commercial ventures of Jeroboam II and Uzziah had not proven abortive, Yahweh might have become a god of commerce, and all the luxury and all the social injustices and inequalities of Canaanite civilization might have been perpetuated under the aegis of Yahweh's approval. As it was, the eighth century prophets spoke to ears apparently deaf. The nation was too prosperous to believe that the sins which the prophets criticized were serious offenses.

An interesting and instructive parallel to the history of the Hebrew religion is to be found in Assyria. Up to the time of Amos and Hosea the development of Yahweh had paralleled that of Ashur. Olmstead has pointed out that both deities came from the desert. When their followers forced their way into the Fertile Crescent, both gods faced the same agricultural religion and borrowed from it some of its least pleasing features. Each was exalted as national god to a position of supremacy never reached by other deities, each was attacked from without and from within in much the same ways and at much the same time. Each was at the same time well on the way toward monotheism. And then, says Olmstead, Ashur succumbed to the miasma of Sumer, that limitless fear of evil spirits and faith in magic for which Babylonia is notorious.[26] But the religion of Ashur had to face another rival more dangerous and more insidious than Baal or Ishtar, the spirit of Mars. This generation knows well that the moral dangers of victory are greater than those of defeat. For generations the sturdy Assyrian farmers were poisoned by the spoils of victory. Wealth poured in upon them as the result of a ruthlessness which even modern warfare can hardly parallel. No race of human beings has a moral fiber that can resist such assaults. Assyria fell a victim of its own successes.

VI. NATIONAL ADVERSITY

In the eighth century it must have appeared to many Israelites that they were well on the way to become the ruling nation in all the world and Yahweh the great God of all gods. But when the Assyrians captured and destroyed Samaria and reduced Jerusalem to vassalage, the world took on a different aspect. Two alternative explanations of their situation seemed possible. Either Yahweh was angry with his people and was punishing them for their sins, or else he was too weak to protect them. So far as we have evidence, few adopted the latter alternative. But even if one accepted the former possibility, there was room for a startling difference of opinion as to the nature and seriousness of the offenses for which they were being punished and as to the probable outcome of the chastisement. In keeping with their patriotic and religious optimism[27] the people, apparently, believed that the national reverses could be but temporary. The sins for which they were suffering, whatever they might be, were trivial and easily expiated. Yahweh must soon restore them to his favor and to their rightful position of power in the world. The prophets, on the other hand, regarded the national sins as heinous beyond description and the divine punishment as threatening the very existence of the nation.

[26] *History of Assyria,* pp. 612, 616.
[27] See above sec. III, pp. 163-66.

One phrase which belongs to the realm of apocalyptic literature serves to point the contrast between the popular and the prophetic outlook upon the future. The "day of Yahweh" was for the people a time in the future when their national deity would bring to his chosen folk greater glory than they had ever yet known. To the prophets it was a day of "darkness and not light," the time when Yahweh would punish them for all their sins.[28] To be sure, in the prophetic books as they have been handed down to us, threats of punishment are relieved by promises of restoration. Style, linguistic usage, theology, and historical outlook seem to mark some of these hopeful passages as post-exilic interpolations. Yet there is no *a priori* reason why the prophets should not promise a return of the divine favor if the people should repent. Promises of restoration not in the least conditioned upon repentance are found in Egyptian apocalyptic prophecies.[29] The ancient seer cannot be expected to exhibit the ponderous logic and the *ex eventu* wisdom of the modern critic in his study. It probably seemed perfectly logical to Isaiah, in view of the wickedness of the nation as a whole, to announce a salvation for a remnant only. It was natural that he and Jeremiah with all their colleagues and successors should believe that, after the "day of Yahweh" with its purifying punishments, the nation would be restored and would continue to grow under the rule of God. Thus a divine act of chastisement, catastrophic and terrible, but not necessarily magical or supernatural, was expected to cleanse and revitalize the nation and produce within it the ideals of morality and religion which the prophets proclaimed. Jeremiah, Ezekiel, Second Isaiah, Haggai, and Zechariah believed that this catastrophic punishment was to be identified with the Babylonian captivity and that, after it, the purified nation must realize her high mission. These great Hebrew preachers of righteousness, then, in spite of occasional glimpses of sunlight on the distant horizon, were prophets of gloom. National disasters were for them *prima facie* evidence of national guilt.

[28] Am. 5.18; for discussion and references to literature see *The Promise of His Coming,* Chap. II and Index, *s.v.,* "Day of Yahweh."

[29] Cf. *HTR,* 18 (1925), 407 f.

When Isaiah and Micah began to preach, they could command a partial hearing for their message because recent catastrophes gave point to their denunciations. Hezekiah and the court adopted the prophetic view of the situation and attempted reforms which the prophetic party urged as calculated to regain the favor of Yahweh. Fortunately for them, a lucky accident as we would say, a sudden disaster to the Assyrian army, saved Jerusalem at the moment when the Rabshakeh was on the point of proving that Ashur was greater than Yahweh.[30] It seemed that the God of the Hebrews had been proved to be the most powerful deity in the world and that the prophetic party and its reforms had been justified. But at what a cost!

The mass of the people read history with different eyes. The retirement of Assyria and the immunity of Jerusalem which had meant so much to Isaiah were only temporary. The growing power of Assyria seemed soon to prove the superiority of Ashur to Yahweh. When Hezekiah died, Manasseh accepted the obvious logic of events and chose the easier alternative, as his grandfather, Ahaz, had done. As his long reign slowly passed, Assyrian civilization came more and more to dominate the little land. Complete submission to Assyria probably brought peace and prosperity in its train. Ahaz had erected an altar after a pattern he had seen in Damascus, doubtless because he believed it the part of wisdom to worship a god more powerful than Yahweh and with rites more efficacious, just as he paid tribute to the Assyrian monarch's overwhelming might. Manasseh did the same and more. From his time the hosts of heaven and the "Queen of heaven," Ishtar, were worshiped in Israel as they were in Assyria. If Israel belonged to the Assyrian nation, it was necessary to worship its gods in order to share in its prosperity. Yahweh's loss of prestige had further consequences. The high places and the Canaanite practices, which Hezekiah had attempted to banish, were restored, and the worship of Yahweh according to Canaanite rite, as Melek, or king, involving the sacrifice of children, was officially introduced. Apparently all the work of the prophets was more than undone. It was blotted out in the blood of the innocent.

[30] 2 Kg. 18.19-35; Is. 36.4-20.

There were those who attempted to preserve on parchment the truths which were being erased from Israel's heart. During this period of reaction, according to the usually accepted theory, the Book of Deuteronomy, or the kernel of it, was composed. It was a thoro-going attempt to put into the law of the land the principles of the eighth century prophets, to transform mere blind custom into the higher form of conscious morality, sanctioned by Yahweh. Since religion and morality, divine and civil law, were essentially identical, it was necessary to reform the cultus as well as to inculcate the moral principles of the prophets. Deuteronomy represents, therefore, a compromise between the prophetic party on the one hand and on the other the priests whom Isaiah and his colleagues had so bitterly criticized. It combined inner ethics with outward form. To eliminate the irregularities and immoralities associated with the high places, it centralized all worship at Jerusalem and declared that city, as the seat of Yahweh, inviolable.

With the best of intentions, the writings of Deuteronomy introduced the germs of as many ills as lurked in Pandora's box. It was a conscious and intelligent attempt to raise morality to a higher level, to purify the nation. Not custom, handed down from remote antiquity and slowly modified by the haphazard experiences of the social group, was the will of Yahweh, but the clear-eyed morality of those best qualified to speak for him, the leaders in thought and religion. Yet its result was to petrify both morality and religion at the stage then reached. The acceptance of the book by Josiah and the people as the law of the land was a long step toward the worship of the letter rather than of the spirit, toward the casuistry and legalism which Jesus so unsparingly criticized. The attempt to make the will of Yahweh national law resulted in making the Jewish law the will of God. A priestly-prophetic compromise of the seventh century B.C. became the highest morality even for modern Christian nations.

The problem of the eighth-century prophets had been the temptations of prosperity. That of the seventh century was to maintain faith under adversity. The seventh-century prophets, moreover, had to face the attack of a civilization overwhelmingly superior in all externals, in military prowess, in wealth, art, and literature, in age, and in the prestige of immemorial tradition. The Deuteronomic antidote had come too late. The reign of Manasseh had introduced the foreign virus into the very bones of the people. To the poor refugees in Egypt after the fall of Jerusalem it seemed that all their woes had dated from the Deuteronomic reformation. Before Josiah, under Manasseh, when they had worshiped the Queen of heaven unhindered, all had gone well with them. All that Jeremiah could do was to reiterate his belief that they were suffering, not on account of the ill-starred Deuteronomic reform, but because it had not gone far enough. How could he, the "calamity howler," "the traitor," convince them of his prophetic authority when all that they could see contradicted his claim? His promise of eventual restoration probably seemed to them small consolation.

Jeremiah counselled submission to Babylon, submission to the inevitable punishment at the hands of Yahweh. After that, a purified remnant, purged by the sufferings of the nation, should eventually take the place which Yahweh had promised them and carry on the racial name and task. Jeremiah does not indicate the practical means by which it was to be accomplished. But he sets forth the inner nature of morality in terms which admit of no ambiguity. The law which was to govern the restored nation was not to be a code, put together by learned priests and zealous prophets, but God himself would write it on men's hearts. No one should teach another, but all equally should know Yahweh and his will.[31] He who achieved the conception of this "new covenant" had reached the highest possible comprehension of religion and morality. He pictures an ideal of democracy which we shall never reach, but toward which we shall ever be striving. It is the legitimate development of the fundamental prophetic idea. It finds its fullest embodiment, as the writer of the Epistle to the Hebrews was quick to see, in Jesus.

[31] Jer. 31.31-34 (30-33). Some deny the passage to Jeremiah.

VII. SACERDOTALISM AND LEGALISM

Post-exilic Judaism unfolds the principles of Deuteronomy in both their worse and their better aspects. Jeremiah's younger contemporary, Ezekiel, with all his high conceptions of individual responsibility, marks a distinct decline below the conception of religion and morality found in the few verses regarding the "new covenant." His long and detailed scheme for a Palestinian Utopia, while it differs in details, is based upon the same principle as Deuteronomy and the Holiness Code of Leviticus. Written law is to guard so completely against the possibility of error that men will have no alternative but to do God's will. Legislation is to achieve a perfect society, static and sin-proof. This became the normative idea of Judaism. It produced a church-state, governed by priests, taught by lawyers, and ruled by the past. According to this conception, the observance of the divine law as recorded in the Torah and interpreted by the scribes was the whole duty of man. It included his obligations to the state and to God; it was both patriotism and religion. Unfortunately, ritual law entered so largely into the ancient codes that the proper observance of rules which had their origin in primitive tabus seemed as important as justice and mercy. Mere blind customary morality was a stage long past for the student of the Law, yet he had no right to choose a higher ethic, except as his ingenuity could coax it out of some ancient formula. This principle killed the seeds of progress before they could germinate. There could be no prophecy, because the Hebrew scriptures were a complete and final revelation of the divine will. In a sacerdotal state where the law gave the priest every advantage, in a so-called theocracy where God could not speak except thru the official scribal interpreter of traditional law, there was small chance for moral development and every possibility of social deterioration and moral stagnation. That the outcome was not worse was due to the preservation of prophetic ideals within the shell of legalism.

Most of the prophets immediately following the Return were concerned primarily with the re-establishment of the Jewish community in the ancient home-land. Their problem was the preservation of the nation and the religion of Yahweh from extinction. They had no strength left to consider the larger problems of morality, nor to attempt to provide an antidote for the legalism which the priests were introducing. They saw religion neglected. They took the shortest and most direct method to restore it. They supposed that if the outward forms were observed, the inward spirit would develop as a natural consequence. Funds were necessary for the rebuilding of the Temple and the proper celebration of its rites. The prophets of the Exile and the Return, Haggai, Zechariah, and Malachi, were far from laying the emphasis on social morality that one finds in Amos and Isaiah. They were more concerned with bringing all the tithes into the store-house. "Pay God his dues in taxes, gifts, and offerings and he will prosper you," is the oft recurring idea. Where Amos ascribes "cleanness of teeth and want of bread" to the moral laxness and the social injustice of a people who are ardent in worship, Haggai lays the lack of material prosperity to the neglect of ritual. He promised them full granaries and wine vats from the very day they began to build God's house. Thus cultus was preserved at the expense of morality and religion. One can well believe that good and bad crops did not often enough synchronize with priestly and prophetic promises and threats to keep interest fully alive.

A similar short cut was taken to national self-preservation. Instead of attempting to save the nation by developing a moral superiority which would make it insensible to the seductions of other civilizations, the priests, under the leadership of Ezra and Nehemiah, put barriers around to shut all other peoples out and to keep Judaism uncontaminated within its shell of social peculiarities. The priest planned this enormity of a self-contained sacerdotal state scornfully exclusive in its religious pride. The efficient layman blindly followed priestly guidance and, in his business-like manner, "put the scheme across." The one genius who made a real contribution to the interpretation of the nation's past and the mapping of its future, Second Isaiah, was a voice crying in the wilderness. His conception of the nation as the "servant of

Yahweh," trained in the school of suffering to carry the knowledge of the true God to the ends of the earth, was lost in the bitter struggle for mere existence. The priestly method of preserving the nation by putting walls of social exclusiveness around it was chosen instead of the prophetic idea of stimulating its moral life. Judaism became a bank vault instead of the "Garden of God."

Yet the priestly, legalistic method did protect the nation and its faith. Along with the evil it saved the good. The writings of the prophets were preserved along with the legal codes, and even into the codes enough of the prophetic spirit had penetrated to prevent the legalistic tendencies of scribal and rabbinic Judaism from entirely quenching its torch. The "two great commandments" came from Deuteronomy and Leviticus. The moral teachings of the earlier prophets were not entirely forgotten in the difficult days of the Return. Zechariah reminds his audience that the "former prophets" had denounced the oppression of the widow, the fatherless, the sojourner, and the poor. They had demanded "true judgment and kindness and compassion every man with his brother." Because their fathers had not harkened, they had been scattered among the nations. Now Yahweh, in restoring them to their own land, demanded the same moral qualities.[32] Malachi likewise threatens that Yahweh will come near to judgment and will be a swift witness against the sorcerers and adulterers and the false swearers, against those that oppress the servant in his wages, the widow and the fatherless, and that turn aside the sojourner from his right, and fear not Yahweh.[33]

The singers of Israel, the Psalmists, preserved the same values. The extremes of conservative and liberal opinion have probably both been wrong as to the Psalms, the one putting too large a proportion in pre-exilic times, the latter ascribing too many to the Maccabean era. The Book of Psalms, however, in its present form, is certainly the prayer book of the Second Temple, perhaps largely the work of Levitical poets, and it reflects the religious and social problems and ideals of the post-exilic period.

[32] Zech. 7.7-10; 8.14-17.
[33] Mal. 3.5 f.

With all their emphasis on the values of ritual and worship, an emphasis entirely natural in view of their origin and purpose, the Psalms are a repository also of moral ideals. Complaints of the unjust oppression of the poor and needy, bitter outcries against the proud and mighty who exploit and defraud their helpless neighbors, are too numerous to require quotation.[34] They often breathe a devout and poignant longing for the reign of God on earth. Their picture of the coming of a righteous prince who shall put an end to wrong and misery and inaugurate a social order of pure religion and unmixed righteousness is deeply colored by the struggle, both theological and moral, thru which Judaism had to pass in the post-exilic period.

The power of Jeremiah's idea of an inner law was nullified in part by the reaffirmation and reapplication in the post-exilic writings of the old belief that adversity was a sign of divine displeasure, prosperity of his favor. With the individualizing of religion and morals after the Exile, this became a most serious problem for personal faith. The Book of Job is a valiant effort to solve it and indeed to meet the whole problem of physical suffering, but like Jeremiah's concept of the inner law, it was too individualistic and too mystical for the majority. Yet there were large numbers of Jews who, like Job, could maintain their integrity altho their outward circumstances, according to the theory, gave the lie to their protestations. There were many wicked who prospered all their days. The Psalmists solve the problem by calling attention to the "latter end" of the righteous and the wicked. But if by that they mean their fate on earth, they are denying facts that were too patent to be gainsaid. The struggle of theory and fact in this field also contributed to progress.

If righteousness is not rewarded and wickedness punished in this life, they must be recompensed in the future. The belief in heaven and hell was one answer to the problem of earthly wrongs and injustices. The old idea of the day of Yahweh was converted into what had been only one of its connotations in pre-exilic times, into a day of judgment. But if that were to be a purely heavenly

[34] On the "poor and humble" in the Psalms see below, chap. VIII, pp. 266-74.

and individual matter, what was to become of the kingdom of Israel? Many Jews could not take the step into a thoroly ethereal world. Perhaps they felt, as we do, that a future spiritual punishment of evil was not a satisfactory vindication of God's governance of this present physical earth. Their first solution of the problem was a day of judgment followed by the physical resurrection of the righteous dead and a complete reversal of present conditions, the elevation of the poor and humble, the casting down of the rich and the proud, and the establishment of the reign of God on earth. Thus they saved their faith in the moral unity of the universe.

This solution of the problem of moral evil is the special contribution of the apocalyptic writers. The sense of present wrongs and the hope of future redress permeates all the apocalypses. The peculiar forms in which the apocalyptists cast their message do not now concern us, nor are we interested in the strange immoral and anti-social philosophy of history which they developed.[35] It is important to notice that they did preserve the old prophetic moral ideals like genuine antiques in a mass of rubbish. While the disagreeable anti-foreign polemic, the ungoverned hatred of their oppressors, the natural chauvinism, and the narrow ecclesiasticism which animates many of them exactly suit the social exclusiveness of the Levitical laws and the misguided, puritanical legalism of the Pharisees, they are the true bearers of the prophetic torch. They insist, albeit in strange symbols and under uncouth forms, that the spirit of God still speaks to men. They keep alive the sense of the enormity of evil. Indeed, using Mazdian conceptions of the two kingdoms, one of good and one of evil, they enhance the sense of the enormity of sin and evil and the consciousness of personal responsibility for their overthrow. They raise and repeat from age to age the old prophetic denunciation of injustice and oppression. They are, indeed, as we later shall see, the spokesmen of the poor, the depressed, the economically underprivileged, in their age-long conflict with the mighty, the haughty, and them that possess the earth. They believed that

[35] On this see *The Promise of His Coming*, pp. 130-136.

soon conditions would be reversed, that the poor would get their deserts and the rich theirs. They preserve and develop the idea of the reign of God on earth and the advent of a righteous prince as his vicegerent who should bring all joy and righteousness to men. Unfortunately they once more identify the nation, or at least the faithful part of it, with the kingdom of God on earth. Religion for most of them, as for the scribes, was identified with Judaism and its laws.

This does not by any means imply that they were patriotic in the sense that they gave blind obedience to the powers that be. Rather just the contrary. Because they preserved the prophetic ideals, they were usually bitter critics of things as they were. Like the prophets they were in opposition to the government. Except for brief intervals, such as the beginning of the Maccabean dynasty, their rulers, whether native or foreign, seemed to the apocalyptists to embody all the evils which their ancient prophetic predecessors had denounced. Their Macedonian and Roman overlords and governors, their Maccabean princes, their Sadducean priests, and even their rabbinic teachers were targets for their shafts of denunciation. The idealist must always be a revolutionary at heart because he sees how far the actual falls short of his aspirations. Christianity was born in this atmosphere of apocalyptic idealism. Even if Jesus does not share its narrow nationalism, his attitude toward society and its institutions belongs to this atmosphere and apart from it is unintelligible.

In addition, then, to the nomadic ideal reinterpreted as a life of democratic simplicity and equal opportunity for all, the Hebrews used certain other concepts in their attempt to formulate their developing ethical notions. They held the idea of the nation as a group in which the will of God should govern men's actions and be the standard for their conduct, the conception of the coming of a divine or divinely guided prince who should introduce and govern a kingdom of righteousness, the hope of an eventual vindication of the righteous, a compensation to the poor, when the new reign of God should be inaugurated. They harbored the expectation of the coming of another Golden Age, when men, beasts, and nature should enjoy the restoration of the Garden of Eden. These conceptions had long been handed down among the two nations who were neighbors to the Hebrews, the Egyptians and the Babylonians. To them, therefore, we must turn for the materials necessary to make clear what the Hebrews made of the pattern ideas they thus inherited. First, as the most inclusive of the three, we turn to the Golden Age, or the "Recovery of Paradise."

CHAPTER VII

THE RECOVERY OF PARADISE

RECENT history has conclusively shown how great political crises and social upheavals kindle ardent hopes that a new age is dawning. So it has been in the past. Almost every nation has had its struggles, its revolutions, and its reformations, which have been, partly the source, and partly the product, of ideals of better government and social progress. Almost every people has its legends or mythologies which enshrine and preserve its aspirations for a fuller and happier life.

When history begins, the world was already old and miserable. One of the earliest historical records, from the Sumerian kingdom of Lagash nearly three thousand years before Jesus, tells of the reforms of Uru-kagina.[1] At the very dawn of history we find oppression and injustice, and the reformer's conscience which attempted to end them. According to one of the earliest of their myths, the Babylonians believed evil to be inherent in human nature. Man was made from the blood of the god Kingu "who caused the strife, led the rebellion, and brought on the battle" which almost resulted in the destruction of the gods,[2] just as the earth and the heavens were made from the body of the other arch-conspirator, the dragon Tiâmat. Men never lose this sense of the evil in the universe and in human society and of the tragedy of the struggle against it.

In attempting to reach a satisfactory interpretation of the involved complex of ideas behind these hopes as they are found in Judaism, we cannot neglect the vast stores of suggestive materials which other religions have to offer. These faiths represent the

[1] See below, chap. IX, pp. 245 ff.

[2] Creation Tablet, VI, 27-32, Barton, *Arch. and the Bible,* p. 263.

greater part of the human race, for Christian nations are now but one third of mankind and until recently were an almost negligible part of it. The religious myths and sacred writings to which we now turn are not some summer poet's fantastic dream. A very superficial knowledge of non-Christian mythologies and religions reveals in most of them the same great hope that is held by Christians, based on the same fundamental ideas. William James spoke of the Bible as the record of great souls struggling with the crises of their fate. These myths are the records of great races struggling with the crises of their fate. They are the fruit, not of a life-time, but of generations of thought and suffering. Nearly all of them are older than Jesus, many more ancient than Moses. If we believe that among all these peoples God did not leave himself without a witness, then we must search to see what the Spirit did signify when he wrote on the hearts of the nations ineffaceable hopes of a better time to come. If we find ideals which testify to almost universal longings in the human soul, then we must consider well whether our interpretations of Christian truth are such as to satisfy these fundamental aspirations.

yes

I. THE MYTHS AND CODES OF BABYLONIA

Until quite recently no Babylonian[3] myth of the Garden of Eden and the Fall of man was known. The wide prevalence of a myth of the Golden Age in Hindu, Persian, and Greek mythology proves its existence in the Aryan world, but aside from the biblical story, no Semitic parallel was known. Now texts have come to light that tell not only of Paradise, but also of its loss. The gods placed the man created out of Kingu's blood in a garden, "laid on him the service of the gods" and stationed twenty guarding spirits around so that he might not escape. A beautiful temple whose *ziggurat* reached the celestial ocean was built and here the gods dwelt in glory and feasted in joy with man to minister to them.[4] Other documents have been discovered which tell

[3] I use Babylonia for the people of the Tigris-Euphrates Valley since there is no better inclusive term.

[4] Barton, *op. cit.*, p. 263 f., ll. 34-72, and p. 270 f.

of the Fall of man.[5] The fragmentary condition of the tablets found does not permit a full reconstruction of the story, but the expulsion of man from the Garden is in one account certainly due to disobedience and rebellion. Its consequences are sin, disease, and want.[6]

Unfortunately, the descriptions of Paradise in the accounts thus far published give us little information as to the moral and social conditions which the ancient Sumerians and Babylonians associated with a paradisiacal state. A less theological description might reveal much as to social ideals. What is told us concerns the gods and their worship almost exclusively. It has no social implications except for one or two indefinite hints. It proves that the people of the Babylonian plain, like the Hebrews, believed that in the beginning the gods ruled on earth, and men and gods lived together in peace and happiness. The ills and miseries of human society were not man's original lot. What is, is not what the gods intended when they created the world and man. With all their limitations, these lines render us one further service. They allow us to use certain other documents from the Euphrates valley to fill in what the Paradise myth lacks in content.[7]

Men could not believe that there was no remedy for the evils and miseries which they endured. An important element in the thinking of the earliest peoples in Babylonia, both Sumerian and Semitic, was their conception of a divine law given to bless mankind. Far earlier than any of the discovered accounts of the myth of Paradise regained is the story of the first reformer, Uru-ḳagina of Lagash. The circumstances with which he dealt and the meas-

[5] Barton, *op. cit.*, pp. 283-288.

[6] The first translation of Creation Tablet VI made it include an account of man's rebellion against the gods, the loss of Paradise, and its recovery. But this interpretation is now abandoned. Compare Barton, *Arch. and the Bible*, 3 ed. (1920), pp. 456-459, and 4 ed. (1925), pp. 270 f.

[7] Prof. Stephen Langdon, *The Sumerian Epic of Paradise, the Flood, and the Fall of Man*, Philadelphia, 1915, discovers a Sumerian myth of Eden. See also his *Le poème Sumerien du Paradis*, Paris, 1919, and *CAH*, I, pp. 456 f. Since its interpretation is disputed and it adds nothing to our knowledge of Sumerian social ideals, I have not discussed it. See Barton, *Arch. and the Bible*, pp. 309-315 for a translation and a different interpretation.

ures he undertook will occupy us later. It is important now to notice that he possibly introduced a new code of laws or reintroduced an old one in order to give effect to his reforms. It appears that Uru-kagina made on behalf of his people a covenant with Ningirsu, the city's god, who, he claims, had made him ruler, and his reforms or laws were part of the compact [8]—a remarkable parallel to the Book of the Covenant of the Hebrews. Other Sumerians, Ur-engur and Gudea, also gave their people divinely approved codes of laws, but the most startling parallel to Moses in both idea and content is Hammurapi. He is installed as king at the command of the gods, as were all the Sumerian and Semitic monarchs, and from Shamash, the sun-god, god of righteousness, he receives the code he gives his people. This primitive and powerful conception of a divine law runs thru the whole of the third millennium in Babylonia.

Other documents throw further light on these ancient ideals. Three hundred years after Uru-kagina, five hundred before Hammurapi, Gudea became priest-king of Lagash. Natural inclinations or perhaps international conditions seem to have circumscribed his political ambitions and influence and to have confined his activities to literature and architecture. Accordingly, he had a profound effect upon Sumerian religion and was long remembered, being worshipped three centuries later at Ur as a divine being. His greatest building enterprise was the restoration of Eninnu, the temple of Ningirsu, the city's chief deity. Inscriptions on a statue of Gudea and especially two huge cylinders of clay recount the erection of the building and the ceremonies connected with its dedication. It was undertaken in obedience to a dream which came to the king during a prolonged period of drought supposedly due to the anger of the gods. In preparation for the building of the temple and still more during its dedication, the king put into effect the laws of Ningirsu and of Nina, the great goddess. His account of the ordinances observed and the resulting social conditions which prevailed during this period may, therefore, be regarded as portraying the chief features of what Gudea and his age regarded as an ideal social order.

[8] See below, chap. IX, pp. 245 ff.

Having received full instructions by temple incubation, "wrapped in sacred sleep, startled by a dream," as he expresses it, Gudea, the "faithful shepherd," performed a sacrifice, observed the omens, and then, to quote his words,

"Great in wisdom, great in ambition, the patesi, for his city, inaugurated a general cleaning-up. In Lagash they were united as children submissive to one mother. The 'rod' and the 'thorny switch' he caused to be laid aside, and the 'cudgel' he caused to be put away. He executed orders. He allowed no distressing things about the temple. The language (=lash) of the whip the overseer prohibited. Lamb's wool he bound on it. The mother did not speak a cross word to her child; (if) the child broke out against its mother, she spoke not a word. If a servant had evidently done wrong, his lord took no further thought thereof. The slave-maid who had done some wrong act, her mistress did not strike her at all in the face. To the patesi, builder of Eninnu, to Gudea, no one brought his complaint. The patesi cleaned up the city, with fire he purified it."[9]

More significant still is the account of some celebration in the temple which is contained in an inscription on a statue of Gudea which was set up in the temple. Price takes it as part of the dedicatory ceremonies, perhaps the observance of the feast of the full moon. Others have regarded it as a parallel to the above account of the ceremonies of purification at the beginning of the enterprise. Unfortunately several lines (included in parenthesis) are quite uncertain in meaning. The section runs as follows:

"The city he cleansed, with fire he purified it. A wooden brickmold he prepared; the omen-tablet was selected. (The terrible necromancer, the justice of the peace . . . the holy man, who carefully carries out commands,) went out of the city. The sacred basket which a woman dares not carry, the hero put upon his head. The temple of Ningirsu like

[9] Cyl. A, 12.20-13.13, as translated by Ira Maurice Price, *The Great Cylinder Inscriptions A & B of Gudea,* Part II (Assyriologische Bibliothek, herausgg. von F. Delitzsch u. P. Haupt, Bd. XXVI), Leipzig: Hinrichs, 1927, pp. 16 f.; cf. the older and in some cases very different renderings of Thureau-Dangin, *Königsinschriften,* p. 103, King and Hall, *Egypt and Western Asia,* London, 1910, pp. 207 f., *CAH,* I, pp. 427 f. See now G. A. Barton's review of Price in *JAOS,* 48 (1928), 84 ff.

that of Eridu on a spotless place he built. No one was struck with a whip, no one was struck with a strap, no mother beat her child with anything; the governor, the overseer, the superintendent, (the officer,) the one who assigned tasks, the one who treats wool, . . . their hands (ceased to work). The graves of the city were not dug, no corpse was buried, no musician played the lyre, no wail broke forth; (even) the sorrowing mother shed no tears. In the district of Lagash no one with a case at court went to the place of rendering justice. The tax-collector entered no one's house."[10]

Most significant of all is the account of the ceremonies of dedication given in Cylinder B. They began on the third day of the new year and included numerous sacrifices and feasts, the induction of numerous officials into their new duties, and the blessing of the temple by various gods. Then at length Gudea rested and with his people celebrated a seven days' feast, for which the king had prepared by bringing in sumptuous provisions, freeing prisoners, and remitting taxes. It was a brief but notable period.

"On the days when the king entered the temple,—during those seven days, a maid was on an equality with her mistress, the servant walked on an equality beside his lord; in his city the mighty and his subordinates lay side by side; on every evil tongue (evil) words were changed (to good); everything evil at the temple he ban(ished); by the decrees of Nina and Ningirsu he was directing (affairs). The scantily clothed were not disturbed by the (well) clothed; the widow suffered not at the hands of the strong; in the house where there was no son, its daughter became the heir. The sun caused everything just to shine forth; its wicked things the Sun-god trod under foot."[11]

The significance of such an account in a document dating 2500 years before the time of Jesus can hardly escape the reader. It is in effect the affirmation of very definite and concrete ideals that strongly remind one of the more general and poetic description of

[10] Gudea Statue B, 3.12-5.11, Price, *op. cit.*, pp. 60 f., cf. p. XIV and p. 60, n. 1; Thureau-Dangin, *op. cit.*, p. 69; King and Hall, *op. cit.*, pp. 207 ff.; *CAH,* I, pp. 427 f.

[11] Gudea Cylinder B, 17.18-18.13, restored in part from the shorter parallel text in Statue B, 7.30-46; Price, *op. cit.*, pp. 54, 65; cf. Thureau-Dangin, *op. cit.*, pp. 73, 139; King and Hall, *op. cit.*, pp. 207-215; *CAH,* I, pp. 427 ff.

the deeds of the "shoot out of the stock of Jesse" which is attributed to the Hebrew prophet Isaiah:

> He will judge the poor in righteousness,
> And give judgment to the meek of the land in equity,
> but he will strike down the violent by the rod of his mouth
> and slay the wicked by the breath of his lips.
> And righteousness shall be the girdle about his waist,
> And trustworthiness the girdle about his loins.
> Then will the wolf dwell with the lamb,
> and the leopard will couch with the kid;
>
> . . . .
>
> The heifer and the she-bear will graze together,
> Together will their young lie down
> and the lion will eat straw like an ox.
>
> . . . .
>
> None will injure, none will kill
> in all my holy mountain,
> for the land will be full of the knowledge of Yahweh
> as the waters cover the sea.[12]

The ancient Sumerian ruler claims actually to have established for a very brief time what was the dream of the Hebrew seers, a kingdom under divine laws in which there were no social distinctions, dissensions, nor oppressions, and where there was abundance for all.

When, shortly after Gudea's death, the hegemony of the Tigris-Euphrates valley fell to the ancient city of Ur, the traditions of Uru-kagina and Gudea seem to have been followed. In the energetic king Dungi three separate motifs are combined: The hope (1) of the coming of a divine deliverer as king, (2) of the restoration of the Paradise lost at the beginning of human history, and (3) of the realization of the ideals long held as to even-handed justice for the poor and oppressed. According to Langdon, the people believed that in him they had found the champion who would restore the primeval Paradise which had been lost by the sin of the divine Tagtug, and the theologians of Nippur wrote

[12] Is. 11.4-9.

the long epic describing this Paradise and how thru jealousy of the goddess Ninharsag it was lost. Hymns written for the cult of Dungi or in his honor express faith in him as son of the earth-mother Ninsum of Erech, sent to restore the age of peace and happiness. They emphasize his love of justice and institution of laws. "He that tirelessly causeth anarchy to depart art thou," they say.[13]

Did Dungi realize popular expectations? Certainly he harbored no ideals of peace, for he was one of the greatest of Sumerian conquerors, and his records, quite in contrast to Gudea's, recount campaign after campaign. The fragments of Sumerian laws thus far recovered from his age do not exhibit remarkable idealism. The important fact is that he appears as another witness to the certainty that in the land of Sumer twenty-four hundred years before Christ men believed that the gods had established laws which made for the protection of the poor against the rich, which provided for justice, and which made universal happiness possible, and that they were appointing kings who should realize these ideals on earth.

One important element in the ethical thinking of the peoples of the Tigris-Euphrates valley was the connection they made between justice and religion. The king was thought to be called by the gods to shepherd the people and to establish justice. Gradually the oversight of righteousness and justice came to be the peculiar prerogative of Shamash, the sun-god. It was from his hands that Hammurapi received his code, as the relief on his *stela* indicates. "By command of Shamash, the great judge of heaven and earth, may I make righteousness to shine forth on the land," Hammurapi prays.[14] Other hymns to Shamash indicate how the light of the sun symbolized justice and righteousness. One runs thus:

"Oh Lord, illuminator of the darkness, who opens the face of the heaven,
Merciful God, who lifts up the lowly and protects the weak,
For thy light even the great gods wait,

[13] *CAH,* I, pp. 456 f. But see above, p. 189, n. 7.
[14] Stela, col. 40, in the Epilog.

All the Anunnaki watch for thy face.
Thou guidest all men as one group,
Full of hope, they look with raised heads for the light of the sun." [15]

Another hymn indicates how the sun came to be so regarded. Its light reveals the truth, the right, and guides the wanderer.

"Thou guidest the lot of mankind,
Eternally just in heaven art thou.
The just ruler of the lands art thou.
Thou knowest what is right, thou knowest what is wrong.
Shamash anoints the head of the just.
Shamash binds the bad as with a leather strap.
Oh, Shamash, the power of Anu and of Enlil is thine,
Oh, Shamash, supreme judge of heaven and earth art thou." [16]

This passage explains the lines from the prolog to Hammurapi's Code which run:

"Anu and Enlil called me to cause justice to prevail in the land, . . . to go forth like the Sun, . . . to enlighten the land and further the welfare of the people." [17]

Another hymn rises to a still clearer conception of the righteousness of God in relation to practical affairs:

"Him whose thought is directed to iniquity thou destroyest;
Him also who unjustly endeavors to alter boundaries.
The unjust judge thou restrainest through imprisonment.
The one who accepts bribes, who does not guide justly, on him thou imposest sin.
But he who does not accept bribes, whose concern is for the oppressed,
Is pleasing to Shamash, his life will be prolonged.
The judge who renders just decisions,
Will end in a palace, the habitation of princes will be his dwelling place." [18]

Shamash is "the Judge," "the Guardian of justice," "the One who

[15] Jastrow, *Heb. and Bab. Trad.*, p. 258.
[16] *Ibid.*, p. 259.
[17] Col. I.
[18] Jastrow, *op. cit.*, p. 259.

pronounces just decrees." Thus social ethics received a powerful religious sanction.

With the fall of Babylon into the hands of the Kassites her progress in both material and moral culture ceased for many generations. The rise of Assyria to power brought a certain type of artistic excellence and a mighty impulse to conquest, but under the Assyrians no developments of the higher or finer elements of human thinking could center around the king. Ideals such as the protection of the weak against the strong were absolutely foreign to the ruthless Assyrian. Yet religion, righteousness, and prosperity were still regarded as the necessary marks of an ideal reign, and the blissful administration of a powerful king was expected to introduce a new age of happiness. Ashur-bani-pal describes the time when he was proclaimed crown prince as one of "almost millennial felicity." The gods had selected him for the throne and they regarded his good works with pleasure. Nobles, high officials, and subject kings welcomed him. The four world regions rejoiced. Enemies, rebels, and evildoers dropped their weapons and ceased to plan mischief. Thieving and robbery ceased, no man provoked to evil, nor was any evil deed perpetrated. The lands dwelt in peace, the four world regions were happy as fine oil.[19]

When his father Esarhaddon dies, he describes again a period of millennial bliss:

How?

"When I assumed my seat on the throne of my father, Adad poured out his rain-storms, Ea opened his springs, the grain grew fifteen inches long, it increased, the cypresses were always green, the orchards bore their fruit in rank profusion, the cattle brought forth their young with ease. During my period of rule, fulness rained down; during my years abundance was heaped up." [20]

A courtier of Ashur-bani-pal greets his accession with fulsome praise:

"The king of the gods has proclaimed the name of the king my lord for the dominion of the Assyrian land. Shamash and Adad . . . have

[19] From a paraphrase of the prince's inscription, Olmstead's *Hist. of Assyria*, pp. 391 f., Luckenbill, *ARA*, II, 987.

[20] Olmstead, *op. cit.*, p. 399, Luckenbill, *op. cit.*, II, 769.

established a gracious reign, ordered days, years of righteousness, abundant rains, copious inundations, fair prices. The gods are revered, the fear of God is strong, the temples flourish. The great gods of heaven and earth are propitious towards the king my lord. The old men dance, the young men sing, the maids and matrons are gaily decked. They take in marriage the women . . . reproduction is blessed. To those who have sinned and looked for death the king has given new life; those who were long captive thou hast set free; those who for many days were sick are become well. The hungry are satisfied, the lean grow fat, the naked are clothed with garments."[21]

We have followed, as carefully as the fragmentary records allow, the development in Babylonia of the idea of the establishment of the reign of the gods on earth. We have noted the few but definite hints of the belief which was probably universal that the lost Paradise was to be restored. We have tried to follow the development of the hopes of the peoples in the Tigris-Euphrates valley traced by fragments scattered over twenty-five hundred years from Uru-kagina to Ashur-bani-pal. The road is long and like the paths in Palestine it wanders in and out, up and down, over rugged mountains and thru narrow wadis. Whither has it led us? At the beginning there stands the belief that once the gods lived with men and ruled the earth they had made. Sin had destroyed this early Paradise, but the gods would find means to restore it. King after king claimed to re-establish the divine rule by introducing and enforcing the laws of right and justice which the gods enjoined. Later monarchs, living in the time of the Hebrew prophets, claimed that their reigns also brought fertility, prosperity, and happiness under the divine blessing. One monarch, Gudea, sets before us a really Edenic ideal of universal equality and good will. This court language, found in the bombastic boasts of monarchs and in the fulsome adulation of subjects, was fully discounted in experience. It was like the party platforms and the pre-election promises of modern politicians. But like the modern campaign documents, it testifies to certain fundamental ideals commonly recognized, if never realized. Mankind is hope-

[21] Olmstead, *Hist. of Assyria,* pp. 408 f., Gressmann, *Ursprung der isr-jüd. Eschat.,* p. 260 f., cf. Is. 61.

lessly optimistic. It insists on believing that Eden will return. We shall have to study more carefully the perfect king who is supposed to accomplish this, and the ideals of justice involved. But first we must turn to the Egyptians, Israel's neighbors on the south.

II. THE EGYPTIAN PARADISE

No explicit myth of Paradise, or the Garden of Eden, has come from ancient Egypt. Yet there are references enough in the Pyramid Texts to prove that long before 3000 B.C. the Egyptians must have had such a myth. The texts mention "that first body" of the "company of the just." There was a time before strife and blasphemy arose, before the fearful struggle between Horus and Set, a time "before death came forth." The indications are slight, but sufficient. Already in the Pyramid Age men had come to look back upon a primitive age when sin and strife were not known.[22]

These phrases are supplemented by meager references to the time when Re ruled over men. The oldest of these, and the fullest description of that Golden Age are thought by many to be found in the "Admonitions of Ipuwer."[23] Nearly two thousand years before Jesus was born, the author of this apocalypse voiced his disillusionment in a long poetic complaint, closely akin to the utterances of the Hebrew prophets in its spirit. First he describes the sad condition of the land. All is in confusion; blood is everywhere; the lawless overthrow the kingship; robbery, arson, and banditry make the land unsafe; the social order is overturned; commerce and trade are stopped; the land has fallen into moral decadence:

"righteousness is in the land only in name; what men do, in appealing to it, is iniquity."

[22] Breasted, *RTAE,* p. 166.

[23] Cf. *HTR,* 18 (1925), 371-79, Gressmann, *Altor. Texte,* 2 ed., pp. 3 f. (Ranke). See Erman, *LAE,* pp. 47 ff., 83, 105 f., and also above pp. 112 f.; *HTR,* 18, p. 381.

Quite naturally, then, men are in despair;

"mirth has perished, it is no longer made; it is sighing that is in the land, mingled with lamentation; indeed, great and small say, 'I would that I might die.'"

The sage himself is so overcome with the abject misery of the land that he cries out,

"Would that there might be an end of men, that there might be no conception, no birth. If the land would but cease from noise, and strife be no more."

Like the Hebrew prophets the sage turns from the unrelieved picture of dismal gloom to paint the Golden Age. Unfortunately the papyrus is badly mutilated at this point, but it would appear that he sketches the wonderful time before human history began when the sun-god Re ruled Egypt, and the document, as we have it, seems to say:

"He (Re) brings cooling to the flame. It is said he is the shepherd of all men. There is no evil in his heart. When his herds are few, he passes the day to gather them together, their hearts being fevered. Would that he had discerned their character in the first generation. Then would he have smitten evil. He would have stretched forth his arm against it. He would have smitten the seed thereof and their inheritance. . . . Where is he today? Doth he sleep perchance? Behold his might is not seen."[24]

Brief as the passage is it tells a long story. Once the sun-god, Re, shepherded men, but their hearts were fevered. Evil was present undiscovered. It came forth and bore its fruit. Now the god is asleep and his might, for which men long, is not seen. But eventually Re will send a king to shepherd men and to restore order in the land. That the words of Ipuwer were rightly so understood seems to be proved by the subsequent discovery of another papyrus containing the "Vision of Neferrohu." It is a document belonging to the same age, nearly 2000 B.C., in which

[24] Quotations from Breasted, *RTAE,* pp. 204-11, cf. Erman, *LAE,* pp. 105 f. See above chap. IV, p. 112; but see Ranke's translation in Gressmann, *Altor. Texte,* pp. 52-55.

we indubitably have a pessimistic prophecy describing the woes and wrongs from which the land suffers, succeeded by a specific prediction of the coming of a king who should right all wrongs.[25] This and the other documents that reveal Egyptian social ideals center so exclusively around the ruler that we shall consider them in the next chapter. Only one need be quoted here for its description of the conditions which the ideal ruler was expected to cause to prevail. The famous *stela* of Merneptah, on which Israel is mentioned as already inhabiting Palestine (c. 1225 B.C.), describes in grandiloquent language the benefits which that weak king had conferred upon his people. One cannot for a moment suppose that he had actually done so. The account is of value as an example of court language in Egypt and as a sketch of social conditions which were regarded as ideal.

It is a hymn of victory over the Libyans, in which the closing strophe summarizes the victories of Merneptah in other lands. The result is represented as a condition of millennial happiness and blessing in the land of Egypt. The great god Re himself has intervened thru Merneptah whom he appointed. Two significant paragraphs run as follows:

"The All-Lord (Re) has said: 'Give the sword to my son, the upright of heart, the good and kindly Merneptah, the champion on behalf of Memphis, the advocate of Heliopolis, who opens the towns that were closed up. Let him set free multitudes who are bound in every district, let him give offerings to the temples, let him send in incense before the god, let him cause the princes to recover their possessions, let him cause the poor to re-enter their cities. . . . Give him duration like Re, let him be the advocate of him who is oppressed in every country.' . . . Great joy has come in Egypt, rejoicing comes forth from the towns of Tomeri (Egypt). . . . 'Sit happily down and talk, or walk far out upon the way, (for) there is no fear in the heart of the people. The strongholds are left to themselves, the wells are opened (again). The messengers skirt the battlements of the walls, shaded from the sun, until their watchmen wake. The soldiers lie sleeping, and the border scouts are in the field at their (own) desire. The herds of

[25] Gardner, in *JEA*, I, pp. 100 ff., cf. *HTR*, 18 (1925), 383 ff., Gressmann, *Altor. Texte*, pp. 47 f., Erman, *LAE*, pp. 110-15. See below, pp. 220-26.

the field are left as cattle sent forth, without herdmen, crossing (at will) the fulness of the stream. There is no uplifting of a shout in the night: "Stop! Behold, one comes, one comes with the speech of strangers!" One comes and goes with singing, and there is no lamentation of mourning people. The towns are settled again anew; as for the one that ploweth his harvest, he shall eat it. Re has turned himself to Egypt: he was born, destined to be her protector, the king Merneptah.' "[26]

Egypt, then, adds few new details to the picture of the Golden Age. That the people in the Nile valley had a myth of the time when the gods ruled on earth is perfectly clear, and that this idea has decidedly affected their conception of the ideal Pharaoh we shall see in the next chapter. That evil crept into the herds which Re shepherded we learn from Ipuwer. Document after document describes these evils. A characteristic feature of Egyptian prophecy we have seen to be the motif of "darkness before dawn," the sudden transition from denunciation of present evils to the promise of future good.[27] It appears in document after document, from the twentieth century B.C. to the first century A.D. This feature, so prominent in Hebrew prophecy and apocalyptic, is hardly to be discovered in any documents from Babylonia. The fact that it has not been discovered there does not prove that it did not exist. The fragmentary character of the picture which discovered materials allow us to draw must never be forgotten. The argument *e silentio* is never more dangerous than in matters depending upon excavation. Yet Egypt does contribute this parallel to the form of Hebrew apocalypticism. Insofar as descriptions of evils allow us to judge what was considered right, what Ipuwer, Neferrohu, and other documents say of disorder, injustice, oppression, and disturbances of the economic order enables us to determine the Egyptian ideal. Merneptah adds another feature which belongs to the time of Egypt's decadence rather than her prime, the longing for escape from the alarms of war, the desire to sleep in peace. It lacks the heroic note. It is the natural reaction of a peace-loving, non-military nation to centuries of

[26] Breasted, *AR,* III, 613-16; Gressmann, *Altor. Texte,* pp. 23 f.

[27] See above, chap. IV, pp. 111 ff., and *HTR,* 18 (1925), pp. 378 f.

foreign wars, enemy invasions, and internal feuds. Perhaps it is something more. About this time the religion of the poor begins to emerge in Egypt, as we shall later see. This is the reaction of the poor man who has the privations and dangers of war to face, while the king and his nobles receive the wealth and the glory. Has the religion of the poor made an impression on court style?

III. PERSIAN MYTH AND ESCHATOLOGY

When we turn from Babylonia and Egypt to Persia we find ourselves in a very different atmosphere. As we have noted, it is difficult to discern clearly the form in which the Jews of the Exile and the post-exilic period came to know the Persian faith.[28] We know, however, that the Persian myth of Paradise and the Fall was pre-Zoroastrian. The fall of Yima is mentioned by Zarathushtra and in the same connection it is said that the Daêvas deceived men and deprived them of immortality.[29] The legend in its larger form as found in the Yashts and the Vendîdâd relates that Ahura Mazda asked Yima to become the bearer of the revelation which was later given to Zarathushtra. When he refused, he was appointed guardian angel and overseer of Ahura's creation, to prosper and increase it. He did so with such excellent results that, for three hundred years,

> "Then the earth became abounding,
> Full of flocks and full of cattle,
> Full of men, of birds, dogs likewise,
> Full of fires all bright and blazing,
> Nor did men, flocks, herds of cattle,
> Longer find them places on it."[30]

To find room for the increase the earth is enlarged by one third, and this suffices for another three hundred years, when the procedure must be repeated to provide for another three hundred

[28] See above p. 114 f.

[29] *Yasna,* 32:5, 8.

[30] *Vend.* 2.8, A. V. Williams Jackson's translation, quoted in Moulton, *Early Religious Poetry of Persia,* p. 155.

years. Such was the Persian Paradise, a pastoral and agricultural Eden.

According to the oldest account, Yima sinned by giving mortals cow's flesh to eat, hoping thereby to make them immortal.[31] A later story runs thus:

"From the devils plundered Yima
Riches, welfare, flocks, and fatness.
Peace and honor bare he from them.
By his sovranty abounded
Ever food and drink unfailing.
Flocks and men were all undying,
Water, plants, no fell drought touched them;
Neither cold nor hot wind blowing,
Neither eld, nor death, nor envy
Devil born were . . .
Ere he first to lies and untruth
Bent his thought and tongue . . .
Then before all eyes the Glory
Bird-like flew away from Yima.
When he saw the Glory vanish,
Yima Khshaêta, noble shepherd,
Rushed he round distraught, and smitten
By his foes on earth he laid him."[32]

Zarathushtra's expectations with regard to the salvation of the world when the *frashôkereti,* "advancement," or "regeneration," should come were moral and spiritual, yet not entirely other-worldly. The theory of the coming of *Saoshyant,* "Savior," or "Deliverer," does not appear in documents that can be certainly assigned to him. Indeed, he and his followers are *Saoshyantô,* "those that will deliver," and he is *Saoshyant.* The "restoration of all things" was to come in his own lifetime, as a result of his teachings.[33] As to the physical nature of this new world we are left in uncertainty, yet Zarathushtra seems to believe that the bodies of the faithful will pass thru the fiery ordeal of molten

[31] *Yasna* 32.8.

[32] *Yasht* 19.32 ff., Moulton, *op. cit.,* p. 150.

[33] Moulton, *op. cit.,* pp. 106 f., *Early Zoroastrianism,* pp. 158, 372, n. 4.

metal. The conclusion follows that it is a material world in which those who "help make the world advance" will enjoy the new life. A quotation will illustrate the nature of the evidence:

"And to him (mankind) came Dominion, Good Thought, and Right: and Piety gave continued life of their bodies and indestructibility, so that by thy retributions through the (molten) metal he may gain the prize over those others. So when there cometh the punishment of these evil ones, then, O Mazdah, at thy command shall Good Thought establish the Dominion in the Consummation, for those who deliver the Lie, O Ahura, into the hands of Right. So may we be of those that make the world advance!"[34]

The idea of the millennium receives tremendous development in later Zoroastrianism, but the stage of its evolution in pre-Christian times cannot be definitely established. The *motif* of four world empires, gold, silver, brass, and iron mixed with clay, as found in Daniel, appears in later Parsi writings, but long after the Maccabean age. Since it appears among Hindus, Greeks, and Persians, it may well be proto-Aryan, yet direct evidence fails. It is probable that the idea was borrowed by Judaism from Mazdaism, but it cannot be conclusively proved. Possibly the Jews took it from the Greeks, but in any case the Book of Daniel has borrowed it.[35]

Tho we can only suspect that Judaism and Christianity owe much in their conceptions of the "last things" to Mazdaism, a comparison of Zarathushtra and Jesus is most instructive. Both spoke as if the great change they proclaimed were to come at once and they and their followers would have a part in it. But the precise intentions of both on this subject are uncertain because of the refraction of the media thru which they have come to us, the ungoverned imaginations of their followers. Both Christianity and Mazdaism were forced to adjourn their expectations of an immediate advent of the New Age. The latter was the wiser in laying out its scheme of the ages, for it developed a system of cycles

[34] *Yasna* 30.7-9, Moulton, *Early Zoroastrianism,* p. 350.

[35] Cf. Meyer, *Ursprung und Anfänge des Christentums,* II, pp. 189 ff., with Moulton, *op. cit.,* pp. 243, 404 f.

aggregating 12,000 years so allocated that the time of the end falls about the year 2398 A.D.[36] For our purpose, however, it is sufficient to remember, as we noted in a previous chapter,[37] that the great contribution of Mazdaism lay in its ethical emphasis. In the great conflict between good and evil there could be only two sides. Man must choose whom he would serve. And there could be no doubt as to the final outcome. The good would certainly triumph, the evil would be completely and eternally defeated and destroyed. Persia agrees with Babylonia and Egypt that the present is evil, but that God must and will intervene to vindicate the right.

IV. HEBREW HOPES

That the Hebrews, at least in post-exilic times, were familiar with the story of Eden is proved by allusions in Ezekiel, Second Isaiah, and Joel to Eden, the Garden of God.[38] Yet there is no expressed expectation of its restoration.[39] It is named simply as a synonym of unlimited abundance. However, nearly every prophet does picture the restoration of the nation, when salvation shall follow punishment, as a pouring forth of physical plenty in unlimited measure. For Micah the swords are to be beaten into plowshares and the spears into pruning hooks and every Israelite is to sit under his own vine and fig tree—a perfectly natural ideal for a prophet from Mareshah, whether the passage be authentic or not.[40] Jeremiah draws a similar picture of pastoral peace and plenty:

"Thus saith Yahweh: In this place which is desolate, without man and without beast, and in all its cities, there shall yet again be a habita-

[36] Moulton, *op. cit.*, pp. 310 f., quoting West, *SBE*, vol. 47, p. XXXI. Of course these similarities, especially those between Zarathushtra and Jesus, are due to parallelism not to diffusion, or borrowing.

[37] Above, p. 115.

[38] Ez. 28.13-16; 31.8, 9, 16; 36.35; Is. 51.3; Joel 2.3.

[39] Two passages, Is. 51.3 and Ez. 36.35, promise that the restored Palestine shall be like Eden, but that is not restoring Eden, though it may suggest it.

[40] Mic. 4.3 f.

tion of shepherds causing their flocks to lie down. In the cities of the hill-country, in the cities of the Shephelah, and in the cities of the Negeb, in the land of Benjamin, in the environs of Jerusalem, and in the cities of Judah, the flocks shall pass under the hands of him that numbereth them, saith Yahweh."[41]

Later prophets are less restrained in their imagination. Second Isaiah sees the whole desert transformed. Yahweh promises:

"I will open rivers on bare heights, and fountains in the midst of valleys; I will make the wilderness a pool of water and the dry land springs of water. I will put in the wilderness the cedar, the acacia, and the myrtle, and the wild olive; I will set in the desert the fir-tree, the pine, and the cypress together."[42]

According to Joel,

"It shall come to pass in that day that the mountains shall drip wine and the hills shall flow with milk and all the brooks of Judah shall run with water, and a fountain shall spring forth from the house of Yahweh and shall water the valley of Acacias."[43]

This picture of the physical abundance that was to characterize the new age was gradually enlarged into the ridiculously hyperbolical. John and "the elders" are said to have ascribed to Jesus a description of the millennium like that in Syriac Baruch, a veritable wine-growers' paradise. The alleged saying runs thus:

"The days will come in which vines shall grow, each having ten thousand branches, and in each branch ten thousand twigs, and in each true twig ten thousand shoots, and in each one of the shoots ten thousand clusters, and on every one of the clusters ten thousand grapes, and every grape when pressed will give two hundred twenty-five gallons of wine."[44]

One can hardly doubt that, whatever these products of oriental hyperbole may have meant to their authors, there must have been many a poor, sad, hungry Jew who understood it all in a literal

[41] Jer. 33.12 f.; see also 31.24, 27.

[42] Is. 41.18 f.; see also 43.19 f.; Ez. 36.8-11.

[43] Chap. 3 (4). 18.

[44] Irenaeus, *Adv. haer.*, V, 33, 3; see 1 En. 10.17 ff.; 25.4-7; 1 Bar. 29.5.

sense and looked forward to the time when he should hunger no more neither thirst any more, when there should be neither mourning, nor wailing, nor pain.

From Uru-kagina to Jesus, however, it is clear that it was not mere physical abundance for which men longed. The Jew as well as the Babylonian believed that the Fall meant a departure of peace and good-will, the entrance of strife and murder. It was not so much the curse on the ground that needed lifting; it was the curse on human relationships. Isaiah puts into mythological language what may well be regarded as one of the most beautiful descriptions of the peace ideal that has ever been written. When the wolf shall dwell with the lamb and the leopard couch with the kid, then surely man can live without strife. And this shall come to pass when "the earth shall be full of the knowledge of Yahweh as the waters cover the sea." [45] The passage found in both Micah and Isaiah sets forth the ideal of law and justice as a result of the Restoration:

> "Many peoples shall go and say, Come and let us go up to the mountains of Yahweh, to the house of the God of Jacob; and he will teach us his ways and we will walk in his paths; for out of Zion shall go forth the law, and the word of Yahweh from Jerusalem." [46]

The result is to be the beating of swords into plowshares, the bringing of peace and good-will to men as portrayed in Is. II. Second Isaiah puts his version of the ideal in much the same way:

> "He will faithfully set forth justice; he will not fail nor be discouraged till he has established justice on the earth, till the isles wait for his laws." [47]

Still more beautiful and suggestive and infinitely more profound is Jeremiah's idea of the "new covenant" which will write the law in the heart so that each will know God for himself, and will obey, not because of legal compulsion or the force of public opinion, but of his own good-will.[48]

[45] Is. 11.6-9; see above, p. 193.

[46] Is. 2.3 ff.=Mic. 4.2 f.

[47] Is. 42.3 f.

[48] Jer. 31.31 ff.

The idea of God as the Shepherd of men was a most natural one for the semi-pastoral Hebrews to emphasize. One need suppose no literary connection between the Twenty-third Psalm and the legend of Re as the shepherd of men. All the neighbors of the Hebrews used the figure, for all were familiar with shepherd life. Perhaps the Hebrews simply inherited it from their Semitic ancestors. Post-exilic prophecy in pastoral language represents Yahweh as himself ruling the earth in the new era that is just ahead. Micah prays:

"Feed thy people with thy rod, the flock of thy heritage, which dwell alone like a thicket in the midst of a garden. Let them feed in Bashan and Gilead, as in days of old."[49]

In the words of the "Great Prophet of the Exile,"

"Like a shepherd he will feed his flock, he will gather the lambs in his arms and take them in his bosom and will lead the ewes gently."[50]

There can be little doubt that the pre-exilic prophets expected the "day of Yahweh" in the immediate future, and, therefore, looked for the dawn of the new age within a very short time, perhaps within their own lifetimes. Such is the most natural interpretation of Isaiah's Immanuel prophecy, and of his charming pictures of the wonderful child that was to be born, for he says "unto us" a child shall be born. Jeremiah, believing that the nation must be thoroly cleansed by a severe punishment, prophesied a seventy-year period of desolation, but as evidence of his faith in its eventual restoration, he bought his cousin's field in Anathoth while the fall of the city was imminent.[51] If he had no doubt of the physical restoration of Jerusalem and Judah, all his promises of future blessedness that are genuine must be supposed to apply to the actual land of Palestine. That in such matters one must not measure an ancient prophet by a modern yardstick is shown by the language of Second Isaiah. Exaggerated and mythological turns of expression are found in every paragraph, yet he was

[49] Mic. 7.14, probably a late passage.

[50] Is. 40.11; see below, chap. VIII, pp. 228 f., 233, 235.

[51] Is. 7.13 ff.; 9.6; Jer. 29; 32.6-15.

plainly thinking of an actual return to the hills of Palestine. Haggai and Zechariah could talk of a restoration of Zion in all her glory while the people were too poor and disheartened to rebuild the Temple. Again, a few centuries later the Maccabees could be hailed as messianic princes who were bringing the reign of God to earth.[52] Josephus tells of six thousand people who perished on the Temple roof in the flames of the house of God when the city was captured by the Romans. A prophet had enticed them into the Temple with a pretended divine oracle which promised that now, in the extremity of their need, God would intervene with a miraculous deliverance from the Romans.[53] Sixty years later the famous Rabbi Aqiba gave his adherence to the adventurer Bar-Kochba in an ill-starred attempt to overthrow the Romans and set up the divine kingdom. There can be little doubt that thru all Hebrew history the idea of a reign of God on earth was the dominant, even if not the universal, conception.

It must not be forgotten, to be sure, that Jewish conceptions of the kingdom of God were far from uniform. Some supposed that it would be of eternal duration on this earth; some looked for a temporary kingdom on earth, others for an eternal life of bliss in a new heaven and a new earth. How large a number the third type were we have no means of knowing. The chief literary representatives of this view are the Similitudes of Enoch (37-70) and certain passages in the third division of Isaiah.[54] Even the Isaianic descriptions of the new heaven and new earth so combine earthly and other-worldly traits that it is extremely difficult to determine whether the writer is merely giving a poetic and imaginative picture of an ideal society or has reached the conclusion that an ideal life on this present earth is impossible.[55] We may be sure that before the time of Jesus there were many Jews so infected

[52] 1 Mac. 14.8-12 (see above, pp. 84, 134 f.); Test. Reub. 6.7-12; Levi 8.14; 18; Josephus, *Ant.*, XIII, 209 (10, 7).

[53] Josephus, *War*, VI, 283-86 (5, 2).

[54] See R. H. Charles, *Critical History of the Doctrine of a Future Life*, Index, s.v. "Kingdom"; McCown, *Promise of His Coming*, pp. 110-30, esp. pp. 123 f. Zech. 14.6 is not to be included.

[55] Is. 65.17-25; 66.22; 60.15-22; cf. 60.10-22.

with Greek or Oriental-Gnostic conceptions of the evil in matter that they could not believe in a physical resurrection—as Paul did not—or in a reign of God on earth. To men of a philosophical turn of mind a more spiritual view would make a strong appeal. But their number must have been comparatively small. The typical Hebrew-Jewish view of the world was that

> "The earth is Yahweh's and all its fulness,
> The world and they that inhabit it."
> "In his hand are the deepest recesses of the earth;
> The heights of the mountains also belong to him.
> The sea is his and he made it,
> And his hand formed the dry land." [56]

It was, therefore, only a question of time until Satan, the interloper, should be overthrown and "the isles wait for his law."

The expectation of a divine rule on earth, no matter what the mythological basis for it, or the mythical traits which enter into the descriptions of it, has most positive and entirely non-mythical implications. It grows out of a keen feeling of dissatisfaction with things as they are, a bitter sense of wrongdoing in society, and a profound belief that in some way evil must be abolished and righteousness displace unrighteousness. There are those who are so keenly sensitive to any criticism of the American Constitution or the present economic order that they cry "Anarchist" or "Bolshevik" at anyone who dares to suggest that these institutions are not perfect. For such people the very phrase, "kingdom of God," should be anathema. It has been the expectation of the radicals thruout all history. It was the hope, if not in word, yet in fact, of those revolutionaries, those bitter opponents of "one-hundred-per-cent patriotism," the ancient prophets of Israel. Indeed, the great service of the prophets was their attempt to transfuse the mythical elements of popular expectation with ethical and social content.[57] Likewise, the kingdom of God was the ardent

[56] Ps. 24.1; 95.4 f. This seems a denial of the view held by some of the biblical writers that the sea, or the Abyss, belonged to Tiâmat and her brood, Leviathan and Rahab. See *The Promise of His Coming*, pp. 48 f., and n. 3.

[57] *The Promise of His Coming*, pp. 60-88.

hope of the apocalyptists who thru the days of the Jewish sacerdotal state kept alive the social ideals of Judaism. It was the battle-cry of the founders of Christianity, John the Baptist, Jesus, and his earliest Jewish disciples. The ethical content which is inherent in its criticism of present injustice and in its expectation of the establishment of God's laws as the rule of life in the earth which he has made is the basic idea of the social gospel.

The practical implications of the hope of the kingdom of God and its effect upon the political situation in Palestine in Jesus' day must not be overlooked. If such an idea takes deep hold upon a people, it must profoundly affect their attitude towards things as they are. Its political consequences will be in proportion to its influence upon the popular mind. If people believe that they are controlled by an inexorable necessity, if they think of the world as essentially static or as hopelessly deteriorating, if they suppose it to be under the control of capricious deities and malicious demons, they will accept what comes with fatalistic resignation. Floods, tempests, earthquakes, famine, plague, tyranny, social injustice, and political oppression are all alike "acts of God." But if men believe that a righteous God rules the universe and that sooner or later he will interfere in the affairs of men to overthrow wickedness and establish righteousness, they will view their rulers with very different eyes. They may resort to various expedients to explain the physical disasters and social ills from which they suffer, but they will not accept them, especially those that are caused by man's inhumanity to man, with submission and resignation. The idea of social progress, in part the product of the evolutionary complex in the modern mind, has created a readiness for change and an openness to suggestions for improvement that makes western society today totally different from that of any other age. Modern society is dynamic as never before.[58] The expectation of the coming of the kingdom of God, since it was largely quietistic, did not create a dynamic society in the modern sense. But it did away with hopeless, fatalistic resignation. It operated as a constant criticism of the *status quo*. Coupled with

[58] Balz, *Basis of Social Theory*, pp. xv-xviii.

the Jewish racial complex, that is, the belief in the divine mission and assured glorious future of the chosen people, it necessarily bred a spirit which could not sit quiet under any foreign overlordship nor tamely submit to social injustice.

As many references to this social hope in the literatures of Babylonia, Egypt, and Israel show, the expectation of the coming of the reign of God was usually connected with the anticipation of the advent of an ideal ruler. Since the conception of the Prince of Peace plays so large a part in Christian literature, it is necessary to follow this idea also thru the centuries in order to determine its social significance and its influence on the thinking of Jesus and early Christianity.

CHAPTER VIII

THE PERFECT PRINCE

"HAMMURAPI, the perfect king, am I," said the Babylonian lawgiver in the epilog to his famous code, with the modesty that marks ancient monarchs.[1] He was far from being the first to harbor the aspiration to be so regarded. It is older than history. In both Egypt and Babylonia we discover the expectation of the coming of an ideal ruler. He is described in various terms, and various traits, human and mythical, ethical and religious, individual and social, attach themselves to him. Some understanding of them is necessary to an interpretation of the Hebrew-Christian ideal of the messiah, the Prince of Peace.

I. EGYPT

The "Admonitions of Ipuwer" and other Egyptian documents refer to the myth, nowhere related in detail, of Re's rule over men. He is

"the herdman of all men. There is no evil in his heart. When his herds are few, he passes the day to gather them together, their hearts being fevered."[2]

Once the sun-god had been the shepherd of men; now the king is ordered, "Command thou men, the flocks of God."[3] According to priestly fiction, the king was himself the son of Re, and, as such, he must continue the divine vocation. He is

[1] Col. 40, 11, Harper, *Code of Hammurabi*, p. 99; cf. col. 3, 37.

[2] See above, p. 199; Breasted, *RTAE*, p. 211.

[3] "Admonitions to Meri-ke-re," Gardiner, *JEA*, I (1914), 34, but cf. Erman, *LAE*, p. 83.

"Son of Re . . . shining upon the Horus-throne of the living, like his father Re, every day; Good God . . . Horus of Edfu, of brilliant plumage, beautiful hawk of electrum. He protects Egypt with his wing, making a shade for the people, as a wall of might and victory."[4]

He was the "good shepherd," or "good herdman," as once the god had been.[5]

The king, therefore, must see to it that impartial justice is administered in all the realm. To this end he made use of the vizierial installation and inculcated a high conception of official obligation.[6] It does not really matter that the Egyptians had only one word, *maat,* for truth, right, and righteousness. We may not be able to decide which meaning belongs to a particular passage, but the context in many instances shows that all three ideas were in the Egyptian's mind. *Maat,* "truth," demanded that every man be treated according to his real deserts, that the wicked should be punished and the good and obedient protected and helped.

Two thousand years before Paul, the Egyptian expressed his attitude toward the powers that be almost in the language of the great apostle. Paul insisted that the good man need have no fear of the authorities, "But if you do wrong you may well be afraid, for they do not carry swords for nothing."[7] Looking at the matter from the standpoint of the ruler, not the subject, the king, in his address to the vizier, set forth strict justice without undue severity as the means to inculcate this "godly fear":

"Cause thyself to be feared. Let men be afraid of thee. A prince is a prince of whom one is afraid. Behold, the dread of a prince is that he does justice. Behold, if a man causes himself to be feared a multitude of times, there is something wrong with him in the opinion of the people. They do not say of him, 'He is a man (indeed).' Behold, the fear of a prince (deters) the liar, when he (the prince) proceeds according to the dread of him. Behold, this shalt thou attain by administering this office, doing justice."[8]

[4] From Ramses II's Kubbân stela, Breasted, *AR,* III, 285.

[5] Breasted, *RTAE,* pp. 245, 337.

[6] See Breasted, *RTAE,* pp. 238-46.

[7] Rom. 13.3 f.

[8] Breasted, *RTAE,* p. 242.

Many other passages inculcate the obligation to seek the golden mean in the administration of justice. The king says to Meri-ke-re:

"Do justice, that thou mayest endure upon earth. Calm the weeper. Oppress not the widow. Expel no man from the possessions of his father. Degrade not magistrates from their posts. Take heed lest thou punish wrongfully. Slaughter not, for it doth not profit thee. . . . Excepting only (?) the rebel who has devised his plans, for God knoweth the froward, and God requiteth his sins in blood."[9]

The honest man, therefore, need have no fear, for every man is to be patiently heard. In lines which exhibit remarkable insight into the psychological reactions of the man with a sense of injury, Ptahhotep advises his son and successor thus:

"If thou art an administrator, hear quietly the speech of the petitioner. He who is suffering wrong desires that his heart be cheered to do that on account of which he has come. . . . It is an ornament of the heart to hear kindly."[10]

The good administrator will never be arrogant or overbearing. The monarch told his vizier, "Behold, it becomes the arrogant that the king should love the timid more than the arrogant."[11] The "Wisdom of Ptahhotep" says, "If thou findest a man wise in his time, a poor man and not thy equal, be not overbearing against him when he is unfortunate."[12]

There was no sickly sentimentality in the Egyptian's conception of justice. He might decry undue severity, and especially the death penalty, except for treason. But he could not brook disorder and violence. The good ruler will "cause himself to be feared" by evildoers. Ramses II was "a protector of his people against unrighteousness."[13] Intef, the herald of Thutmose III, seems almost

[9] Gardiner's translation, *JEA,* I (1914), 26.

[10] 9.3-6, Breasted, *RTAE,* p. 233. "Pass not over a petitioner without regarding his speech," "Installation of the Vizier," *ibid.,* p. 242.

[11] *Op. cit.,* p. 243.

[12] Breasted, *RTAE,* p. 231.

[13] "Poem of Pentaur" (so-called), *SBELE,* II, p. 361; cf. Breasted, *AR,* III, 305-15; but see Erman, *LAE,* pp. 258 ff.

to usurp the duties of the vizier and certainly takes a leaf from the ideals that appear in the "instructions" to his superior. He describes himself as,

> "leader of leaders, guide of millions of men . . . who places every man in his father's seat, . . . the counterpoise of the balances of the Good God, . . . who binds the rebellious, who quiets . . . from the hostile, strong-armed toward robbers, applying violence to them that apply violence, mighty-hearted against the mighty-hearted, . . . lord of fear among rebellious-hearted, who binds the adversary, and repels the violent, the safety of the palace, the establisher of its laws, who quiets the multitude for their lord, the chief herald of the judgment-hall, . . . protector of the seemly, hearer of his prayer, gentle toward the cold-hot one, interceding for him, who does according to his plans, . . . understanding the heart, . . . turning his face to him that speaks the truth, disregarding him that speaketh lies, . . . not mild toward the loquacious, . . . going about after the truth, giving attention to hear petitions, judging . . . for him who is without offense and for the liar, free from partiality, justifying the just, chastizing the guilty for his guilt, servant of the poor, father of the fatherless, . . . of the orphan, mother of the fearful, dungeon of the turbulent, protector of the weak, advocate of him who has been deprived of his possessions by one stronger than he, husband of the widow, shelter of the orphan, making the weeper rejoice. . . ." [14]

As the above quotations suggest, one of the outstanding demands of the Egyptian social code was impartiality. Ptahhotep said: "Be not partial. Beware lest (the multitude) say, 'His plan is that of princes. He utters the word in partiality.'" [15] When the new vizier was inaugurated the king impressed this obligation upon him:

> "Behold (the vizierate) is not to show respect-of-persons to princes and councillors; it is not to make for himself slaves of any people. . . . Forget not to judge justice. It is an abomination of the god to show partiality. This is the teaching. Therefore do thou accordingly. Look upon him who is known to thee like him who is unknown to thee; and him who is near the king like him who is far from (his house).

[14] Breasted, *AR,* II, 767 f.

[15] 13, 1-4, Breasted, *RTAE,* p. 234.

Behold, a prince who does this, he shall endure here in this place. . . . Behold when a petitioner comes . . . see thou to it that everything is done in accordance with law, that everything is done according to the custom thereof, (giving) to (every man) his right. Behold a prince is in a conspicuous place, water and wind report concerning all that he does. For behold, that which is done by him never remains unknown."[16]

Tomb inscriptions show that this ideal had become a part of the official standards of the nobility. The lordly Amenemhet claimed the credit of "judging without partiality."[17] Ameni of Benihasan, under Sesostris I, says, "When years of famine came, . . . I gave to the widow as to her who had a husband; I did not exalt the great above the small in all that I gave."[18] The balance and moderation of this conception of impartiality is shown by the warning drawn from "a saying which was in the vizierial installation of Memphis" relating how a certain vizier Kheti "had discriminated against his own kin (in favor of) strangers, for fear lest it should be said of him that he (favored) his (kin dishonestly)." Such conduct is not commended, for "that is more than justice."[19] Quite in contrast to the code of Hammurapi, the "Admonitions to Meri-ke-re" say, "Distinguish not between the son of a noble and him of lowly birth."[20] A deep sense of official obligation permeates many of the inscriptions the Egyptian nobles and kings have left behind. A fine nuance of kindliness also is found in the ninth or tenth dynasty. Three monarchs bear the same title, are buried in adjoining tombs, and hold much the same ideals of society and their official duties. Tefibi, among other things, says:

"I was open-handed to everyone. . . . I was one of excellent plans, one useful to his city . . . one of open face to the widow. . . . I was a Nile . . . for his people. When night came, he who slept on the road

[16] Breasted, *RTAE,* pp. 240, 242, 241.

[17] Breasted, *AR,* I, 445.

[18] Breasted, *AR,* I, 523, *RTAE,* p. 248, see below, p. 225.

[19] Breasted, *RTAE,* pp. 241 f.

[20] Sec. 15, 11.61 f., *JEA,* I (1914), 27.

gave me praise, for he was like a man in his house; the fear of my soldier was his protection. . . . Any noble who shall do good to the people, . . . he shall be . . . blessed in the hereafter, his son shall abide in his father's house, his memory shall be pleasant in the city, his statue shall be glorified and carried by the children of his house."[21]

Tefibi's chief service seems to have been a victory over the southern nomes and the pacification of the country, with resulting prosperity to his people and especially to the temples.

In these men we have a picture reminding us of Sumer and Akkad under the patesis before it had been unified into one empire. By victories over neighboring nomes, the local chieftain secures peace; by digging a canal he adds immensely to the wealth of his land. He enriches the temples and claims that nature herself brings forth more abundantly because of his goodness and wisdom.

Similar ideals of the monarch's obligations appear repeatedly in the "Admonitions." Meri-ke-re's father urged him:

"Make a lasting monument for thyself in the love of thee. Multiply . . . ., show kindness(?) to the city. . . . Show consideration to the nobles and prosper thy people. Make firm thy boundaries and thy borders(?)."[22]

Amenemhet I, founder of the Twelfth Dynasty, says to his son, Sesostris I (c. 2000 B.C.):

"Harken to that which I say to thee,
That thou mayest be king of the earth,
That thou mayest be ruler of the lands,
That thou mayest increase good.

. . . .

I gave to the beggar, I nourished the orphan,
I admitted the insignificant as well as him who was great of account,

. . . .

I was one who cultivated grain and loved the harvest-god;
The Nile greeted me in every valley;
None was hungry in my years, none thirsted then;

[21] Breasted, *AR,* I, 395.
[22] Gardiner, *JEA,* I (1914), 25 f., secs. 9 f.

One dwelt in peace through that which I did; conversing concerning me.
All that I commanded was correct."[23]

Other parts of the poem, which describe the king's wars, his administration, and the attempt on his life which led him to his misanthropic advice to Sesostris, do not concern us. Almost all of what he says is a mere echo of what has already been quoted for previous dynasties. But one line puts the matter in a fresh light. Sesostris is to make himself an absolute ruler, hard to subordinates, without friends or intimates, "in order that he may increase good." The ideal of the benevolent despot could hardly be more clearly expressed. Says Hall:

"We meet, in the mind of Amenemhet, for the first time, the conception of single-minded public duty, and the obligation of the king to benefit his subjects, which became the tradition of his descendants."[24]

Sesostris I says that Amon-Re had appointed him shepherd of the land.[25] Such was the perfect ruler of his age.

These ideals are set forth with remarkable vividness in that interesting short story with a purpose which comes from the Middle Kingdom, the "Complaint of the Eloquent Peasant," Khunanûp.[26] The peasant addresses the high steward, Rensi, to whom he has come to make complaint of the injustice he has suffered, as

"a ruler void of rapacity, a magnate void of baseness, a destroyer of falsehood, a fosterer of justice, one who comes at the voice of the caller."

When the great man seems not to heed him, he strikes a higher and higher note:

[23] Breasted, *AR,* I, 478-483.
[24] *CAH,* I, p. 303. Hardly "for the first time."
[25] Breasted, *AR,* I, 502.
[26] Translated by Gardiner, *JEA,* IX (1923), 5-25; Erman, *LAE,* pp. 116-31; Breasted, *RTAE,* pp. 216-26.

"Thou rudder of heaven, thou beam of the earth, thou plumb-line that carries the weight. Rudder, diverge not; beam, tilt not; plumb-line do not swing awry. . . . Guider to port of all who are drowning, rescue one who is wrecked. . . . Restrain the robber; take counsel for the poor man; become not an inundation against the petitioner. Take heed to the approach of eternity. Will to live long, according to the saying: 'the doing of justice is the breath of the nose.' . . . The true balancing of the land is the doing of justice. Speak not falsehood, being great. . . . Behold, thou art a hawk to the common folk, living upon the meanest of birds. . . . Helmsman, let not the boat drift. Life-giver, suffer one not to die. Destroyer, let one not be destroyed. Shade, act not as the sun-heat. Shelter, let not the crocodile seize. . . . Despoil not a humble man of his possessions, a feeble man with whom thou art acquainted. The poor man's possessions are breath to him, and one who takes them away stoppeth up his nose. . . . Thou wast set for a dam to the poor man, take heed lest he drown; behold, thou art a swift current to him. . . . Magistrates are the expellers of mischief and the lords of good, are artists to create whatever is and joiners together of the head that is cut off. . . . Do justice for the Lord of Justice, the justice of whose justice exists. Thou reed-pen, thou papyrus, thou palette, thou Thoth, keep aloof from the making of trouble. . . . But justice shall be unto everlasting. It goes down into the necropolis with him who doeth it; he is buried and the earth envelopes him; and his name is not obliterated upon earth, but he is remembered for goodness. Such is the norm in the word of god. . . ." [27]

With these ideals of official obligation in mind one must read the Egyptian documents which may be called messianic. Both the "Admonitions of Ipuwer" and the "Vision of Neferrohu" [28] begin with bitter arraignments of the evils that are to be found in the land. Some of the "Admonitions" have already been quoted. The "Vision of Neferrohu" is found almost entire in a Petrograd papyrus of the Eighteenth Dynasty and several fragments are known, which assist somewhat in determining the text and also prove that it must have been one of the popular pieces of Egyptian literature. As to its date there can be little doubt, for it names

[27] Papyrus B 1, ll. 66 ff., 91 f., 137 f., 145 ff., 157 f., 175, 221 ff., 231-239, 288 f., 305-13, in Gardiner, *op. cit.,* pp. 9-20.

[28] See above pp. 111-14, 198-201.

Ameny, that is Amenemhet I, and his building of the "Wall of the Prince," mentioned in the story of Sinuhe as "made to repel the Beduins and to crush the Nomads."[29] It describes, therefore, the social disintegration and disorder consequent upon the breakup of the Old Kingdom and its accompanying Asiatic invasion.

Neferrohu repeats, in much briefer compass, all the characteristic features of Ipuwer's lamentation. He sees realized that terror of an Asiatic invasion which ever haunted Egypt. As the Hebrew apocalyptist proclaimed the dread foes from the North, so for Egypt they come from the East.

"The earth is fallen into misery for the sake of yon food of the Beduins who pervade the land. For foes are in the East, and Asiatics shall (?) descend into Egypt."

There is no safety, for government is completely disorganized, and the social order is utterly subverted.

"I show thee the land upside down, happened that which never (yet) had happened. Men shall take weapons of warfare; the land lives in uproar. Men shall fashion arrows of bronze; they crave for the bread of blood."

On the one hand, joy has fled, on the other, the customary mourning for the dead is neglected:

"Men laugh with the laughter of pain. None there is who weepeth because of death. None spends the night hungry because of death."

Hypocrisy, indifference to wrong, and family quarrels are common:

"(Every) man's heart careth for his own self. . . . A man sits in his corner careless while one slayeth another. I show thee the son as enemy, the brother as foe, a man slaying his father. Every mouth is full of 'Love me!' All good things have departed."

Men refuse to listen to reproof; misgovernment prevails:

"The discourse of speech in men's hearts is as fire. No utterance of the mouth is tolerated. The land is minished, its rulers multiplied."

[29] Gardiner, *JEA,* I (1914), 105.

The resulting non-production and desolation are pictured:

"The beasts of the desert shall drink from the rivers of Egypt, and take their ease on their sand-banks in the lack of (any) to scare them away (?). . . . Little is the corn, great the corn-measure; (yet) it is measured to overflowing."[30]

Twice Neferrohu uses the phrase, "I show thee the land upside down." In the first case, already quoted above, he has crime, lawlessness, internecine strife, and want in mind. In the second he complains of the elevation of the poor and the abasement of the rich:

"I show thee the land upside down; the man weak of arm is (now) possessor of an arm; men do the bidding of him who (once) did (other men's) bidding. I show thee the undermost uppermost. . . . Men live in the Necropolis. The poor man will make (his) hoard. . . . The pauper eats offering-bread."

He adverts also to the resulting reversal of social and economic position:

"Men take a man's possessions from him; they are given to him who is a stranger. I show thee the possessor as one needy (?), while the stranger is satisfied. He who never was one who filled for himself is one who is empty."[31]

Neferrohu adds a series of features which are entirely lacking in Ipuwer but are the common stock in trade of Hebrew apocalypse, signs and portents in the heavens, and physical disasters on the earth:

"The sun is veiled and shines not (in) the sight of men! None can live, (when the sun?) is veiled (by?) clouds (?). The sight of all is dulled through want of it. . . . The river is dry, (even the river) of Egypt. Men cross over the water on foot. Men shall need water for the ships and for the sailings thereof. Their course is become a sand-bank. And the sand-bank shall be a stream, . . . The South wind shall blow against the North wind, the sky shall not have one wind alone. A fearsome bird shall be born in the swamps of the Delta; it makes a

[30] *Op cit.*, pp. 103 f., ll. 31 ff., 38-50, 35 f., 50 f.
[31] *Loc. cit.*, ll. 54-57, 47 f.; cf. *HTR*, 18 (1925), 385.

nest on either side. . . . Re removes himself from men. (If) he shines, it is (but) an hour (?). None knoweth that midday is there; his shadow is not discerned. Not dazzled is the sight when he is beheld; the eyes are not moist with water. He is in the sky like the moon. . . ." [32]

If the familiar phrases of Hebrew apocalypticism are wanting, it cannot be denied that some of its characteristic *motifs* are present. The moral passion of the Hebrew prophet does not appear. There is no suggestion that the gods have sent all this as a punishment for sin. Indeed, the seer's vision never penetrates beyond the lawlessness and crime which is the outward expression of inner ethical disorder. He makes also a totally different use of some of his *motifs* from that which we discover in Jewish apocalyptic. The overthrow of the rich and the elevation of the poor is to the Jewish prophet of social righteousness, as it was to the Sumerian reformer, not a mark of disorder, but one of the chief features of the restoration of the righteous *régime* of the Golden Age. The scenes of nature which furnished the Hebrew prophet his brilliant figures of speech are familiar in our own experience and current in our literature. His literary technique appeals to us, partly because we are accustomed to it, partly because it really is superior to that of the Egyptian. But making due allowance for these factors, one cannot deny the startling similarity of these prophetic literatures, written tho they are in different languages, under very different skies and nearly fifteen hundred years apart. It would take much less of originality and imagination for a Hebrew of the eighth century to transform the "Vision of Neferrohu" into a chapter of Amos than to sublimate the Babylonian Tiâmat myth into the first chapter of Genesis.

These are striking resemblances. But there is still another which, for the outward form and the inward philosophy of the Hebrew apocalyptic, is still more significant and fundamental. The human mind is thoroly convinced that out of evil good must come. One of the characteristic features of Hebrew apocalypse is the sudden transition from woe to weal, from the period of

[32] *Loc. cit.*, ll. 24-30, 51 ff.

indescribable evil to that of superabounding good.[33] It is finally stereotyped into that philosophy of history which sees the whole story of mankind and the universe under the form of recurring cycles, good turning to bad, and bad to worse, until out of the worst a new beginning of the best is reborn. The Egyptian prophets of the twentieth century B.C. had already adopted this strange device for contrasting the evil with the good and urging men to reform.

Like the Hebrew prophets, Ipuwer and Neferrohu turn from their pictures of hopeless gloom to proclaim the dawning of a new day. In other words, they do what it is said Amos and Hosea cannot have done, they seem to predict the total destruction of the nation, and then most inconsistently to promise a happy future as yet in store for it. Such sudden transitions are by no means uncommon in Egyptian literature. The warnings of Ipuwer and the visions of Neferrohu themselves are far from showing logical arrangement or progress of thought. Especially in the "Complaint of the Eloquent Peasant" one finds the constant alternation of flattering appeals to the high steward's better nature and scornful denunciations of his baseness. Only if these documents be read with constant attention to the dramatic adaptation of tone and manner to the thought, will their apparent inconsistency be neutralized.

In the case of Ipuwer we cannot say how the transition from despair to hope was made, for there is a large *lacuna* in the text. But in any case he uses the same method to picture the happy future which we find sometimes in the prophets; he suggests a return of the primeval Golden Age when the sun-god Re ruled on earth. The land would be restored under an ideal ruler like Re.[34]

There has been much discussion as to the "messianic" character of this passage, first suggested by Lange.[35] Even its pseudo-predictive element has been questioned. As the document stands,

[33] Am. 9.8; Hos. 13.14.

[34] See above chap. VII, pp. 198 f.

[35] "Die Prophezeiungen eines ägyptischen Weisen," in *SBA,* 1903, pp. 601-10.

it cannot be proved to be predictive. But in the larger meaning of prophecy, as an indictment of social evils, certainly the "Admonitions of Ipuwer" can claim a place beside the great sermons of Israel's prophets. Moreover, in this picture of the ideal ruler, he points the way by which the king before whom he is speaking may realize the restoration of the land. And after boldly charging the king with being himself responsible for the evil that now reigns, he closes with eight strophes which describe the joy and prosperity which shall eventually come.[36]

If there may be some uncertainty with regard to the predictive element in Ipuwer, there is no such doubt in the case of Neferrohu. Without the slightest preparation or transitional phrase the prophet of ill becomes the predicter of good. After its long description of the evils of the land, the document closes thus:

"There is a king shall come from the South, whose name is Ameny, son of a Nubian woman, child of Chen-khon. He shall receive the White Crown; he shall assume the Red Crown; he shall unite the Two Powerful Ones; he shall propitiate Horus and Seth with what they love, the 'Surrounder of fields' in his grasp, the oar. . . . The people of his time shall rejoice, (this) man of noble birth shall make his name (endure) for ever and ever. Those who turn to mischief, who devise rebellion shall subdue their mouthings through fear of him. The Asiatics shall fall by his sword, the Libyans shall fall before his flame, and the rebels before his wrath, and the froward before his majesty. The Uraeus that dwelleth in front shall pacify for him the froward. There shall be built the 'Wall of the Prince,' so as not to allow the Asiatics to go down into Egypt, that they may beg for water after (their) wonted wise, so as to give their cattle drink. And Right shall come into its place, and Iniquity be cast (?) forth. He will rejoice who shall behold and who shall serve the king. And he that is prudent shall pour to me libation when he sees fulfilled what I have spoken."[37]

One can well understand how some student of the social problems of the twentieth century B.C. saw in the rise of the new

[36] See discussions of the "messianic" character of this document in Lange, *loc. cit.*, Breasted, *RTAE*, pp. 211 ff., Gardiner, *JEA*, I, pp. 100 f. Another theory has been suggested by Erman, in *SBA*, 1919, pp. 804-15, *LAE*, pp. 92-108; cf. *HTR*, 18 (1925), 377 f.

[37] Gardiner, *JEA*, I (1914), 105.

Theban dynasty the promise of better days, and sought to further the measures he desired and to encourage the new monarch in his reforms by presenting to him this vivid description of the black evils that had once covered the land and that still persisted perhaps in many places, with an accompanying picture and promise of the better times that were coming. Its force naturally was many times multiplied when, like a Jewish pseudepigraphic apocalypse, it was put into the mouth of a wise man who had lived hundreds of years earlier.

In Egypt, then, we find not only the form but also the content of Hebrew prophecy and apocalypticism paralleled to a remarkable degree. As the messianic being is hailed "Thou art my son, this day have I begotten thee," so in Egypt, by a well understood fiction, the king is regarded as the son of Re, the sun-god, by a human mother, the Pharaoh's queen. He is expected to emulate his divine father in that he exercises a benevolent autocracy, striving to "increase good," to use Amenemhet's expressive phrase. Good government, eventuating in order and in prosperity, strict justice, immovable impartiality, kind-hearted benevolence, particularly to the poor and unprotected, are the ideals which these divinely appointed kings were expected to set before themselves. Finally, when periods of unusual distress and disorder arose, when all the world was disintegrating in violence and wrongdoing, the Egyptians looked for the coming of a perfect king who would restore once more the social order they loved.

II. BABYLONIA

Ideas of the kingship were fundamentally alike in all oriental countries. Among the peoples of the Babylonian plain, as among the Egyptians, kings were regarded as divinely appointed guardians and executives of God-given laws. The earliest title, *patesi,* seems to mean priest-king. Far more than in Egypt the early Sumerian and Semitic kings in the Tigris-Euphrates city-states give attention to the worship of the gods and the building of temples. It would almost seem that the great temple-building activity of the eighteenth dynasty in Egypt may have been suggested by the example of the Babylonian monarchs. Life in Egypt, especially in the earlier days, was dominated by the desire for a happy fate after death. In the Euphrates region, men were far more concerned with happiness and prosperity in this life and the worship of the gods was the most important means to that end. Already at the beginning of history, worship was also connected with moral conduct. It was the king's duty to see that the laws of the gods were enforced in society as well as to provide for the proper places and ceremonies of worship.

From the beginning Sumerian monarchs claimed to be given their thrones by the gods. Ura-kagina, the first reformer in history, was only a noble and not the son of his predecessor. His wife, Shagshag, is often named along with him and not infrequently alone in business documents and is apparently given divine honors as the "Goddess Bau." Uru-kagina, therefore, may have owed his throne to a fortunate marriage,[38] but he claims it was given him by the great god of the city, Ningirsu, and the terms he uses have been held to imply that he did not reach it without a struggle. With the god, and not with the people, he made a covenant to reform abuses, end oppression, and re-establish the divine laws in the land.

Gudea, whose brief Paradise we have described,[39] in claiming divine parentage, follows a custom that may have been already many centuries old. In his inscriptions he does not refer to his father, and the natural conclusion is that he was a man of obscure origin. In his prayer on his two great cyclinders to the goddess Ga-tum-dug he exclaims

> "I have no mother, but thou art my mother! I have no father, but thou art my father! In a holy place hast thou produced me. . . . Thou hast given me the breath of life. Under the protection of my mother, in thy shadow I will reverently dwell."[40]

[38] *CAH,* I, p. 386.

[39] See above Chap. VII, pp. 191 ff.

[40] Jastrow, *Civilization of Babylonia and Assyria,* p. 466, Cyl. A, iii, 6-15; Thureau-Dangin, *Königsinschriften,* p. 93. Cf. Barton in *JAOS,* 48 (1928), 85.

In spite of this fiction of divine descent and in spite of the fact that Akkadian monarchs had been accorded divine honors before death, Gudea does not seem to have been deified during his life, tho there was a cult in his name still carried on two centuries after his death.[41] He repeatedly calls himself "the shepherd." He regarded himself as the special favorite of the gods "whose orders whatever they may be" he would carry out.[42] The laws of Nina and Ningirsu he would enforce. Likewise Ur-engur of Ur claimed to be the son of the mother-goddess, Ninsun, and to have been selected by the Moon-god of Ur to rule over "the dark-headed people." Hymns in his honor call him the merciful lord who brought prosperity to Ur, the shepherd of Ur. "Wickedness tarried not before him." [43]

The monarchs of the First Dynasty in Babylon did not perhaps maintain the custom of claiming divine descent but apparently they did claim and receive divine honors.[44] Hammurapi represented himself as the special choice of the gods for the purpose of championing social justice. In the prolog to the code he says:

> "Anu and Bel called me . . . to cause justice to prevail in the land, to destroy the wicked and the evil, to prevent the strong from oppressing the weak, . . . and to further the welfare of the people. Hammurapi, the governor named by Bel, am I, who brought plenty and abundance . . . to E-gis-sir-gal; . . . the divine protector of the land; who collected the scattered people of Nisin; . . . who helps his people in time of need; who establishes in security their property in Babylon; . . . who made justice to prevail and who ruled the race with right; . . . the powerful king, the Sun of Babylon, who caused light to go forth over the lands of Sumer and Akhad, . . . am I. When Marduk sent me to rule the people and to bring help to the country, I established law and justice in the land and promoted the welfare of the people."

The Epilog is equally emphatic and definite in its claims:

[41] Langdon in *CAH,* I, p. 426.

[42] Jastrow, *Civ. Bab. and Ass.*, p. 465, from his cylinders, Thureau-Dangin, *Königsinschr.*, pp. 90-141.

[43] Langdon in *CAH,* I, p. 435.

[44] Olmstead, *Hist. of Assyria,* p. 600.

"The righteous laws, which Hammurapi, the wise king, established and he gave the land stable support and pure government. Hammurapi, the perfect king, am I, . . . The great gods proclaimed me and I am guardian governor, whose sceptre is righteous and whose beneficent protection is spread over my city. In my bosom I carried the people of the land of Sumer and Akkad; under my protection I brought their brethren into security; in my wisdom I restrained (hid) them; that the strong might not oppress[45] the weak, and that they should give justice to the orphan and the widow, in Babylon; . . . for the pronouncing of judgments in the land, for the rendering of decisions in the land, and for the righting of wrong, my weighty words I have written upon my monument, and in the presence of my image as king of righteousness have I established. . . . By command of Shamash, the great judge of heaven and earth, may I make righteousness to shine forth on the land. Hammurapi is indeed a ruler who is a real father to his people."[46]

This selection of phrases from both prolog and epilog is made partly for the purpose of indicating how many of the ideals of kingship in the minds of the Babylonians of 2000 B.C. were the same as those which we find in the great Hebrew prophets, and how many of the expressions which later characterized the messiah of both Jews and Christians are to be found in this ancient code. The implications of this fact are to be considered later. The chief point for the present is that Hammurapi acknowledges the same fundamental ideals as Uru-kagina, Gudea, and Dungi. The righteous king was he who established justice, who defended the poor from the oppressions of the rich.

That the content of this ideal consisted mainly in the defense of the material possessions of the king's subjects, in "establishing in security their property in Babylon," as we have already seen, need not surprise us. Thru long, dull millennia the peoples of the Babylonian plain had struggled with recurrent conditions of anarchy when might was right and none could hope to enjoy in peace the fruit of his labors. We can well understand, therefore, how highly they appreciated the social value of permanent

[45] "Oppose" in Harper's translation is a misprint for "oppress".

[46] Harper, *Code of Hammurapi,* pp. 3-9, 99-109.

material wealth and stable economic well-being. It is not at all strange that they overestimated these relatively unusual values. Hammurapi and all his predecessors were paternalistic autocrats. Ideas of political democracy and of the rights of the human personality were shrouded in the mists of the far-off future. In one particular there is retrogression. The ideals of social and economic equality, which had flourished in Sumerian Lagash under Gudea, had been swept away by the floods of commercial prosperity and the avalanche of conquest. The Amorites of Babylon were too recently come from the wild, free nomadic aristocracy of the desert to lord as conquerors over a nation of farmers and shopkeepers, to harbor any such soft nonsense as the paradisaical ideal of human equality which even to Gudea was a counsel of perfection. Tho Hammurapi claims to be a father to his people and a protector of the weak, and tho many provisions of his code are intended to limit the strong, yet in its provisions "the advantage is always on the side of the stronger, except where fraudulent intent or deliberate injury can be proved." [47]

When the custom arose of deifying the reigning monarch we do not know. Apparently it was practiced by Naram-sin, the Semitic king of Akkad. Certainly it became universal in the Sumerian kingdom after the time of Gudea. Possibly Dungi was the first Sumerian ruler to adopt the idea. Gudea and Ur-engur, kings of Lagash before him, had claimed to be of divine parentage in terms which perhaps are to be figuratively understood. Shagshag, the Queen of Uru-kagina, is called the Goddess Bau. Thus our meagre records show that the ground had long been prepared for the introduction of the usage.[48] Dungi's long and prosperous reign may well have appeared to justify his deification. It is possible, indeed, that Ur-engur was deified during his life-

[47] Jastrow, *Civ. Bab. and Ass.*, p. 300.

[48] King, *Hist. of Sumer and Akkad,* pp. 274, 288, 298 f., Index, s.v. "Deification"; *CAH,* I, p. 386 and "Index", s.v. "Kingship"; L. Waterman. *AJSL,* 37 (1920), 77 f., reviewing S. Langdon, *Sumerian Liturgical Texts* ("Univ. Mus. Publ. of the Bab. Sec.," X, ii, 1917), doubts that the evidence proves the deification of Dungi, but does not deny that other Sumerian kings were deified.

time instead of posthumously.[49] It seems fairly certain that Dungi was deified while still alive, and that the practice was kept up by his successors until the dynasty ended with Ibi-sin. This being true, we find on the east of the Hebrews, as well as on the south, the conception of the deified king. It was found in both the civilizations to which they owed most. So universal was it in antiquity, indeed, that the evidence adduced above is hardly necessary. One need only refer to that collected by Frazer in *The Golden Bough*. This well recognized fiction must be borne in mind in estimating the language of the Hebrews when it seems to imply supernatural traits in the Davidic dynasty.

Except for the half-Sumerian dynasty of Isin, one cannot, at least at present, find evidence for high social ideals among the Semites of Babylonia before Hammurapi. The Semitic dynasty of Akkad which arose a hundred and fifty years after Urukagina represents one of the earliest expansions of the Sumerian-Akkadian civilization. Its kings were famous as conquerors, not as reformers or lawgivers. Yet here also one discovers an interesting *motif* that belongs in the history of the development of social ideals.

Its most famous king was Sargon. The only inscription which names his father gives him no title whatever, and the inference is inescapable that the new king, who was destined to carry the arms of Akkad from the mountains of Elam to the Mediterranean and possibly to Cyprus, rose from the ranks. It may have been this humble ancestry coupled with his brilliant conquests which made him a popular hero in succeeding generations and led to the development of the legend of Sargon, which appears in late Assyrian texts. The story runs:

> "Sargon, the mighty king, king of Agade am I. My mother was lowly; my father I did not know (in another tablet: a father I had not). The brother of my father dwelt in the mountain. My city is Azupiranu, which is situated on the bank of the Euphrates. My lowly mother conceived me, in secret she brought me forth. She placed me in a basket of reeds, she closed my entrance with bitumen, she cast me

[49] S. Langdon, in *CAH*, I, p. 435.

upon the river, which did not overflow me. The river carried me, it brought me to Akki, the irrigator. Akki, the irrigator, as his own son . . . brought me up. Akki, the irrigator, as his gardner appointed me. When I was a gardner the goddess Ishtar loved me, and for four years I ruled the kingdom."[50]

Parallels to various features of the legend will occur to every reader. Moses was born in secret and placed in an ark of bulrushes smeared with bitumen. He was also rescued and loved by the daughter of the divine Pharaoh. Romulus and Remus were sons of a vestal (!) by Mars, were thrown into the Tiber, or placed in a little boat, whence they were rescued and, after the wolf had nursed them, raised by a shepherd whose wife's name is Acca. The infant god Dionysus was put upon the sea in an ark. Krishna, the son of a prince, is saved from death at the hands of a jealous king and brought up by a cowherd,[51] among lowly peasants. As Monier Williams remarked, it was this feature of his legendary biography which especially endeared him to the lower classes,[52] and the same remark applies to the other popular heroes of this class. Just as today the American public delights in the stories of the poor newsboy who has become president of a great railway system, so in all ages the popular mind has rejoiced in tales of the tables turned, of the discomfiture of the rich and powerful by the prowess of a lowly hero, a divinely favored child, who has risen to power in spite of apparent handicaps. For there is an instinctive faith in the mass of mankind that the wicked auto-

[50] Barton, *Arch. and the Bible,* p. 337; cf. King, *Chronicles of Early Babylonian Kings,* II, p. 87 ff., *History of Sumer and Akkad,* p. 216-228. See below, p. 233 f.

[51] The legend is fully developed in the Vishnu Purana, which dates from about the fourth century A.D., but reflects earlier legends already referred to in the Bhagavad Gita; J. N. Farquhar, *Outline of the Religious Literature of India,* London, 1920, pp. 143 ff. Other parallels are found in Alfred Jeremias, *O. T. in the Light of the Anc. East,* II, pp. 93-96; *Das Alte Testament in Lichte des alten Orients,* 3 ed., 1916, "Motiv-register," s.vv. "Retter," "Geburt," "Hirt," etc.

[52] *Brahmanism and Hinduism,* 4 ed., London, 1891, p. 112.

crat, the oppressive rich man, must some day be overthrown and the poor man come to his just, but long withheld deserts.[53]

There is scholarly difference of opinion as to Sargon. Probably there were two kings of the dynasty, Sharru-kîn and Shar-Gali-Sharri, whose names were confused and whose histories were conflated into one heroic character. The legend certainly, in its known form, is late. Yet the fact that Ur-engur and Gudea a little later seemed to pride themselves on being "fatherless, motherless, without genealogy" like Melchizedek,[54] makes it more than probable that the popular joy in the overthrow of the mighty and the success of the man of lowly origin was as common in the third millennium as it was at the origin of Christianity [55] or is today. Many of these stereotyped, traditional *motifs* were already presented in the Etana myth, which told of the divine choice of the first earthly king, or shepherd of men.[56] They certainly appear in the Sargon legend. He whom the gods love best is apparently not to be found among the powerful and the mighty who are already lording it over the earth, but in some hidden, humble place; among the young, the weak, the lowly.

In later times many of these *motifs* constantly reappear. Almost every Assyrian monarch from whom inscriptions of any length have been preserved claims to be the favorite of the gods and to act always at their command.[57] Not a few claim to be "humble" or of obscure origin, yet to have been exalted by the deity.[58] Each of them is a shepherd, or the "rightful shepherd." [59] In many cases the king claims that his destiny was determined while he was still in his mother's womb.[60] Some say that they have ruled "with righteousness." [61]

[53] For Deliverer *motifs* see Jeremias, *op. cit.*, Eng. Tr., II, pp. 90 ff., German, "Motiv-register", s.v. "Retter".

[54] Heb. 7.3.

[55] Lk. 1.48, 51 f.

[56] Zimmern, *KAT*, 382 f. and n. 4.

[57] Luckenbill, *ARA*, I, 43A, 63, 73, 113, 148, 163, *et passim.*

[58] *Op. cit.*, I, 63, 356, 419.

[59] *Op. cit.*, I, 113, 118, *et passim.*

[60] *Op. cit.*, I, 209.

[61] *Op. cit.*, I, 236.

In the period when Assyria and Israel were in contact the same *motifs* appear in even more explicit terms. In a tablet from Ashurbani-pal's library, Ashur-nasir-pal I (1049-30 B.C.) is represented as putting the traits of obscure origin and divine favor into a prayer to Ishtar:

"The son of Shamsi-adad, who adores the great gods, I was born in the midst of mountains which no one knoweth; I was without understanding, nor did I ever pray to thee; the people of Assyria did not know and did not receive thy divinity. But thou, O Ishtar, fearful mistress of the gods, in the lifting up of thine eyes, didst teach me and didst desire my rule; thou didst take me from out of the mountains and didst call me to the threshold of the peoples. Thou didst preserve for me the scepter."[62]

If Olmstead's interpretation of the texts is correct, Ashur-nasir-pal cannot be adduced as a parallel to the Sargon of the legend. He mentions his father; he makes no claim of divine birth, but he does pretend that his origin was obscure and that he had been chosen by the deity and raised from this obscurity to his lofty position as monarch. Since his father apparently did not come to the throne till late in life, it is possible that the child was born and grew to manhood in exile. If so, his case fitted the already stereotyped and familiar *motif*.

When a nameless usurper came to the throne in 722 B.C., he adopted the name of Sargon of Akkad and apparently took the legend of his namesake as a prophecy of his own career. Adroitly he turned his unknown ancestry into an asset, but he does not boast of it. His son, Sennacherib, claimed descent from semi-divine heroes such as Gilgamesh and Enkidu.[63]

Sargon writes himself down as

"favorite of the great gods, (he) who established the freedom of Sippar, Nippur, and Babylon, who repaired their decay, helper of the poor, who made good their losses."[64]

[62] Olmstead, *Hist. of Assyria,* pp. 72 f., Zimmern, *KAT,* p. 382, cf. A. Jeremias in *ERE,* I, p. 186.

[63] Olmstead, *Hist. of Assyria,* p. 206.

[64] Luckenbill, *ARA,* II, 104.

He is the "rightful shepherd," "the guardian of justice." [65] Sennacherib also is

"the wise shepherd, favorite of the great gods, guardian of the right, lover of justice, who lends support, who comes to the aid of the needy, who turns (his thoughts) to pious deeds." [66]

Ashur had looked on him among all princes with sure favor, all the gods chose him as ruler, the queen of the gods presided over his birth.[67] Esarhaddon succeeds him with the same grandiloquent claims, sometimes in even more extravagant phraseology.[68] In one of several oracles addressed to him we read,

"Fear not, Esarhaddon, it is I, the Lord (Bel), who is speaking with thee, the 'beams' of thy heart will I strengthen, like thy mother, who brought thee into existence." [69]

Ashur-bani-pal (668-626), in whom culture and manly vigor, literary zeal and military ability were united with inhuman ferocity, in more than one text claims divine kinship, tho he also states over and over that Esarhaddon was his father.

"I (am) Asur-bani-pal, offspring (creature) of Ashur and Bêlit, the oldest prince of the royal harem, whose name Ashur and Sin, the lord of the tiara, have named for the kingship from distant days, whom they formed in his mother's womb, for the rulership of Assyria, whom Shamash, Adad, and Ishtar, by their unalterable decree, have ordered to exercise sovereignty." [70]

The claim that he was especially chosen of the gods to rule the land of Ashur recurs even more frequently. A council of the great gods, decreed for him a favorable destiny and granted him a receptive mind.[71]

The religious, or, if you prefer, mythological, atmosphere ap-

[65] *Op. cit.*, II, 77, 92, 107, 117, 119.

[66] *Op. cit.*, II, 233, 256, *et passim.*

[67] *Op. cit.*, II, 407.

[68] Cf. *op. cit.*, II, 574.

[69] *Op. cit.*, II, 624.

[70] *Op. cit.*, II, 765; cf. also II, 986.

[71] *Op. cit.*, II, 843.

pears, most clearly in the "Dialog Between Ashur-bani-pal and Nabu" in which the god finally replies thru a priest to the king's repeated appeals by saying,

"Small were you, Ashur-bani-pal, when I left you to the Queen of Nineveh (Ishtar). Weak were you, Ashur-bani-pal, when you sat on the lap of the Queen of Nineveh. Four were the nipples that were placed in thy mouth; two thou didst suck, in two thou didst hide thy face." [72]

The last king of the line to reign in Nineveh, Sin-shar-ishkun, claims he has been blessed with the same divine favor and help. In his hands "Nabu, guardian of all things, placed a righteous scepter and a just staff for the government of the (widespread) people." [73]

In Babylon the same traditions prevail. Of Merodach-baladan, the contemporary and would-be ally of Hezekiah, we read:

"Marduk inclined his heart toward the land of Akkad (i.e. Babylon), from which in anger he had turned away; he surveyed all peoples, he assembled all mankind; among all men, all abodes he made choice with fixed determination; upon Merodach-baladan, king of Babylon . . . he looked with joy . . . and proclaimed his decision: 'This is the shepherd who shall gather the scattered together.'" [74]

Tho Nabopolasser was of the house of Merodach-baladan and son of the well known viceroy, Bel-ibni, in the presence of Marduk he calls himself "son of nobody, the little, the unknown among the people." [75]

The facile and servile priests of Babylon could quickly ingratiate themselves with a new conqueror by applying to him the same language that had long been customary in the courts of Assyria and Babylonia. Of Cyrus they wrote in his cylinder inscription:

"Marduk . . . took pity [upon the people, whose sufferings had just been narrated]. He surveyed all lands together, assembled them and

[72] *Op. cit.*, II, 1129.

[73] *Op. cit.*, II, 1156.

[74] Gressmann, *Ursprung der israel.-jüd. Eschat.*, p. 251; Zimmern, *KAT*, p. 382.

[75] Olmstead, *Hist. of Assyria*, p. 633.

sought a righteous prince after his own heart, to take him by the hand. Cyrus, king of Anshan, he called by name, he proclaimed his name to supremacy over the totality of all things." [76]

The Semitic monarchs of the first dynasty of ancient Babylon, then the later kings of Assyria's prime, the rulers of the brief glory of New Babylonia, and finally in the sixth century the conquering Persians carry on *motifs* that belong to the legend of the divine Savior-king. After the time of Hammurapi they make little or nothing of the idea of justice for the poor and protection for the weak against the rich and powerful. Yet these ideals are not forgotten. The traits of a lowly, or at least an unknown, origin, of a choice by the gods, and of the inauguration by each new monarch of a new age of order, justice, prosperity, and universal happiness come to belong to the stock phraseology of court language and were ascribed to every monarch. Tho these documents were lacking in ethical power, yet they witness to ideals of society which could not be erased from men's minds. The living germs had been planted. They would eventually grow and fructify.

It is among the Sumerians that we have discovered the first uncertain heralds of the messianic idea. There is difference of opinion among Assyriologists as to whether one may properly speak of a messianic hope among the early Sumerians and Akkadians. One may agree that the term is used "virtually in the sense that makes every reigning king a messiah or a potential messiah." [77] And that certainly is not the sense in which it is common to interpret the messianism of the Hebrew prophets. But is not the process to be reversed and the messianic hope of the Hebrews to be interpreted first of all in the light of the ideals which had so long antedated it? It seems to me significant that the royal scholar, Ashur-bani-pal, who did so much to preserve the ancient literary lore of his peoples, is the one who most frequently uses language reminiscent of the paradise legend to describe what he has done for his people, and thus virtually claims to be a messiah.

[76] Zimmern, *KAT*, p. 381. Gressmann, *op. cit.*, p. 251. The marked similarity to the language of Is. 45.1 has often been noted.

[77] Leroy Waterman, *AJSL*, 37 (1920), 77 ff.

There can be little doubt that the Hebrew prophets were familiar with this type of hope among the nations around them. It is highly improbable that a nation which had been paying tribute for generations to the growing power of Assyria should be unfamiliar with the court language of the one dominating nation in all the world. If Ahaz borrowed an altar from Assyria, is it unlikely that his courtiers borrowed the language of Assyria to flatter their weak but aspiring monarch? That Isaiah should have adopted it and adapted it to a higher purpose is entirely in keeping with the keen social perceptivity and practical sagacity of the statesman prophet. The antiquarian labors of the scribes of Ashurbani-pal and Nabonidus can hardly have been absolutely unique. And even if the copying of ancient legends had not been carried on, all that we know of the preservation and travels of folklore and mythology argues that the myths of the ancient Sumerians would have been handed down unaltered in their fundamental characteristics by the popular traditions of nations which came within the sphere of influence of the civilization of which they were the founders. And one cannot deny for a moment that the Hebrews came within the circle.

It is, therefore, quite probable that the cycles of myths and legends concerning the divine Savior-hero, Marduk, the dying and rising Savior-god, Tammuz, and the kings who had in some measure emulated them were familiar to the Hebrew people and became the basis for the popular hope for the "day of Yahweh" and his eventual rule upon earth. Out of this expectation the prophets and apocalyptists of Judaism and Christianity constructed the messianic hope. With its eschatological vagaries we are not now concerned. But the social implications of these age-long protests against continued wrong and unceasing demands for redress cannot be overlooked.

III. THE MESSIANIC HOPE AMONG THE HEBREWS

It is unnecessary to discuss at length the messianic hope among the Hebrews. It is essential, however, to note the bearing of the materials from Egypt and Babylonia upon the interpretation of the messianic passages in Hebrew and Jewish writings. Isaiah's beautiful description of the child that should be born does not use language more exaggerated than we find applied to Babylonian or Egyptian monarchs. Understood as reflecting the "court style" everywhere common in oriental palaces, it can certainly be applied to a child whom he expected to be born in the Hebrew royal family.[78] The lines of Isaiah carry many of the ideas that we have discovered in the other monarchies.

"For unto us a child is born, unto us a son is given; and the government shall be upon his shoulder: and his name shall be called Wonderful Counsellor, Mighty God, Everlasting Father, Prince of Peace. Of the increase of his government and of peace there shall be no end, upon the throne of David, and upon his kingdom, to establish it, and to uphold it with justice and with righteousness from henceforth even forever. The zeal of Yahweh of hosts will perform this."[79]

It is not difficult to understand how Jeremiah, Ezekiel, Haggai, and Zechariah would look back upon the half millennium of the Davidic dynasty and expect it to continue indefinitely, even as did the author of Samuel.[80] Ezekiel is fond of the very phrase that so often recurs in the Assyrian documents. David is to be restored as the shepherd of his people.[81] Haggai and Zechariah believe Zerubbabel to be God's chosen.

Strangely enough, Second Isaiah borrows in part the words of the Babylonian priests in greeting Cyrus as the Lord's anointed. Yahweh says of Cyrus, "He is my shepherd and shall perform my pleasure." He is Yahweh's anointed, whose right hand he has held, to subdue nations before him.[82] The resemblance of language cannot be a mere coincidence. It would seem that there was in his words an intentional polemic against the claim that Marduk had called Cyrus. For the great Prophet of the Exile, the Davidic

[78] Cf. Gressmann, *Ursprung der. israel.-jüd. Eschat.*, pp. 250-270.
[79] Is. 9.6 f.; cf. 4.2; 11.1-5.
[80] Jer. 23.1-8; Hag., 2.23; Zech., 4.7-10; 2 Sam. 7.16.
[81] Chap. 34.23; 37.24 f.
[82] Is. 44.28; 45.1, cf. above p. 237. But see Torrey in *SEC*, pp. 287 f.

prince is of no importance. It is his concern to waken the nation again to a sense of its value and mission.[83]

It was quite natural, when the Davidic line had long since ceased to be a factor in the political life of the nation, that other ideas of the coming of the "perfect prince" should arise. Under the stress of the Maccabean struggle, when finally the nation had been freed, the people took the only reasonable course when they chose Simon, the last of the brave band of brothers, as hereditary high priest and ethnarch. Neither he nor his immediate descendants were ever officially recognized as anything more, but popular opinion, according to Josephus and the Testament of the Twelve Patriarchs, discovered in John Hyrcanus the fulfillment of the old prophecy of the coming prophet, priest, and king.

Into the expectations of the coming deliverer, it was almost inevitable that mythical traits should creep. Marduk had delivered the gods from the attack of Tiâmat, according to Babylonian myth. But the brood of the dragon was still on earth. Its power was to be seen in all the suffering thru which God's chosen people must pass. Yahweh must overthrow these demonic powers to save his people. Since post-exilic theology had risen above primitive anthropomorphism, Yahweh could no longer enter the battle in person, as he once had been thought to do. From the good spirits of Mazdaism, Judaism took Michael and the other angels and archangels. They appear in Daniel and in Ethiopic Enoch as the champions of the people of God, as God's emissaries and servants. They are a rationalization of the "hosts" whom Yahweh had once commanded. The "Son of man," who appears as the special angelic representative, or personification, of the Jewish people in Daniel, appears in the Similitudes of Enoch also as the Elect One, chosen of God, like the Semitic and Egyptian monarchs, and like them charged with the task of judging and punishing the wicked, rewarding the good, and establishing the divine laws.

The idea of a dying and rising Savior-god never interested official Judaism. In the Talmud the "suffering and dying messiah" does receive enigmatic mention, but long after the time of

[83] But see Cook in *CAH,* III, pp. 488-498.

Jesus.[84] The conception was foreign to the cult of the Law and to the transcendental theology of the rabbis. It does not appear in the pre-Christian literature that has been handed down by any branch of the orthodox church; the apocalypses know nothing of it. That Jewish sects in various corners of the ancient world may have adopted such ideas is apparent from the study of strange documents like those of the Mandeans.[85] But we have no evidence of the currency of these speculations in Galilean or Judean Judaism in the time of Jesus.

In first-century Judaism there is no deep sense of a stain of individual sin, no insatiable longing for escape from the evil world. The Jew was too socially minded to be other-worldly. He was conscious of the evil that was in society, but he did not think of it in the abstract as some taint to be removed by sacrificial expiation, but concretely as wrongs to be righted, as sinners to be punished, as evil to be overcome with good. Judaism had not abandoned its faith that God ruled the world. There was a profound consciousness of individual and national shortcomings. How else could the national inferiority, the national failure, the high-handed oppressions of their enemies, be explained? Therefore prayers, fastings, sacrifices, the fastidious observance of the Torah! God must be the one to save them from their enemies and the hands of those that hated them. The Shemôneh-'esrêh, the Eighteen Benedictions, which by the end of the first century A.D. had assumed practically their present form and were used almost as universally as the Lord's Prayer is among Christians, are a standing monument to the fundamental spirit of Judaism in the century when Christianity began. Eight of the nineteen prayers (10-17) as they are now used have to do with the restoration of Israel. The tenth blessing reads:

"Proclaim with great trumpets our freedom and lift up a banner to gather our scattered and to collect us from the four ends of the earth. Blessed be thou, Lord, who gatherest the exiles of thy people Israel. Restore our judges as before and our counsellors as at the beginning,

[84] See Weber, *Jüdische Theologie,* Leipzig, 1897, pp. 359 ff.

[85] See for example Reitzenstein, *Das iranische Erlösungsmysterium,* Bonn, 1921.

and take from us sorrow and sighing; and rule over us, thou, Lord, alone, in grace and pity, and justify us in the judgment. Blessed be thou, Lord, O King, who lovest righteousness and judgment."

The blessings with which the prayers close, which in the main agree with the oldest manuscript known,[86] summarize the aspirations of the people when the prayer was composed. Some of them are:

"Blessed be thou, Lord, who breakest enemies in pieces and bowest down the haughty. . . . Blessed be thou, Lord, stay and confidence of the righteous. . . . Blessed be thou, Lord, who hearest prayer. . . . Blessed be thou, Lord, who allowest thy Shekinah to return to Zion."

The fifteenth prayer, which mentions the house of David, is not in the Genizah text. It runs thus:

"Let the shoot of David, thy servant, spring forth quickly, and lift up his horn by thy help; for upon thy help we wait continually. Blessed be thou, Lord, who lettest the horn of salvation spring up."[87]

If we may not be sure as to the exact time which produced these prayers, with their longings for the coming of God in power to overthrow the oppressor and restore righteousness and judgment, there is no lack of other evidence for the presence of this mood at the time of Jesus. The many messianic disturbances of which Josephus gives us hints[88] are not entirely unambiguous evidence. It can hardly be gainsaid that in the expectations of the people there must have been many fantastic, mythical traits—expectations that God would work miracles in the overthrow of their enemies, in the glorification of the nation, and in the fructification of its land. How could the unreflecting read the Old Testament without harboring delusions of that kind? However metaphorical or poetically imaginative the prophets and apocalyptists may have intended to be, ordinary folk, even in the Orient, may sometimes

[86] That from the Cairo Genizah. Schechter, *Jewish Quarterly Rev.*, X, 1898, p. 656.

[87] In the above I follow Schürer, *Geschichte des jüdischen Volkes im Zeitalter Jesu Christi,* 4 ed., 1907, II, pp. 538-544.

[88] See below, chap. X, pp. 308-13.

have been prosaic enough to take their glowing phrases literally. Surely the six thousand who perished in the flames of the sanctuary praying for the promised miraculous deliverance may have been looking for a "Son of man" to appear on the clouds of heaven as the Book of Enoch had promised, or for some other equally supernatural intervention from on high. Yet with all that was supernaturalistic and fantastic in Jewish expectations, the basic conception was the hope for the establishment of divine justice on the earth. The Jews had the Psalter before them. One need but refer to the second and the one hundred and tenth Psalms. When the kings of the earth set themselves in array, he that sitteth in the heavens laughs at them. He sets his king on the holy hill of Zion and proclaims his decree:

"Thou art my son;
This day I have begotten thee.
Ask of me, and I will give thee the nations for thine inheritance
And the uttermost parts of the earth for thy possession.
Thou shalt break them with a rod of iron,
Thou shalt dash them in pieces like a potter's vessel."

If, as is generally maintained, the one hundred and tenth Psalm is Maccabean, addressed to Simon, the "hereditary high priest and ethnarch" by the will of the people, it is particularly instructive. He is to sit at Yahweh's right hand until God makes his enemies a footstool for his feet. Yahweh at his right hand will strike thru kings in the day of his wrath. He will judge among the nations.

Mythical and actual, spiritual and ethical traits are best summarized and combined in the seventeenth Psalm of Solomon:

"O Lord, thou art our King for ever and ever,
For in thee, O God, doth our soul glory.
How long are the days of man's life upon the earth?
As are his days, so is the hope (set) upon him.
But we hope in God, our deliverer:
. . . .
Behold, O Lord, and raise up unto them their king, the son of David,
At the time in which thou seest, O God, that he may reign over
Israel thy servant.

And gird him with strength, that he may shatter unrighteous rulers,
And that he may purge Jerusalem from nations that trample (her) down to destruction.
Wisely, righteously he shall thrust out sinners from (the) inheritance,
He shall destroy the pride of the sinner as a potter's vessel.
With a rod of iron he shall break in pieces all their substance,
He shall destroy the godless nations with the word of his mouth;
At his rebuke all nations shall flee before him,
And he shall reprove sinners for the thoughts of their heart.
And he shall gather together a holy people, whom he shall lead in righteousness,
And he shall judge the tribes of the people that has been sanctified by the Lord his God.
And he shall not suffer unrighteousness to lodge any more in their midst,
Nor shall there dwell with them any man that knoweth wickedness,
For he shall know them, that they are all sons of their God.

. . . .

And the blessing of the Lord (will be) with him: he will be strong and stumble not;
His hope (will be) in the Lord: who then can prevail against him.
(He will be) mighty in his works, and strong in the fear of God,
(He will be) shepherding the flock of the Lord faithfully and righteously,
And will suffer none among them to stumble in their pasture.
He will lead them all aright,
And there will be no pride among them that any among them should be oppressed."[89]

[89] Ps. of Sol. 17.1-3a, 21-27, 38-41. Charles, *APOT,* II, pp. 647 ff. (Gray).

CHAPTER IX

THE HOPE OF THE POOR

LIKE an angry crimson stain, the oppression of the poor and the helpless by the proud and the powerful overspreads the pages of history. Like a discordant diapason the cry of the wronged sounds thru ancient literature. But thru and above it all there shines, now dimly, now brightly, the hope of eventual vindication and compensation. The faith is never lost that God reigns and that at last righteousness and justice must triumph in his world. In all that has been recorded above as to the longing for the recovery of Paradise and for the coming of the perfect prince, the confidence that God will some day avenge the poor by the overthrow of their oppressors has again and again appeared.

I. THE PROTECTION OF THE POOR IN BABYLONIA

The first reformer in history, Uru-kagina of Lagash, appeared nearly three thousand years before Jesus as the champion of the oppressed. His chief concern was to do away with tyrannous taxation and to free the people from the high-handed exactions of dishonest government officials and rapacious priests. In a series of striking texts we have three versions of what he undertook to accomplish. His accounts reveal a depth of injustice and misery which could not be suspected from the pious votive texts and the boastful royal records of other reigns. He tells us that the land had suffered wrong and oppression "since distant days, from the beginning." The temples and the offerings due them must always have been a considerable burden upon the Sumerians. By this time the patesi had developed from a simple chieftain into a proud, ambitious, and luxury-loving monarch surrounded by a numerous and highly organized court that had been corrupted by wealth due to the conquest of neighboring cities and to the growth of commerce. To the temple tithes and offerings was added a burden of taxation to support the ruler and his court, and to the priests were added a horde of officials to collect the taxes and a host of inspectors "down to the sea" to insure their payment. The rulers did not hesitate to appropriate the lands and flocks of the temples, perhaps on the ground that they were patesis, or viceroys of the gods, and the priests, who made the temples into powerful commercial corporations, recouped themselves by demanding heavy fees for their services and by accepting bribes in the administration of justice, which seems to have been largely in their hands, often "splitting" with the patesi and his officials.

To these abuses Uru-kagina put an end. Most significant were his efforts to relieve the poor of oppression. He says that after his reforms:

> "The high-priest . . . came not into the garden of a poor mother and took not wood therefrom, gathered not tax in fruit therefrom. . . . If to the subject of the king a fair ass be born and his overlord say, 'I will buy it,' when he buys it, let him say, 'Pay in silver as much as satisfies my heart.' . . . If the house of a great man joins the house of a (humble) subject of the king and the great man say to him, 'I will buy it,' let him say to him when he buys it, 'Pay in silver as much as satisfies my heart and my house.'"

It is added that if the poor man refuse to sell, the overlord or the great man shall not be angry with him.[1] Evidently ancient Sumer knew its Naboths and its Ahabs. Another example of Uru-kagina's reforms in the interest of the poor had to do with the *corvée*. Apparently when men had been engaged in forced labor, they had not been supplied with drinking water or even allowed to fetch it for themselves, an evil which the great reformer set himself to remedy. It would seem to have been no idle boast when Uru-kagina claims to have been the champion of the weak against the

[1] Langdon, *CAH,* I, p. 387; Thureau-Dangin, *Königsinschriften,* pp. 47-57, esp. p. 47, Cone A, 5, 1 ff.; p. 53, Cones B and C, 11, 11-12, 11.

strong, and to have established liberty in the place of servitude. He insists that in his reign the strong man did no wrong to the widow and the orphan.[2]

It is significant that Uru-kagina suffered the fate which has so often befallen reformers, a sudden and complete overthrow. It came from without, by the attack of the inveterate enemy of Lagash, the city of Umma, under the leadership of Lugal-zaggisi, one of the greatest of Sumerian conquerors.[3] The records do not make clear the circumstances of the defeat of Uru-kagina, but one is justified in supposing that the radical reforms of the new ruler of Lagash had alienated large numbers of his subjects, especially those military and civil officials upon whom the defense of the city would largely devolve in case of attack. Armies are made up of the strong, of those who are most inclined to prey upon the poor, the widow, and the orphan. The weak whom Uru-kagina had befriended were least able to help their king and their city in time of attack.

Like Uru-kagina, later Sumerian and Semitic rulers were social reformers. In fulfilling the will of Nina and Ningirsu it was the care of Gudea to see that the strong man did not oppress the widow nor wrong the orphan. He took it for granted that the patesi, the earthly representative of the gods, was the protector of the weak and humble against the rich and powerful, who are regarded as their inevitable oppressors. From the nature of the patesi's words we may well assume that they had need of whatever help he could give them.[4] Of Ishme-dagan it is said,

> "That the rich man do not whatsoever be his desire,
> That one man to another do nought disgraceful,
> Wickedness and hostility he destroyed,
> Justice he instituted."[5]

Hammurapi, likewise, was called of Anu and Enlil "to prevent

[2] King, *Hist. of Sumer and Akkad,* pp. 184 f., Thureau-Dangin, *Königsinschriften,* p. 55, Oval Tablet 2, 4-8; p. 53, Cones B and C, 12, 12-28.

[3] Thureau-Dangin, *Königsinschriften,* p. 57 f.

[4] See above pp. 189 ff., 227 f.

[5] Thompson in *CAH,* I, p. 474.

the strong from oppressing the weak." In his wisdom he restrained the people of Sumer and Akkad that "the strong might not oppress the weak, and that they should give justice to the orphan and the widow." His code was written "for the righting of wrong."[6] It has been pointed out that Hammurapi, the capable administrator, did what no Hebrew legislator ever thought of attempting. In his code he protected the rights of the widow to her dowry and to a son's share in the inheritance, and he restricted her right to remarriage for the sake of her minor children. The Hebrews exhorted, but they did not provide specific legislation to enforce the exhortation.[7]

In one particular Hammurapi's code differs *toto cœlo* from Egyptian and Hebrew standards. The organization of Babylonian society was thoroly aristocratic. The code knows three classes, the patricians (*amêlu*), plebeians, or workingmen (*mushkênu*), and slaves (*wardu*). The differences in status before the law seem unique to one accustomed to the Hebrew emphasis on one law for all and to the modern practice of favoring the rich. Offenses against the first class, the Semitic aristocracy, were more severely punished than those against the other classes. For example, if a man destroyed the eye or broke the bone of a patrician, his eye was to be destroyed, his bone was to be broken. If he destroyed the eye or broke the bone of a plebeian, he was to pay one *mana* of silver. If he caused the same injury to a slave, he was to pay the owner half of his value. Unintentional killing of a patrician cost one half a *mana* of silver, of a plebeian one third of a *mana*. Thus far the standard is not unlike that of modern society. But if the patrician received greater compensation for injuries suffered, he also paid higher fees and penalties. For saving a patrician's life or eye by an operation, a physician was to receive ten shekels of silver. The same service earned only five shekels in the case of a plebeian, and only two in that of a slave. For setting the broken bone of a patrician, the physician was to receive five shekels. The like service for a plebeian and the slave of a patrician was valued

[6] Harper, *Code of Hammurabi,* p. 99; see above chap. VIII, pp. 228 f.

[7] S. A. Cook, *The Laws of Moses and the Code of Hammurabi,* London, 1903, p. 275.

at three shekels. A gentleman who stole from temple or palace had to make restitution thirty fold, a plebeian only ten fold. Likewise, for his divorce the patrician had to pay three times as much as the plebeian. Apparently on the principle of *noblesse oblige,* the patrician was compelled to give out of his abundance far more than was demanded of the plebeian out of his poverty, while at the same time his personal and property rights were accorded a higher value.[8] Plainly on one side at least, this is much more just than our principle of assessing the same fees and fines upon the poor and the rich, for the demand which means nothing to the rich may confiscate all that a poor man has.

We cannot doubt that the poor must have suffered from oppression constantly. Already in Sumerian times there are numerous references to the large estates belonging, some of them to the temples, some to the king, some to private individuals. Under Kassite rule this process of creating large holdings went on more rapidly. The foreign rulers were not solicitous of the rights of their conquered subjects, but were glad to concentrate wealth in the hands of their families and favorites.[9] The Assyrian monarchs have little to say about the underprivileged except to boast that the abundance which the gods have granted them feeds the hungry and clothes the naked. Two or three of them claim to be protectors of the poor.

Without being in the least pessimistic as to social progress or harboring a hatred of culture, one is compelled to admit that the development of civilization in the Tigris-Euphrates valley did not make marked improvement in the economic or social condition of the majority of the people. Cultural gains in some directions were balanced by losses in others. One of the losses seems to have been the disappearance of the strong sense of the rights of the common man. In the old days of the Sumerian patesis there rested on each city ruler a feeling of obligation to dig canals and otherwise promote the prosperity of his land and to bring peace and

[8] For discussion of the meaning of "amêlu" and "mushkênu," see Johns, *The Relations between the Laws of Babylonia and the Laws of the Hebrew Peoples* (Schweich Lectures, 1912), London, 1917, pp. 7-10.

[9] King, *History of Babylonia,* pp. 249 ff.

comfort to all. The Kassite monarchs knew nothing of this ancient tradition of the ruler's fatherly duty to his subjects. The Assyrian monarchs are famous for their grandiloquent boasting and among their claims they include the bringing of liberty, prosperity, and happiness to their people. But the insatiate ambition for foreign conquest which possessed the rulers of Ashur drove such modest and kindly obligations as the Sumerian patesis practiced into the background. It was left for the Hebrew prophets once more to champion the rights of the poor and oppressed.

II. THE POOR IN EGYPT

The thoroly undemocratic mind of the Egyptian has appeared again and again in the documents which have been quoted. How transparent is the smug, self-satisfied complacency of the royal father in the saying to Meri-ke-re that the poor man cannot tell the truth because he is pressed with want.[10] The rich man, who is above need, is thought to be above temptation. Even when they are commanded not to be arrogant to the poor man because the king loves the timid more than the arrogant, the patronizing condescension of the privileged classes to those under them is evident.[11] Tho in the time of the New Empire the Pharaoh descended from the lofty pinnacle of deified seclusion to become a warrior and a man among men, there is no intimation that the courtier ever dreamed that the poor man was as good as he. It was a subversion of social order that the poor man should become rich and the rich man poor.[12] Even tho the poor man, by dint of ability and good fortune, might become one of the privileged group about the king, the shepherd and the sheep belonged to different worlds.

Granted all this, yet the concern everywhere expressed for the poor, the hungry, the thirsty, the naked, the orphan, the widow, the weak, the weeper, brings us very near to that conception of benevolence and charity which has all too often been regarded as a

[10] Sec. 11, *JEA,* I (1914), 26.
[11] Breasted, *RTAE,* pp. 243, from the "Installation of the Vizier."
[12] See above Chap. VIII, pp. 220 ff.

full discharge of one's social obligations, both in Judaism and Christianity. The attitude of much of the Old Testament to the poor, the widow, and the orphan is practically the same as that of the Egyptian. A passage like Job's protestation of integrity might almost have been copied from an Egyptian tomb.[13]

Thus Ameni of Beni-hassan on the walls of his tomb proclaims:

> "There was no citizen's daughter whom I misused, there was no widow whom I afflicted, there was no peasant whom I repulsed (evicted?), there was no herdman whom I repelled, there was no overseer of five whose people I took away for (unpaid) taxes. There was none wretched in my community, there was none hungry in my time. When years of famine came, I plowed the fields of the Oryx barony (his estate) as far as its southern and its northern boundary, preserving its people alive, furnishing its food so there was none hungry therein."[14]

The eloquent peasant appeals to the high steward thus: "Thou art a father to the orphan, a husband for the widow, a brother for her that is put away, an apron for him that is motherless."[15] Intef, the herald of Thutmose III, claims to be, not only a terror to the wicked, but a protector and helper of the weak.[16] Amenophis, son of Kanakht, urged his son, "Receive not the gift of a strong man, nor repress the weak for him." One must be kind to the widow and charitable to the stranger. "God loveth the happiness of the humble more than that the noble be honored."[17] Two thirds of a poor man's debt are to be forgiven.

Not only are there Egyptian parallels to the language of the prophets, but also to that of the Psalms. Eventually the social ideals of the twelfth and eighteenth dynasties penetrated into the world of theology, and a religion of the poor, comparable to that of the post-exilic Jewish community, made its appearance.[18] Sev-

[13] Job 31.5-23; see below, p. 265.

[14] Breasted, *AR,* I, 523; *RTAE,* p. 248; see above p. 218.

[15] *JEA,* IX (1923), 9, ll. 64 f.

[16] See above, pp. 216.

[17] Griffith's translation in *JEA,* XII (1926), 21.3; 26.8-14; 16.5 ff.

[18] See Breasted, *RTAE,* chap. X; Battiscombe Gunn, "The Religion of the Poor in Ancient Egypt," in *SBELE,* II, pp. 309-23, slightly enlarged in *JEA,* III (1916), 81-94; cf. *CAH,* II, pp. 160 and 208.

eral of the hymns which were produced by these poor folk are worthy of comparison with the literature of the Hebrews on account of their similarities both in content and in phraseology.

Two poor necropolis workmen, father and son, dedicate a *stela* of thanksgiving for the recovery of another son which begins:

> "Amon-Re, Lord of Karnak,
> The great God within Thebes;
> The august god who hears prayer,
> Who comes at the voice of the distressed humble one,
> Who gives breath to him that is wretched." [19]

The long hymn which follows is full of phrases that might have come from one of the Psalms, and it repeats again and again the idea of Amon's readiness to hear the wretched and the humble.

A Cairo papyrus contains a long hymn to Amon, employing the phraseology of the old mythology and that of Ikhnaton's Aton theology apparently without an inkling of inconsistency. It runs in part thus:

> "Hail to thee! Re, lord of truth,
> Whose sanctuary is hidden, lord of gods,
> Khepri in the midst of his barque,
> Who commanded and the gods became;
> Atum, who made the people,
> Who determined the fashion of them,
> Maker of their sustenance,
> Who distinguished one color (race) from another;
> Who hears the prayers of him who is in captivity,
> Who is kindly of heart when one calls upon him,
> Who saves the timid from the haughty,
> Who separates the weak from the strong,
> Lord of knowledge in whose mouth is Taste;
> For love of whom the Nile comes,
> Lord of sweetness, great in love,
> At whose coming the people live." [20]

Other lines which follow, evidently borrowed from the Amarna hymns to Aton, suggest that possibly Ikhnaton's reformation had

[19] *JEA,* III (1916), 83.

[20] Breasted, *RTAE,* p. 347 f.

contributed to this conception of God as a kindly father. The god who cared for the worm and the gnat might well be supposed to look with solicitude upon the "silent," "the poor," or "humble," "the timid," the wretched inarticulate masses, and be ready to save them from the haughty, the rich, and the powerful. Gardiner has made the suggestion that Egyptian *nmḥ,* "humble," may be the general name for the poorer population above the slave class, like Babylonian "mushkênu."[21]

The ancient myth, as old certainly as the Middle Kingdom, which tells of the reign of Re on earth at the dawn of history, when he was shepherd of men, is drawn upon to furnish a still further expression of the social hopes of the poor. On that writing material of the poor, an *ostrakon,* is preserved a hymn that reminds one of the twenty-third Psalm. It runs:

"O Amon, thou herdman bringing forth the herds in the morning, leading the suffering to pasture; as the herdman leads the herds (to) pasture, so dost thou, O Amon, lead the suffering to food, for Amon is a herdman, herding him that leans upon him. . . . O Amon-Re, I love thee, and I have filled my heart with thee. . . . Thou wilt rescue me out of the mouth of men in the day when they speak lies; for the Lord of Truth, he liveth in truth. I will not follow the anxiety in my heart, (for) that which Amon hath said flourisheth."[22]

Another figure of speech, likewise biblical, to describe the communion of the worshiper with his god is found in Papyrus Sallier:

"Thou sweet Well for him that thirsteth in the desert; it is closed to him who speaks, but it is open to him who is silent. When he who is silent comes, lo, he finds the well."[23]

One might well consider the "silent," as well as the "poor," as a technical term for those classes who had little chance to be heard in the courts amid the noise made by the great ones. But if they could not speak for themselves, their Lord, the good shepherd, could. He would not only comfort their hearts; he would also plead their cause. The god is "a just judge, not accepting a bribe, uplift-

[21] *JEA,* III, p. 83, n. 3.
[22] Breasted, *RTAE,* p. 355.
[23] Breasted, *op. cit.,* p. 356.

ing the insignificant, (protecting) the poor, not extending the hand to the rich." Amon is "the vizier of the poor man." The injured and neglected mother "raises her arm to God, and he hears her cry," for he is "the loving god who heareth prayers, (who giveth the hand) to the poor, who saveth the weary." The poor man can appeal to Amon as his champion and advocate when he must plead his cause before the courts:

"O Amon, lend thine ear to him who stands alone in the court (of justice), who is poor while his (opponent) is rich. The court oppresses him (saying), 'Silver and gold for the scribes! Clothing for the servants!' But Amon transforms himself into the vizier that he may cause the poor man to triumph; the poor man is just and the poor man (overcomes) the rich. Pilot (in) front who knoweth the water, Amon, thou rudder, . . . who giveth bread to him who hath none, and preserveth alive the servant of his house."[24]

In the Greek and Roman period the one striking difference between Hebrew and Egyptian apocalypse seems to have disappeared. The argument *e silentio* is always uncertain, but it is an interesting fact that the old Egyptian fear of a rising of the common people is not to be discovered in documents after the Persian period. When the ruling classes were foreigners, when all Egyptians suffered more or less from the oppression of alien conquerors, the native apocalyptist no longer saw the advance of the lower classes as an evil, for their common sufferings tended to obliterate class distinctions among the native Egyptians. The revolutionary temper of the so-called "Demotic Chronicle" and the "Apology of the Potter" has its close parallel in the Jewish apocalypses from Daniel on. Thus in various ways the Hebrew and Egyptian outlook came to be more and more alike.[25]

Eduard Meyer and Breasted have called attention to the close parallel between the religion of personal piety which developed in Egypt in the priest-ruled state of the period of her decadence and restoration, and the individual religion of Judaism in post-exilic times when Judea was also priest-ruled and decadent for a

[24] Breasted, *RTAE,* p. 353.

[25] Cf. *HTR,* 18 (1925), 387-405, cf. above, pp. 220 ff., 251.

time, and then revived somewhat under the Maccabees, but looked always to the past, not the future. It is significant that during these similar periods in both Egypt and Palestine the religion of the poor developed with its demands for divine communion, divine justice, and divine protection against the rich. Since the fundamental conditions were so similar in the two nations, it would be too much to claim that Israel was dependent in a literary way upon Egypt in this matter, that Judaism borrowed directly from the social prophets of Egypt and the humble spokesmen of the poor whose hymns and prayers have been preserved. Yet with such excellent opportunities for contacts between the Hebrews and Egypt, it would be hazardous to deny the possibility that the hopes and aspirations of the poor in Egypt may have been communicated to their neighbors in Palestine.

III. THE POOR IN NORTH SYRIA

Instead of speaking of the influence of the Babylonians and Egyptians upon the Hebrews, we should rather think of a Near East in which, with many varieties of custom and belief, there was a culture fully as uniform as that of Europe today. Intercommunication was constant, and, indeed, had been so since long before the beginning of written history. Certain outstanding religious and ethical ideals were almost everywhere accepted. Among these, regard for the poor was one and to it rulers in every land paid at least lip service. This was true of the little kingdoms as well as of the great.

Our knowledge of the Near East in ancient times depends largely upon the literatures of the Hebrews, the Babylonians and Assyrians, and the Egyptians, for from them alone have masses of documents been preserved. To these we shall be able to add, ere long, the Hittites, upon whose documents an impressive beginning has been made. But it is, in the main, to the three literatures mentioned above that one is compelled to turn for information as to ancient beliefs and ideals. But occasional happy discoveries show that the ancient world was a unit and that other smaller nations lived in the same atmosphere and harbored the same ideals as those peoples whom we know more fully.

One of the most interesting and in some ways most puzzling of these smaller nations has been Samal, or Ya'di, whose records were uncovered by the German excavations at Zenjirli. Kalamu, a king of the eighth century, who first of his line became voluntarily a vassal of Assyria, appears on his *stela* with a flower in his hand instead of sword or scepter and with a most unconventional record:

"I, Kalamu, son of Hayya, sat on the throne of my father. In the presence of the former kings the *mushkabîm* [the 'prostrated' peasantry] had gone about like dogs; but I, to one was a father, to another a mother, to another a brother. He who before me had not seen a sheep, him I made the owner of a flock; he who before me had not seen an ox, him I made the owner of cattle, of silver, and of gold. He who from his youth up had not seen a coat in my days was clothed with fine linen. And I took the *mushkabîm* by the hand and gave them an affection (for me) like the affection of the fatherless for his mother. And whoever of my sons shall sit (on the throne) after me and shall injure this inscription, may the *mushkabîm* not honor the *ba'rîrîm,* and the *ba'rîrîm* not honor the *mushkabîm.*"[26]

The inscription affords an interesting glimpse into conditions which must frequently have prevailed in the Syrian coastal regions, the *ba'rîrîm,* the "wild folk," the nomadic conquerors, at strife with the conquered sedentary peasantry upon whom they had imposed their rule. Kalamu had reconciled the conquered to their lot by making it endurable. A later king, Panammu I, following the Assyrian model, claims to have brought prosperity and plenty to his land, and Panammu II, who in 732 died, a loyal vassal of Assyria, in Tiglath Pileser's camp before Damascus makes somewhat similar claims. He had freed captives and made his people to revel in plenty.[27]

[26] Olmstead, *Hist. of Assyria,* pp. 184 ff.; C. C. Torrey in *JAOS,* 35 (1915), 364-69, Enno Littmann, *SBA,* 1911, pp. 976-85; Mark Lidzbarski, *Ephemeris für semit. Epigraphik,* III, Giessen: Töpelmann, 1915, pp. 218-38; Gressmann, *Altor. Texte,* 442 f.

[27] Olmstead, *op. cit.,* pp. 186 ff., G. A. Cooke, *A Text-book of North Semitic Inscriptions,* pp. 159 ff., 171. Whether Azriau of Iaudi in the

The thoroly materialistic outlook of these boasts need not surprise one. Do not the Hebrew prophets as well as the Assyrian monarchs use similar language? Does not each political party in every national election engage to inaugurate an era of national prosperity if given the reins of government? The significant element in Kalamu's record of his achievements is the claim to have served the peasantry. The full dinner pail has been given to the working classes. The implication of the allusion to the mutual respect due between the peasantry and the nobility is equally instructive. Evidently the existing social stratification was to last forever. The ideal condition is mutual honor, or respect, between the high and the low, the nobles and the people, capital and labor, each in its place. Is this a reminiscence of the recognized class distinctions of Hammurapi's code and the Egyptian monuments, or is it the natural outcome of historical circumstances similar to those which produced the *amêlu* and *mushkênu* of Babylon? However skeptical one may be as to the reality of this boasted prosperity of the poor, these inscriptions vouch for the wide diffusion of those ideals which we have seen first among the Sumerians in Babylonia in the third millennium B. C. and for their persistence during two thousand years. At the very time when the prophets of Israel were proclaiming God's care for the poor, we discover a similar concern for their welfare at the other end of Syria.

IV. THE POOR IN MAZDAISM

Very little has come from the writings of Zarathushtra or any of his successors that bears upon the rights of the poor. The duties

annals of Tiglath Pileser III was king in a "Northern Judah," as Winckler supposed, is now generally doubted. See D. D. Luckenbill in *AJSL*, 41 (1925), 217-32, Sidney Smith in *CAH*, III, pp. 35 ff., S. A. Cook in *CAH*, III, p. 378, G. A. Driver in *JTS*, 27 (1926), 412; but favoring Winckler's hypothesis Olmstead, *loc. cit.* and Hogarth in *CAH*, II, p. 142. The controversy concerns the present argument in that Winckler's theory implies a worship of Yahweh in Samal and it might be supposed the social ideals noted above were connected with him. However all three of the kings mentioned were anything but worshipers of Yahweh.

of lending neighborly help and hospitality, of laboring to master the earth, of tending the kine, of being fruitful and multiplying were emphasized.[28] God was one "whose first care was to relieve suffering and shelter the honest and industrious poor."[29] This, to be sure, means little more than pity for the unfortunate and the inculcation of the duty of giving alms and caring for the needy. There are, however, significant passages which seem to go somewhat farther. Of special interest is a stanza in *Yasna* 53, the *Gatha Vahishto-ishti,* which runs as follows:

> "To them of evil belief belongs the place of corruption. They that go to despise the worthy, contemners of Right, who forfeit their own self—where is the righteous Lord that shall rob them of life and freedom? Thine, Wise One, is the Dominion, whereby thou canst give to the right-living poor the better portion."[30]

Clearly the prophet of Mazdaism has in mind the contrast, which so often stirs the hearts of Israel's prophets and psalmists, between the proud, the haughty, the scornful, who prepare the pit into which they themselves fall, and the righteous poor for whom God has prepared adequate compensation for their sufferings.

Again in the prayer *Ahuno Vairya, Yasna* 27.13, Zarathushtra is called

> "He that bringeth the life-works of Good Thought unto the Wise One, and (so) dominion unto the Lord, even he whom they made shepherd for the poor."[31]

The lines illustrate, in the first place, how widespread was the tradition upon which the Fourth Gospel takes its stand when it makes Jesus the good shepherd. In the second place they bring the shepherding of the poor and the establishing of "dominion for the Lord" into significant connection. As has already been indicated, the social history of Mazdaism was quite different from that of Judaism so far as the influence of nomadism is concerned.[32] It

[28] L. T. Hobhouse, *Morals in Evolution,* p. 470.
[29] *Ibid.,* p. 466.
[30] Moulton, *Early Religious Poetry of Persia,* p. 114.
[31] Moulton, *op. cit.,* p. 115.
[32] See above, pp. 149 ff.

seems to have been different also in this, that it did not suffer from opposition as did the prophetic faith in the Hebrew monarchy and the religion of the poor in post-exilic Judaism. It was, perhaps, too soon adopted and emasculated by priests and princes. It did not live thru the transition from nomadism to agriculture and from argiculture to commerce, certainly not in the days of its founder or other creative religious thinkers. Yet even Mazdaism raises its voice, tho never so faintly, in recognition of the right of the poor to Ahura's special care and connects the establishment of the divine dominion with their protection.

V. THE POOR IN ISRAEL

1. *In Pre-Exilic Times*

The complaints of the poor and needy at the oppressions of the proud, the haughty, the rich, and the mighty are too numerous in the Bible and too well known to require quotation here. Tho there is no reference to either poor or rich in the Ten Commandments, yet the Book of the Covenant, the earliest collection of Hebrew laws, exhorts that justice be done the poor man and provides that interest shall not be exacted for loans nor harshness practiced in the taking of security. It prescribes that the products of the fallow fields of the sabbatical year shall be left to the poor. The fatherless, the widow, and the sojourner shall not be wronged or oppressed.[33]

Deuteronomy and Leviticus develop these injunctions still farther in the interest of the poor and unfortunate. The Hebrew laws go far beyond the code of Hammurapi in their evident concern for the underprivileged of every kind, for the dependent, such as servants, slaves, captives, and those without legal or natural defenders, such as orphans, widows, and foreigners. Their exhortations to justice, kindness, and philanthropy are without parallel in the Babylonian code. They have their nearest counterparts in the "Admonitions" and the epitaphs of Egypt. The inclusion of the sojourner, the *gêr,* or resident alien, and the slave among the objects of special

[33] Ex. 22.25 ff.; 23.6-12; 22.21 ff.

consideration puts the standards of the Hebrews on a distinctly higher level than those of their neighbors.

The laws that occur in various strata of the Hebrew codes forbidding the taking of interest are patent evidence of the regard for the poor which marked the moral leaders of Israel.[34] They are beacons that signalize a long and bitter contest between an agricultural and a commercial civilization. It is illuminating to discover that another nomadic people which became agricultural followed the practice which the laws of Exodus and Deuteronomy inculcate. In Assyria the landlord loaned to his tenant without interest on condition that repayment be made immediately after harvest. Olmstead contrasts the practice of commercial Babylon which made no such provision for the needs of the farmer, and consequently the peasant in the late Babylonian documents has become a slave.[35] No one will deny that one of the most difficult problems in an agricultural community is to find means by which the farmer may tide himself over the long period of waiting between harvests without falling into the hands of the usurer. Israel's prohibition of the taking of interest was intended to provide such means, but no doubt it was more remembered in the breach than in the observance. It was this very use of the power of ready money which gave the rich in the days of Amos and Isaiah the power to sell the needy for a pair of shoes and to join house to house and field to field. In a purely commercial society and for business purposes the loaning of money is quite another matter, and Babylonia had known and legalized the practice probably long before the time of Hammurapi. The Hebrew laws against interest are another example of the conflict between agricultural and commercial civilizations.

The inculcation of the sabbatical year of release and of the year of Jubilee is yet another example of Hebrew idealism. We have no evidence that the latter was ever observed. That slaves were not always released, altho the obligation to do so was recognized, is clear from the actions of Jeremiah's contemporaries in a

[34] Cf. Driver on Ex. 22.25.

[35] *Hist. of Assyria,* pp. 520 f.

time of threatened danger.[36] The much more humane Babylonian law which allowed a person to be sold for debt for only three years proves that such legislation was not unusual. There is no doubt also that there was some widely recognized custom or law intended to prevent the permanent alienation of a man's ancestral property. The incident of Naboth's vineyard and the laws regarding the redemption of land are sufficient evidence. Altho it cannot be proved that such laws were actually observed, the data are sufficient to indicate the accepted ideal and the prevailing sentiment in favor of the man who was unfortunate. As to a sabbatical year for the fields, it is to be said that a custom of fallowing must be followed in a land such as Palestine unless artificial fertilizing is extensively practiced. But it would be much wiser if it were not concentrated into a single year. Imagine the economic consequences for the poor peasant and the landless proletariat if no fields were cultivated in the whole country for a year. Moreover, many fields in the dry-farming area needed to lie fallow every other year. We may well doubt whether such a seventh-year fallowing would profit either the land or the poor, but the precept, as well as that permitting the poor to glean in the fields at every harvest, indicate the direction of Israel's thought, and the latter privilege must have been of no small value to those who were on the edge of want. If different portions of the fields and vineyards were left uncultivated on successive years, as a verse in the "Book of the Covenant" may be held to indicate, this provision for gleaning in fallow fields must also have mitigated the hardships of the poverty stricken. The strongly humanitarian tone of the command is striking. The land is to lie fallow "so that the poor of your people may eat." [37]

In Israel this regard for the poor and unfortunate was coupled with no aristocratic disdain, no superman contempt. The motive urged in the case of sojourners and slaves is noteworthy. The Hebrew was to be merciful because he had been an alien and a slave in Egypt, because of sympathy born of similar experiences,

[36] Jer. 34.8-17.
[37] Ex. 23.10 f.

not because of immeasurable superiority.[38] The nomadic ideal also gives a special coloring to the Hebrew conception of justice for the poor. Like Gudea of Lagash, the moral leaders of Israel believed that the divine laws demanded the essential equality of the maid and her mistress, the man and his slave. Luxury for the few, want for the many, this was not the will of Yahweh. Every Israelite family was to have its own patrimony and dwell under its own vine and fig tree. Insistence upon equal privilege for all and upon simplicity of life gave bitterness to the prophetic invective against luxury. The wrongs of the poor were the inevitable result of the wealth of the rich.

The very words used for the underprivileged classes in Hebrew, as in other languages, convey in many instances a connotation of oppression on the part of those who enjoy the advantages of life. *'Ebyôn,* the common word for "poor," "needy," comes from *'âbâh,* "to long for." *Dâl* is from *dâlal,* meaning to "totter," to "hang." *'Anî* is from *'ânâh* in the sense of to "bend, labor, toil." In the intensive and causative stems the verb means to "afflict, oppress," a connotation which the substantive never loses. *Miskên,* used a few times in the sense of "poor," comes from *sâkan* in the sense of "stooping, crouching, being bowed." The related Arabic root means to be needy. The Babylonian *mushkênu* and the *mushkabîm* of Ya'di [39] are "plebeians," a conquered peasantry and proletariat ruled by the higher classes. In Assyria they are serfs.[40] It is not without significance that πτωχός is from a root which means to "cower, cringe," and so to "beg." In prehistoric times when language was in the making, men realized that poverty did not mean mere lack of goods; it involved a deprivation of that for which one naturally and legitimately longed; it meant weakness and dependence; it implied cringing and cowering before rich conquerors who forced the poor man to bend his back to labor.

The classical description of the woes of the poor is to be found in the prophets of the eighth century, Amos, Micah, and Isaiah.

[38] Dt. 5.15.
[39] See above, pp. 248 and 256 f.
[40] Olmstead, *Hist. of Assyria,* p. 518.

In no other literature can such flaming denunciation, such biting invective against those who enrich themselves at the expense of the unfortunate be found. The glorious prosperity of the land between the Syrian wars and the advance of Assyria resulted in shameless exploitation and oppression. Amos returns to the matter again and again:

> "They sell honest folk for silver,
> the needy for a pair of shoes;
> they trample the heads of the poor [into the dust of the earth],
> and make the knees of the lowly to tremble." [41]

Isaiah, who belonged to the class he was denouncing, is not less bitter. Addressing the elders and princes of the people Yahweh says:

> "And it is you who have eaten my vineyard bare.
> The plunder of the poor is in your houses.
> What do you mean that you crush my people
> and grind the face of the poor?" [42]

Micah cries out to the "heads of Jacob and the rulers of the house of Israel,"

> "Ought you not to know justice,
> you haters of good and lovers of evil?
> But you pluck their skin off from them
> and their flesh off from their bones.
> You devour the flesh of my people
> and flay their skin off from them,
> You lay their bones bare
> and chop them up like flesh in a pot,
> Like meat in the midst of a cauldron." [43]

If, as Old Testament scholars have long held, Deuteronomy was written under the influence of the eighth-century prophets in an attempt to put the prophetic spirit into the civil and sacerdotal laws of the nation, we should expect to find it going beyond the

[41] Am. 2.6 f.; 5.10 ff.; 8.4 ff.
[42] Is. 3.12 f.; cf. 1.17.
[43] Mic. 3.1 ff. See above pp. 138 ff.

Book of the Covenant in efforts to protect the poor and unfortunate. And this seems actually to be the case. The Deuteronomists repeat the Covenant laws intended to protect the weak. They do not seem to fear that the poor man will be unduly favored in his lawsuits.[44] They insist upon regard for the orphan, the widow, and the resident alien until these three terms come to be a shibboleth of their reform. Their exhortations carry a note of humanitarian motivation and prophetic urgency. But they advocate charity more often than justice. Tho moved by the prophetic spirit, the Deuteronomists already begin to water down the ideals of their teachers.

2. *The Poor in Early Post-Exilic Judaism*

In post-exilic Jewish literature there is a remarkable variety of attitudes. The Priest Code differs totally from the Book of the Covenant and Deuteronomy. The widow and the fatherless are not mentioned, the alien only to insist that he must observe all the law. The sabbatical year is a purely religious institution. No mention is made of the poor or the release of debtors. That is postponed to the year of Jubilee. Except in the provision for the return of a man's ancestral lands in the fiftieth year, there is no recognition of a social problem.[45] Charity and the gleanings of the fields are the only provisions made for the poor. Clearly the priestly attitude in social matters is very different from that of the prophets.

Much of post-exilic canonical literature is concerned solely with the restoration of Jerusalem and the Jewish nation. Here we may class such works as Second Isaiah and Joel. Third Isaiah, Zechariah, and Malachi plainly and bluntly insist upon the prophetic and Deuteronomic ideals of social righteousness, but these are not their chief interest.[46] Nehemiah also, as will be readily admitted, has other matters closer at heart, but, with masterful emphasis, he demands the actual practice of the prophetic ideals.[47]

[44] Cf. Ex. 23.3, Dt. 1.17; 16.19; Lev. 19.15.
[45] Lev. 25.1-55.
[46] Is. 58.1-12; 59.1-15; Zech. 7.8 ff.; Mal. 3.5.
[47] Neh. 5.1-13.

In Job and in Proverbs one finds a continuation of various nuances of the pre-exilic social attitude, in Job more in the prophetic spirit, in Proverbs rather in the legalistic, along with the calculating, practical wisdom of the East. Few passages in literature state more powerfully a high ideal of conduct for a man of wealth and social position than Job's asseveration of innocence, with its startling reminiscences of Egyptian modes of thought.[48] Job claims with passionate insistence that he has never ignored the rightful claim of any servant, man or woman. He has never grudged a poor man what he desired, nor made a widow pine in want. He has never eaten his morsel alone, but shared it with the fatherless. The naked he has warmed with fleeces from his sheep. He has never brought false suit against anyone, nor taken land by fraud or violence. He has never relied upon his gold, nor rejoiced because his wealth was great. He implies also that the motives for his kindly and upright conduct had not been merely fear of God's anger. He has remembered that God had made the slave also and formed them both alike in the womb. His care for the fatherless has grown out of his recognition of God's fatherly care in his own life.[49]

Equally remarkable are the sympathy and understanding as well as the poignant bitterness of Job's description of the woes of the poor. Why, he asks, does not the Almighty hold regular sessions of court and dispense justice to mankind? There are those who remove the landmark, plunder flocks, drive off the orphan's ass, and seize the widow's cow for debt. They tear the very infant from the breast as a pledge for the poor man's loan. They evict the needy, and the homeless unfortunates must huddle away in caves and wander like wild asses in the wilderness in search of food, stealing or gleaning to feed their children. They lie all night uncovered, drenched by mountain downpours, clinging to rocks for shelter. They starve while they carry the sheaves and press the olives, and thirst while they tread the winepress. The writer of the Book of Job was no communist; he doubtless believed that

[48] See above, p. 251.

[49] Chap. 31.13-31.

rich and poor must always live side by side. But with unerring instinct he saw and pictured the evils of society.[50]

Even less than Job does the Book of Proverbs display impractical idealism. The average common sense of Israel's wise men recognized the practical advantages of wealth and the handicaps which poverty imposes. But the rich are painted with no halo. Materials preserved from the days of the prophets are combined with observations marked with the cynicism of Koheleth.[51] He who oppresses the poor for the sake of gain and he who gives presents to the rich shall both alike come to poverty. The rich man thinks he is wise, but the wit of the poor man sees thru his pretense.[52] The poor are peculiarly the clients of God and He will defend them.

> "Rob not the poor because he is poor,
> neither wrong the unfortunate in lawsuits;
> For Yahweh will act as their advocate
> and rob of their lives those who rob them."[53]

The book repeatedly enjoins charity and justice to the poor, the weak, and the unfortunate, and in general recognizes the prophetic standards without passionately championing the lower classes.[54]

3. *The Party of the Poor in the Psalter*

If there is one book in the Bible which seems thoroly alive to the sufferings of the poor, it is the Psalter. Yet how peculiar it is! The prophets of the eighth and seventh centuries reveal to us the wrongs which were inflicted upon the poor under the monarchy. The Psalter, the hymnbook of the second temple, paints in lurid

[50] Chap. 24.1-12.

[51] Chap. 14.20; 18.23; 19.7, 22; 22.1.

[52] Chap. 22.16; 28.11.

[53] Prov. 22.22 f. V. 22 is paralleled by the "Maxims of Amenophis," 4.4 f. (*JEA*, XII, p. 199), v. 23 by Pap. Anastasi, II, 8, 5-9, 3; Breasted, *RTAE*, p. 353. See above, p. 254.

[54] Chap. 14.31; 17.5; 19.17; 21.13; 22.2, 4, 9; 28.8, 14 ff., 27; 29.13; 30.14; 31.8 f.

colors their sufferings under the theocracy of sacerdotal Judaism after the Exile. The poor, the needy, the humble, groan under the injustice and oppression of the proud, the rich, the violent. One of the serious problems of the psalmists is the fact that the wicked are rich and prosperous, while the pious are poor and needy. Not gentleness and humility, but pride and violence seem to have God's approval. Yet the confidence that God will eventually intervene to give justice its due always rises above all doubts. God will avenge the poor, the humble shall inherit the land.

> "Happy is he whose help is the God of Jacob,
> whose hope is in Yahweh his God,
> the maker of heaven and earth,
> the sea and all that is in them.
> He keeps faith for ever,
> he executes justice for the wronged,
> he gives food to the hungry.
> Yahweh looses the captives,
> Yahweh opens the eyes of the blind,
> Yahweh raises those that are bowed down,
> Yahweh preserves the alien,
> the fatherless and widow he maintains.
> Yahweh loves the righteous,
> but the life of the wicked he ruins.[55]

Why is it that in a large number of the Psalms the poor and the needy, the meek and the oppressed, are always identified with the righteous servants of Yahweh, while the rich, the proud, and the powerful are always represented as wicked and godless? Hebrew historians have no direct light to throw upon the question, but the literature of post-exilic times supplies a general answer, which seems to run somewhat in this wise.

The prophets had made themselves the special advocates of the peasantry, the common people, who were always threatened with poverty and who suffered from the exactions and injustices of

[55] Ps. 146.5-9; cf. 9.12, 18; 10.2, 9, 12, 14, 17 f.; 12.5; 18.27; 22.24; 34.19; 35.10; 37.14; 40.17; 41.1; 68.5 f., 10; 70.5; 72.2, 4, 12 ff.; 74.19, 21; 79.11; 86.1; 94.6 f.; 102.17, 20; 103.6; 107.41; 109.16, 22; 113.7; 140.12. Cf. Hannah's song, 1 Sa. 2.1-10.

the princes and the powerful. The prophetic ideals of industry and simple living, of justice and mercy, were written into the legal codes and into the traditional history of the race. Thus all pre-exilic Hebrew literature was permeated by the social attitudes and ideals for which the prophets had pleaded. But it is worth noting, by way of contrast to later notions, that the prophets never represented the common people or the poor as righteous. Indeed, Jeremiah finds the lowly as well as the great all alike hopelessly ignorant of God's law.[56] For the pre-exilic prophets, moreover, the nation was a unit and was treated by Yahweh as such. There were rich and poor, there were righteous and wicked, but all must suffer together for their collective sins. The doctrine of the "remnant," which Isaiah seems to have originated, and that of individual responsibility and divine discrimination, which first appears in Jeremiah and Ezekiel, made possible a very different development of thought in post-exilic times.

The catastrophe of the Exile must have temporarily effaced social distinctions. But such a state of equality could not last long. Doubtless many of the exiles were soon able to find opportunities for advancement in their new home. Whether in devastated Judea there arose marked differences between families among the miserable folk who were left behind we cannot say. In any case post-exilic Judaism soon came to exhibit the same classes of the rich, the moderately well-to-do, and suffering poor as had existed in pre-exilic Palestine.

The social and religious situation soon developed so as to cause the formation of two leading groups, or parties, partly political, partly religious in their aims and principles. On the one hand there were the aristocratic, the rich and well-to-do families, who were brought into relations with the surrounding non-Jewish peoples partly by their political positions as heads of the Jewish community, partly by the commercial intercourse thru which their wealth came and into which in turn it forced them the more deeply. On the other hand there were religious conservatives, strictly pious folk, represented in the first instance by some of the returning exiles

[56] Chap. 5.4.

from Babylon, whose sole interest lay in the maintenance of their ancestral faith. Men like Nehemiah had made great sacrifices in coming back to barren Judea. Wealth meant nothing to them. When in power they put restrictions upon the intercourse between their fellow countrymen and the neighboring peoples which raised a distinct barrier to the growth of the Jewish people in wealth and influence. Thus they awakened bitter resentment among those whose religious interests were outweighed by other considerations. The fanaticism of the stricter party made them poor politicians. Foreign rulers would naturally prefer to have in power men who were more pliant and friendly. The moral strictness and the racial separativeness of the pious handicapped them financially, and they were usually, therefore, among the middle or lower classes and would with difficulty maintain their status, being always in danger of falling lower and lower in the economic and social scale.

The classes which were economically and socially higher were much more open to the seductions, first of Persian, and then of Greek civilization. The disadvantage of the strict observance of Ezra's laws seemed to fall heaviest upon them. The poor found it easier to keep themselves clear of foreign influences, for exotic civilization and luxuries cost money. Moreover, the upper classes were always inclined to enrich themselves at the expense of their poorer brethren, as Nehemiah discovered and as Zechariah and Malachi bear witness.[57] Thus the poor and the righteous tended to fall into one class, the rich and the wicked into another. All during the period when the Psalms were being written, down to Maccabean times, this situation continued. With few exceptions the occasional pictures which the historical works give us show the richer Jews conforming to the civilizations around them, while the lower and middle classes were inclined to remain true to their ancestral faith and their national customs. The true servants of God were, therefore, so often poor that pious and poor seem to us to be used almost interchangeably.

The stricter party had more than one reason for regarding themselves as the true people of God. First, they had truly taken the

[57] Neh. 5.1-5; Zech. 7.10; Mal. 3.5.

prophetic message to heart, which, for them, meant that they were ardently devoted to God's Law. The nation had suffered endless misery, according to the prophets, because of the hard-heartedness, the stiff-neckedness, the disobedience of the fathers. Therefore the pious of the post-exilic period bow themselves before the divine will. Their pride and disobedience should not again bring the nation into danger of his wrath. They are, accordingly, the humble, the teachable. The word *'ânâw,* "humble," which they often use as a self-designation, does not describe one who is servile in the presence of men, nor one who is afflicted or bowed down by external circumstances, or even an inner sense of guilt, but rather one who voluntarily humbles himself before God. In this sense the pious poor and oppressed were also the humble, and "humble" becomes almost a synonym for "pious," or for "poor." Various other terms emphasizing this meekly receptive attitude are used to describe these pious, God-fearing folk. They are once called the "quiet in the land," reminding one of the "silent" who prayed to Amon in faith that the Lord of Truth would hear and speak for them.[58] They are the "broken and contrite of heart," the "broken in spirit," those who "wait for Yahweh."[59] The passage quoted in Luke's gospel from the latter part of Isaiah as describing Jesus' ministry is particularly significant in its combination of various expressions to characterize those who are to hear the prophetic message.[60] The variety and frequency of words which describe the faithful as silent before God, as waiting for him, and longing for him, show how inevitably the attitude of humble teachableness passed over into one of absolute social and political quietism.[61]

Their poverty and persecutions, in the second place, convinced the pious that they were God's chosen people. According to accepted Hebrew theology, peace and prosperity ought to mark all God's true followers. Making a virtue of necessity, the pious poor

[58] Ps. 35.20. See above, p. 253 f.

[59] Ps. 34.18; 51.17; 109.16; 147.3; Is. 57.15.

[60] Is. 61.1 f.; Lk. 4.18. Cf. Is. 42.2 ff.; Mt. 12.19 f.

[61] Is. 8.17; 30.18; 64.4; Mic. 7.7; Ps. 25.3, 5, 21; 27.14; 33.20; 37.7, 9; 39.7 f.; 40.1; 52.8; 62.1, 5; 69.3, 6; 130.4 ff.

transmuted their disability into a glorious epithet of praise by developing the doctrine that God's chastening was a sign of his love. It is in the Septuagint, and not in the Gospels, that the Greek word for "beggar," πτωχός, is first ennobled, largely as a result of this doctrine. The conception of the Suffering Servant in Second Isaiah marks a long step in the progress of this theology for the unsuccessful. But perhaps the chief reason for the growth of this peculiar Jewish idea was the belief, which we have been following thru its many ramifications in the literature of the Near East, that the poor are peculiarly under the divine protection. The idea had been implicit in the thinking of countless generations of poor folk. It was a part of the atmosphere of the ancient world. It had been accorded written expression in most emphatic language in all the divinely inspired literature of the Hebrew race. Small wonder that the poor and persecuted, but pious and law-abiding, Jew of the Persian and Greek periods was confident that he had a special claim upon the divine favor. The fact that he could say, "I am poor and needy" (*'ânî we-'ebyôn*) constituted a requisition upon God's care which could not be denied. Poverty and need were enough to open God's ears to any man's cry.[62]

In what sense there was a party of the poor, a sect, an *ecclesiola in ecclesia,* it is difficult to say. Since the poor are so often mentioned in the Psalms, and on the assumption that the Psalter was largely the work of the Levites who chanted its hymns in the Temple services, it has been concluded that we have to do with a party of Levites, who suffered under the oppression and exploitation of the rich high-priestly families.[63] It seems a probable assumption, but it is only an assumption. That there must have been Levites among them one cannot deny, but how large a number were of this calling cannot be determined from the known data. Some who deny that the poor were a Levitical party still insist that the term is a party epithet like *Chasid* or *Chaber.* In this case the Hebrew words for poor must have passed thru the same evolution as the Arabic *faqîr,* which, starting as "poor," has

[62] Ps. 40.17 = 70.5; 86.1; 109.22.

[63] So Causse, *Les "pauvres" d'Israel,* pp. 95 f.

come to mean also a member of a dervish order, not to mention its farther development into "faker." The word *'ebyôn* has passed thru exactly such a history in coming to be the favorite designation of non-catholic Jewish Christians. But if there was a party which called itself by such a name in pre-Christian times, it must have used interchangeably the Hebrew words, *'ebyôn, dâl,* and *'ânî,* for all appear in parallelism in the Psalms. Such a procedure is extremely improbable, and therefore it seems to me that the "party of the poor" under that designation should disappear from the descriptions of Jewish society.

One cannot deny that there were groups with some cohesion and permanence centering around this or that leader, as in the dervish orders of Islam. Indeed, it is not to be doubted that there was a party, persisting thru generations, that made use of the various terms under discussion as partisan shibboleths and regarded itself as the true Israel of God, while it decorated its opponents, the priestly aristocracy which ruled the nation, with epithets of execration. But it need not be supposed that all the inhabitants of Judea or all the Jewish population of Palestine were divided between the two parties. There must have been a large number, doubtless a majority, of the peasantry and proletariat who were as sheep having no shepherd. They were the "people of the land'" the *'ammê hâ-'âres,* of the Talmud. Since the aristocratic rich who were in power collected taxes from the people and secured their wealth largely at their expense, any opposition party which made capital of the oppression of the poor would attract the sympathy and support of the great mass of the population. This does not mean that the poor were pious any more than they had been in Jeremiah's day, but rather that the pious, who were also poor, had interests in common with the lower classes and that both, by force of circumstances, were thrown into opposition to the aristocratic, wealthy, and culturally liberal party.

In post-exilic Judaism there were, then, two parties which in periods of stress came into violent opposition. The historical records reveal them especially in the time of Nehemiah and again in the Greek period. The Hellenists and the Chasids, the Sadducees and the Pharisees, are their later representatives. The open-minded, forward-looking group, who were ready to adopt foreign ideas, unfortunately went so far as to be willing to give up what was distinctive of the Jewish religion. Being priests in a sacerdotal state, they present the anomally, unfortunately not otherwise unknown, of an ecclesiastical leadership which abandoned its religious principles while it used its position to exploit the people. It was inevitable that they should hate and persecute the opposition party which thwarted their plans, challenged their leadership, and denounced their wickedness and oppression. The party of the pious sometimes included priests. Simon the Just may serve as an outstanding example. Many may have been Levites. There is no reason why the majority, like Nehemiah, may not have been laymen. They were zealous, doubtless over-zealous, for the law of God, and partly on that account, they were scorned, defamed, and persecuted. For the same reason also they were unable to win for themselves an economic competence, for the law forbade the contacts with the heathen and the unbrotherly practices by which their opponents became rich. Conditions made them the natural leaders of the middle and lower classes in opposition to the aristocratic party. Moreover they not only delighted in calling themselves holy and righteous, lovers of the Law, men that feared God, but also poor, needy, afflicted, humble, making these terms party cries.

From men of this party came no small number of the Psalms as well as other portions of the literature of post-exilic Judaism. In consequence, Hebrew literature as it came to be canonized and read in the synagog gave the words "poor and needy," "afflicted," "humble," a distinctly ethical coloring. They seem to belong to those who are righteous and God-fearing in contrast to the rich, the proud, the violent, who were represented as oppressors of men and contemners of God. Yet the words for "needy," "poor," and "afflicted," *'ebyôn, dâl, 'ânî,* never lose their economic meaning. The poverty of the pious was not fictitious; not every rich man was wicked, nor every poor man righteous. However, so large a proportion of the righteous were poor that both qualities belonged to the word, while the rich and the powerful, those who enjoyed the good things of life, had been so often denounced in both the prophets and the Psalms that the very word "rich" carried with it a connotation of wickedness. Still another connotation belongs to the word *'ânî*. The basic meaning of the word is "afflicted," "oppressed," and the afflictions of the people had so often been due to the oppressions of the rich and the proud, that the word always carries with it this atmosphere of injustice and oppression. It must not be forgotten that this ethical coloring was in no small measure due to the idea widely prevalent in the ancient Near East that the poor and helpless were especially under the protection of the gods, who would eventually intervene to see justice done. The evidence does not lead to the conclusion that any of the words used in the Psalms to designate or describe the party of the pious ever became a party name. There may have been a poor man's party, but there was no "party of the poor." [64]

4. *The Attitude of the Scribes and Rabbis*

In the present state of uncertainty as to the date of many of the Psalms, it is impossible to determine definitely to what periods belongs the party strife which they so vividly suggest. Doubtless some of them belong to the period of rapid Hellenization just before the Maccabean war. Strangely enough, there are no documents of this conflict which can be confidently dated to that time, while those which probably or certainly belong here do not show traces of it. Such are Daniel, Judith, Tobit, and especially the Wisdom of Jesus son of Sirach. Between 200 B.C. and 100 A.D. the Hellenizing tendencies of many Jews, the attempt of Antiochus Epiphanes to Hellenize the nation by force, the early successes and the final abject deterioration of the Maccabees, and then the Roman conquest with its complete frustration of the national hopes, introduced a bitterness into much of the literature peculiar to this period, the apocalypses, which cannot be paralleled in the Psalter. The apocalypses record the aspirations and the disappoint-

[64] In this I take distinct issue with Causse, *Les "pauvres" d'Israel.*

ments of those who were ardently waiting for the consolation of Israel during this period when the civilization of the West was more and more distinctly threatening to blot out the "chosen people" and their religion. Probably some of the literature of this period, such as Daniel, the original Testaments of the Twelve Patriarchs, and the two Books of Maccabees, were too deeply concerned for the nation to note any party strife within it. They may indeed have been written when the common danger was so great that party differences were forgotten or when, as under John Hyrcanus, just government left no serious cause for complaint.

Yet during this period which seemed to the apocalyptists so evil that they believed God could no longer endure its iniquity, but must intervene, as he had once done in the Flood, to destroy all the workers of unrighteousness, we discover a new group arising, the scribes, who found in the study of the Law a way of escape from the evils of the world. While they were zealous for the faith of the fathers, none more so, many of them found some means of rising above the group of the poor and oppressed or evading its disabilities. Some of them doubtless were priests or Levites. Some probably came from among the small landholders; they were perhaps children of village sheikhs, or judges, and knew the legal precedents and the oral wisdom current in middle-class circles. It was such men in part who had collected the gnomic sayings of Israel and Egypt into the Book of Proverbs. For them poverty was the result of slackness; it was God's punishment on drunkenness, gluttony, and late sleeping. Still, they echo the phrases of the prophets with regard to the oppression of the poor and needy and most earnestly commend justice and benevolence. The poor present an opportunity for the wise and just to serve God and earn his commendation. Proverbs doubtless represents the commonly accepted standards of society at their highest level.

Jesus ben Sira may be taken as a representative of the new class of scribes in the Hellenistic age. He stands in succession to the wise men of Israel who had written her proverbs. In their spirit he looks upon wealth as good. It is the reward of temperance and industry.[65] Riches bring anxiety and sleeplessness, yet

> "Gold and silver will make the foot stand sure."
> "Riches and strength will lift up the heart."[66]

Ben Sira fully recognizes the disadvantages under which the poor man suffers. He pities him and decries the oppression which he must endure. He believes that God hears the prayer of the poor and that the lowly will eventually be raised up, if he is also wise, that is, doubtless, if he has learned wisdom of the scribe.[67] Ben Sira can write passages of almost prophetic fervor. God is a judge, he tells us, who will not respect persons and especially will not respect anyone's person against a poor man. He hears the prayer of him that is wronged and does not despise the supplication of the orphan and the widow. The prayer of the humble pierces the clouds. God will judge righteously. He will not be slack nor long-suffering till he have crushed the loins of the unmerciful and taken vengeance on the heathen, till he have taken away the multitude of the haughty and broken in pieces the scepters of the unrighteous.[68]

Yet it is a complacent and supercilious sympathy he bestows on the unfortunate lower classes. Take one of the many passages in which he contrasts the rich and the poor:

> "What peace is there between a hyena and a dog?
> And what peace between the rich and the poor?
> The prey of lions are wild asses in the wilderness,
> So the pastures of the rich are the poor.
> An abomination to a haughty man is lowliness,
> So an abomination to a rich man is a poor man.
> When a rich man is shaken he is held up by his friends,
> But when a lowly man falls he is thrust away by his friends.
> When a rich man is fallen there are many helpers,

[65] Chap. 13.24; 19.1.
[66] Chap. 31.1; 40.25, 26.
[67] Chap. 21.5; 4.1-10, 10.30-11.1.
[68] Chap. 35.12-18.

He says unmentionable things and men justify him:
A lowly man falls, and men rebuke him;
He utters wisdom, and no attention is given him." [69]

For ben Sira the study of the Law is the one occupation that is worthy of the true Israelite. He approves of agriculture and recognizes the value of various crafts. After describing the work of the farmer, the signet maker, the smith, the potter, he says:

"Without them a city shall not be inhabited,
Nor men sojourn nor go about their business therein."
"They will maintain the fabric of the world's life,
And their prayer is in the work of their hands."

But all these workmen have no leisure for the acquisition of wisdom. They toil and sweat for long hours and never are sought in the council of the people.

"Not so he who applies his soul
And meditates in the Law of the Most High.
He will seek out the wisdom of the ancients
And occupy himself with prophecies."
"Many shall praise his understanding."
"His name shall live from generation to generation." [70]

The scribe had inherited the social standards and moral ideals of former generations, and the good within him responded to their natural appeal. But the point of interest had shifted from present problems to an ancient literature. His heart was not fired by the sight of wrong and injustice. It warmed only at the acute and subtle interpretation of the Law.

The attitude of ben Sira seems to have been that also of the scribes and rabbis of Jesus' day. It is set forth with appropriate quotations from the Talmud by Abrahams in a chapter on "Poverty and Wealth" in his first series of *Studies in Pharisaism and the Gospels.* In the Talmud "there is no cult of poverty, neither is there a cult of wealth." Some of the rabbis were rich, the majority were poor. Many of them had been or were laboring men.

[69] Chap. 13.18-22.
[70] Chap. 38.24-39.9.

Their emphasis on the duty of every Israelite to learn a trade is well known. Neither asceticism nor luxury was the rabbinic ideal, but a life of moderation and "calm joyousness." He is really rich who rejoices in his lot. Wealth may easily become an evil. "The more wealth, the more care," said Hillel, who had been so poor that he worked for half a dinar a day. To some men God sends riches as a test of character. They become an evil if made an instrument of oppression or if their possession leads to neglect of the Law. Yet wealth is a necessary part of the divine order, else who would give alms? The rich maintain the order of the world by turning their possessions to the service of their fellows. The rich support the poor, the poor support the world. There must be poor people, else how could any one perform the loving kindness of truth? To be sure, too many of the rabbis had been poor for them to idealize poverty as have so many Christian exegetes. They quoted the saying of Proverbs 15.15, "All the days of the poor (*'ânî*) are evil," and added, "Ben Sira said, 'The nights also. The lowest roof is his roof, and on the highest hill is his vineyard. The rain off (other) roofs (falls) on his roof, and the soil from his vineyard on (other) vineyards,' " a trenchant saying not found in our copies of ben Sira. "Poverty in the house of a man is more distressful than fifty plagues." Its sufferings are so intense that they save a man from Gehinnom. Yet poverty is not the worst of evils. "There is no poverty but poverty of mind." Poverty might be necessary if one would follow the highest ideals.

> "This is the path to the Torah: A morsel with salt shalt thou eat, thou shalt drink water also by measure, and shalt sleep upon the ground, and live a life of hardship, and labor in the Torah. If thou doest this, happy shalt thou be and it shall be well with thee." [71]

The real evils, or dangers, of poverty were that a man might complain against God or be hindered in the study of the Law. Poverty, like wealth, was sent by God, not necessarily as a punishment for sin, but as a test of character. In either case God chose the fitting test and it was not for man to complain.

[71] Mishnah, *Aboth,* vi. 4. Cf. *Baba Qama,* 92a.

The great difference between the rabbis and the prophets lies in the rabbinical emphasis on charity. The complacency of the argument that there must be poor and rich in order that works of charity may be performed as God has enjoined is anything but attractive. We much prefer the prophetic demand for justice. Yet one cannot but admire the careful organization and regulation of charity by the rabbis, who went far beyond the Law itself in providing for the needs of the poorer members of the Jewish community.[72] Their practical good sense is seen in such laws as the so-called *prosbul* of Hillel, by which it was made possible for needy borrowers to secure loans even tho the Sabbatical year was near.[73]

The rabbis also did not forget that God demanded justice and protection for the weak. As Katz has shown, "the religious principles of justice and righteousness advocated by the prophets were duly and zealously upheld by the scribes and rabbis and by them duly incorporated into the Talmudic codes."[74] The rabbinic interpretations of the laws of the Old Testament were intended to render more effective their provisions for the protection of the poor and to adapt them to changed conditions. They provided legislation on behalf of skilled and unskilled laborers, Jewish and non-Jewish slaves, minors, women, debtors, and tenants, and ordered for each Jewish community a committee to collect and distribute poor-relief, besides enforcing the Old Testament regulations with regard to the gleanings of the fields and vineyards and the giving of the tithe of every third year to the poor. Tho the rabbis adjusted their standards to developing commerce and industry, they tried to prevent profiteering and even to exclude the middleman. If they did not protest against economic injustice in the impassioned language of the prophets, they nevertheless do show a sincere desire to protect the poor and helpless from the rapacity of the rich and the strong.[75]

[72] See G. F. Moore, *Judaism,* II, pp. 162-79.

[73] *Op. cit.,* I, pp. 259 f.

[74] *Protection of the Weak in the Talmud,* p. 84.

[75] Quoted largely from article, "The Beatitudes in the Light of Ancient Ideals," *JBL,* XLVI (1927), 57 f. Cf. also, Moore, *op. cit.,* II, pp. 180-83.

It is clear, therefore, that one does not do justice to the scribes and rabbis if he indiscriminately applies to them the words of Jesus that they had forgotten the weightier matters of the Law, justice, and mercy, and faithfulness, in tithing mint, dill, and cummin. There may have been many who honored the Old Testament laws and the prophetic exhortations more in the breach than in the observance, but they do not represent the true character of Judaism. Without unduly praising or blaming the rabbis, one may say two things: They had not by any means forgotten the rights of the poor. The refreshing stream of social justice had not suddenly disappeared in desert sands. Yet their enthusiasms were not those of the prophets and apocalyptists. They were not ardently longing and praying for divine judgment to right the social wrongs of their times. The fact that they were dealing with the practical problems of a Jewish community ruled by a foreign power necessarily limited their social interests and activities. Even more than this, their preoccupation with the *minutiæ* of scriptural exegesis and with legal technicalities blinded them to the social problems they should have attempted to solve. They were more concerned to put a hedge about the Law than to protect the poor.

5. *The Poor in the Apocalypses*

How different is the attitude of the rabbi and scribe from that of the apocalyptist? The scribe is calm, cool, and calculating, somewhat cynical withal, and disdainful alike of the hyena-like rich and the dog of a poor man. The apocalyptists are hot with indignation at injustice and evil, which rule the world. They long for the consolation of Israel with a poignancy born of bitter experience with the wrongs and oppressions of the mighty who control the affairs of this age. In wealth, pride, and power they see, not only the cause of misery and ungodliness, but their very essence.

At first sight it seems strange that little of the literature which breathes this spirit comes from the second century before Christ, if the Psalms be excepted, and little from the first century of our era, if the gospels and the teachings of Jesus be not included. The explanation, possibly, is that Daniel and those portions of Ethiopic Enoch which belong to the earlier period, and the apocalypses of Ezra and Baruch in the second are so deeply concerned with the national salvation that all internal social problems and party struggles are forgotten. Books like Jubilees and 1 and 2 Maccabees reflect the happy and prosperous years of good government under the earlier Maccabees. But the books which have been assigned to the years of misgovernment and civil strife under Alexander Jannaeus, Hyrcanus and Antipater, Herod, and the Roman governors, the period for a century before the birth of Jesus, reveal all the bitterness of the Psalms, with added nuances of unrestrained vindictiveness.

All of the books which manifest this spirit appear to have come from a pious, conservative, legalistic party in Judaism who are in opposition to the party in power, which was latitudinarian, irreligious, and oppressive. It is the conflict between Chasids and Hellenists, between Pharisees and Sadducees, that they portray. On the whole it is a conflict between a popular party which claims to stand for the poor and the oppressed and an aristocratic party which enriches itself by misgoverning and exploiting the people, almost exactly the same party division which has already been discovered in the Psalter.

The Testaments of the Twelve Patriarchs, which in their original form are attributed to an ardent adherent of the Maccabean dynasty in the reign of John Hyrcanus, represents much the same point of view as Proverbs and Ecclesiastes. The writer had a simple agricultural ideal of life.[76] Riches and unseemly and wicked luxury belong together; the good man will avoid both. Wealth easily becomes a means of injustice and oppression.[77] There is none of the prophetic bitterness against injustice. Charity toward the poor, the needy, the weak, and the oppressed is repeatedly urged, but there is no excoriation of their oppressors.[78]

[76] See above, p. 151 f.

[77] T. Benj. 6.2 f.; T. Dan. 3.4; T. Ash. 2.8.

[78] T. Iss. 3.8; 5.2; 7.5; T. Ash. 2.5 f.; T. Jos. 3.5; T. Benj. 4.4.

In one quaint and vigorous passage, however, the author shows a fine discrimination as to moral values and a keen sense of social evils. Almsgiving, fasting, and keeping the laws as to foods, he insists, cannot compensate for stealing, dealing unjustly, plundering, defrauding one's neighbor, and swearing falsely.[79]

A very different spirit rules the Similitudes of Enoch (1 Enoch 37-71) and the Exhortations, or Book of the Two Ways (1 Enoch 91-104), the Psalms of Solomon, the Book of the Covenanters of Damascus, and the Assumption of Moses. The authors of these writings are confident that wealth and wickedness are synonymous. The wicked who are to be given over to the sword, according to the Damascus Covenanters, "have made themselves strong with a view to wealth and unjust gain." In the stubbornness of their hearts they have cast off restraint with a high hand to walk in the ways of the wicked, to drink the poison of the kings of the Gentiles and the venom of the kings of Javan.[80] In other words they were the progressive, Hellenizing party. There are three nets of Belial, fornication, the wealth of wickedness, and the pollutions of the sanctuary. Twice elsewhere the Covenanters refer to the "wealth of wickedness." [81] The Book of Jubilees makes the same charge against the Hellenizing priesthood.[82] Ethiopic Enoch speaks of "sinfully acquired wealth," and "unrighteous gain," which cannot help one in the fires of Sheol.[83] A few years before Jesus denounced the scribes who "devour widows' houses and for a pretense make long prayers," the Assumption of Moses makes charges, apparently against the Sadducees, that they were destructive and impious rulers who say they are just, "devourers of the goods of the poor, saying that they do so on the ground of their justice, but really to destroy them."[84] On the other hand, according to the Covenanters of Damascus,

[79] T. Ash. 2.5-8.
[80] Zadok. Frag. 9.17-20.
[81] *Ibid.*, 6.10; 8.12; 9.14.
[82] Chap. 23.21.
[83] 1 En. 103.5; 63.10.
[84] Chap. 7.3, 6.

"They that give heed to (the messiah) are the poor of the flock. They shall escape during the period of visitation, but the rest shall be handed over to the sword when the messiah comes."[85]

The same sense of a division of the nation into rich and wicked on the one hand, and righteous and poor on the other pervades Ethiopic Enoch, especially the two sections which date from the early part of the first century before Christ. It is difficult to determine from what class of society the authors of these writings came, but it is clear that they did not belong to the master-class. They who are God's favorites are referred to as holy, elect, righteous, they that cleave unto the Lord, and call upon his name. On the other side are the sinners, the evildoers, the ungodly, the unrighteous, those who deny the Lord of Spirits. Such general epithets throw no light on the moral standards or the social ideals of the writers. But one group of expressions makes the class consciousness of the writer of the Similitudes perfectly plain. He refers again and again to "the kings, the mighty, the exalted," to "the kings, the mighty, and them who possess the earth," as those whom God will relentlessly punish.

In the later section called the Book of Exhortations, we find a description of the "two ways," the way of the righteous and the way of the wicked. The two groups are so sharply contrasted and so clearly described that their chief characteristics are plain. The righteous are represented as saying,

"In our troubled days we have toiled laboriously and experienced every trouble,
And met with much evil and been consumed,
And have become few and our spirit small."

"We hoped to be the head and have become the tail:
We have toiled laboriously and had no satisfaction in our toil;
And we have become the food of the sinners and the unrighteous
And they have laid their yoke heavily upon us."[86]

Other passages tell how the righteous are persecuted, afflicted, and oppressed by the mighty. Those who exploit, oppress, and de-

[85] Zadok. Frag. 9.10.
[86] 1 En. 103.9, 11.

stroy them are in favor with their rulers, who aid and abet the wicked, instead of defending the innocent. The little book draws a picture of a group of pious folk who are trying to live according to the laws of God, but, instead of reaping the fruits of their righteousness, are toiling in vain for the good things of the earth, while the wicked prosper.

Yet in spite of their unhappy lot, their confidence in God is unshaken. The day is surely coming when there will be a complete reversal of present conditions. The woes pronounced upon the wicked are important both because they reveal the mind of the writer and his party and because they often resemble those which Jesus pronounced upon the unrighteous. We may quote only a few of the most striking:

"Woe to you, ye rich, for ye have trusted in your riches,
And from your riches shall ye depart,
Because ye have not remembered the Most High in the day of your riches."

"Woe unto you, ye sinners, for your riches make you appear like the righteous,[87]
But your hearts convict you of being sinners,
And this fact shall be a testimony against you for a memorial of your evil deeds.

Woe to you who devour the finest of the wheat,
And drink wine in large bowls,
And tread under foot the lowly with your might."

"Woe to you, ye mighty,
Who with might oppress the righteous;
For the day of your destruction is coming."

"Woe to you who build your houses through the grievous toil of others,
And all their building materials are the bricks and stones of sin;
I tell you ye shall have no peace."

[87] That is, it appears as if God were prospering them because of their righteousness.

"Woe to them who work unrighteousness and help oppression,
And slay their neighbors until the great day of judgment." [88]

As a result of their identification of the rich, the proud, and the wicked on the one hand, and the poor, the humble, and the righteous on the other, Jewish apocalyptists gave a peculiar reinterpretation to the "hope of the poor." The basic idea was that God would punish the wicked, no matter how high they had risen.[89] All the ancient world, moreover, believed with Seneca that "an avenging god follows behind the proud," [90] or, as the Book of Proverbs has it, "Pride goeth before destruction and a haughty spirit before a fall." [91] All human pride must be laid low before Yahweh. [92] All the ancients also believed with Amenophis,

"Verily man is clay and straw,
God is his fashioner;
he pulls down and builds up each day,
he makes a thousand dependents at his will,
(or) he makes a thousand men into overseers (?)
when he is in his hour of life." [93]

As one of the Hebrew psalmists expressed it,

"God is judge,
He puts down one and raises another." [94]

There was another element which doubtless entered into this complex of associated ideas. In all ages men had rejoiced at the rise of the obscure poor man, the man of lowly birth, to power and authority.[95] The historical writers and psalmists of Israel had delighted in representing David as rising from the sheepfold to the

[88] 1 En. 94.8; 96.4, 5, 8; 99.13, 15.
[89] Ps. 52.5 ff.
[90] *Hercules furens,* II, 385. Cf. Is. 5.15 f.; 13.11.
[91] Chap. 16.18; cf. 11.2; Jer. 49.15 f.; Ob. 3, 4.
[92] Is. 2.9-17; 5.15.
[93] *Maxims,* 24.13-18, Griffith, *JEA,* XII (1926), 221.
[94] Ps. 75.7.
[95] See above, pp. 231 ff.

throne.[96] So a late author represents the messiah as coming into Jerusalem in lowly and peaceful guise, riding on an ass.[97] Various writers had emphasized the original obscurity and weakness of the Hebrew clans as a reason why God had chosen them. He could and would show his might by using instruments which were helpless in his hands and had no glory or power of their own.[98] Combined with the interpretation of trouble and suffering as a test of character or a penance for sin which, humbly and steadfastly endured, must be suitably recognized and rewarded, the idea enters into the Suffering Servant songs of Second Isaiah.

Again, as we have seen, there ran thru all the thinking of the ancient world the faith that in the Golden Age, or whenever the divine laws were in force, the poor man was as good as the rich man, the slave the equal of his master. The festival at the dedication of Gudea's temple suggests it,[99] as do also the harvest festivals of the Cronia at Athens and the Saturnalia at Rome, during which rich and poor, bond and free, feasted together, and the slave was even served by his master. The Hebrew prophets and apocalyptists had long pictured the new age for which they longed as exactly the opposite of the present. High hills would be made low, the deserts turned into springs of water. In Psalm 107.33-41 is a typical combination of these various ideas:

> "He turns rivers into a wilderness
> and springs of waters into arid desert,
> an oasis into a salt waste,
>   because of the wickedness of the inhabitants.
> He turns a wilderness into pools of water
> and dry land into springs of water,
> and there he settles the hungry
>   that they may build a city to dwell in,
>   and sow fields and plant vineyards
>   and gather the fruits of their increase.

[96] 1 Sa. 16.6-12; 18.18; Ps. 78.70.
[97] Zech. 9.9 f.
[98] Dt. 8, esp. vv. 3, 16 f.; Ps. 44.2 f., 105.12 f.; Hos. 1.7; Zech. 4.6.
[99] See above, pp. 191 f.

And he blesses them so that they multiply greatly
 and their cattle do not diminish.
He pours contempt upon princes
and makes them wander in a pathless waste
till they grow few and are bowed down
 under restraint, adversity, and affliction.
But he lifts the needy up out of his woes
 and makes their families like a flock."

The Jewish apocalyptists went but a step farther, then, when they insisted that, as a preliminary to the new age, God would raise up the humble and abase the proud; he would enrich the poor and impoverish the rich.[100]

The party of the pious, therefore, having come to regard themselves as the true Israel, applied all these hopes and promises to themselves. Just because their opponents were rich and proud and powerful, God would pull them down. Just because they themselves were humble, despised, poor, and weak, God would raise them up. No mere equality with the rich and the powerful could satisfy them. The wicked rich, the oppressing rulers, must be fearfully punished, while the exploited poor, the suffering humble, must receive glorious compensation for all they had endured. The later portions of the Old Testament prophecies and Psalms were full of this hope.[101] The apocalypses of the first century before Christ go far beyond the canonical scriptures in the vehemence and vindictiveness of their language.

The pride of the mighty is soon to be brought low. Passage after passage in both of the first-century sections of the apocalypse of Enoch emphasizes this heartening message that the wicked will be overthrown and the righteous will be exalted.

"Woe to those who build unrighteousness and oppression
And lay deceit as a foundation;
For they shall be suddenly overthrown,
And they shall have no peace."

[100] Cf. 1 Sa. 2.1-10; Ps. 18.27; 147.6; Prov. 18.12; 29.23.

[101] Is. 35; 40.1-11, 27-31; 41.1-20; 49.24 ff.; 52.13-55.13; Ps. 37; 109; etc.

"Fear not the sinners, ye righteous;
For again will the Lord deliver them into your hands,
That ye may execute judgment upon them according to your desires."

"Be hopeful, ye righteous; for suddenly shall the sinners perish before you,
And ye shall have lordship over them according to your desires."

"Woe to you who love the deeds of unrighteousness: wherefore do ye hope for good hap unto yourselves? know that ye shall be delivered into the hands of the righteous, and they shall cut off your necks and slay you, and have no mercy upon you." [102]

The Similitudes of Enoch have been of especial interest to the students of the messianic idea because they present a "Son of man," an "Elect One," who forms the bridge apparently between the angelic Son of man of Daniel and the Son of man in the Synoptic Gospels. He is the judge who comes to vindicate the righteous and overthrow the wicked. Several passages refer to these mighty who are to be brought low.

"And this Son of Man whom thou hast seen
Shall put down the kings and the mighty from their seats,
And shall loosen the reins of the strong,
And break the teeth of the sinners."

"He shall be a staff to the righteous whereon to stay themselves and not fall,
And he shall be the light of the Gentiles,
And the hope of those who are troubled of heart."

"And all the kings and the mighty and the exalted and those who rule the earth
Shall fall down before him on their faces,
And worship and set their hope upon that Son of Man,
And petition him and supplicate for mercy at his hands.

Nevertheless that Lord of Spirits will so press them
That they shall hastily go forth from his presence,
And their faces shall be filled with shame,
And the darkness grow deeper on their faces.

[102] Chap. 94.6; 95.3; 96.1; 98.12.

And he will deliver them to the angels for punishment,
To execute vengeance on them because they have oppressed his children and his elect,
And they shall be a spectacle for the righteous and for his elect:
They shall rejoice over them,
Because the wrath of the Lord of Spirits resteth upon them,
And his sword is drunk with their blood." [103]

The spirit of these lines is too vindictive to be impressive: it is too full of impotent hate to be strong. Yet one cannot but sympathize with these honest, devoted people who felt that the future of the kingdom of God depended upon them. They were the seven thousand who had not bowed the knee to Baal, the remnant of whom the prophets had spoken, the chosen people to whom the promises belonged, for they were those who had not hardened their hearts, but bowed their spirits in contrition before their Maker. They were the flock of the poor: he was their Shepherd. Surely he must lead them beside still waters and restore their souls.

The spirit of the prophets, psalmists, and apocalyptists had not entirely departed from official Judaism, as the numerous enactments in the Talmud which we have noted prove. Important as coming from this very period is a passage from the Jerusalem recension of the Shemôneh-'esrêh, the Eighteen Benedictions. The second prayer contains this ascription of praise to God:

"Mighty art thou, abasing the proud,
Strong and judging the ruthless." [104]

The Psalms of Solomon insist that God is gracious and merciful, the hope and refuge of the poor; he is gracious and gentle to rejoice the soul of the lowly by opening his hand.[105] Yet the great apocalyptic psalm (17), which so beautifully portrays a non-warlike messiah, contains no reference to the poor. Both the Eighteen Benedictions and the Psalms of Solomon are full of poignant longing for the reign of God, yet they have little to

[103] 1 En. 46.4, following Charles' emendation; 48.4; 62.9-12.
[104] Burney, *Poetry of Our Lord,* Oxford, 1925, p. 163.
[105] Chap. 5.2, 13 f.; 10.7; 15.2; 18.3.

say of the great reversal of the social classes. The overthrow of Israel's enemies they confidently expect, but they do not pray for the elevation of the poor and the weak.

In such apocalyptic writings as the Similitudes and the Exhortations of Enoch there is a spirit that differs *in toto* from that revealed in Pirqe 'Abôth, the Eighteen Benedictions, and the Psalms of Solomon, which may be regarded as products of official Judaism and the party of the Pharisees. They show, not cool calculation, reasoned argument, and seasoned common sense, such as one discovers in the Mishna, but profound and bitter hate, enthusiastic loyalty, and ardent hope. Was Jesus a rabbi or an apocalyptist? The alternative, put thus baldly, is manifestly unfair. But there can be little doubt as to which group he more closely resembles. He follows in the train of the prophets, the psalmists, and the apocalyptists who had proclaimed deliverance to the bound, who had preached good tidings to the afflicted.

There is every reason to say, with Causse, that the apocalypses which we have been quoting were "the popular books of edification of the time, the books which people read at Nazareth, at Capernaum, and at Bethsaida, when Jesus was a child."[106] All this being so, we can understand the ardent hopes with which the common people of Galilee received the proclamation of John and of Jesus that the kingdom of God was at hand. We can understand too with what joy the poor, humble folk who made up the persecuted bands of early Jewish Christians sang such songs as the Magnificat:

"He has done a mighty deed with his arm;
He has scattered the proud with the evil purposes of their hearts.
He has put down princes from their thrones,
And he has exalted the lowly.
The hungry he has filled with good things,
And the rich he has sent away empty."

For it was written in the Book of Enoch in the seventh generation from Adam,

[106] *Les "pauvres" d'Israel,* p. 139.

"See! The Lord comes with his holy myriads
to execute judgment upon all
and to destroy all the ungodly,"

and likewise.

"Be hopeful; for aforetime you were put to shame thru ill and affliction;
but now you shall shine as the lights of heaven,
you shall shine and you shall be seen,
and the portals of heaven shall be opened to you."[107]

[107] 1 En. 1.9 = Jude 14 f.; 1 En. 104.2.

CHAPTER X

THE SON OF DAVID AND THE SON OF MAN

How did the social and ethical developments which in the preceding chapters have been sketched at length, and yet inadequately, affect the task which Jesus set himself to accomplish? To answer this question we must ask another. What was that task? The answer to this question involves a survey of the political, social, and religious conditions which Jesus faced. With the situation clearly defined we shall be in a position to interpret the Gospel statements as to Jesus' aim and as to the methods by which he attempted to realize it.

The variety of answers which Jesus received when he asked his disciples what the popular opinions about him were is indicative of the uncertainty that prevailed in the minds of his contemporaries as to his purpose. As a previous chapter indicated to satiety, there seems hardly to be less division of opinion today. The two titles most frequently applied to Jesus in the Synoptic Gospels epitomize the difficulty Jesus had in making his meaning clear. The variety of parties and opinions and the complexity of the social situation in his day were the causes of the misunderstanding and opposition from which he suffered and they are partly the cause of our modern difficulties in understanding him. The subsequent developments of Christian theology have added tremendously to an already complicated problem. To forget his theology is one of the most important, as it is one of the most difficult, tasks of the modern historical student as he approaches the problem of Jesus. The *sine qua non* of success is that one immerse himself in the historical situation of Jesus' time. Insofar as he does that, he will approximate a true answer to the old question of Jesus, "Who do you say that I am?" We turn first to the political situation.

the foundations for the "fourth sect," as Josephus names them, the revolutionaries who were eventually to bring on the Jewish War. After the revolt against the census, so far as our records go, serious difficulties disappear for a time.

There is apparent reason for the comparative quiet of the next quarter of a century—just the period when Jesus was growing to manhood. It cannot be supposed that the Roman governors and their dependent kinglets were inhumanly oppressive. The imperial rule in the provinces was infinitely better than that of the Roman oligarchy commonly called the Republic. Under the latter, the proconsul and the host of dependents who followed him were under the necessity of recouping their fortunes in the single year of office allowed. They had no concern for the welfare of the subject peoples they exploited. The stories of Verres, Scaptius, and even of Cicero's own year in Cilicia are excellent illustrations of a calculated robbery which the Spaniards in the New World could hardly equal.[2] The emperor, with his own future and that of his dynasty in mind, had a purely selfish interest in the development and permanent productivity of every part of the empire. And Augustus applied his remarkable organizing ability to the task of perfecting the machinery by which the provinces might be sanely, profitably, and continuously exploited. This involved so governing that there should not be expensive rebellions and other disturbances to interfere with business and the collection of taxes. The emperors often remitted taxes and made gifts to aid areas stricken with famine or other disasters. They were not insusceptible to flattery and preferred that people speak well of them. Some of them were moved by natural feelings of kindliness and a sense of duty. Particularly Augustus must be credited with real magnanimity, and there can be little doubt that Tiberius was not so bad as his prejudiced biographer, Tacitus, has painted him. The attention which, according to Josephus, the emperors gave to the Jewish complaints against Herod, Archelaus, and Pilate, is evidence that the feelings of subject peoples were considered and

[2] For a fine picture of Roman exploitation see Cicero's letter to Atticus, VI, 1, 16. Cf. V, 21.

that not a little thought and care were expended in seeing that justice was done.

According to Josephus there was much dissatisfaction during the procuratorship of Pontius Pilate. Agrippa, as quoted by Philo, gave him a most evil reputation for obstinacy, corruption, insolence, robbery, and inhuman cruelty.[3] Yet the actual counts in the indictment hardly substantiate the charges. To be sure, he more than once aroused the stoutest opposition on the part of the Jewish population. Yet the incident of the votive shields related by Philo and that of the Roman standards as told by Josephus[4] suggest obstinate, blundering, and tactless ignorance, rather than evil intention. In using the Temple treasures to provide water for Jerusalem he doubtless believed he was rendering the people a real service. According to Josephus' account in the *Jewish War*[5] the massacre which followed was due to the undue zeal of the soldiery, not to Pilate's orders. It does not require the brutality and stupidity of a Sarail to set an insurrection in motion. The well-meaning tactlessness of a Curzon is almost equally irritating, as India knows. Pilate, as it seems to me, is to be placed between the two, not absolutely brutal and stupid, but also not keen and skilful, not always sincere, nor above cupidity and ruthlessness. It can hardly have been due solely to the misgovernment, even of a Felix, a Cumanus, or a Florus that Judea saw a constant succession of insurrections and finally the desperate war that ended in the destruction of Jerusalem.

Certainly in Jesus' day there had been as yet no serious occasion for alarm on the part of the Jews. Jesus' reference to the Galileans whose blood Pilate had mingled with their sacrifice does not imply that they were regarded by his hearers as martyred saints, but rather as desperate sinners. Pilate's rule had only begun when Jesus died. Since the accession of Augustus the country had been much better governed than it had been under its own Maccabean kings. Nothing half so serious had occurred as during the civil

[3] Philo, *Leg. ad Caium*, 38.

[4] *Ant.* XVIII, 3, 1 = *War*, II, 9, 2 f.

[5] II, 9, 4 = *Ant.*, XVIII, 3, 2.

wars of the reign of Alexander Jannaeus. The desires of the Jews had been observed, somewhat tardily to be sure, in the deposition of Herod's son and successor in Judea, Archelaus. Antipas seems to have governed the revolutionary Galileans without serious opposition. When he was deposed after a reign of forty years, it was for no fault of his administration. Philip ruled the regions east of the Sea of Galilee for almost as long a period with no serious disturbances. Up to the time of Pilate, Josephus has nothing to record in Judea and Samaria but an occasional change of high priests and a not too rapid succession of procurators.

These years of comparative quiet are followed by a series of outbreaks culminating in the Jewish War. Mommsen well says that the war began, not in 66 A.D., but in 44 A.D., on the death of Herod Agrippa. It must be admitted that during those years the Jews were given repeated provocation to revolt, if Josephus has not seriously exaggerated. Some of the most serious disturbances were caused by Roman soldiers who took occasion to show their contempt for the people whom they were policing. More dangerous was the dissatisfaction caused by the cupidity, rapacity, and cruelty of the procurators Cumanus, Felix, Albinus, and Gessius Florus. Yet it can hardly be supposed that Palestine alone among the widespread provinces of the empire suffered from incapable or predatory governors. Tho Roman pride, obstinacy, and injustice played their part, more fundamental causes must have been at work to have occasioned the series of outbreaks which Josephus describes. As it seems to me, they are to be classed under two heads, economic and psychological difficulties.

II. THE ECONOMIC SITUATION

It has been supposed, especially by social radicals who have espoused economic determinism, that the fundamental causes of the difficulties from which the Jewish people were suffering were economic. This aspect of the case has too often been ignored by "regular" theologians, but not without reason. The data at present available with regard to economic conditions in Palestine in the first century of our era are not sufficient to make the situation entirely clear. The complaints of the prophets give us a more complete picture of the eighth century before Christ than we have of the first century after his birth. Recent studies, however, are beginning to clarify the problem.

We know that the reigns of Augustus and Tiberius were, on the whole, prosperous. All the data point to a general increase of commerce and wealth during the greater part of the century, in spite of occasional depressions due to famines, overexpansion, or other temporary misfortunes. Whereas there is definite evidence that prices were rising rapidly and the common people suffering seriously in the fourth and third centuries B.C., and we know there must have been widespread want during the period of the civil wars of the Republic, all the world seems to have taken a new lease on life with the accession of Augustus.

In Palestine, also, if we may judge by the archeological evidence, the Greek and Roman periods seem to have been times of expansion and prosperity. During this period the cities of the Decapolis came to their prime. They had extended the borders of cultivation two or three days journey beyond their present limits.[6] The stately ruins of Jerash (Gerasa), which are now being brought more fully to the light, are sufficient evidence of the wealth and culture of these cities in the second century. But some of them had long been important centers of Greek civilization. Strabo names four famous men of Gadara, the Cynic Menippus, the Epicurean Philodemus, the poet Meleager, and the rhetorician Theodore, the teacher of the Emperor Tiberius, all belonging to the three centuries before the birth of Jesus.

Perhaps even more significant are the cities west of the Jordan. Anthony thought Jericho a gift fit for Cleopatra. Three cities in the Maritime Plain and the Jordan Valley, Jamnia, Phasaelis, and Archelais, with their surrounding territories, were a worthy legacy for the Empress Julia, wife of Augustus.[7] Sebaste-Samaria, Askalon, and Caesarea Stratonis were among the cities which had

[6] Guthe, *Die grieschisch-römischen Städte des Ostjordanlandes,* pp. 6 ff.

[7] Josephus, *Ant.,* XV, 4, 2; XVIII, 2, 2.

arisen into new beauty thru the building enterprise of Herod. Many other cities, some of them apparently of no small importance, had been built by the Hasmoneans or Herod. Antipas rebuilt Sepphoris, which had been destroyed in the disturbances following Herod's death, and later erected for himself a magnificent new capital at Tiberias. The employment of from ten to eighteen thousand workmen on the Temple at Jerusalem—if we may trust Josephus' account—, workmen and the work supported by Herod's munificence and later by the Temple treasury, must have brought an increase in the economic activities of the Holy City such as would send a modern chamber of commerce into Babbitic ecstasies.[8] One cannot look at the beautiful drafting and magnificent stones of Herod's buildings in Jerusalem and Hebron or the colonnades of Sebaste and Askalon without feeling that the civilization which could produce such works was vigorous, dynamic, and self-consciously prosperous.

One can hardly accept at its face value the assertion of Josephus that in Galilee there were two hundred forty cities and villages, each with a population of at least 15,000.[9] Today the largest city in Galilee, Tiberias, has little more than half as many inhabitants, and the district all told only a few hundred thousand. Yet the archeological and historical evidence leaves no doubt that the population was far greater than it is now. The western shore of the sea was practically a continuous city, as the ruins testify. Sennabris with perhaps other cities lay at the southern end, a short distance north Hamath with its famous baths, then almost without a break Tiberias, Tarichaea, Magdala, perhaps Dalmanutha, Heptapegon, Capernaum, and Chorazin, the last a little back from the shore. There is a short space about the head of the lake which seems to have been unoccupied, but Bethsaida-Julias lay on the east side of the river. These cities were not unknown to international fame and to commerce. The fish that were pickled at Tarichaea and the baths of Hamath are mentioned by Pliny the Elder.[10] With the sails of countless fishing smacks dotting its

[8] *Ant.*, XV, 11, 2; XX, 9, 7.
[9] Combining *Vita*, 45, and *War*, III, 3, 2, as Josephus hardly intended.
[10] *Hist. nat.*, V, 15; cf. G. A. Smith, *Historical Geography*, p. 451.

surface, with the caravans of all nations thronging its markets, with thousands of people crowding its cities, the little sea, now so solitary, must have been the center of a vigorous and prosperous life in the days of Jesus.

The highlands west of the lake were equally busy. Their widespread plains and valleys provided a basis for rewarding agriculture. The trade routes that crossed Lower Galilee, from Damascus toward Egypt, from the fertile fields and growing cities of the Ḥaurân and the Decapolis to the ocean, to Caesarea, Haifa, Ptolemais, and Tyre, are evidence that it was in the full current of world commerce and culture. The tells which dot its surface are mute testimony to its departed glory. Unfortunately, almost no excavating has been done in Galilee, but the potsherds that sprinkle the surface of its mounds show that the greater portion of them were inhabited in Jesus' day. The many names which Josephus and the Talmud give us can be assigned in a large number of instances to their proper sites without uncertainty. The scattered references of Greek and Roman writers, the allusions of the Gospels to the multitudes that thronged Jesus, the accounts which Josephus has left us of his activities among these busy villages and cities during the Jewish War, the statements of the Talmud covering the first century, all point to a large population and an active and happy economic life.

Under these circumstances how could there have been such frequent and bitter revolts against Roman authority? People do not engage in riots and insurrections when they are busy, well fed, and happy. There must have been festering sores underneath the outward show of well-being. One needs but to step behind the beautiful façade of temples and forums built by Herod and his kind to discover the hovels of the poor out of whose sweated labor the appearance of prosperity was so vaingloriously created. The archaeological remains we have mentioned, temples, forums, theaters, stadia, are not all there was in the ancient city.

yes.

A road built in 1921 by Jewish *ḥallûṣîm* ("pioneers") along the shore of the Sea of Galilee between Tiberias and Magdala cut thru an ancient village of Roman times which, after it had fallen in ruins, had been covered by the earth washed down from the hill above. In the freshly cut bank one could see the rough walls of the little rooms that must have been the homes of the ancient lowly. One could almost span them with outstretched arms.[11] Wherever an ancient city has been excavated such buildings have been discovered, at Tell Sandaḥanneh, Gezer, Tell Ḥûm, at Athens itself. The life of the ancient poor, whether in village or in city, was meager beyond description.

The first century represents much the same stage of economic and social development as the twentieth. There had been the ancient period of art and commerce which we call the Mycenaean, or Aegean, civilization. It had been followed by the dark ages of migrations and the feudal period of Homeric times, the mediaeval period of commercial and industrial cities reaching its climax in the great days of Athens, and finally, after wars innumerable, an era of world commerce, of unlimited luxury, and of artistic, intellectual, and industrial development much like our own.[12] To be sure, certain of the most potent causes of economic injustice and maladjustment which the modern world suffers were lacking. Machinery had not brought about our absurd division of labor, extraordinary concentration of populations in manufacturing centers, nor tremendous centralization of wealth and power in the hands of the few. Yet to a certain extent the slave took the place of the machine. He was employed in great numbers in factories, on country estates, in mines, and on public works to develop an incipient mass production and to provide a condition of comfort for the well-to-do and luxury for the rich, very much as machinery does today. If that was not an age of machinery, it was an industrial and pre-eminently a commercial age. Business was the making of Alexandria, Corinth, Ephesus, and Rome.

It was, therefore, above all else an age of cities. They had attracted great hordes of former peasants, who thought to share in the joys of urban diversions and the wealth of urban commerce. The literary men of Greece and Rome constantly sing the praises

[11] Cf. Albright's description in the *Annual of the American School of Oriental Research in Jerusalem,* Vols. II and III (1921-22), 43.

[12] Cf. Eduard Meyer, *Kleine Schriften,* Halle, 1910, pp. 90-145.

of the country. Xenophon represents agriculture as the proper occupation of the gentleman, its management, rather than the actual holding of the plow.[13] Cicero says:

"Of all the means of acquiring gain, nothing is better than agriculture, nothing more productive, nothing more pleasant, nothing more worthy of a man of liberal mind."[14]

But this praise of the bucolic ideal was only a psychological compensation for their failure practically to promote country life. The country could not compete with the city either in pleasures and diversions or in opportunities of gain. All the graceful encomiums of the poets, the earnest exhortations of the moralists, and even the laws passed by emperor and senate could not keep either the rich or the poor in the country. The fulminations of a rhetorician like Dion Chrysostom, tho exaggerated, have a large element of truth. The country was being deserted and the cities crowded with idle citizens. Commerce was a path to wealth so much shorter and easier, even if less sure and safe, that landowners preferred to abandon their broad acres and remove to the city to engage in business. Land could be profitably used only as *latifundia,* large estates worked by slave labor under overseers, or stewards, or as small farms rented to *coloni,* tenants who lived in the direst poverty and squalor.

Various causes contributed to the abandonment of the country. Some have suggested that mosquitos and malaria played no small part in the decay of country life. It is quite probable that a progressive impoverishment of the soil was a large factor in producing the economic difficulties which the world then faced, for while the ancients understood the necessity and the methods of fertilization, they did not put their knowledge into practice.[15] Moreover, as Ferrero insists, the governments and rulers of the

[13] *Oec.,* IV, 2 and 4; V, 17; XV, 4 ff.

[14] *De off.,* I, 42. Cf. Mahaffy, *Silver Age of the Greek World,* pp. 326-38, 422 f., H. E. Barnes, *The New History and Social Studies,* p. 547; Simkhovitch, *Toward the Understanding of Jesus,* pp. 84-124, in the essay "Rome's Fall Reconsidered."

[15] Simkhovitch, *op. cit.,* pp. 84-139.

city states of antiquity always favored the city at the expense of the country, just because they lived in the cities.[16] They had to feed and amuse the rabble of the city. The peasants in the country could not gather under palace windows to cry for bread and circuses. Besides its natural economic drawing power, then, the city had the artificial advantage of its doles and the attractions of its pleasures and excitements, its busy market places, its theaters, its stadia, its circuses.

For a century or more before the period we are now discussing slave labor had offered a means of offsetting the economic disadvantages under which agriculture suffered. In Italy the former holdings of the Roman citizens who had been the mainstay of the early Republic were consolidated into *latifundia,* vast estates owned by senators and other capitalists of the cities and worked by slaves, a dozen to one hundred and sixty acres—human machinery that was almost as cheap as oxen and no more highly regarded. They were worked in gangs under overseers and shut at night into barracks, often underground.[17] Such cheap labor could partially overcome the handicap of impoverished soil. Other countries like Egypt, where the Nile annually brought new fertility and the soil was tilled by a serflike peasantry which from time immemorial had been accustomed to semi-slavery and semi-starvation, might appear to be going on prosperously. A new region recently subjected to cultivation, like the Ḥaurân and the Ledja, might also grow and prosper.[18] Yet even in Egypt there was deep-seated unrest and ardent hope of miraculous release from Roman oppression.[19]

How did a land like Palestine and an agricultural population such as the Jews fare in an empire where such conditions pre-

[16] *Ancient Rome and Modern America,* New York-London: Putnam, 1914, pp. 77-96.

[17] Woodhouse, art. "Slavery (Roman)," *ERE,* XI, p. 623; Fowler, *Social Life at Rome,* New York, 1910, pp. 217-22; Rostovtzeff, *Social and Economic History of the Roman Empire,* Oxford, 1926, pp. 61-65.

[18] Guthe, *Die griechisch-römischen Städte des Ostjordanlandes,* pp. 6 f., 36-41.

[19] See *HTR,* 18 (1925), 397-400; Rostovtzeff, *op. cit.,* p. 301.

vailed? Obviously, they were not prepared to fit happily into their niche in the new Golden Age which Augustus had created to suit the commercial and financial aspirations of the money aristocracy of Rome. By tradition, even by divine law, they were largely agricultural. Theirs was an ancient land. It had been farmed without scientific refertilization for over three thousand years.[20] The little Jewish peasant holdings in the mountains of Judea, and even in more fertile Galilee, were in no position to compete with the *latifundia* of Italy, the Nile-fed soil of Egypt, or the fresh acres of the Ḥaurân. The Jews of the Dispersion, living in great Hellenistic or Roman cities and engaging in business on a larger or smaller scale, were prepared to profit by the new commercial prosperity which the *pax Romana* had introduced. The well-to-do Jews of Jerusalem, Joppa, Sepphoris, and Tiberias likewise, who were not dependent on the land alone, but lived largely from trade or commerce, did not suffer. They profited also by the general tendency toward urbanization. But the artisan and the farmer, competing with the enormous slave labor of the Roman Empire, were necessarily reduced to the most serious straits. The empire truly had introduced an era of unheard-of prosperity thruout the whole Mediterranean basin. But prosperity following interminable wars does not necessarily benefit the lower classes, nor the nations which are unable to meet world competition. If we may judge by analogy from other similar situations, we must conclude that prices were rising; luxury and poverty were increasing together. The underprivileged suffer first in such eras of expansion and development. The Jews who remained in little Palestine, unless they had the advantage of wealth and position, were compelled to meet competition which was too strong for them. They had not only foreign competition to meet. They lived in the roughest and poorest part of the country; at their very doors, all around them, occupying the richest sections of their land, were Greek cities, such as Scythopolis and the other cities of the Decapolis in the rich land of Gilead, and Gaza, Askalon, and many more in the Maritime Plain. In resources the Jews were sadly handicapped.

[20] See above, Chap. II.

They suffered peculiarly from taxation. Above them was the power of Rome, concerned only to secure its taxes and promote business. If, following Tiberius' expressive dictum that "a shepherd does not flay his sheep, but only fleeces them," the Roman Empire improved upon the unbelievable rapacity of the Republic, the purpose was solely to prolong and increase the efficiency of the process of "fleecing." How deeply the Jews felt the burden of Roman taxation is shown by their complaints of Herod's exactions and their stout resistance to the census of Quirinius. But it cannot be supposed that Roman demands were relatively higher in Palestine than in other subject lands. The difficulty lay in the fact that the Jews suffered a double taxation. They labored under a handicap that is often ignored. The Temple dues, which scribal punctiliousness had fastened upon the people, must have been enormous. Two tithes each year, gifts, offerings, and sacrifices in addition, not only laid a heavy load upon the conscience, but constituted a burdensome levy upon the economic abilities of the pious, and they supported in idleness a great group of priests, so many, in fact, that two weeks in the year was the time required of each for actual service in the Temple, a service in itself morally valueless and religiously questionable. If they had served as pastors or teachers of the people, one might forgive something of their exactions, but those duties they had long ago shifted to the willing shoulders of the scribes.[21] The Jews, then, had to bear this heavy burden of religious taxation in addition to that imposed by the government. As Grant had recently pointed out, the extreme difficulty of their situation lay in the fact that each system of taxation was imposed without reference to the other, and each was calculated to extort from the people all they could possibly contribute. The tithes and offerings prescribed by the Law had originally been levied when the priests were also temporal rulers. Now the support of a greedy foreign government was super-

[21] Cf. C. G. Montefiore, *Lectures on the Origin and Growth of Religion as Illustrated by the Religion of the Ancient Hebrews,* 3d ed., 1897, pp. 473 f.; J. Jeremias, *Jerusalem zur Zeit Jesu,* II, A, pp. 13 f., 19-24.

imposed upon a taxation that was sufficiently burdensome in itself.[22]

The Jewish peasant, therefore, was in a peculiarly evil plight. One expression, found often in the Talmud, is taken by Christian scholars as typifying the social situation of the majority of the Jewish people, the phrase, *'am hâ-'âreṣ*. In the Talmud the *'ammê hâ-'âreṣ,* the "people of the land," are again and again placed in contrast to the Pharisees, the "brothers" of the rigorist group, and to the learned. The term was taken from the use of the Hebrew phrase in Ezra and Nehemiah to designate the inhabitants of the land of mixed ancestry who did not observe the Hebrew laws.[23] In the second century of our era it means the Jew who does not observe the rules as to tithing and ceremonial cleanness. There was a period when he was heartily despised by the rabbis and their pupils and reciprocated with an almost unlimited hatred. However, this second century group cannot be exactly identified with the common people who flock about Jesus. An *'am hâ-'âreṣ* might be rich as well as poor; he might be a priest or a Levite. Moreover, no first century rabbi speaks of this group in the scathing terms employed by second-century rabbis, and, so far as clear evidence is obtainable it appears that the laws which the "people of the land" are accused of disregarding in the second century were not yet fully developed, or at least applied to laymen, in the first century.

Yet Hillel, who bears the reputation of having been one of the mildest and kindest of the rabbis, said, "no uneducated man (*bôr*) fears to sin, and no *'am hâ-'âreṣ* is a saint (*ḥâsîd*)."[24] In other words, no Jew who was ignorant of or ignored the law could be truly pious. It may be safely affirmed that the separatist tendencies which come to such vigorous expression in the second century were already at work in the first. Owing, as Montefiore long ago pointed out, to the "burdensome agrarian and purity laws,"[25] there was arising a great group, doubtless including the

[22] See Grant, *The Economic Background of the Gospels,* pp. 92-104.
[23] Ezra 9.1, 11; Neh. 10.28-31.
[24] *Aboth,* II, 5 (6). But cf. Julius Boehmer in *JBL,* 44 (1926), 298-304.
[25] *Op. cit.,* p. 502.

majority of the common people, whom their more rigorous co-religionists placed outside the pale of the true Israel because they would not accept the new and stricter standards which scribal legalism was developing. Despised by those whom they regarded as their leaders, dragged hither and thither by impostors who arose to persuade them that God would now intervene to save them from their enemies and oppressors, they made up the great crowds upon whom Jesus "had compassion because they were mangled and prostrate as sheep having no shepherd." To this group belonged Jesus and his disciples, representing those who wished to love and serve God. At the other extreme were the publicans and sinners. They had sought escape from economic helplessness and the burdensome exactions of scribal rigorism by deserting their religion and their people. Over against them stood Pharisaic pride and self-righteousness, and in addition there was the injustice that devoured widows' houses, while for a pretense it made long prayers. Economic exploitation on the part of Rome was matched by grasping injustice on the part of the leaders of the nation.

If, therefore, we lack exact and extensive documentary evidence to prove that the peasantry of Palestine were suffering under serious economic disadvantages and injustices, yet the inferences legitimately drawn from the general economic situation in the Roman Empire and from conditions in Palestine itself justify the conclusion that the Jewish agricultural population and the poorer classes in general were far from fortunate. There were just grounds for the bitterest dissatisfaction on the part of the mass of the population, who not only suffered, but also saw before them no hope of improvement or escape, but rather progressive and inevitable enslavement.

Yet we cannot escape the further conclusion that other and less material causes were at work. If it had been purely a matter of political dissatisfaction or of economic disabilities, Greece or Egypt or Asia Minor would have had grounds for revolt against Rome. That the unrest which existed in these countries never succeeded in making itself seriously felt indicates the presence of other factors in the Jewish situation. In Palestine there were psychological causes at work which did not exist elsewhere.

III. THE PSYCHOLOGICAL PROBLEM

One may truly say that the problem of the Jewish people was largely psychological. Why could the Jew not accommodate himself to the new situation in which he found himself? Why did not the discontented move to the cities and seek the commercial prosperity that so many of their brethren of the Diaspora enjoyed? To no small extent it was the ideals of their fathers, the pattern ideas inherited from previous generations, that kept the faithful remnant in their own land and made it impossible for them to submit to the new economic and political situation.

Over against the wealth and luxury which the new world offered stood the old nomadic-agricultural ideal of democratic simplicity and manual labor. The hope of Israel was that every family should dwell under its own vine and fig tree with none to molest or terrify. How impossible to realize in a word of *latifundia,* villas, and Hellenistic cities! The stern repression of the desire for wealth and luxury, a desire as natural to Jews as to others, and the sense of inferiority due to economic failure necessarily worked a compensatory aversion for all of the culture that went with these rejected goods and for the people who were associated with them. The sense of frustration which the Jewish farmer felt, the absurd discrepancy between the ideal of life which his religion taught him and that which he could achieve, worked a dichotomy in his temper which was far from wholesome. The ordinary citizen accepted the Pharisaic ideal as theoretically right. Practically, he found it impossible to achieve. He stood self-condemned for sins he could not avoid. And the easy scape-goat was the foreign civilization which everywhere flaunted its power and wealth in his face and put its political and economic shackles upon him. It was not merely an economic, but also a cultural, problem. There is no inescapable contradiction between a relatively simple agricultural life and a large measure of intellectual and artistic development. It was the racial, moral, and religious concomitants of Greek civilization which made its intellectual and artistic elements anathema to the Jew. It seemed impossible to separate them. Yet many a Jew, on a visit to Sebaste or Scythopolis or Askalon, must have felt the superiority of Greek culture, *as culture,* and have departed with a haunting, bitter sense of inferiority. If he learned of Platonic philosophy and Stoic morality, he could either claim that they were borrowed or he could criticize their weakness in order to maintain for himself a superiority he secretly doubted. The inevitable outcome of this inferiority complex was that he should denounce the wickedness of the civilization he secretly or unconsciously admired.

Inherited racial and political ideals were equally fruitful in dangers. The national pride was fed by the familiar stories of the empire of David and Solomon and the military prowess of the Maccabees. A nation with such a history must still have a glorious future before it. The particular circumstances of international politics which made the former successes possible were of course forgotten or unknown. The belief, now fully accepted by all, that they were a distinct race derived from one great ancestor combined with national spirit to produce a type of patriotism hard to excel in tenacity and blindness.

Worst of all, this whole system of economic, racial, and political ideas with its vaulting ambition and its hatred of foreigners was sanctioned by religion. The Jew had every reason to feel himself ethically and religiously above the Gentiles. Had not the best of their philosophers acknowledged Jewish superiority by reaching substantially similar views long after Moses was believed to have given the Law on Sinai? The hoary age of his race, his nation, and his religion, in an age that worshipped antiquity, gave the Jew every reason, so he felt, for despising the Gentile. The fact that he was mistaken in much of his history did not matter, for there was no one to prove him wrong. His faith was substantiated by the Holy Scriptures which contained his admittedly superior revelation. In the Law it was written that he should extirpate the people who tried to share the promised land with him. All other nations were to serve him, for he was of the chosen race, and the predictions of the prophets foretold the time when all nations should flow to Jerusalem and the sons of the aliens should be his plowmen and vinedressers. The fact that Jewish religion and morality actually were far superior to any other known rendered the situation far worse, for it lent a semblance of right to all that Jewish racial pride claimed.

yes.

The sanctions of religion applied in double measure to the hopes of the Jews regarding the new age and the advent of a heaven-sent ruler to realize all these national ambitions. Even the realistic Greeks and the prosaic Romans shared these expectations. But the Jews had made them a part of their religious inheritance as had no other race. For the average Jew the hope of the coming of God's reign was, no doubt, an intensely practical matter. The rabbis and apocalyptists might develop their various refinements or sublimations of the idea. It seems hardly possible that the ordinary Jew who heard the prophets read from time to time in the synagog could have understood them in any way but literally. Doubtless he believed that a ruler would be sent by God to overthrow the heathen and to establish the divine reign on earth. Then there would be enough for all. There would be no more taxes, no more injustice, no more oppression. The discrepancy between the miserable present and the glorious future suggested no doubts, for God's power could accomplish the impossible. Had not the Almighty stepped in again and again to save his people in times of distress? Indeed, only a century and a half before he had miraculously saved the nation from annihilation by the Syrians. It did not matter how great Rome was. God's arm was not shortened. The heathen might rage. He that sitteth in the heavens would laugh.

That this is not a fanciful picture is proved by Josephus. This astute Jewish historian, knowing that his Graeco-Roman audience could have but scorn for such fantastic ideas, has tried to cover up the spirit which animated the insurrectionists who constantly disturbed the peace during the century before the fall of Jerusalem by calling them robbers and bandits, but he constantly betrays the real facts. The Hezekiah whom the youthful Herod destroyed along with his band could hardly have been a mere robber or the Sanhedrin would not have indicted Herod for his murder.[26] The "band of robbers" whom Herod ingeniously dislodged from the caves in the Wâdî el-Ḥamâm were not ordinary bandits. Does a robber kill his seven sons and his wife one after another when they wish to accept an offer of clemency and finally cast himself over the precipice where he has thrown their bodies? Mere bandits do not usually prefer suicide to captivity.[27] On Herod's death Judas, son of Hezekiah, seized Sepphoris and raised the standard of revolt. The fact that the Romans burned the city and sold its inhabitants into slavery argues that they must have joined Judas and put up a stout resistance to the Romans.[28] Ten years later Judas of Gamala, who may be the same man, and Saddok, a Pharisee, roused the people to resist the census taken by Quirinius on the introduction of direct Roman rule into Judea. The high priest at the time persuaded the nation to submit to the census, one of the wisest administrative reforms of Augustus. But Judas argued that it was an introduction to slavery, and that God would not help them unless they took desperate measures to help themselves. Religious sanctions, then, surrounded the birth of the "fourth sect" of Josephus, the revolutionary movement which culminated in the Jewish War. So closely were religion and revolution connected that the preaching of John the Baptist was suspected of having a political animus. Josephus ascribes Herod's execution of John to fear of a revolution, not to the hatred of Herodias, as in the Gospels.[29] Jesus died under the same charge. Barabbas was an insurrectionary.[30] A little later two sons of Judas were crucified, doubtless because they were following in the footsteps of their father.[31] Tho Josephus' sources are meager for the period just before his own birth, that during which Jesus grew to manhood and preached the coming of the kingdom of God, it is evident that the Jewish historian was right in regarding it as a time during which the spirit of revolution seen in the "fourth sect" was steadily

[26] *Ant.*, XIV, 9, 2-5.
[27] *Ant.*, XIV, 15, 5.
[28] *Ant.*, XVII, 10, 5 and 9.
[29] *Ant.*, XVIII, 1, 1-6; XVIII, 5, 2.
[30] Mk. 15.7.
[31] *Ant.*, XX, 5, 2.

growing. He was aware that the numerous insurrections which he himself had seen could not have begun without previous preparation in the spirit of the people. According to Josephus the Jewish War began, not with the death of Herod Agrippa in 44 A.D., but with the census of Quirinius almost forty years earlier.

One of the outstanding features of the popular psychology was belief in the miraculous. Judas and Saddok had argued that God would help them if they did their part. Doubtless everyone saw with perfect clearness that a little people such as the Jews could not hope to develop the military strength necessary to defeat the Romans, but it was the general belief that, at the proper time, God would intervene. The insurrections which the Romans put down one after another usually show some trait which reveals this hope of miraculous divine aid. Theudas promised to divide the Jordan as Joshua had done.[32] Various impostors and deceivers arose to lead the multitude into the wilderness with promises of signs and wonders. An Egyptian prophet drew a crowd of followers to the Mount of Olives with the promise that the walls of Jerusalem would fall down at his word and they should march victoriously into the city.[33] The ardency and tenacity of this hope among the people were almost incredible. On the very day the Temple was burned a prophet went about the streets proclaiming that the people should go to the Temple, for there they would receive miraculous signs of their deliverance. According to Josephus six thousand men, women, and children crowded into the outer court of the Temple in this faith and perished in the conflagration and massacre that followed the Roman entry.[34] In an age when miracle was regarded as the rule and not the exception, such infatuation was entirely natural.

The social situation in Palestine, then, was a most complex one. It was further complicated, as has already been noted, by another problem which is mainly psychological in its social effects, the peculiar importance of religion in Jewish thinking. A people's

[32] Josephus, *Ant.*, XX, 5, 1.

[33] Josephus, *Ant.*, XX, 8, 6; *War*, II, 13, 4-6.

[34] *War*, VI, 5, 2.

attitude toward religion determines their reactions to a large proportion of the stimuli which social contacts provide. Religion deeply affects the subconscious undercurrents of character. People are inclined to be happy and hopeful or bitter and morose according as they have a bright and helpful religion or one that hampers and represses them. Nothing is so harmful to the spirit as a sense of failure, of frustrated powers and unattainable ideals. Such an experience breeds restlessness and dissatisfaction. Sooner or later it will demand compensations in some wild outbreak against hindrance and restraint. The fundamental demand of the soul is peace. A fighting spirit is often due to some inner disharmony that expresses itself in outward conflicts. The Jewish religion did not offer a path to peace in the first century of our era. The god whom it worshipped was not commonly pictured as a kind and benevolent creator and preserver of all mankind, but as a just but stern autocrat, a transcendant tyrant, who kept careful account of men's faults and sins and weighed out impartial justice. His chosen people were suffering for the sins of their fathers and of the wicked who were still among them. The majority, in fact, were far from fulfilling his exacting demands, and the future was far from hopeful. Indeed, many taught that still greater wickedness and severer sufferings were in store for the nation of his choice before they could expect the glorious future of prophetic promise to be realized. Some insisted upon the punctilious observance of impossible scribal traditions as an indispensable condition of his favor. The present was unendurable, the future held little promise of relief.

IV. PROPOSED SOLUTIONS

The complexities of the situation are best realized when we turn to consider the solutions which were proposed for the political, economic, and religious problems of the nation. An unique difficulty lay in the fact that all of these problems were essentially one, so far as anyone could see. The nation's political and economic ideals were also moral ideals held under the sanctions of religion. Now, it cannot be denied that all social problems are religious problems insofar as moral elements enter into them. Religion cannot be indifferent to wrong wherever it appears, a fact which many modern religionists wish to suppress. Yet one can imagine the confusion in the United States if, as an Italian correspondent recently declared, all liberals had to be "wets," and all fundamentalists "drys," if the political parties had to declare themselves for or against evolution. The ancient Jews had not learned the simple expedient of committing to different organizations within the group the solution of the various problems which confronted them. All matters had to be settled by the committee of the whole. This characterization of the ancient point of view must not be pressed too far. It is not probable that all of the Sadducees held identical views on all questions of theology, morals, and politics. The literary evidence makes it clear that men whose attitude toward the Law was that usually called Pharisaic entertained most diverse opinions as to the coming of the kingdom of God. Yet in general there was a certain consistency in the views which Josephus imputes to each of the "four philosophies" of his people. Each of them was, in a certain sense, a religious sect, a political party, a social "set," and an economic "school."

The solution which the Essenes proposed for the national difficulties was flight. According to Philo and Josephus, they dwelt in villages and cities with the rest of the people, but led a communistic life, meeting together for meals and worship. The majority, at least, did not marry. They severed themselves from society by strict rules as to food and ceremonial purity, so much so that a member could not live outside the community. They offer an extreme example of industry and of simplicity of life as to food and clothing. Aside from their ascetic avoidance of women one could hardly discover a more faithful adherence to the old Hebrew agricultural ideal. Their religious and philosophical ideas, however, do not seem to be Jewish, but oriental or perhaps Hellenistic. In Josephus' accounts one seems to hear echoes of Mazdian or Pythagorean doctrines. The ideas and ideals of Jesus and the early Christians, contrary to the opinion of some, resemble those of the Essenes only as each movement adopted much of the best in Judaism. The Christian church cannot be supposed to be in any sense derived from them. For the national problem they offered no solution whatever. Pliny, who had perhaps visited a community living a monastic life high above Engedi, caught the secret of their attraction. "There flock to them from afar," he says, "many who, wearied of battling with the rough sea of life, drift into their way of living." A few thousand men could escape from the insistent conflicts of the existing social order by taking refuge in this asylum, but for the great majority, including women and children, they offered no help.[35]

The Sadducees' solution consisted essentially in yielding to the forces that opposed the national ideal. There can be little doubt that they represented on the whole the party of cultural compromise and accommodation. Doubtless there were many differences of opinion as to how far a Jew might wisely go in accepting Greek customs. Doubtless there were many Jews not of the Sadducean party who were philhellenes. Yet it is inevitable that the aristocracy which rules should be so brought into contact with their foreign overlords as to become infected with the virus of alien culture.

The Sadducees may be described as a party of priestly clans and their immediate dependents who gathered around a nucleus consisting of the families from among whom the high priests and other Temple officials were chosen. They were a political aristocracy because their priestly position made them the official leaders of the nation and its spokesmen in negotiations with foreign rulers. They were a social aristocracy also. Since at this time the racial purity of the priestly clans was carefully guarded, they were a separate caste, elevated by both blood and office to a position superior to their compatriots of other birth. An aristocracy is usually conservative, and, in the nature of the case, a priestly group would be inclined to allow full weight to the priestly law which

[35] Philo, *Quod omnis probus liber,* 12 f. (75-91); fragm. in Eusebius, *Praep. evang.*, VIII, 8; Josephus, *Ant.*, XVIII, 1, 5; *War,* II, 8, 2-13; Pliny, *Hist. nat.*, V, 17; cf. above, p. 154 f.

magnified their office and to neglect or despise the supposedly later national literature, some of which regarded sacerdotal rites as unimportant or valueless. By a perfectly intelligible polar reaction they stigmatized as illegitimate and unauthoritative the scribal traditions upon which the party of their rivals, the Pharisees, was founded, even tho many a scribal rule confirmed their own priestly prerogatives and perquisites. By so doing they escaped not only a belief in the relatively modern idea of a bodily resurrection and its concommitant ideal of a messianic or heavenly kingdom on earth, but also the prophetic ideals of social morality. They were apparently literalists in their interpretation of criminal law and therefore savage and brutal in its enforcement.

Their social, political, and ecclesiastical position made them also the financial aristocracy in Judea. They had everything to gain by the maintenance of "normalcy," everything to lose by disturbances and insurrections. The messianic hope could have held out little attraction for them, in the form of a hope of a Davidic prince none at all. The priest, as Ezekiel's Utopia shows, preferred to subordinate the prince to himself. Why should they wish a change? The enormous Temple income prescribed by the Law assured them no small wealth. Their position opened to them great commercial advantages. The apocalyptic literature proves that they did not neglect their opportunities.[36]

One could not expect that such a party should have any deep moral convictions or any sympathy for the need and sufferings of the people. Such a group could discover no remedy except stern repression by force for the dissatisfaction that was everywhere rife. Religious officials always tend to become mere ecclesiastics, interested in the outward forms and visible institutions of religion rather than its inner spirit. How much more must this be true of a group whose tasks had to do with forms alone, who never became responsible for teaching morality or religion, who had no pastoral duties, no preaching to do, but only during two weeks in the year to perform certain perfunctory rites! Since, moreover, their political, social, and economic position set their

[36] See above, pp. 282-85.

interests largely in opposition to the people as a whole, it is not strange that the nation received no leadership from the Sadducees. Their abuse of their position rendered the economic condition of the masses infinitely worse. According to Josephus they were extremely quarrelsome, even among themselves. Their whole spirit and practice divided and weakened the nation to an incalculable degree.[37]

According to Josephus, the real leaders of the people were the Pharisees, the group to which he, by birth a priest, joined himself on coming to years of discretion.[38] It can hardly be claimed that the Gospel picture of the Pharisees is to be taken as complete. Jesus was criticizing certain evil tendencies in the religion of his people, tendencies which were most clearly manifested among some of the scribes and Pharisees. The criticisms are not to be taken as fully describing the whole group. Naturally Jesus did not stop to enumerate their good qualities. If one combine the Gospel accounts with those of Josephus and the materials found in the Talmud, he will construct a very different picture from that commonly drawn. Among them there must have been many who combined their rigid formalism with a deeply religious spirit and a high morality.

Such a combination of qualities made it inevitable that the Pharisees, almost as truly as the Essenes, should solve the problem of the nation by flight into unreality. Instead of yielding to the temptations of cultural assimilation as did the Sadducee, the Pharisee tried to raise an insuperable barrier between himself and the world. His innumerable petty rules of purity put a tremendous burden upon time, strength, and purse. It must have been much easier and less costly for the Essene, living in his communistic brotherhood, to keep his rules of purity than for the Pharisee. In a group made up of Pharisees alone the program would perhaps have been feasible. But even if his sense of religious superiority gave him emotional relief from the strains of the social conflicts he endured, even if his political quietism served

[37] Josephus, *Ant.*, XIII, 10, 6; XVIII, 1, 4; *War*, II, 8, 14.

[38] *Vita*, 1-2.

to remove occasions for irritating contacts, the Pharisee could not escape the world of Pilates and Caligulas. His religious scrupulosity made him the more easily subject to irritation. The invasion of his rights, of his religious privacies, was the harder to bear because of his stiff defense against it.

For the common people such a solution was no solution at all. The ordinary peasant could not keep the letter of the scribal rules of conduct. Too many circumstances in his life brought him in contact with that which was ritually defiling. The demands upon time and property were too heavy. Even the demands upon understanding and memory were beyond the majority. If in modern America a large proportion of the supposedly normal in mind and body are found to have the intellectual capacity of thirteen years or less, may we suppose that a large per cent of the farmers, fishermen, and artisans of Jewish Palestine were equal to the task of understanding and observing the rules which the scribes had evolved with no little exegetical subtilty? The *'am hâ-'âres* was the ignorant man, doubtless often because he would not learn, but more often, perhaps, because he had never been able to give the necessary time to the study of the Law and because he could not have understood and remembered if he had tried.

Even if all the people had been able to follow the Pharisaic example, it is certain that the difficulties in the social situation would not have been overcome. The formalistic, or legalistic conception of religion could satisfy some, but not all the people. To many it must have been decidedly irksome. With such it inevitably led to that type of divided and frustrated personality which Paul describes so vividly in the autobiographical sketch of the seventh chapter of Romans. It did not, therefore, meet the religious needs, and it was decidedly modified in later Judaism. It could not permanently solve the political and cultural problems because of the divisive spirit it engendered. A claim to moral and religious superiority is always in danger of developing religious snobbery. How much more when it is partly based upon purely formal and external criteria and actively furthers racial and national animosities! The Pharisaic scheme offered no solution whatever for the economic problem but rather made it more difficult, while it added to the social problem by creating new divisions and hatreds within the Jewish group itself.

There was another type of solution, another party, or tendency, to which Josephus does not explicitly allude. As the documents which have been preserved prove, the apocalytic movement must have influenced great multitudes. Certainly it played a large part in the beginnings of Christianity. Partly in agreement with the scribes and Pharisees, partly differing from them were the men who wrote and read the apocalypses. Their attitude, like that of the "fourth sect" of Josephus, was that of the Pharisees in their respect for the Law and their thorogoing nationalism. Like the "fourth sect" and unlike the Pharisees, they were not so completely immersed in the observance of the Law that they could ignore everything else. They believed and taught that the "last days" were come. The times were so evil that God could no longer endure the sins of the unrighteous and the sufferings of the pious. Their works, which no doubt were widely read outside of the official circles of the Sadducees and the rabbinic schools, did much to provide the foundation of dissatisfaction and fanatical faith upon which the revolt of 66 A.D. was based.[39]

As we have noted, this movement had many nuances of thought and hope; it was anything but homogeneous. But it continually emphasized three points: (1) the national superiority of Israel, (2) the certainty of divine intervention on their behalf, and (3) the overthrow of the rich and mighty and the elevation of the poor and weak. Here, then, was promise of a real solution of the whole complicated series of problems which the nation faced. Its political future was assured; evil and irreligion were to be miraculously overthrown; want and injustice were to come to an end. This solution did not appeal to the Sadducees, perhaps not to the majority of the Pharisees, for they belonged to the rich, the proud, the mighty who were to be overthrown, or else expected the reign of God to be introduced in some other manner. But it did attract

[39] See above, pp. 282-91, and McCown, *The Promise of His Coming*, pp. 92 ff., 141 f., 143 ff.

All were wrong in their solutions, The true + only way is the way of love, cooperation mutual understanding, friendlyness i.e. J. way.

the multitude. Properly understood, it was essentially quietistic. Man must wait for God to act by his own might and in his own time. But the apocalyptist was convinced by his reading of the signs of the times that the hour of destiny was near at hand. Many and various as were the types of apocalyptic thought, their total effect was to increase the tension, to stimulate hope, to embitter class and race feeling, and to make any rational solution of the difficult problems of the nation inacceptable. It was a flight from reality into a land of dreams. It could bring temporary forgetfulness of pain, but in the end it made the disease worse.

If the basic idea of apocalyptic theology tended toward quietism, there was much in its message which worked in the opposite direction. It was one of the important elements in the situation which rendered inevitable the rise of the revolutionary movements which have already been described. To vigorous and ardent spirits, riot and insurrection offered a necessary emotional outlet in action. But revolution involved a vast increase of all the racial animosities and cultural rancors which were in a measure sublimated in Pharisaism. Indeed, Josephus describes the "fourth sect," to which he gives no name, as being like the Pharisees in everything except that they had an unconquerable love of liberty. They were bitter racialists, ardent nationalists, strict religionists, thorogoing apocalyptists, but unable longer to endure inaction. So far as they were sincere in their patriotism and in the hope of divine aid, theirs was a solution of the national problem which was emotionally satisfactory. It is better to take up arms against a sea of troubles than to attempt weakly to rationalize them. Here, at least, is not divided personality, but self-conscious unity and power. Socially, however, it could not succeed, however much it might satisfy certain individuals. It ignored too many factors, and it postulated a fictitious element, the expectation of miraculous aid. It almost cost Judaism its existence.

To discerning eyes it was plain that Palestinian Judaism was hastening toward a catastrophe. Her internal bitterness and divisions, the sufferings and wrongs of her peasantry, and the revolutionary unrest of the more vigorous elements in her population could not be hidden by the glory of Temple ritual. What remedies had her leaders to propose? The Sadducees saw no evils which needed remedy except lawlessness, which must be put down by force. Aristocracies are inclined to deal with symptoms, not with diseases. The Pharisees saw the evils in part at least, but they also merely proposed to deal with the symptoms. The Law was not being observed; then persuade the people to observe the Law. The synagog was not being attended; then urge the people to attend. The Sabbath was being violated. The rabbis averred that if all Israel should keep two Sabbaths or even one completely, the Kingdom of God would come. They did not stop to inquire why the Law was neglected. They refused to see the social difficulties and injustices, the very burdens due to the yoke of the Law, which were causing the decay of Jewish ideals. As to the remedy of rebellion, anyone not completely blinded by hatred or fanaticism could see whither that would lead. It was equivalent to cutting off the head to cure the disease. The apocalyptist, if he was not a revolutionary, merely handed an opiate to the people. The sufferings of the last days they must endure. The end was at hand. He that endured to the end would enjoy the glories of the new age. In the end the opiate aggravated the disease.

V. JESUS' SOLUTION

At first glance Jesus' remedy does not seem to have been essentially different from that of the apocalyptists. He used many of the terms that we find on the lips of the prophets and apocalyptists. He proclaimed the imminent coming of the reign of God, the advent of a Son of man on the clouds of the heavens, and a great reversal in which the first should be last and the last first. He summoned his people to return to their ancient ideals. What did he mean? We cannot understand his solution of the problems of his time without clearly defining the terms he used in the light of the meanings and the associations which they had in Jewish minds.

What did Jesus mean when he heralded the imminent coming of the reign of God and allowed himself to be hailed as the messiah?

The history of three thousand years is compressed into those terms. We may rest assured that the people in general looked for the overthrow of the Romans and the establishment of a Jewish empire over the whole world. They expected the annihilation of all evil and the destruction of evildoers; the rich and the mighty of whatever race were to be humbled; the poor and the suffering were to escape their age-long travail; they were now to be fed. The messiah would reign in abundance and in righteousness. It was a strange combination of moral and material elements. But Jesus only partially fell in with these conceptions. He counseled submission to Rome: "Pay Caesar his dues," was his advice. When tempted to turn stones into bread, he refused on the ground that man had more important needs. His was not to be a reign in which free bread should be the distinguishing feature. Yet, on the surface at least, he promised the apocalyptic reversal of conditions and the righting of immemorial wrongs. The poor were to come into possession, the hungry to be fed, the sad to rejoice. The old idea of Gudea's dedicatory festival, the promise of Urukagina's reform, was to be realized.[40] They were to be realized by the labors of a personal representative of God, one especially anointed for his task.

What form were these labors to take? What sort of a messiah did Jesus expect to be? That is the crux of the question.[41] The solution lies in accurately defining the use of two terms employed to describe his messianic mission, the phrases "Son of David," and "Son of man."

As to the title "Son of David," it is not used by Jesus himself, but by others. Once he seems distinctly to discount its significance, if not to disclaim it. His unanswerable question put to the Jewish authorities, "How can the scribes say that the messiah is David's son?" certainly seems to imply that he did not accept the designation as fitting or adequate for the mission he had

[40] See above, pp. 191 ff., 245 ff.

[41] I am assuming that the Gospel accounts are substantially accurate. The basis for this assumption will appear in the following argument.

envisaged.[42] It could hardly have implied less than a renewal of David's kingdom based on military force. Even in its finest expression as seen in the seventeenth Psalm of Solomon this ideal could hardly have been satisfactory to Jesus. As a designation of the messiah the term was so common in Jewish literature that inevitably his contemporaries and his disciples after his death applied it to him, once they were convinced that he had been the "anointed." They would not discover its essential inconsistency with his moral and spiritual ideals. In any case the Gospels often represent him as using another self-designation with a very different set of connotations, the term "Son of man."

That Jesus ever actually referred to himself as the Son of man has been frequently denied on various grounds. That in a number of instances Matthew and Luke have interpolated the phrase into the records is evident from a comparison with Mark. That in some instances it has no messianic connotation seems reasonably certain. In Hebrew and Aramaic the phrase was used simply for "man" in a generic sense, for "mankind." The term may have been used in this sense in Jesus' saying, "The son of man is lord of the Sabbath." It has been alleged, tho apparently on insufficient grounds, that the phrase, *bar nashâ,* which Jesus must have used, could be employed as a substitute for "I" and "me," as "one" is sometimes modestly used in English. However it certainly was used for "anyone," "some one." Again, granting that it is a messianic title, some have argued from the fact that Jesus always uses it in an impersonal way, and does not say, "I am the Son of man," that he was referring to a messiah who was to come in the future, and did not intend to refer to himself as this coming one. Formerly it was commonly argued that Jesus used the term in reference to himself with the connotation of humility and frailness, as it appears to be applied to Ezekiel, or as if he were man *par excellence,* the true representative of mankind.

In finding a way thru this maze of arguments and assertions the first point that needs to be fixed is that, whatever other uses the term had in the Aramaic of Jesus' day, it had come to be used

[42] Mk. 12.35 ff., and parallels.

in a messianic sense. Its application in Daniel 7 to a heavenly or angelic being who represents the people of Israel and its subsequent repeated use in the Similitudes of Enoch in a plainly messianic sense preclude its employment in New Testament times, in some of the connections in which it appears in the Gospels, in any other than a messianic meaning. The idea of a primeval, perfect man, a man from heaven, appears in various quarters of ancient literature to reinforce and explain this interpretation.[43] When we read in the Gospels of the Son of man coming on the clouds of heaven, there can be no doubt that a heavenly messiah is intended.

Did Jesus, then, use the expression in reference to himself? No one who studies 1 Enoch and its fellows carefully and without prejudice can conclude that the writers of the Gospels were unfamiliar with the apocalyptic ideas and language of these works. For several decades it has been widely acknowledged that Jesus could not have lived in the first century of our era and preached the coming of the reign of God without constantly using these same ideas and language, even as the Jews used Greek and Roman coins. There had been no other terms minted to express the moral and religious ideals which Jesus was attempting to convey. The reaction of the scholar against the various millennial extravagances has made him slow to admit that Jesus could have been an apocalyptist. Yet we must face the facts; we do not need to steady the ark.

The most original and creative, the most intensely moral and most profoundly spiritual portions of the Old Testament, the prophets and the Psalms, were shot thru with apocalyptic expectations. Apocalypses constituted a considerable portion of the most influential literature of contemporary Judaism. The New Testament is full of these hopes. Primitive Christianity was essentially and predominantly an apocalyptic movement. If Jesus did not use the language of apocalypticism, if he did not call himself the Son of man in the apocalyptic sense, we have to eliminate very large and important sections of the Synoptic records as unauthentic

[43] See, for example, 4 Ezra 13.3 ff.

interpolations due to the perverted views of his earliest and most intimate disciples. We have to believe that these early Christians adopted a view of Jesus which they believed him to have taught, but which they constructed out of their own imaginations, with little or no warrant from his language. It is interesting to note a meticulous accuracy in this wrong-headed faith of theirs: they never represent him as calling himself the son of David, altho others repeatedly address him as such; they constantly represent him as referring to himself as the Son of Man, altho others never address him or refer to him as such. Most impossible of all, we are forced to the conclusion that Jesus lived and died entirely outside the currents of thought that dominated his contemporaries. If he was an apocalyptist, he fits into his age; if he was not, he becomes, not so much a real person, as a mythical, unreal man from heaven.

The hypothesis, recently defended with great plausibility by S. J. Case, that Jesus was an apocalyptic prophet who proclaimed the coming of the reign of God by direct divine act and without the intervention of a messiah, is much more probable, but it labors under many of the objections just mentioned. How can we suppose the disciples to have misunderstood him so completely? If he did think of himself as the messiah, we can easily understand how the disciples should have imported into the word connotations which were not in his mind, just as the term Son of God has been egregiously misinterpreted. If he did not, all Christianity has been founded upon a misapprehension.

On the other hand, I cannot see serious difficulties in the way of the hypothesis that Jesus did believe himself to be the messiah. All the New Testament records favor it. If John Hyrcanus, tho he was of the tribe of Levi, had been heralded as messiah, which, in the eyes of most scholars, is the view of the author of the Testaments of the Twelve Patriarchs, there is no reason why any Jew who seriously believed himself commissioned to cause the will of God to be done on earth should not interpret his task in these terms, particularly if, as seems possible in the case of Jesus, he was of the Davidic line. Jesus very properly interpreted his sense of communion with God and his devotion to the divine will in terms of the heavenly voice, "Thou art my beloved Son, in whom I am well pleased." If Jesus had pondered long and deeply upon the salvation of his nation from the difficulties that beset them, how natural, in view of the ideas which were rife among his people, for that conviction to be understood in terms of a call to messiahship! Once we disabuse our minds of the connotations which Christian theology has erroneously read back into the various titles applied to Jesus, such a conviction on his part becomes perfectly intelligible in the mind of a sane man with an unique sense of the divine Fatherhood. It seems much more natural that Jesus should have reached this conviction in the strength of his devotion to a superhuman task than that his disciples should have evolved the idea after the nation had rejected and crucified him.

If, now, Jesus was an apocalyptist and used the title "Son of man" of himself, what did he mean by it? The probable explanation is that he chose the title as the best available to indicate his conception of the messianic office. It had several advantages over "messiah" or "son of David." First of all, it had other meanings and could not be pounced upon as prima facie evidence of messianic claims, a wise precaution in view of the delicate political situation. It would not arouse undue expectations in the minds of ardent but unwise friends. It could not be used against him by his enemies. Moreover, it had never been connected with mundane politics or materialistic measures for realizing the reign of God, and its use, therefore, gave Jesus a considerable initial advantage when he should attempt to explain to his disciples his conception of the kingdom. Not that it necessarily implies a kingdom in heaven or a purely spiritual kingdom of God. Various views as to the messianic and the ensuing divine kingdom were expressed in Ethiopic Enoch, where the messianic Son of man is most fully portrayed. Certainly the Similitudes and the Book of Exhortations, the two portions which have most points of resemblance with the teachings of Jesus, tended to remove the emphasis from the earthly and sensuous and to place it upon the moral and spiritual. Such an emphasis would exactly suit the purpose of Jesus.

Finally, and most important of all in view of our present argument, the Son of man of 1 Enoch is the great judge who is to overthrow oppression and injustice and inaugurate an age of righteousness. He is to put down from their thrones the kings and the mighty and those that possess the earth, but he is to be a staff to the righteous, a light to the Gentiles, and the hope of those who are troubled of heart.[44] He was to bring about the fulfillment of the hope of the poor.

It has been argued with great vigor that, if Jesus believed in the apocalyptic scheme, his morality has no force for us today. The apocalyptist believed the "present age" to be wholly evil. Only in the "next age" was righteousness possible. If Jesus adopted this view, it is urged, then his instructions to his disciples were only an interim morality intended to preserve his followers from evil and prepare them for the new age that was soon to dawn. He could, therefore, have planned no new moral order for existing human society.

How far Jesus went in accepting the apocalyptic scheme for the future it seems to me impossible to determine. That the term "Son of man" fully expressed his conception of his mission or that we must read into his purpose and expectations all that the term includes in 1 Enoch seems to me entirely improbable. Indeed, that temptation in which he refuses to cast himself down from a wing of the Temple reads like a definite repudiation of a suggestion that he attempt to appear in the guise of one coming on the clouds of the heavens.[45] The idea of the second advent, which played so large a part in the thought of the early church, may have had no place in the mind of Jesus. It was quite natural for the early Christians to discover this explanation of the manner in which his claim to be the Son of man from heaven should be eventually fulfilled. Hellenistic Christians like Paul would be prepared to look for a heavenly kingdom in which flesh and blood

[44] See above, pp. 288 f.

[45] See the writer's article, "The Temptation of Jesus Eschatologically and Socially Interpreted," *Biblical World*, 53 (1919), 402-07. For a fuller discussion of the apocalypticism of Jesus see *The Promise of His Coming*, pp. 144-66. On *Interimsethik* see above, pp. 22 ff.

should have no part. But evidence is lacking in the Synoptic Gospels for a purely transcendental view of the reign of God. It was not a common view among the Jews. The end of the age was not necessarily the end of the world. The kingdom of heaven does not imply a kingdom in heaven. Over against passages that suggest a future, transcendental kingdom [46] are others that just as emphatically suggest a kingdom on earth or one already in some sense present.[47] It is, however, a spiritual kingdom in the truest sense, for it is not a matter of material blessings, of earthly government and glory, or of external and physical force. Its sanctions were purely inward and moral; it was to be a product of social forces.

One has good grounds, then, for concluding that Jesus expected the reign of God here upon this earth. The principles of conduct he enunciated were preparatory to a new life here. His teachings are not an *Interimsethik,* but represent his ideals of life. They were his solution of the social problems of his people. In the light of our previous studies, what were his ideals and how did he expect them to be realized?

[46] Mk. 12.25; 10.30.
[47] Mt. 6.10; Mk. 3.24-27; 9.12 f.; Lk. 7.22.

J. reign of G in Earth was not like Pharisees obedience to Ch rules, laws etc. but to service of love to human welfare + growth of Persons.

CHAPTER XI

THE SHEPHERDS AND THE MAGI

History is full of remarkable coincidences. One of these is the fact that Christmas comes at practically the same time as the Roman *Saturnalia*. During the week of that festival, December 17-24, the whole population gave itself to unrestrained jollification. The feature of the celebration which has been thought most significant was the liberty allowed to slaves, for the festival was supposed to recall the happy days of the Golden Age when, under Saturn's mild rule, all men were equal and there was abundance for everyone. As Accius put it in his versified *Annals*,

> "The greater part of the Greeks and especially Athens keep in honor of Saturn a religious festival which by them is said to be the Cronia. And thus they celebrate that day: in country and city almost all give themselves joyfully to feasting, and they provide for their slaves; each for his own; and likewise also thence has been handed down that custom of ours that slaves shall feast at the same time with their masters."[1]

It is certain that the earliest Christians knew nothing of the birth of Jesus on December 25, and it seems probable that the celebration of that date as Christmas began about the middle of the fourth century. It is also clear that many of the customs connected with the *Saturnalia* found their way into the Christmas celebration, for example the joyful feastings, the giving of presents to children, and the burning of candles. Was the choice of date originally determined by a desire to replace with Christian customs the objectionable features which the day had licensed, or by a recognition of the fitness of the coincidence? We cannot say.

[1] Macrobius, *Sat.*, I, 7, 37.

Yet by a happy chance (shall we call it?), this old pagan celebration that recalled the Golden Age of peace, good will, equality, and abundance was brought into connection with the time when the angels sang their song of peace and good will to the shepherds in the fields of Bethlehem. The birth of the King who should rule in righteousness was a fitting fulfilment of the wistful prophecy of the legend of the Golden Age.

It is also a significant coincidence that brings the simple shepherds from Bethlehem's rocky plains with their homely gifts into the company of the wise astrologers of the Orient with their splendid presents of gold and frankincense and myrrh to bow together before the manger-cradle at the season when the Romans celebrated the equality of the slave and his master. The shepherds and the magi represent two strands that we find tightly woven together in the thinking of Judaism and Christianity, obsequious worship of wealth and position, and the glorification of poverty and simplicity. Very early in the history of the new religion appears the desire to prove that people of wealth, respectability, and influence must recognize the right and accept the truth when it is presented to them.[2] Perhaps the story of the visit of the magi is a result of this tendency.

In striking contrast to this obsequiousness in the presence of wealth and position is the Jesus of the Gospels. He stands in direct succession to the prophets who championed the cause of the poor, the fatherless, the widow, and the stranger against the rich and the powerful. He champions them, not as one who holds himself aloof outside their ranks and reaches down the pitying hand of condescending charity, but as one of them. He stands in direct succession to those apocalyptic writers who looked for a complete and catastrophic overturning of the present world order when the reign of God should begin. Does this seem a startling statement? In the light of our previous studies the evidence in the Gospels is clear.

[2] Acts 6.7; 17.4, 12, 33 f.; 18.8; 19.31; 21.39; 22.28.

I. THE ECONOMIC AND SOCIAL CONDITIONS OF JESUS' LIFE

The conditions under which Jesus was born and grew to manhood are a sufficient indication that he had understanding and sympathy for the lower classes. According to Luke he was born in a stable, cradled in a manger, and reared in a carpenter's home in a small and unknown town of Galilee, surrounded by an atmosphere of simple, unofficial piety. The lowly station of Joseph and Mary is shown plainly enough by the lodgings with which it is said they were forced to content themselves at Bethlehem. Any important member of the Davidic line would have had connections at the ancestral seat which, according to the hospitable customs of those days, would have made it unnecessary for him to seek a place in the inn. If Jesus did belong to the royal line, he certainly never made the slightest use of the fact, and his one reference to the theory that the messiah was to be of Davidic lineage indicates how little he valued such ancestry.

The fact that Jesus was reared in a little Galilean town is not without significance. Nazareth was so unimportant that Josephus, who, as Jewish generalissimo a generation later, organized the whole region for defense against the Romans, never mentions it. So unknown is it to history that a considerable body of critical opinion has denied its existence in the days of Jesus. It was not an auspicious center from which to inaugurate a world revolution. Yet the quiet country village was for all that the kind of place best suited to train the leader of the new "proletarian movement" which was intended to transform human society.

Jesus was a man of the country. It is said that there is a country mind and a city mind. The latter demands for its enjoyment constant titillation by the multifarious and constantly recurring sights and sounds of the city. The movement and hum of multitudes, the sense of activity, the nearness of one's fellows, the bright lights, the accidents, the meeting with strangers, the hearing of news from many lands, and, not least by any means, the amusements, the theater, the arena, the stadium, all these are demanded by some natures to stimulate their minds into pleasurable activity. On the other hand, there are those who have resources of enjoyment within themselves. The bleating of the sheep, the lowing of the cattle, the bark of a dog, the cry of a jackal, the soughing of the wind, the twitter of the birds, the green of the grass, the colors of the flowers, the waving of the grain fields, such sights and sounds suggest joys to the country-minded which are more satisfying than the exciting pleasures of the city. Jesus was country-minded. The commonest incidents of village and country life had for him the highest significance. In the falling bird, the blooming flower, the sower broadcasting his seed, the shepherd seeking his sheep, the poor woman hunting her coin, he saw the deepest meanings. One of the great services which he has rendered the world is that he has thus dignified and glorified the ordinary experiences of life. True to his way of looking at life is the Oxyrhynchus saying,

"Raise the stone, and there thou shalt find me,
Cleave the wood, and I am there."

This characteristic of the mind of Jesus becomes the clearer when we compare him with Paul, the man of the city. The apostle's figures of speech are borrowed from the market-place and the arena just as those of Jesus come from farm and field. Paul proved that the gospel could migrate to the city and thrive there also. But it was not born there. Jesus first saw the light in a country town and the first thirty years of his life were spent in a village home.

"Where the patient oxen were, by the ass's stall,
Watching my Lord's manger knelt the waking cattle all;
'Twas a little country maid vigil by him kept—
All among the country things my good Lord slept.
Fair was Rome the city on that early Christmas morn,
Yet among the country-folk was my Lord born!"[3]

Life in the Galilean countryside conveyed many impressions which could not come to one born and reared in Judea and Jeru-

[3] From Margaret Widdemer's "A Country Carol," *Everybody's Magazine*, January, 1913.

salem. Its people escaped many influences of the Judean environment. There is an openness and attractiveness about Galilee's landscape of rounded hills and rolling plains which symbolize, if they did not produce, the less conservative and sunnier temperament of the Galilean as compared with the Judean. The accessibility and the mixed population of Galilee, the caravans which crossed it from Damascus to Egypt, and from the Ḥaurân and Gilead to the sea at Ptolemaïs and Tyre, the presence of numerous Greek cities on all sides, guaranteed that any man reared in that section of Palestine should be entirely familiar with the predominant qualities, both good and bad, in Hellenistic civilization. It could not save him from an intense patriotism. The fact that a little more than a century before this time the Jews had returned as colonists to Galilee after an enforced removal during the Maccabean wars of independence suggests something as to the character of the fellow countrymen among whom Jesus lived. They were pioneers or children of pioneers in a Galilee *irredenta*, with some of the energy, enterprise, adaptability, liberality, and love of independence that characterize the pioneer on a new frontier. Judea more easily bred cultural exclusiveness and religious fanaticism. Jerusalem, the place of shrines, pilgrimages, and sacred festivals, was the natural home of legalistic conservatism and sacerdotal pride. Galilee, being farther from the religious center where scribes and priests gathered, was less under the influence of the bigoted ecclesiastics who just then dominated Jewish life. It more easily preserved the best moral and spiritual elements in the Jewish inheritance.

Tho Galilee was a hotbed of revolutionary patriotism according to Josephus, it might well be that men of penetrating mind learned from the experiences of that section of the country at the hands of Herod and the Romans that armed revolt was not only futile but reacted most unfavorably upon morality and religion. In particular the revolt and destruction of Sepphoris, which lay only four or five miles from Nazareth, may have made a deep impression upon Jesus. It occurred when he was but a child, and he could hardly have escaped repeatedly seeing the evidences of its devastating effects, the more so if, as has been suggested, he assisted in the rebuilding of the city.[4]

The carpenter's home in Nazareth of Galilee, again, gives bond for the sympathies of Jesus. His nights were passed in a windowless stone hut along with the ass and goats, if the family was rich enough to own them, and a considerable brood of smaller children. His days were given to the rough work of the country carpenter. In a land where all the buildings are of stone or brick, a carpenter is not likely to be a building contractor of large enterprises or extensive means. A careful survey of the usage of the words for carpenter in both Aramaic and Greek does not support the suggestion that Jesus was perhaps a mason or some other kind of artisan.[5] He was rather an ordinary worker in wood. In a little town where all life must have been of the simplest possible description he is not likely to have been an artist in cabinetwork and fine inlaying. Often, possibly, he found no work in Nazareth and journeyed to Sepphoris to assist in its rebuilding under Herod Antipas. Possibly he went to Ptolemais or Capernaum to engage in building ships, for "carpenter" in both Aramaic and Greek is often "shipwright." Who knows but that it was on such journeys that he first came to know Peter and Andrew and James and John? Did he build the boats from which he later taught the multitudes? In any case, tho his very trade tended to increase his knowledge of people and of the great world that throbbed around him, Jesus was merely a simple, country working man. After the death of Joseph he was evidently the head of the house and charged with the responsibilities of a father. He knew both the work and the worries of a laboring man's life, the terror of war, the pinch of poverty, the haunting fear of unemployment, the long anxiety of years of drought, the grim spectre of famine, the insolence of the wealthy employer, the callous heartlessness of the successful merchant. His living was earned by hard, rough labor with the simplest and crudest of tools in shaping rude beams and doors and rustic yokes and plows such as the Orient still uses. His sym-

4 S. J. Case, in *JBL*, 45 (1926), 14-22, and *Jesus*, pp. 208-12.

5 See the writer's article, "'O Τέκτων," in *SEC*, pp. 173-89.

pathies would naturally lie with simple, hard-working people and with unostentatious ways of living.

Unequivocal evidence as to Jesus' sympathies and as to the purport of his message is provided by the people whom we find around him. His following was of peasants from Galilee.

> "Country lads that followed him, blithe they were and kind,
> It was only city folk were hard to him and blind."

He was bred in the country; he carried on his ministry in the country. He chose his disciples from common working men, so far as we know their callings, with one exception. And this one was an outcast from Jewish society and from the synagog. Hegesippus knew a significant story regarding two grandnephews of Jesus, grandsons of Jude. They were hailed before the Emperor Domitian as possible leaders of insurrection, but they were found to be only simple, hard-working men, so manifestly harmless that they were quickly dismissed.[6] Jesus came from the class that had suffered poverty, privation, and oppression since society began. He belonged to those about whom Sumerian patesis, Egyptian pharaohs, and Hebrew prophets had declaimed as the helpless who needed protection from the rapacity and cruelty of the rich and powerful. He came from among those to whom the ideal of simple agricultural life made the strongest appeal. Was he class-conscious? Not in the sense in which the term is often used by those who advocate class war and class hatred, but in the very true sense that he knew the life of the lower classes from bitter personal experience and believed that they were not destined to remain forever the pastures of the rich.

II. JESUS' ATTITUDE TOWARD THE RICH AND ARISTOCRATIC

Jesus' attitude toward the pretensions of wealth and aristocracy is quite unequivocal. To be sure, it must not for a moment be forgotten that he shows none of the doctrinaire hatred of the

[6] Eusebius, *Hist. Eccles.*, III, 19, 20, 32.

bourgeoisie and the *intelligentsia* that marks a certain type of modern socialistic propaganda, nor does he exhibit in his actions any such aversion for the rich and the powerful as appears in the apocalypses. He does not in the least discriminate against the upper classes. He is as ready to answer the request of the centurion and recognize his faith as to listen to the cry of the blind beggar. He heals Jairus' daughter as gladly as the poor, unclean woman on the street. He accepts an invitation to the house of the rich Pharisee just as graciously as to that of Levi, to dine with tax-gatherers and sinners. Perhaps it should be added that what he says at such dinners, for example to Simon the Pharisee,[7] need not be construed as a rebuke or an attack on his host. The rich Zacchaeus, tax-gatherer and outcast tho he was, is especially chosen as Jesus' host and then highly commended for making full restitution for any wrongs he had committed and giving half his goods to charity. Jesus, according to Mark, loved the rich young man who came seeking eternal life. But he showed no trace of servility or obsequiousness in the presence of these of the better sort.

Remembering, then, that Jesus is never a literalist, that he never mistakes the outward appearance for the inward spirit, that he never confounds possessions and personality, we must not for a moment ignore the fact that few public speakers in any age have denounced wealth so unsparingly:

> "How hard it is for those that have property to get into the kingdom of God! . . . It is easier for a camel to pass thru the eye of a needle than for a rich man to get into the kingdom of God."[8]

> "A man's life is not in having a superabundance from his possessions."[9]

> "Do not store up treasures for yourselves on earth."[10]

[7] Lk. 7.36-50.
[8] Mk. 10.23, 25.
[9] Lk. 12.15.
[10] Mt. 6.19.

"Sell your property and give alms." [11]

"You cannot be a slave to God and to Mammon." [12]

In the parable of Dives and Lazarus the rich man goes to Hades as a matter of course, because he has been rich and has had his fill of good things on earth. Doubtless he had neglected poor Lazarus and had many other sins to his account, but that did not need to be stated. Likewise, the only sin mentioned against the man who planned to tear down his barns and build greater was his possessions. It could be taken for granted that any person who lived in luxury and had far more than he needed was "not rich unto God." [13]

Montefiore has confessed that he was wrong in saying that Jesus had a bias against the rich.[14] But there can be no doubt that he had a bias against riches. Loisy is right in representing Jesus' attitude toward Mammon thus:

"It is wealth in itself and not merely wealth dishonestly acquired, rather it is to be said that wealth honestly acquired was not conceived of. If it is called 'Mammon of iniquity' (Lk. 16.9), it is considered as a sovereign force in a world given up to injustice, and so much the more because injustice is as if naturally bound to the pursuit, the possession, and the use of wealth." [15]

This is exactly the view of the Damascus Covenanters, the Similitudes and the Exhortations of 1 Enoch, and the Assumption of Moses.[16] Jesus did not regard wealth as the unpardonable sin, but he did agree with the Psalms and the apocalypses in thinking it wholly evil in its effects upon the person who maintained his hold upon it. He doubtless believed that it was almost invariably wickedly acquired and wickedly used.

If one were to stop here, the impression might easily be created that for Jesus wealth was not merely the chief but, indeed, the

[11] Lk. 12.33.

[12] Mt. 6.24 = Lk. 16.13.

[13] Lk. 16.25; 12.13-21.

[14] See above, p. 11, and cf. *Synoptic Gospels,* 2 ed., II, p. 33.

[15] *Évangiles synoptiques,* I, p. 614.

[16] See above, pp. 282-285.

only sin. In fact, he has been portrayed as the leader of a great proletarian revolution against the economic exactions of Rome. Such a picture of him is as false as the one so common in evangelical circles which makes him a meek and mild ascetic and mystic who walked thru a troubled life to death on the cross like an automaton moved by the springs of Old Testament prophecy. There were other qualities beside mere possession of wealth which Jesus unsparingly condemned, and, while many of them are characteristic of the rich, they are not all the product of riches. There were other classes beside the rich whom Jesus denounced. To understand the position he took as to the social and religious problems of his day we must place these others along beside the rich in order to determine what were the fundamental qualities which drew the fire of his fearless tongue.

Upon the scribes and Pharisees Jesus oftenest poured forth the lightnings of his scorn. He openly flaunted in their faces his supreme disregard of their petty legalism. For the rich man's blindness Jesus has a half pitying, "Thou fool." What can be more withering than the pitiless, often repeated, "Woe unto you, scribes and Pharisees, hypocrites"? They had forfeited their places as husbandmen in God's vineyard.[17] Indeed, they had committed the unpardonable sin, in their failure to recognize the spirit in which he was working.[18]

When one turns to the records which the rabbis of Jesus' time have left behind them, the *Sayings of the Fathers* and other quotations handed down from them in the Talmud, one finds it hard to understand how Jesus could have taken an attitude of such uncompromising hostility toward men who showed so much good sense and true piety. To be sure, the medium in which their wit and wisdom has been preserved is to us unattractive and even repellent. Yet, half obscured by their long-winded and wearisome discussions, sometimes of pettifogging, legalistic trifles, there often shine mental keenness and moral and spiritual insight such as have made the Hebrew prophets a part of the world's permanent

[17] Mk. 12.1-12.
[18] Mk. 3.23-30.

literature. Nearly everything that Jesus himself said can be paralleled in the Talmud. How then are we to explain Jesus' unsparing denunciation?

Certain fundamental errors, just then apparently in the ascendancy, threatened to destroy the good that was in the Jewish religion. We must remember, first of all, that a mechanical theory of the inspiration of the Scriptures and a consequent necessity for a literal interpretation of the sacred writings placed inescapable shackles on the wings of the spirit. The modern literalist and the ancient Pharisaic legalist are twin brothers in more ways than one. There was little opportunity for them to discover new truth, for the spirit of prophecy was stilled. God had spoken of old time; there was for them no spirit of truth to lead men on to greater things. All the wisdom that God had for the world was hidden in the pages of the Scriptures. It was the task of the scribes to worm it out by various kinds of verbal acrobatics and intellectual legerdemain. Thus literalism and legalism built a hedge about the Law, to use a rabbinic phrase, a hedge so high and thick that ordinary men no longer saw God. Thus they were led to lay heavy burdens upon men's shoulders, burdens so impossible that a great multitude gave up trying to walk in the way of life. But legalism and literalism do not inevitably shut men out of the kingdom, tho they put many stumbling-blocks in the way. Many escape the trammels of their mistaken theories and walk in the free fields of truth and righteousness, just as many Jews and Christians in all ages have risen above the limitations of their theologies into the light of morality and faith.

There were, of course, hypocrites among Jesus' contemporaries. No age is without them. Literalism and legalism always make hypocrites, for they lay impossible burdens on the spirit, and, while some will acknowledge their inability to live up to unattainable standards, others will delude themselves and try to delude their neighbors into thinking that they are satisfying the impractical demands. There is no literalist today who really believes and obeys the Bible from cover to cover. To take but one example, who sees to it that women keep silence in the churches? It is easy to put

J. judgment of men was on the basis of their treatment & attitude toward humanity & Personality. Did their acts enable Persons or degrade?

burdens upon others and to forget to lay our fingers to them. There were scribes who devoured widows' houses and for a pretense made long prayers, just as there are deacons who do the same today. Others no doubt washed the outside of the cup and the platter, making a great fuss about ceremonial cleanness while they entirely neglected the dead men's bones of unspiritual thinking, and immoral, unsocial living. The scribes were lawyers, and the lawyer's besetting sin is to forget justice and mercy and truth in his struggles to observe the technicalities of the law, putting the law before the justice it is intended to achieve.

The hypocrisy and pretense of the Pharisees were inevitable concomitants of what was all in all their fundamental sin, religious selfishness, spiritual pride and self-satisfaction. With what biting irony Jesus set it forth in the story of the Pharisee and the publican at prayer in the Temple! "O God, I thank thee that I am not like the rest of men!" The same irony burns thru the story of the lost sheep. The "ninety and nine just men that needed no repentance" included those same Pharisees. As if there could be any so righteous that they needed no repentance! A vigorous verse in the Fourth Gospel puts it in a nutshell. "If you were blind, you would have no sin. But now you say, 'We see'; your sin remains." He who is blind but insists he sees is hopeless. How often Jesus foretells the doom of those who have exalted themselves! Worst of all, in their spiritual blindness the Pharisees had exalted themselves into positions of religious leadership, but they were not serving, and Jesus recognized no leadership but that of service. They were leading the people into the ditch. They were shutting the door of the kingdom in the face of humble seekers who wished to enter. Theirs was a religion for the few, not for the many. The fundamental error of the scribes and Pharisees whom Jesus denounced—whatever may be true of the rabbis of the Talmud—was that they had adopted a view of religion which made it socially ineffective.

Jesus eventually found himself brought into conflict with another class of people who exalted themselves, the Sadducees, who were in positions of political leadership. In Galilee, where his activities chiefly centered, they were not in power as in Judea, and therefore he had no occasion to attack them. With the purely civil authority of Herod Antipas, his own ruler, he had less reason to deal. One of his chief concerns thruout his ministry was to avoid conflicts with the civil authorities. No unbiased student of the life and times of Jesus can for a moment suppose that his primary aim was either economic or political. His purpose was the transformation of the spirit in which men lived and worked. To have entered the field of economic reform, beside being a ridiculous anachronism, would have obscured the real issue. Even more, it would have frustrated his primary purpose to have given himself out as a political leader in opposition to the Sadducees and the Romans. It was this that made his handling of the messianic idea so difficult and drove him to adopt the Enochic language of the Son of man coming on the clouds of heaven, a conception to which only the grossest misinterpretation could give a political significance.

The spirit of the political aristocracy was such, however, that Jesus could not escape opposing it. It is best characterized in the delicious irony of the Gospel of Luke: "The kings of the Gentiles lord it over them, and those who exercise authority over them are called benefactors." The "benefactors," the philanthropists of those days, after gathering their wealth at the expense of the people, did not build libraries and hospitals and universities; they did not give organs to churches and creed-bound gifts to missionary societies. As it was the fashion for the robber barons of the Middle Ages to build monasteries and endow cathedrals, so it was the custom in Jesus' day to beautify cities with imposing theatres and forums, to restore ruined temples, and to erect sumptuous baths where the rich might disport themselves in forgetfulness of the toiling slaves and degraded freemen whose labor made such magnificence possible. The Testaments of the Twelve Patriarchs [19] and the Gospel references to the charitable who sound trumpets before them suggest that the giving of alms and the payment of Temple vows was the Jewish equivalent of the Gentile

[19] See above, p. 281 f.

x Had J. made all the poor rich what better moved Personality be? no new Shs?

benefactions. Such self-glorifying generosity indicated exactly the opposite of the spirit of Jesus.

Yet it was no childish display of this kind on the part of the political authorities which led Jesus into his final and fatal conflict with them. It was a less striking, but more fundamental, misuse of power, the prostitution of worship itself in the interest of wealth. When Jesus cleared the Temple of all those enterprising traders who were making the house of God a den of thieves, he struck directly at the Sadducean management of the Temple and its worship, for they were using their position as the ecclesiastical heads of the nation to increase their already swollen incomes at the expense of the people. It has been supposed, to be sure, that the money-changers were priests appointed for the purpose and not ordinary merchants or bankers. While this may have assured that "in normal circumstances the people would be fairly treated," as Abrahams says, yet on more than one occasion the rabbis themselves had interfered in less spectacular but equally effective ways with priestly abuses which were causing injustice to the people. At the time Jesus cleansed the Temple, there appears to have been no rabbi to take the part of the worshiper. Jewish authorities assert that "under the aristocratic *régime* of the Temple's last decades" there were instances of priestly exploitation of the poor who came to make offerings there. One need have no hesitation therefore, in accepting the full historicity of the account of Jesus cleansing the Temple of similar abuses only four decades before the final destruction of the city.[20] It was this fearless attack upon graft and exploitation which drove the Sadducees to unite with their hereditary enemies, the Pharisees, in planning Jesus' arrest and crucifixion. And thus Jesus died as the champion of the poor against the exactions and oppressions of the rich.

This examination of the negative evidence as to Jesus' spirit and aim, this scrutiny of the groups whom he criticized and attacked, discovers, as it seems to me, an unchangeable streak of "yellow" running thru the party-colored fabric of contemporary society; the assumption of position and power without considera-

[20] Abrahams, *Studies in Pharisaism and the Gospels,* Series I, pp. 86 ff.

tion, and indeed only with scorn, for the great mass of the common people. Leaders who claimed to be divinely appointed shepherds of the people were little better than wolves. They were hardly so conscientious as the Romans, who undertook not to flay, but only to fleece. They were indeed far worse because of their pretense of righteousness. Jesus condemned the currently fashionable religiosity just because it failed to function in ethical relations. It emphasized external forms and individual worship and salvation while it neglected the wrongs of the people.

III. JESUS' ATTITUDE TOWARD THE COMMON PEOPLE

When, now, we turn to investigate the subject from the positive side, when we study those whom Jesus championed in order to discover the qualities he approved, the reason for his uncompromising hostility to the economic, political, ecclesiastical, and religious aristocracy of his time becomes at once apparent. He was the enemy of the rich and powerful because he was the friend of the poor and oppressed.

It is a motley crowd which the Gospels place about Jesus as his supporters and friends. The Galilean multitude, on whom Jesus had compassion because they were as sheep not having a shepherd, must have included both rich and poor. We know that often the scribes and Pharisees came to hear him. Yet the great mass of his audiences must have been those whom the rabbis called the *'ammê hâ-'âreṣ,* the "people of the land," the ignorant multitude whom the Pharisees despised because they did not keep the Law, whom the rich exploited as their legitimate prey, and whom the Sadducees, the Herodian princes, and the Romans bled for tithes and taxes. From the beginning to the end of his public preaching they followed Jesus. One very popular "life" of Jesus has propagated a fundamental misunderstanding of the course of his ministry. By contrasting a "year of popularity" with a "year of opposition," it has suggested that the popularity of Jesus with the multitude declined, a view to which the Fourth Gospel lends some support.[21] According to the testimony of the Gospel of Mark, Jesus was fully as popular with the crowd, whenever he showed himself to them, at the end of his ministry as at the beginning.[22] The opposition of the leaders increased in bitterness, and there was a period of retirement, even of hiding, it would seem. But Jesus was as high in the favor of the multitudes the day before his arrest as when he began his ministry. The enthusiastic company of country pilgrims who had hailed him on the day of the triumphal entry did not desert him, even in the end. It was a city rabble that cried, "Crucify him, crucify him." The deed was done before his friends could rally from their surprise.

In his contacts with the common people Jesus recognized one of the sure signs of his messiahship. When John the Baptist sent to ask whether he was the long-awaited one, he pointed to his ministries to the suffering and his preaching of glad tidings to the poor as unmistakable evidence. Luke shows a thoro understanding of Jesus' spirit in setting at the beginning of his ministry, as a characterization of the whole, the verse from Isaiah,

> "The spirit of the Lord is upon me,
> because he has anointed me to tell glad tidings to poor folks,
> he has sent me to proclaim liberty to captives and sight to blind folks,
> to set people who were beaten down at liberty,
> to proclaim an auspicious year of the Lord." [23]

Both passages suggest by their form and their content the close connection between the aims of Jesus and the half mythological hopes of the ancient world expressed in the court language of Assyria, Babylonia, and Israel.[24]

If we may trust the records, the company of common folk who crowded around the young Carpenter-teacher from Nazareth included Jews and Gentiles; people from Idumea, Perea, and

[21] Jn. 6.66.

[22] Mk. 7.14; 8.1; 9.14, 25; 10.1, 46; 11.1-10.18; 12.12, 37.

[23] Lk. 4.18, a free rendering of Is. 61.1. The answer to John, Mt. 11.5 = Lk. 7.22, is a combination of Is. 35.5 f. and 61.1.

[24] See above, pp. 196 f., 237 f., 241-48.

Phoenicia rubbed shoulders with men from Judea and Galilee. They were in the main the lower classes, the economically unfit, those who by hard labor and frugal living barely succeeded in making ends meet, and those who thru misfortune or ineptitude were playing a losing game, those who were falling behind in the economic race. The scribes and the Pharisees were never there unless they could sit a little apart from the multitude whose touch would have defiled them. The great mass of the people who hung upon Jesus' words were from that vast group who had nothing to lose and everything to gain by an overthrow of the existing order and who found in an impossible Pharisaism no consolation for the overwhelming spiritual and physical ills of life.

Along with them we find another group whose presence must have seemed an insult to the mass of struggling, exploited farmers and working men who made up the majority of Jesus' followers. What did Jesus have in common with the tax-gatherers and sinners, the agents of the Romans, the Herodians, and the Sadducees in robbing the people, and the rebels against the Law who were living in open defiance of the authority of the synagog? How could Peter eat with Levi who taxed his fish? What common attraction in Jesus was there for blind Bartimaeus and rich Zacchaeus? How could white-souled Mary of Nazareth become the friend of the scarlet-robed Mary of Magdala?

Why did Jesus set himself up as the friend and defender of this motley group of poor, despised, and outcast humanity? There were three factors common to the experiences of this amorphous multitude. First, they were despised, neglected, and oppressed by the leaders of the nation. Second, they were "lost." They were wandering hopelessly befogged, not knowing which way to go in order to find themselves. They were "lost" to society, economically unsuccessful, morally weak, self-condemned, or in revolt, religiously neglected and in danger of complete loss of faith. Unless they could be "saved" to themselves and to society, the nation stood in the gravest danger of extinction. To all the leaders they were mere pawns in the game of politics. Third, they were ready to listen to Jesus. They did not think themselves righteous. They were not satisfied with things as they were nor with themselves. They knew they were "lost." Therefore they could in some measure appreciate the truth of the new message that Jesus proclaimed. In some measure they had the open mind, the teachable spirit. But whatever their spiritual receptiveness, they were at least ready for social and economic revolution.

Are we to suppose, then, that poverty and need open the gates of the Kingdom of God? It has been frequently argued that in the Beatitudes Jesus meant to say,

"not that poverty and suffering are in themselves a title to his blessing, but that they dispose the soul to those meek and lowly dispositions which qualify men to receive it, just as, on the other hand, prosperity and riches dispose the heart to be hard and proud."[25]

This raises two questions, first as to Jesus' estimate of meekness, and second as to the effect of poverty on character.

IV. JESUS AND HUMILITY

Far more has been made of the "meekness and gentleness" of Jesus than the facts warrant. In the New Testament the word πραῢς, "meek," appears three times in Matthew and elsewhere only in 1 Peter 3.4. The noun πραΰτης, "meekness," an often mentioned Christian virtue, is used once of Jesus, in 2 Corinthians 10.1, along with ἐπιείκεια. The latter word means "reasonableness," "fairness," "equity," "clemency," and in that sense is applied to Felix in Acts 24.4. The two Matthean passages in which the adjective πραῢς is applied to Jesus set him in contrast to rough and haughty rulers (21.5) and to hard and exacting teachers (11.28 ff.). The word ordinarily means "gentle," "mild," "humane," not "meek" in the sense of servility.[26] The third passage

[25] Godet, on Lk. 6.20 f.

[26] Zech. 9.9, from which Mt. 21.5 is quoted, has *'ânî,'* "afflicted," "poor," but the Greek, the Targum, and the Syriac agree in translating as if they had read *'ânâw,* "humble," "lowly."

in which the word occurs, Matthew 5.5, is evidently an interpolation from Psalm 37.11 and need not be considered here.

The other word applied to Jesus in Matthew 11.29, ταπεινός, usually has unpleasant or derogatory connotations in Greek literature. It is applied to one who is "low," "mean," "servile," "humiliated," or "of low rank," "lowly." In the Septuagint it translates Hebrew words that mean merely "poor," "of lowly station," "afflicted," or "humble."[27] In the language of the Septuagint, which is normative for the New Testament writers, the word has none of the evil suggestions that surround it in Greek writers, just because the Hebrews had an entirely different attitude toward all the poorer classes. Jesus, then, according to Matthew 11.28 f., is kindly, or gentle, not severe and exacting like the scribes; he is modest, unassuming, and approachable, not haughty and scornful, as men in positions of authority are wont to be.

In a quotation from Isaiah 42.1-4 the writer of Matthew (12.16-21) attempts to characterize Jesus as one marked by quietness and lack of ostentation. The occasion for the remark is the statement that Jesus did not wish those whom he had healed to broadcast the news. He was just the opposite of the modern Babbitt. He went quietly about the task of building up true religion without any attempt to attract attention or arouse excitement. Read in the light of its context and its original meaning in Isaiah, the passage may well be applied to Jesus. Unfortunately the "reasonableness and modesty" of the Galilean Carpenter have been made over into weakness and softness. The facts of his life entirely bear out one of the basic contentions of Bruce Barton's *The Man Nobody Knows,* tho his picture may be unhistorical and overdone and may glorify certain objectionable qualities much prized in modern business circles. Jesus was vigorous and efficient. His acts and words, his flouting of conventional social and religious standards, his fierce invectives against the scribes and

[27] *Râsh,* 1 Sa. 18.23; *dâl,* Is. 11.4; 25.4; 26.6; Zeph. 3.12; *dak* and *dakkâ,* Ps. 10.18; see especially Ps. 34.19, ταπεινὸς τῷ πνεύματι; *'ânî,* Prov. 30.14; Is. 14.32; 32.7; 49.13; 51.21; 66.2; Jer. 22.16; *'ânâw,* Am. 2.7; Is. 11.4; Zeph. 2.3; Prov. 3.34; 16.19.

Pharisees, his cleansing of the Temple, all this proves him to have been no effeminate weakling, mildly sorrowful but helplessly ineffective in the presence of evil.

The average strong man, the dominating personality, rarely understands a strength which does not show itself in the mailed fist. He is constitutionally incapable of admiring the passive resister. That a brave and strong man should be willing to die for his cause without trying to kill someone while he was dying is to such persons inconceivable. Their interpretation of Jesus' conduct is reinforced by the misconceptions, product of the same defective mentality, which can see in the death of Jesus only a lamb led to the slaughter. Unfortunately, the common mind has accepted the strong man's conclusion: Jesus was a languid sufferer, a flaccid, passive non-resister. But the records of Jesus' life in the Synoptic Gospels, read in the light, not of Pauline and Johannine mysticism, not of Platonic and Aristotelian theology, but of the history and ideals of his race, prove him to have been a supremely vigorous and courageous social and religious reformer. His humaneness and lowliness consisted in his sympathy for the lowly and the helpless, in the absence of any aristocratic disdain for their unfortunate weaknesses and incapacities, not in a dumb and nerveless yielding to circumstances or a quietistic waiting for God's own good time.

In the light of his actions and teachings what, then, was Jesus' estimate of that often urged but little-practised virtue, humility? One of the clearest indications is to be discovered in his condemnation of pride. The haughty disdain of the Pharisee and the Sadducee for the multitude constituted a considerable part of their sin. Pride means self-centered indifference to the needs and rights of others; it invariably exalts itself by debasing others; it rises by kicking others down. As to positive testimony, since the authenticity of the Matthean Beatitudes is doubtful, they cannot be used. But there is sufficient evidence that Jesus praised modesty and humility. To deny it is as unnecessary as it is impossible. Lack of ostentation was for him a cardinal virtue, for example in prayer, fasting, and almsgiving.[28] Moreover, he selects a child as the best example of the spirit his disciples should emulate. His kingdom belongs to men of childlike spirit. God has hidden the truth from the wise and learned, and revealed it to the simple-minded. He who would be first in the new order must be modest and become the servant of all.[29] Kindliness, the gentleness that becomes a gentleman, simplicity, open-mindedness, teachableness, these are the qualities he approved as indicated by his reported teachings and actions.

He takes a step farther, a step which few of his professed followers have been willing to imitate. He counsels the patient endurance, without retaliation, of insult and injury and an active, beneficent love for the enemy who inflicts wrong. This, possibly more than any other of his teachings, has been responsible for the picture of the lamblike Jesus and for the rejection of his ideal as impossible. Surely this is "interim ethics." Such a principle of conduct could not be applied thruout the centuries under the various trying conditions that have arisen in developing society!

I do not wish to be guilty of doing what a recent writer has called "putting footnotes to the sayings of Jesus" to nullify their application. That has already been done too frequently. Yet three principles must be borne in mind in interpreting such sayings. (1) Jesus was an oriental, a poet, a popular preacher. (2) It is contrary to his own principles to apply his teachings with legalistic literalism. He did not give a new Law. (3) In these passages he was dealing with men's relations as individuals to their fellows, not propounding rules to govern society or guide individuals as citizens in a democratic age. In his teachings we must seek principles of conduct, not rules of thumb. His own uncompromising hostility to people who wronged their fellows is clear enough evidence that he advocated no mere silent endurance of social evils. On the other hand, his sayings regarding non-resistance and suffering for the right clearly indicate that he did not believe in fighting as the proper way to settle disputes. His attitude toward law and

[28] Mt. 6.1-18.

[29] Mk. 10.13 ff.; cf. Mt. 18.2 ff.; Mt. 11.25; Mk. 9.33-36.

his teachings regarding the inwardness of religion warrant the conclusion that there was no place for force in his plan of action. Now the opposite of external force is not passivity, but inward, spiritual force. Jesus' actions and words indicate plainly enough that he was militant and aggressive in his attacks on social wrong. He shows neither fear nor mercy in his excoriation of wrong-doers. For him "lowliness," "humility," did not mean either weakness or servility.

Oye

V. JESUS' ATTITUDE TOWARD MATERIAL POSSESSIONS

What, now, is the relation between poverty and the qualities which belong to the members of the kingdom of God? Does the absence of material possessions work by some spiritual alchemy to produce them? Is there any necessary connection between poverty and piety? Thru practically the whole history of the Hebrews and the Jews there had been a close relationship.[30] Very few indeed who were truly pious could ever acquire wealth. It is universally true that few who accumulate wealth, even by just means if that is possible, remain strictly pious. Wealth produces wickedness, but the corollary that poverty produces piety does not follow. Piety usually produces poverty, but one cannot turn that sentence around. Does poverty produce humility? Humility, in the sense in which Jesus exemplifies it, as gentleness, consideration for others, a spirit of service and sacrifice, often produces poverty or at least prevents the acquisition of wealth. Wealth usually kills humility. But poverty does not necessarily engender true humility, nor any other qualities that belong to children of the loving heavenly Father.

True

On few topics have Christian exegetes and theologians written more pious piffle, or rather impious cant, than on the blessings of poverty. Want makes dependence and servility. It breeds the "slave morale" which Nietzche rightly decried. It stunts the finer mental and spiritual capacities which might easily develop into

Oye

[30] See above, pp. 266-74.

rich fruitfulness. How many artists, scientists, and statesmen does the world lose because the children of the poor lack opportunities! No one who knows intimately the lives of poor people would deny that beauty of character may develop in spite of dire want and constant adversity. The careers of men like Lincoln prove that the want of material possessions is for some only a handicap to be overcome. Plain living that may seem poverty to some is famous for the company it keeps. But all that one may say does not alter the fact that poverty is a curse which only an infinitesimal portion of those born to it escape. One need but stop to think of the underfed millions of China, India, and Africa, of the city slums of the western world, of famine, filth, disease, ignorance, and immorality that flourish in poverty like bacteria in sewage. Children born to squalor and neglect, reared in hunger and crime, old age dying in loneliness and want, a life of struggle, deprivation, anxiety, and suffering, such are the blessings of poverty! Blind class hatred, inordinate, if unsatisfied, lust for the comforts and pleasures wealth can buy, constant striving to add a little to the little already gained, all this is as subversive of noble character as fabulous wealth and luxury. Poverty does not fit one for the kingdom of God.

Why, then, does Jesus demand poverty of his followers? Why does the church recognize such men as St. Francis and Tolstoi as the truest exemplifications of the spirit of Christ? The answer is that Jesus did not demand poverty, but rather undivided allegiance, of his followers. That which men admire in St. Francis is not his poverty but the devotion of which his poverty was the evidence and the symbol. The fact that Jesus asked the rich young ruler to sell all his property and give it away as alms does not imply that he makes the same demand of others. Even if the Son of man had not where to lay his head, we need not conclude that he expected the same of all who should come after him. There is no evidence that Levi, and Peter and his partners abandoned their families and their property when they dropped their work to follow Jesus.[31] Tolstoi's failure ever to become a true Tolstoian

[31] The phrase "leaving all," found only in Lk. 5.11, 28, is manifestly an editorial addition.

is evidence that his common sense stopped short of the actual practice of a doctrinaire theory. Jesus was not an ascetic; he worshiped poverty as little as Mammon. No, humanity.

The whole tenor of Jesus' teaching makes it clear that he could never have thought poverty to be in itself a qualification for entrance into the kingdom of God, least of all the sole qualification. Rather his attitude toward the entire question of property is based upon a principle which applies without discrimination to rich and to poor. It has been trenchantly stated by Alexander Irvine:

> "The power of Mammon to poison a spiritual atmosphere . . . is subtle, insidious, and deceptive. Millions are unconscious that they are under the spell of it. They think in bulk. Who, being a god, would not rather taint millions with pennies than dozens with millions? No, it is not the amount. It is the spirit." [32]

Jesus said to the rich, "Do not store up for yourselves treasures on earth. . . . You cannot be slaves to both God and Mammon." Then he turned to the poor with equally pertinent advice: "Do not be anxious about the way you live, about food and drink and clothing." The rich man's heart is lost in his treasures, the poor man's heart is lost in his worries. One is as far from the Christian spirit as the other.

Then, as now, the vast majority of poor people were as far from understanding the teachings of Jesus as the most perverse rich man. Jesus demanded of both a devotion to worthier ends than the pursuit of material well-being. "Seek first God's kingdom," that is the basic demand of Jesus. No man could serve God and have his heart immersed in other interests.

The rich man can give his wealth away. How can the poor man escape his worries? When he is already hungry and naked, when the essential lower needs of the body are not satisfied, how can he set his mind on higher things? It is all very well for Jesus to talk to well-fed Galilean peasants in the sunlit glow of the Galilean springtide about living like birds and lilies, without anxiety or foreboding. Can Jesus have meant to say to the vast multitude of the suffering poor merely, "Depart in peace, be

[32] *The Carpenter and his Kingdom,* New York, 1922, pp. 223 f.

warmed and fed"? What was his medicine for haunting, gnawing poverty? If he demands of the rich "not inner freedom in the possession of riches, but full liberation from them," [33] how much more must he demand for the poor, not martyr endurance or Stoic indifference, but the possibility of escape from their cares and sufferings.

Now it appears to me that Jesus clearly recognized the fact that preoccupation with the acquisition and expenditure of wealth was the major social evil. The master iniquities of his age, as of ours, were connected with money-making. Those complaints, so often repeated thru all of the history of the ancient Orient, prove it always to have been thus. In their pursuit of wealth the rich oppressed the poor, the strong the weak. Did Jesus see, as we now do, that the Roman Empire was a great business enterprise? Did he have any inkling of the fact that his people stood for a nomadic-agricultural ideal of simple living, while Rome stood for an industrial-commercial ideal with concomitant wealth, luxury, and wickedness? It is absurd to ask the question. Yet, with that instinct for truth which distinguishes him, he chose the best in the traditions and temper of his people. He saw, what the ancient world had always seen, that wealth and luxury are always accompanied by poverty and suffering. He saw that the pursuit and possession of wealth inevitably produce exploitation and injustice. Wealth is the major cause of social wrong.[34]

VI. JESUS' IDEAL OF LIFE

The recognition of this insidiously poisonous influence of material luxury and culture drove Jesus to his so-called *lebensverneinende,* or anti-cultural attitude. The term is a misnomer, to be sure. Yet, while Jesus gives no systematic teaching of communism, no complete and absolute condemnation of all rich men, expresses no conviction that private property and with it poverty

[33] Weiss-Bousset, *Die Schriften des Neuen Testaments,* 3 ed. (1917), p. 282.

[34] E. A. Ross, *Sin and Society,* Boston-New York: Houghton Mifflin, 1907, p. 97.

are to disappear from the earth, he does exhibit what may very mildly be described as a "negative attitude to property." Jesus has a "non-political and non-cultural standpoint." [35]

This "negative attitude" of Jesus is to be interpreted, however, merely as a natural expression of the nomadic-agricultural ideal which belonged to the cultural tradition of his race. The prophets had voiced the insistent demand that every family should possess its own freehold and should enjoy it undisturbed by want or war. They had recognized the inescapable fact that such an ideal is impossible of realization if a few are to have great estates. Inordinate wealth in the hands of the few necessarily involves unendurable privation for the many. Jesus' so-called anti-cultural attitude must not be misinterpreted as harboring the slightest measure of asceticism. The tendency of Pauline Christianity to emphasize the cross has led to a complete misunderstanding of the spirit of Jesus. The ascetic tendencies which were so strong in the Roman world soon overshadowed the practical Galilean working man who had rejoiced in sunshine and flowers and the pleasures of social living. John the Baptist may have come "neither eating nor drinking," but the Son of man was so often seen at feasts in the company of men enjoying the good things of life that he was called, so he tells us, a "glutton and drunkard." The basic wrong in the society of his age lay in the fact that only a few could thus simply and happily enjoy life. Undue wealth, selfish greed, thoughtless luxury, and religious narrowness all combined to defraud the many of their rights as children of the loving heavenly Father. Therefore Jesus boldly and bitterly attacked the existing social order and proposed that men make a complete about-face in their attitude toward the acquisition and use of wealth.

Those who deny that Jesus had a social message have rightly called attention to the fact that his teachings on social conduct usually seem to consider the effects of conduct on the person acting rather than upon those whom he affects by his action. He says, "Love your enemies that you may be sons of your heavenly

[35] Klausner, *Jesus of Nazareth,* pp. 107 and 376.

Father," not "that you may win your enemies and make them sons of the Father." This may well be due to another of the elements in the nomadic-agricultural ideal of ancient Israel, that emphasis upon the value and rights of each individual member of the nation. It received new emphasis and interpretation in the individualism of Ezekiel and post-exilic Judaism. Jesus' evaluation of the individual life as infinitely precious has universally been recognized as one of his great contributions to the ideals of mankind. His peculiar service, however, lay in extending the application of this valuation. In an effort to teach the moral values of religion the prophets, psalmists, and apocalyptists had narrowed the circle of God's interest down to the small remnant who obeyed the Law. Jesus found a way to maintain the highest ethical standards and at the same time to show that God cared not only for those within the fold but for the lost, the outsiders, as well. The publican, the sinner, and by implication the Gentile, the poorest as well as the richest, the most ignorant as well as the most learned, all were under the care of the loving Father. Jesus' thought is not individual, it is not social; it may properly be called universal humanism.

Whatever, then, worked injury to vast numbers of potential children of God was a terrible wrong. Self-centered pride, preoccupation with legalistic trifles, and undue emphasis on the forms of religion all led to indifference to weightier matters of the Law, justice, mercy, and faithfulness. Much more did the accumulation of wealth not only produce in its possessor a type of character that was the antithesis of God's love, but it also produced poverty as its inevitable fellow, and poverty necessarily involved the limitation and degradation of multitudes who were fully as valuable in God's sight as the rich. There is no respect of persons with God. A simple life rejoicing in the good things of the world and in happy companionship with one's fellows, without envy, enmity, greed, censoriousness, or struggle for precedence and power, such is Jesus' ideal of life as one discovers it in the Synoptic Gospels. And he desires to make this ideal realizable for every individual of every sort.

VII. THE PATH TO THE IDEAL

Such an ideal he found absolutely unattainable in society as it was constituted. Before it could be realized men must tread a difficult, toilsome path. Those who longed for it must abstain from many of the good things of life and must suffer without limit at the hands of the wicked. And the wicked also would suffer endless woes of their own making, for there must of necessity intervene a complete reversal of present conditions, which were wholly evil, the exact antithesis of God's will. The proud must be humbled, the wicked must be put out of their places of power, the rich must be shorn of their riches, for pride that scorned one's fellows, wealth selfishly enjoyed, and power unjustly exercised were the chief blights on individual character and the chief sources of social evil. This overturning of the present constitution of society, this complete reversal of conditions, was the great hope of Jesus. The certainty that it was soon to take place was the dominant note in his preaching. The glad tidings that God's reign was soon to replace the present reign of evil was the central theme of his message.

Sometimes with grim humor, sometimes with biting sarcasm, he proclaims that, when this great reversal takes place, the last shall be first and the first shall be last, the humble shall be exalted, and they that have exalted themselves shall be abased. The king brings in the poor, the blind, the halt, the lame from the byways and hedges to enjoy the feast. The rich were to receive no consideration, the well-fed were to go hungry, the careless revelers were to mourn; but the sad should enjoy the pleasures of life, the hungry should have enough to eat, and the poor should be in possession of all good things when God reigned upon the earth.

The Lukan Beatitudes and Woes are thoroly intelligible and absolutely fitting in the context of this great reversal. They have nothing to do with individual qualifications. They do not mean that every poor person, merely because of his poverty, has the moral and spiritual qualities that characterize the sons of God, nor do they mean that no rich man can hope for a place in the new order.

why his gospel was so revolutionary.

They do not overlook, either in the one direction or the other, the fact that God is a God of justice, that sin must be punished and righteousness rewarded. We must not misunderstand their paradoxical, hyperbolical conciseness. What they do mean to say is that the ancient hope of the poor is to be realized. The Beatitudes are a reaffirmation of that confidence in the divine justice which we have discovered in some of the earliest written documents of the Sumerians and have traced thru all the history of the Near East. When Jesus said, "Happy are you, O ye poor," he meant to say that under the reign of God those who now suffered poverty would have their rights vindicated. When he said, "Woe to you, O ye rich," he included in his condemnation not so much the individual rich man as the social order which made grinding poverty and luxurious wealth necessary concomitants.[36]

The Lukan Beatitudes proclaim Jesus' belief that God should reign upon earth, that his will should be done here as it is done in heaven, as Matthew puts it in the Lord's Prayer. The Matthean Beatitudes surely represent a re-editing of the original sayings of Jesus to introduce ideas which, to be sure, are in the main consistent with his teachings elsewhere in the Synoptic Gospels, but which spiritualize away his original intention. The Lukan Beatitudes are also thoroly in the spirit of other sayings of his, and their concise vigor is much more likely to be original with Jesus than to have come from an editor. Jesus was constantly preaching just such a revolutionary coming of the Kingdom. Taken in this sense the Beatitudes needed no reinterpretation except for those who believe that luxury and want, wealth and poverty, injustice and suffering, and a capitalistic organization of society are divinely ordained to continue to the end of time. When the Beatitudes were put in a thoroly non-eschatological context at the beginning of the Matthean Sermon on the Mount and used to describe the qualifications for entrance into the kingdom of heaven, they had to be reinterpreted, but such was not the original inten-

[36] See above, pp. 245-91, and article, "The Beatitudes in the Light of Ancient Ideals," *JBL*, 46 (1927), 50-61. But see Boehmer, *JBL*, 45 (1926), 298-304.

tion of Jesus. He was proclaiming the principles of justice which should dominate the earth under the reign of God.[37]

How and when Jesus expected the new age to dawn we cannot determine with certainty. His language is highly figurative. We cannot be certain as to the authenticity of all his reported sayings. Admittedly authentic sayings appear in different connections in different Gospels, contexts which vitally affect their meaning. Contemporary Judaism, the New Testament, and the Gospels themselves present such a diversity of views that dogmatism is as impossible as it is undesirable. Previous discussions have indicated that he could not have expected it to be introduced by the revolutionary methods of his Galilean compatriots. The forces in which he trusted were moral and spiritual.[38] The kingdom was God's, and he would accomplish his great purpose by divine, not human, methods. Man's part, so far as he has any, seems to consist in living according to the divine principles of justice and unselfishness, in sacrifice, suffering, and service. These are not the methods the human mind would naturally choose, yet we must admit that, if men would adopt them, the reign of God would be here. In this, as in other matters, Jesus laid down principles, leaving the details to human ingenuity and intelligence. Methods necessarily vary in detail from age to age and from land to land. Only the principles are universally and eternally true.

The present discussion is concerned with ideals, not with methods, and with the principles that are to determine method only insofar as they throw light upon ideals. It is tremendously significant that Jesus rejected all use of force and depended solely upon a direct appeal to the good instincts within the human heart, the foolishness of preaching, as Paul calls it. Otherwise the question as to how and when the reign of God was to begin is relatively unimportant. What must be known in order to determine Jesus' ideal, is its character. If the argument above is correct, the last is reasonably clear. Jesus believed that the eternal principles of

[37] See the various interpretations of the Beatitudes instanced above, pp. 3-11.

[38] See above, pp. 321-28.

divine justice were to be embodied in a social order in which there should be neither poverty nor luxury, neither pride nor servility, neither selfishness nor suffering, but where every person would enjoy all the good things of life so far as that was possible without injury to others. The shepherds and the magi, charmed by the angels' song of peace and good will, would stand together as brethren at the cradle of universal humanity and together they would offer their gifts for the common social good.

CHAPTER XII

THE ESSENCE OF THE SOCIAL GOSPEL

In the preceding chapters an effort has been made to present the chief factors that had entered into the historical development of the numerous ideals of social justice current in Jesus' day, and to indicate their bearing upon the interpretation of the gospel he proclaimed. It now remains to draw together the multifarious threads of this investigation and summarize the elements which, in the light of history, the social gospel of Jesus actually included. This will be done without any attempt to apply his teachings to modern problems, save insofar as occasional reference to present conditions may serve to make clearer the interpretation adopted.

I. THE CULTURAL INHERITANCE

There are to be remembered, first of all, the physical conditions which created the economic and social situation with which Jesus had to deal. A climate that produced vigorous and prolific men and women; a soil which, under that semi-arid and capricious climate, could not provide wealth, but only a bare subsistence, to be won by steady industry and laborious toil; an intermediate position between the desert and the sown that made a constant conflict of ideals inevitable and kept ever before the people's minds the ideals of simplicity and individual initiative that belong to the nomad; a central location on the highways of commerce which exposed the Jewish people to all the cultural winds that blew and made further cultural conflicts inescapable; a little land divided into infinitesimal groups by its diversities—these are some of the geographical factors that entered into the making of the Jewish people.

On the racial and political side there fall to be considered the motley mixture of peoples that entered into the making of the Hebrew nation; economic conditions and political vicissitudes which prevented it from ever enjoying real independence and opportunity for expansion; political and cultural conflicts with other peoples which eventually produced one of the most tenacious race complexes of which history has record, a race complex based upon a conscience of steel and a religious faith of adamant and combined with a dominating patriotism resting upon a supposed covenant between God and his chosen people. The Jews believed, therefore, that they had an assured national destiny. This race complex, in the time of Jesus, was stung to new sensitiveness by sharp divisions. The theoretical solidarity of race, morals, and religion was shattered by innumerable parties, none of which had a program adequate to the situation. The nation's pride, moreover, was sorely wounded by failure to realize any of the high hopes based upon faith in its manifest destiny.

The popular conception of the national destiny was a product of various inherited pattern ideas. From the Arabian desert and the rocky fields of Palestine had come a nomadic-agricultural ideal, a belief in the simple life, in the dignity of labor, and in the value of the individual. In common with their neighbors, the Hebrews believed that on some golden day Paradise with its peace and plenty would return, probably thru the appearance of a just, benevolent, and divinely aided ruler. One of the constantly recurring elements in this expectation was the faith that, since evil was to be overthrown and righteousness triumph, the poor, forever downtrodden and oppressed, would come to their rights and would enjoy the prosperity of the returned Paradise, while their oppressors, the rich, the proud, and the powerful, would suffer fitting punishment. The present relations of the social classes would be exactly reversed.

Hebrew morality and religion, admittedly the highest the western world had then produced, were the outcome of a long series of cultural and social conflicts in which the prophets had stood for the nomadic-agricultural ideal, that is for simplicity of living and the rights of the poor, while they had bitterly opposed the growth of luxury, extravagance, and social injustice which seemed inescapable results of commercialized society. The prophets were spokesmen for economic unrest and social discontent, as well as for pure, spiritual religion, spokesmen for the former, as they would insist, because spokesmen for the latter. They had, therefore, found themselves unpopular, persecuted, even martyred, because the king, the nobles, the priests, indeed all the ruling classes were usually those who profited by the commercialism which oppressed and robbed the mass of the nation. But, in spite of their lack of success and their decided social bias, their words had been faithfully preserved in the national literature and had come to be regarded as God's word to his people. The psalmists and the apocalyptists had succeeded them as spokesmen alike for God and the people. Among the many parties and tendencies of post-exilic Judaism there were numbers of the poor and oppressed who held true to their faith in God and the national future and who counted themselves the true representatives of Israel, voicing their bitter sense of wrong and their ardent hopes of deliverance in the Psalms or in those extravagant flights of fancy which we call apocalypses.

II. THE EXISTING SITUATION

The divisions which in the days of Jesus cut across the theoretical solidarity of the Jewish race were of various kinds. On the economic side the classes consisted of the rich and powerful with their satellites and the laboring masses, and between the two a middle class of uncertain limits and tenure. On the social side the Sadducees claimed superiority because of their birth and position, the Pharisees because of their piety. On the religious side, there were innumerable sects among those who supported the Temple worship and, besides, the Essenes, who, apparently, refused to join in its sacrifices. On the cultural side there were the Sadducees and others of the rich who favored cultural assimilation, the great majority of the nation who were bitterly anti-foreign, and the fairly numerous group of outcasts and strays who had weakly succumbed to the temptations of the more joyful Hellenistic civilization. On the political side there were the Sadducees, the ruling aristocracy, favoring submission to Rome; the Pharisees and rabbis desiring, yet fearing, emancipation and professing political quietism while they satisfied their pietistic libido with cultural separatism and legalistic scrupulosity; the apocalyptists with flaming hopes of an imminent supernatural revolution; and the practical patriots, among whom the Zealots and Sicarii arose, who believed that God would perform his promises when they undertook to free themselves by force.

The national problem was an inextricable tangle of economic, political, and religious factors. There was evident exploitation of the mass of the population by the Romans and by the rich of their own race. Competition with the Romans and with other foreign peoples made the situation of the Jews doubly hard because of handicaps due to lack of natural resources and to burdens and restrictions imposed by their religion. The economic situation must have acted as a constant, even if not consciously recognized, irritant. The occasional mistakes, offenses, and injustices of their Roman governors were magnified into unbearable oppression by the national self-consciousness. Their patriotic pride was fed by a combination of beliefs, in part well founded, in their racial, moral, and religious superiority, and in the certainty of their eventual triumph. Their political dependence and their evident, if unacknowledged, cultural backwardness gave them an inferiority complex that could be removed only by a major operation. Such a situation could not long continue. Some new adaptation had to be discovered. Either the nation's ideals must be changed and unified, or they must be altogether abandoned.

For this extremely difficult problem none of the recognized national leaders had a solution. The Essenes sought escape from the ills of the world in flight to a monastic life. The scribes and Pharisees also saw hope only in flight from the surrounding world, into a life hedged and confined by the Law, a *régime* of impossibly meticulous scrupulosity which involved a virtual abandonment of political ambitions and of all cultural relations with other peoples. The apocalyptist saved his faith by transporting himself into a world of dreams. The "fourth sect" sought emotional relief in action; they urged immediate revolt against Rome, believing implicitly that divine aid miraculously given would enable them to conquer the world and realize the promised reign of Israel, which was the reign of God. Eventually they won to their point of view enough of the nation to precipitate the Jewish War. After its tragic failure and the equally unsuccessful revolt under Hadrian the faithful remnant returned to the scribal ideal and retired within the Chinese Wall of the Law. The scribal ideal was a method of social adaptation which preserved the national self-consciousness and with it the great moral values which Judaism enshrined, but, as modern liberal Judaism recognizes, at the expense of the possibility of growth within the group or service to the world outside. Was there a path by which Judaism might have escaped this long period of misunderstanding, isolation and dormancy?

A satisfactory solution of the nation's problem must offer some medicine for its economic, political, and social ills. It could not consist in specious rationalization or in blind flight into unreality. It was a thorogoing and revolutionary solution which Jesus proposed. What were its essential elements?

III. THE CORRECT APPROACH TO THE INTERPRETATION OF JESUS

If modern scholarship is to make any advance toward a correct interpretation of the teachings of Jesus, it must determine the point from which to approach him. It must discover the cultural background to which he belonged and interpret him as a part of that civilization. The thesis of this study is that his conception of the reign of God, in other words his social ideal, is to be interpreted out of the messianic, or, better, the apocalyptic, hopes of his people, and that these hopes, in turn, are to be understood as part of a vast cultural complex to which the wise men, the psalmists, and the prophets of Israel have made their contributions, but which owes many most important elements to the prophets and social thinkers of Egypt and Babylon and Sumer and perhaps not less to the ill-defined but tenaciously maintained longings of the suffering poor in all the ancient Near East. Judaism had filched certain picturesque superstitions from Mazdaism, it had modified its anthropomorphic conceptions of deity to meet the attack of Hellenism, but there is not evidence sufficient to prove that its essential social ideals had been affected by the vivid apocalyptic conceptions of Mazdaism, the political ideas of the Greeks, or the asceticism and other-worldliness of Hellenistic theosophy.

Jesus constantly uses the language of the prophets, psalmists, and apocalyptists. What he says must be interpreted in the light of their ideas, not according to the mysticism of Paul and the Fourth Gospel. When he condemns luxury and wealth, we are not to turn to Hellenistic asceticism for explanatory parallels, but to the nomadic-agricultural ideal, remembering the conditions of life in Palestine and the history of the development of that ideal. When he denounces pride and power, we must not think of the struggles of the *demos* and the *plebs* in Greece and Rome, but of the prophetic condemnation of social injustice and economic exploitation. When he urges his followers to share their last crumb with the needy, we are not to recall the communistic theories of Greek philosophers, but Hebrew ideals of brotherhood and benevolence. When he promises the coming of God's kingdom and accepts a place as its messiah, we have to remember all that the phrases connote in the literature of his race. We must remember, too, that an almost identical hope runs thru all ancient thinking, and everywhere it implies, not some other-worldly, heavenly happiness, but the righting of wrongs and the cure of sufferings on this earth, by obedience to the laws of the gods.

When he speaks of the poor, we have to interpret his words in the light of what apocalyptists, psalmists, and prophets say about the wrongs of the oppressed. And we must go farther back, to Gudea and Uru-kagina. The whole ancient Orient evidently believed that the rich were the inevitable oppressors, the gods the natural champions of the weak. When the laws of the gods were obeyed, oppression would be at an end. The Hebrews believed that Yahweh was the defender of the poor, the widow, the fatherless. Can we understand the words of Jesus in any other sense? He also, like the prophets and apocalytists, is the champion of the *'ammê hâ-'âres,* the "people of the land," the outcasts and the sinners, the multitude of the neglected and despised, the poor and oppressed. Necessarily, then, he was the enemy of the Sadducees, the Pharisees, the rabbis, the scribes, and all the rulers and the upper classes who were responsible for the evils he saw so clearly, and who ignored these evils while they regarded themselves as the true representatives of religion and arrogated to themselves the position of shepherds of the people.

In adopting this social gospel Jesus had sponsored an ideal that was universally human. The Roman Saturnalia, the Athenian Cronia, the Greek myths of the Golden Age, the numerous literary and practical efforts toward communism among the Greeks, and the democracy of many of the mystery religions show how widespread the same ideas were in all the Mediterranean world. Christianity could hardly have grown as it did if it had been able to offer nothing more than a promise of heavenly bliss to satisfy the ineradicable demand for justice which perennially blossoms in the human heart. It is as a champion of justice that Jesus holds a place in the homage of the modern world.

yes ×

IV. CURRENT MISCONCEPTIONS OF JESUS

This approach to the interpretation of Jesus' teachings at once renders impossible many of the current views as to his plan and purpose. If one accept the central contention of this study that Jesus is to be understood in the light of the social ideals of the ancient Orient, and not in the light of Hellenistic Christianity as it developed out of the work of Paul and his fellows, a considerable number of current conceptions of Jesus are at once revealed as mistaken.

There are those who object to the representation of Jesus as a

+ When say these ideals only in Heaven 2 ans.? If G. cant bring them here with me who to be in H. how is he to bring them in H.?

champion of the masses and a foe of the upper classes because he is meek and lowly, a Prince of peace. There is a militant note in the Carpenter-Prophet's social message that seems out of place in the cathedral's dim religious light. It disturbs the mystical meditations of the trustful saint. A learned and intensely sincere Jewish rabbi insists that Jesus could not have driven the money-changers out of the Temple. It would have been quite inconsistent for a leader, famed for his gentleness and forbearance, one who had just been proclaimed king and deliverer of his people, to inaugurate his messianic reign with a riot, with an open and fierce attack on the priests and teachers of Israel, and on people who were peacefully pursuing a lawful trade. He was not the man to brand the teachers of his people "hypocrites," "scorpions," "whited sepulchres." "There was not enough of gall in him to force such words from his mouth." He who had taught the duty of loving one's enemies, of blessing those that cursed, certainly would not curse and harm.[1]

Entirely apart from the earnest rabbi's surely unfounded assumption that there could have been no evil in ancient Judaism, it is certainly wrong to picture Jesus as a mild-mannered mystic without courage or virility. From what source does such a conception of him come? Certainly it does not fit into the Judaism of the first century. Many an ancient as well as a modern Jewish rabbi who speaks fearlessly of the sins and shortcomings of his own people would be immensely the superior of such a Jesus. Love does not exclude but necessarily includes regard for the sufferings of the underprivileged and oppressed. Moreover, Jesus was not a rabbi. He was a successor of the Old Testament prophets, and surely no one ever spoke more vigorously and courageously of the sins of the chosen people than did they. And their denunciations included priests, princes, and prophets. No undue reverence for authority sealed their mouths.

The evidence completely discredits the spiritualizing and antisocial interpretations which have been proposed for Jesus' teach-

[1] Joseph Krauskopf, *A Rabbi's Impressions of the Oberammergau Passion Play,* Philadelphia, 1907, pp. 63 f. See above, pp. 341 f.

ings. How strangely his words have been tortured to fit current social conventions! When did Jesus ever teach that wealth is good? Rather it is a contaminating evil which can be made to serve the ends of righteousness only as we get rid of it. The unjust steward gave up his profits, the rich young ruler was to sell all his property. The parable of the *minæ* is as far from being an encomium on the ability to make money as that of the eleventh-hour workers is from teaching a minimum wage. Matthew equally perverts the meaning of Jesus with his "poor in spirit," his "hunger and thirst after righteousness." The spiritual outlook of Jesus and the religious element in his teaching are not to be denied. He did believe in trustful teachableness that seeks the truth, in humility that drives to service. The methods by which he expected his ideal to be realized were moral and spiritual. What Matthew makes him say in the Beatitudes he does say elsewhere. But that is not what he meant to say in the Sermon on the Plain. The ideals of Jesus could not be realized in the heart without affecting the outward conditions of life, nor, indeed, could they be fully realized until outward conditions were radically changed.

When, therefore, Jesus said, "Blessed are you poor," he did not mean, "Blessed are the pious," those who are humbly sensible of their spiritual deficiencies. When he promised the poor the kingdom of God, he did not mean that spiritual happiness here and hereafter are intended to compensate for present material sufferings and economic injustices. He did not praise poverty as if there were some virtue in hunger and want. When he prohibited the laying up of treasures on earth, he was not glorifying ascetic self-abnegation, as if there were spiritual values in unhappiness. Jesus was no Cynic. When he called down woes upon the rich, the happy, and the well fed, he was not attacking individuals, but a system. He means that any social, political, or economic organization of society which inevitably perpetuates proud, heartless wealth and dull, grinding poverty is wrong and must be changed if God's will is to be done on earth.

The objections of the religio-historical school to a social gospel are based upon a perverted method. They interpret Jesus by the predominant forms which Christianity adopted in the Roman Empire under the influence of Hellenistic civilization, not by the inherited categories of Jewish-oriental thinking, a procedure which, as I have tried to show, is entirely wrong. Moreover, the idea that religion stands by itself as an underived element, an independent, unrelated area in the human soul, is contrary to all the findings of modern psychology. Religion is not the product of external environment; that can be successfully maintained against the assertions of the geographic and economic determinists. But this does not mean that it is not affected by environment, nor that it can successfully avoid attempting to affect its environment. Religion and morality are indissolubly connected and morality cannot escape responsibility for social conditions. No true worshiper of a loving heavenly Father can avoid duties to his neighbors, and these, according to the teachings of Jesus, include some responsibility for his physical condition and not merely for the heavenly salvation of his soul. So long as Jesus is regarded as the author of the parable of the Good Samaritan and the Matthean picture of the final judgment, he must be supposed to have had some program for ministering to human need.

The pre-millennialist, therefore, who would have all programs of social betterment postponed until the Second Coming, is neglecting his duty even as did the priest and the Levite in Jesus' parable. The thorogoing eschatologist represents Jesus as doing exactly what the consistent millenarian does, advocate an *Interimsethik* valid only for the present evil time before the coming of the New Age. Just what Jesus meant by the coming of the kingdom of God and how he expected it to be brought in we cannot say, but, as I have tried to show, he expected it to come upon this earth and to consist essentially in living according to the rules of conduct which he laid upon his disciples.[2] There is no sufficient evidence that he believed it to be some transcendental mode of life. Paul's saying, "Flesh and blood cannot inherit the kingdom of God," is not an echo of anything we can find in the Synoptic Gospels. In view of the unqualified inwardness, the profound

[2] See above, pp. 326 ff.

spiritual insight of Jesus' conceptions of morals and religion, it seems to me impossible that he should have believed that any external, tho divine, interference with the physical and social order, any miraculous transformation of the world and men, could make men truly children of God, even as forced compliance with civil and ecclesiastical ordinances could accomplish no real change of human character. Rather, to put the matter in modern terms, he expected by his teachings, life, and death to release in the spirits of men and human institutions social forces which God could use to transform the world into a place more in accordance with his will.

If this be true, Jesus was no Marxian revolutionary. He was not planning to lead the world's proletariat against the financial aristocracy of Rome. The whole of Jesus' teaching is so consistently opposed to the use of force that one can hardly understand how his aristocratic enemies could have perverted his message into a seditious opposition to the Empire. If Jesus is right, the use of force can never promote the coming of God's kingdom. The issues of life are out of the heart. Laws cannot affect the will, but only the outward conduct, and outward conduct is of importance only as expressing the will. Jesus had all the sympathy for the wrongs of the poor that any communist could ask. His purpose to do away with these wrongs was steadfast, but his method was poles apart from those of the socialist, the communist, and the modern reformer-by-legislation. Even the best laws are of value only as the concrete and effective expression of the will of the vast majority of the social group. As we are slowly learning, a bad will can wreck any scheme of government. If the boss has no convention to buy, he will overtly or covertly buy the electorate of a whole state. It is the good will that is permanently effective, and that alone.

V. THE PURPOSE AND METHOD OF JESUS

In the foregoing criticism of current misconceptions of Jesus, the essential elements of his purpose and method have been restated. Jesus was neither communist, Bolshevist, nor socialist. He nowhere attempts to lay down a constitution for a perfect democracy. Yet he was a revolutionary, and it was because he was a revolutionary that he was put to death; he was a revolutionary, not against Rome, but against the constituted authorities of his own people. Like the prophets, he rebelled against those who were determined to regiment opinion, to force the nation into a groove. Worse than that, he was no hundred-per-cent patriot. Like Jeremiah he counseled submission to a hated foreign power. He refused to countenance war or revolution. He urged his followers, "Resist not evil. . . . When the Roman soldier forces you to carry his pack one mile, go with him two." He counseled that they should pay their taxes to the empire. He was a defeatist.

I can hardly believe that it was for this reason alone that he was put to death, as has sometimes been argued.[3] There were other factors that were more effective. The revolutionary party was not yet in power. Neither Pharisees nor Sadducees wished rebellion against Rome. What united the two major parties in the Sanhedrin against Jesus was the fear that his attacks upon them would completely undermine their authority over the people. He was exposing their villainy, their weakness, their lack of constructive leadership. They were against him because he was stirring up the masses against them, and their leadership, their privileges, and their emoluments were threatened. They were against him because he was more revolutionary than any Bolshevist. Not only were his social ideals entirely different from theirs, but his methods also were so mysteriously unintelligible to them as to fill them with indescribable forebodings.

In attacking the national leaders Jesus walked in the footsteps of the prophets, who had trod the *via dolorosa* long before him. In his constructive program he went far beyond them. It is possible that at the first he had hoped by his proclamation of the truth to waken the people to the moral attitude which should

[3] So Vladimir G. Simkhovitch, *Toward the Understanding of Jesus*, New York, 1921, pp. 52 ff., 80 ff.

* Followers of Tolstoy & C. O. persecuted in Russia by Soviet.

make them fit citizens for the kingdom of God when it should come. He may have believed that when enough people were ready, it would come. He told his disciples as he sent them out to preach, if we may trust a lone Matthean passage, that they should not have exhausted the cities of Israel until the end should come.[4] When they returned and it had not come, he went away with the chosen few and began to prepare for another step. The kingdom, he now taught, could come only by suffering. He himself must die and all his true disciples must follow in his train. Here he was adopting the view long since proposed by the great Prophet of the Exile in his doctrine of the Suffering Servant. Whether the Servant be the nation or the individual, the lesson is the same. For reasons we cannot entirely understand, suffering is necessary if the world is to be brought to God.

How can suffering advance the cause of social justice? The poor have been suffering thru all the ages, but they have not thereby brought the kingdom of God nearer to actuality. Jesus demands suffering of a different kind. This is a point at which he went far beyond the best of his immediate predecessors. Their righteousness had consisted too largely in personal piousness, ritual observances, and passive submission to the will of God and to the ills of life. Jesus demanded a peaceable and teachable temper, a modesty and kindliness that made aggression and injustice toward anyone impossible; he demanded also the willingness to suffer for righteousness' sake, the readiness to sacrifice all that was dearest in the interest of the kingdom. But his ideal went far beyond mere submission, mere humility, mere suffering, or sacrifice merely for the sake of self-abnegation. The ideal of Jesus was not asceticism but activity, not servility but service.

This is the point at which Jesus made his greatest advance over the prophets whose labors he was continuing. Second Isaiah and the poor who had preserved his idea seem to have thought that by some divine magic their sufferings were to be turned into blessings for the world when the great catastrophic reversal of present conditions should come. Jesus insisted, not on passive endurance,

[4] Mt. 10.23.

but on sacrificial activity for the sake of the kingdom. He came not merely to suffer, but to minister; not merely to deny himself, but to save the world. If he was to save the world, he must include the oppressed poor in his salvation, and the social organization which was responsible for their oppression must be transformed.

We stand related to the oppressing social organization as the common man for whom Jesus spoke never could be in that day. The vast majority had no legal or recognized method by which to express an opinion on public questions. Such expression, indeed, was not desired. Jesus did not contemplate his followers as citizens in a democratic commonwealth. Therefore the duties of the modern Christian cannot be directly inferred from anything he says. But his principles can determine our responsibilities. It is a legitimate inference from his words and actions that we are under obligation to see that justice and righteousness are done. Recognizing the ineffectiveness of the ballot, the insincerity and corruption of politicians, the hypocrisy, heartlessness, and rapacity of commercial life, we will not flee into the wilderness like the Essene, retire within our own righteous group like the Pharisee, or dream our lives away like the apocalyptist, but attack evil wherever it appears in church or state. The sufferings that must inevitably follow we should bear as uncomplainingly as Jesus did his. The disciple is not greater than his Teacher.

There is another point at which Jesus went beyond his predecessors, and it is here that one of the most significant lessons for modern democracy appears. Jesus demanded that the leaders of the people above all others should suffer and serve. No Jew before his time had thought of the messiah as suffering. He was to come in militant pomp and power, or in heavenly glory to rule men with a rod of iron. The supreme contrast between the Christian group and the world lay just in this that

> "The rulers of the nations lord it over them,
> and their great men exercise authority over them.
> It shall not be so among you.
> But whoever among you wishes to become great
> shall be your servant,
> and whoever among you wishes to be first
> shall be your slave."[5]

[5] Mt. 20.25 ff. = Mk. 10.42 ff., cf. Lk. 22.25 f.

Yes

Aye

The democracy of Judaism and of Jesus did not consist in providing ballot boxes. The opinion of the ordinary citizen was not asked on questions of public policy. He had no part in the election of the Sanhedrin. Jesus by force of circumstances was led to trust in moral agencies or to resort to arms. And we are coming to see that all the political machinery of democracy in itself seems to produce little but noise and confusion. With seventy-five per cent of our citizens still children, the ballot can accomplish little. The voice of fifty-one per cent of any electorate is not the voice of God. Moreover, the most intelligent citizen can accomplish nothing by his ballot, for men behind the scenes manipulate the puppets whom they allow to appear as candidates so that the worst appear the best, and the best become the worst. The safety of any group depends upon its leadership. Jesus put his finger on the weakest spot in democracy altho he was speaking of autocracy.

Again, legislation without good will on the part of leaders and people accomplishes as little as did the revolutionaries of 66 A.D. Legislation and all attempts to improve the externals of life, the environment only, is but an effort to save the world by force, and is inevitably doomed to failure. Society and the souls who constitute it can be saved only by a leadership that is so unselfish that it wins by attraction and not by authority. The good that is in men must be discovered and aroused to effective action before we can have a good world.

To turn, now, to another element in the social gospel it is plain in the light of what has been said that a reinterpretation of the nomadic ideal played a considerable part in the teaching of Jesus. It does not appear to me that, as I understand Causse to imply, Jesus and his earliest followers were hostile to civilization as such.[6] The records do not seem to me to indicate that Jesus had either a *lebens-* or a *kulturverneinende* attitude. John the Baptist and many another beside the Essenes may have fled into the Wilderness of Judea, that ancient and honorable refuge of those whom injustice oppressed or luxury distressed. But Jesus, unlike John, came eating and drinking; he was the friend of publicans

[6] *Les "pauvres" d'Israel*, pp. 139 ff.

and sinners; he was even called a glutton and a wine-bibber. He did not forbid marriage. When one reads his exhortations against worry, and against laying up treasures on earth, and even his denunciations of wealth and the service of Mammon, one cannot but feel that he desires the happy use of the good things of the earth without the cares and distractions of undue wealth which make real happiness impossible. The cares of riches choke the word. When one clings to Mammon, he cannot love God. Worst of all, wealth makes poverty; luxury cannot be unless there is want. A social order that produces only superabundance for the few must be wrong, for all have the right to the good things of life.

This is not the place to discuss in detail the application of Jesus' principles to the complex problems of modern civilization. But it cannot be denied that Jesus laid his finger upon the festering sore spot in all civilization as it has developed down to the present day. One of the foremost of American sociologists, E. A. Ross, has said that "the master iniquities of our time are connected with money-making."[7] In a later volume he mentions as the important tasks of our day "the big social services involving questions of fares, prices, wages, hours, and conditions of work, which antagonize prominent people," and concludes:

> "A democracy will use its schools to counteract the anti-social spirit that too often radiates from the big, masterful figures of commercial life. It will rear its youth in the ethics of brotherhood, team-work, and responsibility. In educating for social service, it aims at something greater than lessons in kindness and consideration. It presents life from a new angle. It meets current notions of success and reward with more exacting ideals growing out of a new vision of social welfare. It aims to turn out youth ready not only to make their calling a service but to grapple with the old egoistic, carnivorous type and eject him from places of influence where he can be a sinister model and pace-setter for the next generation."[8]

Is not this putting into terms of modern experience the ideals of Jesus? He looked at the "big, masterful figures," the "old

[7] *Sin and Society,* Boston, 1907, p. 97.

[8] *The Social Trend,* New York, The Century Co., 1922, pp. 181 f.

egoistic, carnivorous type," and said, "It shall not be so among you." Walter Rauschenbusch was justified in asking,

> "Has the teaching of Jesus on private property been superseded by a better understanding of the social value of property? Or has his teaching been suppressed and swamped by the universal covetousness of modern life?"[9]

Jesus does not attack the production of wealth, but the hoarding of it for one's self. He did not criticize the foolish rich man because his fields brought forth bountifully, but because he planned to store his crops for his own enjoyment. From Urukagina to this day the major iniquities of society have been connected with laying up treasures on earth.

Does this seem inevitably to lead to an abandonment of civilization as we know it for something of a vastly different kind? Be it so! There is sociological justification for the ideal of the prophets and Jesus. Charles A. Ellwood has pointed out the fact that social evolution is a matter of pattern ideas which are determined by occupation. When men multiplied and passed beyond the simpler nomadic and agricultural types of society, they began to come into competition for places in the sun. A long series of conflicts arose which developed the predatory ideal, for in the period of "barbarism," only the strong, the predatory, could survive. It was this predatory type, as I have repeatedly pointed out, a type produced by wars and resulting commercial expansion and competition, which produced the poor who suffered from the powerful in ancient Babylonia, Egypt, and Israel. In protest against this "barbarian" civilization the great ethical religions arose, all at about the same time, Buddhism, Confucianism, Zoroastrianism, and the prophetic religion of the Hebrews. The Hebrew religion preserved wonderfully the values of primitive group life, the ideals of the family, fatherhood, brotherhood, service, and love, which were gradually extended to the clan, then to the nation, and finally to the world.[10]

[9] *The Social Principles of Jesus,* New York, The Association Press, 1916, p. 126.

[10] *Christianity and Social Science,* New York, 1923, pp. 37-53; cf. *The Social Problem,* New York, 1915, pp. 48-70.

The Hebrews were able to maintain these ideals, as I have pointed out, because of their peculiar geographic situation and the unusual course of their history. It was the service of the prophets to develop the nomadic ideal, to use the phrase of biblical scholarship, the "values of primary group life," to quote the sociologist. The pious poor and humble of post-exilic times and later the apocalyptists preserved this ideal and handed it on. Jesus took it up and enshrined it in his life and teachings in a form immeasurably superior to its former formulation. He had no sooner done so than, to prove his devotion to his ideal, he died. Within two centuries his followers lost it. The story of that loss is a long and fascinating one, but it cannot be rehearsed here.

The question for us is, Can we find it again? Can we discover the fundamental principles according to which human beings of every sort can associate together in happiness and peace? Can we make it possible for the shepherds and the magi to live together in the world? That is the will of God for the world, to speak theologically. That is the kingdom of God. That is what Jesus meant when he blessed poverty. To the poor belongs the kingdom of God because the oppressions they have suffered, the privations they have endured on account of economic injustice, make a change in the social order imperative, and because the predatory cannot inherit the kingdom. That is what I understand an economist like Thomas Nixon Carver to mean when he insists that the old morality which enabled men to endure privation and hardship without social degeneration must be replaced by a new morality sufficient for an age of unprecendented prosperity. Such a morality surely cannot be based upon the principles of predatory barbarism which now prevail. It is for the leaders of today in economics, sociology, politics, education, and religion to discover the methods by which those principles and ideals that are socially sanative may be embodied in modern civilization, save it from self-destruction, and then leaven it with living forces.

This study was begun with the purpose of discovering what Jesus' ideal for society actually was, and not with the purpose of proving that a certain interpretation of it was a panacea for today's

An ch sold self & authority & war.

SELECTED BIBLIOGRAPHY

DESPITE its length, the following bibliography includes only books frequently cited and those to which the writer owes most or which he believes may be profitably used by students who wish to pursue the subject farther. Its purpose is, first, to aid such students, and, second, to decrease the bulk of the foot-notes. Usually works representing various views on disputed questions are listed. Volumes cited only occasionally or incidentally are sufficiently described in the foot-notes.

ABBREVIATIONS

AJSL = American Journal of Semitic Languages and Literature. Chicago: The University of Chicago Press, 1884-

AJT = American Journal of Theology. Chicago: The University of Chicago Press, 1897-1920

AR. See Breasted, James Henry, in the General Bibliography

ARA. See Luckenbill, Daniel D., in the General Bibliography

CAH = Cambridge Ancient History, ed. by J. B. Bury. S. A. Cook, and F. E. Adcock. Cambridge: The University Press, 1923-

DB = Dictionary of the Bible, 5 vols., ed. by James Hastings. New York: Scribner, 1898-1909

EB = Encyclopedia Biblica, 4 vols., ed. by T. K. Cheyne and J. Sutherland Black. New York: Macmillan, 1899-1903

ERE = Encyclopedia of Religion and Ethics, 13 vols., ed. by James Hastings. New York: Scribner, 1908-27

HTR = Harvard Theological Review. Cambridge: Harvard University Press, 1908-

ICC = International Critical Commentary. New York: Scribner, 1899-

JAOS = Journal of the American Oriental Society. New Haven: Yale University Press, 1843-

JBL = Journal of Biblical Literature. New Haven: Society of Biblical Literature and Exegesis, 1881-

JEA = Journal of Egyptian Archaeology. London: Egypt Exploration Fund, 1914-

JPOS = Journal of the Palestine Oriental Society. Jerusalem: Palestine Oriental Society, 1920-

JR = Journal of Religion. Chicago: The University of Chicago Press, 1921-

JTS = Journal of Theological Studies. London: Milford, 1900-

KAT. See Zimmern, Heinrich, in the General Bibliography below

LAE. See Erman, Adolf, in the General Bibliography

PJB = Palästinajahrbuch des deutschen evangelischen Instituts für Altertumswissenschaft des heiligen Landes zu Jerusalem. Berlin: Mittler, 1905-

QSPEF = Quarterly Statement of the Palestine Exploration Fund. London: Palestine Exploration Fund, 1869-

RTAE. See Breasted, James Henry, in the General Bibliography below

SBA = Sitzungsberichte der preussischen Akademie der Wissenschaften zu Berlin. Berlin: Akademie der Wissenschaften, 1882-

SBE = Sacred Books of the East, tr. by various scholars and ed. by Max Müller. Oxford: Clarendon Press, 1879-1910

SBELE = Sacred Books and Early Literature of the East, ed. by Charles F. Horne. New York-London: Parke, Austin, and Lipscomb, 1917

SEC = Studies in Early Christianity, ed. by Shirley Jackson Case. Presented to Frank Chamberlin Porter and Benjamin Wisner Bacon. New York-London: The Century Co., 1928

ZAW = Zeitschrift für die alttestamentliche Wissenschaft und die Kunde des nachbiblischen Judentums. Giessen: Töpelmann, 1881-

ZDPV = Zeitschrift des deutschen Palästinavereins. Leipzig: Baedeker, 1878-

GENERAL BIBLIOGRAPHY

Badè, William Frederic, The Old Testament in the Light of Today: a Study in Moral Development. Boston-New York: Mifflin, 1915

Barnes, Harry Elmer, The New History and the Social Studies. New York: The Century Co., 1925

Barton, George Aaron, Archaeology and the Bible. 4 ed. Philadelphia: Sunday School Union, 1925.

Bevan, Edwyn, Jerusalem Under the High Priests. London: Arnold, 1912

Breasted, James Henry, AR = Ancient Records of Egypt: Historical Documents. . . . 4 vols. Chicago: The University of Chicago Press, 1906

—— —— RTAE = Development of Religion and Thought in Ancient Egypt. New York: Scribner, 1912

Bristol, Lucius Moody, Social Adaptation: a Study in the Development of the Doctrine of Adaptation as a Theory of Social Progress (Harvard Economic Studies, vol. 14). Cambridge: Harvard University Press, 1915

Brunhes, Jean, Human Geography: an Attempt at a Positive Classification: Principles and Examples: Tr. by I. C. LeCompte, ed. by Isaiah Bowman and Richard Elwood Lodge. Chicago-New York: Rand, McNally, 1920

Causse, (Antonin), Les "pauvres" d'Israel (prophètes, psalmistes, messianistes). Strasbourg-Paris: Istra, 1922. See the review by Adolphe Lods in Revue de l'histoire des religions, 1922

Charles, R. H., Eschatology: a Critical Study of the Doctrine of a Future Life in Israel, Judaism, and Christianity. . . . The Jowett Lectures for 1898-99. London: Black, 1899

——— ——— Religious Development Between the Old and New Testaments. New York: Holt, n. d.

Dewey, John, and Tufts, James H., Ethics. New York: Holt, 1906

Erman, Adolf, LAE = The Literature of the Ancient Egyptians: Poems, Narratives, and Manuals of Instruction, from the Third and Second Millemia B.C. Tr. by Aylward M. Blackman. London: Methuen, 1927

Flight, John W., "The Nomadic Idea and Ideal in the Old Testament," JBL, 42 (1923), 158-226

Gressmann, Hugo, Altorientalische Texte und Bilder zum Alten Testament. 2 ed. Berlin-Leipzig: De Gruyter, 1926-27

——— ——— Ursprung der israelitisch-jüdischen Eschatologie (Forschungen zur Religion und Literatur des Alten und Neuen Testaments, 6). Göttingen: Vandenhoeck und Ruprecht, 1905

Hauck, Friedrich, Die Stellung des Urchristentums zu Arbeit und Geld (Beiträge zur Förderung christlicher Theologie, II, 3). Gütersloh: Bertelsmann, 1921

Hobhouse, L. T., Morals in Evolution: a Study in Comparative Ethics. New York: Holt, 1921

——— ——— Social Development: its Nature and conditions. London: Allen and Unwin, 1923

Hölscher, Gustav, Die Propheten: Untersuchungen zur Religionsgeschichte Israels. Leipzig: Hinrichs, 1914

Jastrow, Morris, The Civilization of Babylonia and Assyria: its Remains, Language, History, Religion, Commerce, Law, Art, and Literature. Philadelphia and London: Lippincott, 1915

——— ——— Hebrew and Babylonian Traditions. The Haskell Lectures, 1913. New York: Scribner, 1914

——— ——— Die Religion Babyloniens und Assyriens. 2 vols. in 3. Giessen: Ricker, 1905-12

Jeremias, Joachim, Jerusalem zur Zeit Jesu: kulturgeschichtliche Untersuchungen zur neutestamentlichen Zeitgeschichte. Leipzig: Pfeiffer, Teil I, Die wirtschaftliche Verhältnisse, 1923, Teil II A, Die sozialen Verhältnisse: Reich und Arm, n. d.

Klausner, Joseph, Jesus of Nazareth: his Life, Times, and Teaching. Tr. from the Original Hebrew by Herbert Danby. New York: Macmillan, 1925

Luckenbill, Daniel D., ARA = Ancient Records of Assyria and Babylonia. 2 vols. Chicago: The University of Chicago Press, 1926-27

Macalister, R. A. Stewart, The History of Civilization in Palestine. Cambridge: The University Press, 1912

McCown, Chester C., "Hebrew and Egyptian Apocalyptic Literature," HTR, 18 (1925), 357-411

—— —— The Promise of His Coming: a Historical Interpretation and Revaluation of the Idea of the Second Advent. New York: Macmillan, 1921

—— —— "The Wilderness of Judea and the Nomadic Ideal," Journal of Geography, 23 (1924), 333-49

Meyer, Eduard, Geschichte des Altertums. 2 ed., Stuttgart-Berlin: Cotta, 1907-

—— —— Die Israeliten und ihre Nachbarstämme: alttestamentliche Untersuchungen, Mit Beiträgen von Bernhard Luther. Halle a. S.: Niemeyer, 1906

—— —— Ursprung und Anfänge des Christentums. 3 vols. Stuttgart-Berlin: Cotta, 1921-23

Moffatt, James, The Holy Bible, Containing the Old and New Testaments, a New Translation. New York: Doran, 1926

Moulton, James Hope, Early Religious Poetry of Persia. Cambridge: The University Press, 1911

—— —— Early Zoroastrianism. The Hibbert Lectures, Second Series. London: Williams and Norgate, 1913

Olmstead, A. T., History of Assyria. New York: Scribner, 1923

Smith, Charles Ryder, The Bible Doctrine of Society in its Historical Evolution. Edinburgh: Clark, 1920

—— —— The Bible Doctrine of Work and Wealth in its Historical Development. London: Epworth Press, 1924. Both volumes contain much valuable matter, but they seem to me to overidealize the ideas of the Bible.

Smith, Sir George Adam, The Historical Geography of the Holy Land, especially in Relation to the History of Israel and of the Early Church. 4 ed. London: Hodder and Stoughton, 1896

—— —— Jerusalem: its Topography, Economics, and History from the Earliest Times to A. D. 70. 2 vols. London: Hodder and Stoughton, 1907-08

Smith, J. M. Powis, The Moral Life of the Hebrews. Chicago: The University of Chicago Press, 1928

Soares, Theodore Gerald, The Social Institutions and Ideals of the Bible: a Study of the Elements of Hebrew Life in their Development from the

Beginnings to the Time of Christ, and of the Social Teachings of the Prophets, of the Sages, and of Jesus. New York-Cincinnati: The Abingdon Press, 1915

Steuernagel, Carl, Lehrbuch der Einleitung in das Alte Testament. Tübingen: Mohr, 1912

Strack, Hermann L., and Billerbeck, Paul. Kommentar zum Neuen Testament aus Talmud und Midrasch. 3 vols. München: Beck, 1922-26

Thureau-Dangin, F., Die Sumerischen und Akkadischen Königsinschriften (Vorderasiatische Bibliothek, Bd. I, Abt. 1). Leipzig: Hinrichs, 1907.

Todd, Arthur James, Theories of Social Progress: a Critical Study of the Attempts to Formulate the Conditions of Human Advance. New York: Macmillan, 1922

Wallis, Louis, Sociological Study of the Bible. Chicago: The University of Chicago Press, 1912

Wallis, Wilson D., Messiahs: Christian and Pagan. Boston: Badger, 1918. An anthropologist's collection of parallels from varied sources.

Zimmern, Heinrich, and Winckler, H., KAT = Die Keilinschriften und das Alte Testament von Eberhard Schrader, 3 Aufl. neubearbeitet. Berlin: Reuther und Reichard, 1902-03

CHAPTER I IS THERE A SOCIAL GOSPEL?

SECTIONS I AND II

Cone, Orello, Rich and Poor in the New Testament: a Study of the Primitive-Christian Doctrine of Earthly Possessions. New York: Macmillan, 1902. By far the most consistent discussion, but it overemphasizes the eschatological point of view and ends by adopting a spiritualizing interpretation of Jesus' teachings.

Driver, Samuel Rolles, art. "Poor," in Hastings, DB, IV, pp. 19 f.

Expositor's Greek Testament, ed. by W. Robertson Nicholl. New York: Dodd, Mead, 1897

Loisy, Alfred, Les évangiles synoptiques. 2 vols., Ceffonds: pub. by the author, 1908, 1914

Montefiore, Claude G., The Synoptic Gospels, ed. with Introduction and Commentary. 2 vols. London: Macmillan, 1909; 2 ed., 1917

Peake, Arthur S., ed., Commentary on the Bible. New York: Nelson, 1919

Votaw, Clyde Weber, art. "Sermon on the Mount," Hastings, DB., V, pp. 1-45

SECTION III

On the history of recent thought on the social question in relation to Christianity see

Church and Industrial Reconstruction, The, by the Committee on the War and the Religious Outlook. New York: Association Press, 1921, esp. the "Selected Bibliography," Appendix II, pp. 273-86

Mathews, Shailer, art. "The Development of Social Christianity in America," in Religious Thought in the Last Quarter-Century, ed. by Gerald Burney Smith. Chicago: The University of Chicago Press, 1927, pp. 228-39

Fiebig, Paul, War Jesus Rebell? Eine historische Untersuchung zu Karl Kautsky, Der Ursprung des Christentums, mit einem Anhang: Jesus und die Arbeit. Gotha: Perthes, 1920

Naumann, Gottfried, Sozialismus und Religion in Deutschland: Bericht und Kritik. Leipzig: Hinrichs, 1921

Rauschenbusch, Walter, Christianizing the Social Order. New York: Macmillan, 1912, esp. pp. 1-39, "The Social Awakening of the Churches"

Soziale Geist in der evangelischen Kirche der Gegenwart, der, und die evangelisch-soziale Arbeit im Freistaat Sachsen. 2. erweitete Auflage, hersgg. vom kirchlichen Ausschuss für soziale Arbeit in den Bezirken Zittau und Löbau, Gerhard Bemmann. Herrnhut i. Sa., 1927, see pp. 212 ff., "Übersicht über die neuere soziale Literatur von kirchlicher Seite"

Ward, Harry F., The Gospel for a Working World, New York: Missionary Education Movement, 1918, esp. "Bibliography," pp. 250-53

Weinel, Heinrich, and Widgery, Alban G., Jesus in the Nineteenth Century and After. Edinburgh: Clark, 1914, esp. pp. 146-284

SECTION IV

Recent volumes discussing Eschatology from various points of view:

Case, Shirley Jackson, The Millennial Hope. Chicago: The University of Chicago Press, 1918

Dougall, Lily, and Emmett, Cyril W., The Lord of Thought: a Study of the Problems which Confronted Jesus Christ and the Solutions He Offered. New York: Doran: 1922

McCown, Chester C., The Promise of His Coming

Rall, Harris Franklin, Modern Premillennialism and the Christian Hope. New York-Cincinnati: The Abingdon Press, 1920

Schweitzer, Albert, The Quest of the Historical Jesus: a Critical Study of its Progress from Reimarus to Wrede. Tr. by W. Montgomery, with a Preface by F. C. Burkitt. London: Black, 1910. Gave the eschatological problem a new prominence in theological controversy.

"Symposium on Eschatology," arts. by various American scholars, JBL, 41 (1922), 1-204

SECTION V

Peisker, M., "Troeltschs Darstellung der Soziallehren des Evangeliums," Theologische Studien und Kritiken, 1922, H. 1-2, Sonderheft "Neutestamentliche Forschungen," pp. 1-54

Troeltsch, Ernst, Gesammelte Schriften, vol. I, Die Soziallehren der christlichen Kirchen. Tübingen: Mohr, 1912

SECTION VI

See the works of Barnes, Bristol, and Todd in the General Bibliography

Grant, Frederick Clifton, "Method in Studying Jesus' Social Teaching," SEC, pp. 239-281

Langlois, Charles Victor, and Seignobos, Charles, Introduction to the Study of History. Tr. by G. G. Berry. New York: Holt, 1898

Scott, Ernest Findlay, "The Limitations of the Historical Method," SEC, pp. 3-18

Teggart, Frederick J., The Processes of History. New Haven: Yale University Press, 1918

——— ——— The Theory of History. New Haven: Yale University Press, 1925

CHAPTER II THE PHYSICAL FACTORS IN HEBREW HISTORY

See the works of Brunhes, J. Jeremias, and Sir George Adam Smith in the General Bibliography above

Febvre, Lucien, and Battailon, Lionel, A Geographical Introduction to History. Tr. by E. G. Mountford and J. H. Paxton. London: Kegan Paul, Trench, Trubner, 1925. See the criticism by Carl O. Sauer, Morphology of Landscape, pp. 50 f.

Koller, Arnim Hajman, The Theory of Environment: an Outline of the History of the Idea of *Milieu* and its Present Status. Pt. I. Dissertation, University of Chicago. Menasha, Wisconsin: Banta, 1918

McCown, Chester C., "Climate and Religion in Palestine," JR, VI (1927), 520-39

Passarge, S., Grundzüge der gesetzmässigen Characterentwickelung der Völker auf religiösen und naturwissenschaftlichen Grundlagen und in Abhängigkeit von der Landschaft. Berlin: Borntragen, 1925

Sauer, Carl O. The Morphology of Landscape (University of California Publications in Geography, II, 2). Berkeley: The University of California Press, 1925

Sawyer, E. R., A Review of the Agricultural Situation in Palestine. Department of Agriculture and Fisheries, Palestine (Introduction dated March 16, 1922)

Schwöbel, Valentin, "Die geographischen Verhältnisse des Menschen in der Wüste Juda," Palästinajahrbuch, ed. G. Dalman, III (1907), 72-132

SECTION II

Blanckenhorn, Max, Syrien, Arabien, und Mesopotamien (Handbuch der regionalen Geographie, V, 4). Heidelberg: Steinmann und Wilckens, 1914

—— —— "Kurzer Abriss der Geologie Palästinas," ZDPV, 35 (1912), 113-39

SECTION III

Exner, Felix M., "Zum Klima von Palästina," ZDPV, 23 (1910), 107-64

Hahn, Julius, Handbuch der Klimatologie, vol. III, Klimatographie. Stuttgart: J. Engelhorns Nachfolger, 1911, pp. 90-99

Hilderscheid, Heinrich, "Die Niederschlagsverhältnisse Palästinas in alter und neuer Zeit," ZDPV, 25 (1912), 1-105

Huntington, Ellsworth, Civilization and Climate. 3 ed. New Haven: Yale University Press, 1924

—— —— The Pulse of Progress, including a Sketch of Jewish History, with a Chapter on Climatic Changes by G. C. Simpson, Director of the British Meteorological Service (Chap. VIII, pp. 109-20, from The Nineteenth Century and After, Jan., 1926). New York-London: Scribner, 1926. In addition to the highly debatable theory of climatic changes here defended, the "sketch of Jewish history" seems to me to overemphasize the racial exclusiveness of Judaism.

—— —— World Power and Evolution. New Haven: Yale University Press, 1919

—— —— and Cushing, Sumner W., Principles of Human Geography. New York: John Wiley, 1921

Ward, Robert De Courcy, Climate Considered Especially in Relation to Man. 2 ed. New York: Putnam, 1918

SECTION IV

See the Bible Dictionaries and the works of J. Jeremias, J. Klausner, and Sir George Adam Smith cited in the General Bibliography

CHAPTER III THE FATHERS ACCORDING TO THE FLESH

Albright, W. F., JAOS, 48 (1928), 183 ff., rev. of A. Jirku, *Die Wanderungen der Hebräer in 3. u. 2. Jahrtausend v. Chr.*

Barton, George Aaron, Archaeology and the Bible, pp. 17-138

Boas, Franz, The Mind of Primitive Man. New York: Macmillan, 1913, chap. I, "Racial Prejudices"

Hall, H. R., The Ancient History of the Near East. 3 ed. London: Methuen, 1916

Huntington, Ellsworth, The Character of Races. New York: Scribner, 1924
——— ——— "The Biological Antecedents of Jesus," Scribner's Magazine, 80 (July, 1926), 53-59. Conforms too closely to the views of the biblical writers.
Kroeber, A. L., Anthropology. New York: Harcourt, Brace, 1923, pp. 34-86
Macalister, R. A. Stewart, History of Civilization in Palestine
Margoliouth, D. S., The Relation of the Arabs and Israelites Prior to the Rise of Islam (British Academy, Schweich Lectures, 1921). London: Oxford University Press, 1924, esp. chaps. I and II
Vincent, Hughes, Canaan d'apres l'exploration récente. Paris: Victor Lecoffre, 1907

SECTION II

Baudissin Festschrift = Abhandlungen zur semitischen Religionskunde und Sprachwissenschraft W. W. Grafen von Baudissin . . . überreicht, hersgg. von W. Frankenberg und F. Kücheler (ZAW, Beiheft 33). Giessen: Töpelmann, 1918
Albright, W. F., "Palestine in the Earliest Historical Period," JPOS II (1922), 110-34
——— ——— "A Colony of Cretan Mercenaries on the Coast of the Negeb," JPOS, I (1921), 187-94
Barton, George Aaron, A Sketch of Semitic Origins, Social and Religious. New York: Macmillan, 1902
Clay, Albert T., The Empire of the Amorites. New Haven: Yale University Press, 1919
Cook, Stanley A., CAH, I, chap. V, pp. 181-237, "The Semites"
——— ——— CAH, II, chap. XIII, pp. 296-351, "Syria and Palestine in the Light of the External Evidence"
Hall, H. R., CAH, II, Chap. XII, pp. 275-95, "The Keftians, Philistines, and Other Peoples of the Levant"
Macalister, R. A. Stewart, The Excavation of Gezer 1902-05 and 1907-09. 3 vols. Published for the Committee of the Palestine Exploration Fund by John Murray, London, 1912
Meyer, Eduard, Geschichte des Altertums, I, 2, pp. 347-97
Myres, John L., CAH, I, pp. 31-41, "Palaeolithic Man in the South and East"
——— ——— CAH, I, pp. 89-93, Culture of the Eastern Mediterranean Lands
Vincent, Hughes, Jérusalem sous terre. London: Cox, 1911

SECTION III

Burney, C. F., Israel's Settlement in Canaan (British Academy, Schweich Lectures, 1917). 2 ed. London: Oxford University Press, 1919

Cook, Stanley A., CAH, II, chap. XIV, pp. 352-406, "The Rise of Israel"

—— —— CAH, III, chaps. XVII-XX, pp. 354-500, History of Israel from the Settlement to the Exile

Fishberg, Maurice, The Jews: a Study of Race and Environment. London: Walter Scott, 1911

Gadd, Cyril J., The Fall of Nineveh: the Newly Discovered Babylonian Chronicle, No. 21,901 in the British Museum: London: British Museum, 1923

Macalister, R. A. Stewart, The Philistines: their History and Civilization (British Academy, Schweich Lectures, 1911). London: Oxford University Press, 1913

—— —— CAH, III, chap. XVI, pp. 333-53, "The Topography of Jerusalem"

Meyer, Eduard, and Luther, Bernhard, Die Israeliten

Olmstead, A. T., The History of Assyria

Salaman, R. N., "What has Become of the Philistines?" QSPEF, 1925, pp. 37-45, 68-79

SECTION IV

Bevan, Edwyn, Jerusalem under the High Priests. London: Arnold, 1912

Cook, Stanley A., CAH, VI, chap. VII, pp. 167-99, "The Inauguration of Judaism"

Lightly, J. W., Jewish Sects and Parties in the Time of Jesus. London: Epworth Press, 1925, pp. 133-265

Montgomery, James Alan, The Samaritans, the Earliest Jewish Sect; their History, Theology, and Literature. Philadelphia: Winston, 1907

Moore, George Foot, Judaism in the First Three Centuries of the Christian Era, the Age of the Tannaim. 2 vols. Cambridge: Harvard University Press, 1927

Schürer, Emil, Geschichte des jüdischen Volkes in Zeitalter Jesu Christi. 4 ed. 3 vols. Leipzig: Hinrichs, 1901-09

—— —— A History of the Jewish People in the Time of Jesus Christ. Tr. by Sophia Taylor and Peter Christie (from the second German edition). 5 vols. New York: Scribner, 1891

CHAPTER IV ISRAEL'S SPIRITUAL ANCESTRY

See the Bibliography for chap. III, and the General Bibliography, esp. the works of Breasted, Gressmann, Meyer, Olmstead, and Zimmern.

Albright, W. F., "Egypt and the Early History of the Negeb," JPOS, IV (1924), 131-61

Gressmann, Hugo, "Foreign Influences in Hebrew Prophecy," JTS, 27 (1926), 241-54

Meek, Theophile James, "The Interpenetration of Cultures as Illustrated by the Character of the Old Testament Literature," JR, VII (1927), 244-62

SECTION II

Wardle, W. Lansdell, Israel and Babylon. The Twenty-fifth Hartley Lecture. 2 ed. London: Holborn Publishing House, 1925. One of the latest of innumerable books on the subject. See the review by G. R. Driver in JTS, 27 (1926), 412 ff.

SECTION III

Breasted, James Henry, A History of the Ancient Egyptians. New York: Scribner, 1908

——— ——— A History of Egypt from the Earliest Times to the Persian Conquest. 2 ed. New York: Scribner, 1909

Budge, E. A. Wallis, Facsimiles of the Hieratic Papyri in the British Museum. . . . Series II. London: The British Museum, 1923

——— ——— The Teachings of Amen-em-apt, son of Kanecht. . . . London: Martin Hopkinson, 1924

Deissmann, Adolf, Licht vom Osten: das neue Testament und die neuentdeckten Texte der hellenistisch-römischen Welt. 4 ed. Tübingen: Mohr, 1923

Hall, H. R., CAH, I, pp. 577-84, "Interrelation with Babylonia"

Langdon, S., JEA, VII (1921), 133-53, "The Early Chronology of Sumer and Egypt and the Similarities in their Culture"

Lefebvre, Gustave, Revue Biblique, 31 (1922), 481-88, "Égyptiens et Hebreux"

McCown, Chester C., "Hebrew and Egyptian Apocalyptic Literature," HTR, 18, 357-441

Mace, A. B., Annals of Archaeology and Anthropology, University of Liverpool, IX (1922), 3-26, "The Influence of Egypt on Hebrew Literature"

Peet, T. Eric, Egypt and the Old Testament. Liverpool: University Press of Liverpool, 1922

Smith, Sidney, JEA, VIII (1922), 41-44, "The Relations of Marduk, Ashur, and Osiris"

SECTION IV

On Mazdian influence, in addition to the works cited in the text, see

Böklen, Ernst, Die Verwandschaft der jüdisch-christlichen mit der parsischen Eschatologie. Göttingen: Vandenhoeck und Ruprecht, 1902

Bousset, Wilhelm, Die Religion des Judentums im späthellenistischen Zeitalter. 3. Aufl., hersgg. von H. Gressmann. Tübingen: Mohr, 1926, esp. pp. 53-96, 469-524

Carter, George William, Zoroastrianism and Judaism. Boston: Badger, 1918

Maynard, J. A., "Judaism and Mazdayasna: a Study in Dissimilarities," JBL, 44 (1925), pp. 163-70. Against Jewish borrowing from Mazdaism.

Söderblom, Nathan, La vie future d'après le mazdéisme à la lumière des croyances parallèles dans les autres religions. . . . Angers: Burdin, 1901

As to Greek influence on Judaism and early Christianity, out of a large and growing literature, see the following:

Bentwich, Norman, Hellenism. Philadelphia: The Jewish Publication Society, 1919, esp. chap. III

Bousset, Wilhelm, above

Fairweather, William, Jesus and the Greeks, or Early Christianity in the Tideway of Hellenism. Edinburgh: Clark, 1924

Gilbert, George Holley, Greek Thought in the New Testament. New York: Macmillan, 1928, esp. pp. 11-33, 101-40

Jackson, F. J. Foakes, and Lake, Kirsopp, The Beginnings of Christianity. Pt. I, The Acts of the Apostles, vol. I, Prolegomena I, The Jewish, Gentile, and Christian Backgrounds. London: Macmillan, 1920, esp. pp. 1-168

CHAPTER V THE DAWN OF DEMOCRACY

See the works by Causse, Flight, Sir George Adam Smith, and Wallis, in the General Bibliography.

Bertholet, Alfred, Die Stellung der Israeliten and der Juden zu den Fremden. Freiburg i. B. und Leipzig. Mohr, 1896

Blunt, A. W. F., Israel Before Christ: an Account of Social and Religious Development in the Old Testament. London: Oxford University Press, 1924. An excellent brief account.

Kent, Charles Foster, "The Birth of Democracy," Yale Review, IX (1919), 131-42

SECTION II

See also the works by Bristol and J. M. P. Smith in the General Bibliography.

Robinson, Theodore H., Prophecy and the Prophets. New York: Scribner, 1923, pp. 1-27

SECTION III

Gressmann, Hugo, Die älteste Geschichtsschreibung und Prophetie Israels von Samuel bis Amos und Hosea) (Die Schriften des Alten Testaments, II, 1). Göttingen: Vandenhoeck und Ruprecht, 1921

Montefiore, Claude G., Lectures on the Origin and Growth of the Hebrew Religion as Illustrated by the Religion of the Ancient Hebrews (The Hibbert Lectures, 1892). 3 ed. London: Williams and Norgate, 1897

Renan, Joseph Ernest, History of the People of Israel. 3 vols. Boston: Roberts Brothers, 1891-92

Schmidt, Hans, Die grossen Propheten (Die Schriften des Alten Testaments, II, 2). 2 ed. Göttingen: Vandenhoeck und Ruprecht, 1923

CHAPTER VI POLITICS AND RELIGION

Barton, George Aaron, The Religion of Israel. New York: Macmillan, 1918

Buttenwieser, Moses, The Prophets of Israel from the Eighth to the Fifth Century: their Faith and their Message. New York: Macmillan, 1914

Fuller, Leslie Elmer, The Historical and Religious Significance of the Reign of Manasseh. Leipzig: Drugelin, 1912

Hölscher, Gustav, Die Propheten: Untersuchungen zur Religionsgeschichte Israels. Leipzig: Hinrichs, 1914

Micklem, Nathaniel, Prophecy and Eschatology. London: Allen and Unwin, 1926, esp. pp. 13-82, 240-44

Robinson, Theodore H., Prophecy and the Prophets. New York: Scribner, 1923, esp. pp. 28-49

Smith, Henry Preserved, The Religion of Israel: an Historical Study. New York: Scribner, 1914

Smith, J. M. Powis, The Prophets and their Times. Chicago: The University of Chicago Press, 1925

CHAPTER VII THE RECOVERY OF PARADISE

SECTION I

See in the General Bibliography the works of Barton, Gressmann, Jastrow, Luckenbill, Olmstead, Thureau-Dangin, and Zimmern-Winckler, also the Bibliographies for chaps. III and IV

SECTION II

See in the General Bibliography the works of Breasted, Erman, and Gressmann, and the Bibliographies for chaps. III and IV

SECTION III

See the Bibliography for chap. IV, sec. IV

Meyer, Eduard, Ursprung und Anfänge des Christentums. 3 vols. Stuttgart-Berlin: Cotta, 1921-23, esp. vol. II.

SECTION IV

See the Bibliography on chap. I, sec. IV, and works by Charles and Gressmann in the General Bibliography

Balz, Albert George Adam, and Pott, W. S. A., The Basis of Social Theory. New York: Knopf, 1924

Dietrich, E. L., Schub Sch'but. Die Endzeitliche Widerherstellung bei den Propheten. Beiheft zur ZAW, 40, 1925

Torrey, Charles Cutler, "Outcroppings of the Jewish Messianic Hope," SEC, pp. 285-310

Volz, Paul, Jüdische Eschatologie von Daniel bis Akiba. Tübingen-Leipzig: Mohr, 1903

CHAPTER VIII THE PERFECT PRINCE

SECTION I

See the Bibliography for chap. VII, sec. II

SECTION II

See the Bibliography for chap. VII, sec. I

Harper, Robert Francis, The Code of Hammurabi. . . . Chicago: The University of Chicago Press, 1904

Jeremias, Alfredt, art., "Ages of the World (Babylonian)," ERE, I, pp. 183-87

King, Leonard William, A History of Babylon from the Foundation of the Monarchy to the Persian Conquest. London: Chatto and Windus, 1915

SECTION III

See the Bibliography for chap. VII, sec. IV

Messel, Nils, Der Menschensohn in den Bilderreden des Henoch. Beiheft zur ZAW, 35, 1922. Takes a view contrary to that here adopted.

CHAPTER IX THE HOPE OF THE POOR

SECTION I

See the Bibliography for chap. VIII, sec II

King, Leonard William, A History of Sumer and Akkad. . . . New York: Stokes, 1910

SECTION II

See the Bibliography for chap. VIII, sec. I

SECTION III

Cooke, G. A., A Textbook of North-Semitic Inscriptions. . . . Oxford: Clarendon Press, 1903

SECTION IV

See the Bibliography for chap. VII, sec. III

SECTION V

Significant literature on the "poor" in the Psalms and other post-exilic Jewish literature:

Baudissin, Wolf Wilhelm Grafen, "Die alttestamentliche Religion und die Armen" (Vortrag, gehalten im Theologischen Studentenverein zu Berlin), Preussische Jahrbücher, 149 (Juli bis Sept., 1912), 193-231; references to earlier literature, pp. 194 f.

Causse, (Antonin), Les "pauvres" d'Israel (prophètes, psalmistes, messianistes. Strasbourg-Paris: Istra, 1922. See the review by Adolphe Lods, Revue de l'histoire de religions, 1922

Driver, S. R., art., "Poor," Hastings, DB, III, pp. 19 f.

Loeb, Isidore, "La littérature des pauvres dans la Bible," Rev. des études juives, 20 (1920), 161-98; 21 (1890), 1-42, 161-206; 23 (1891), 1-31, 161-93, with additions pub. Paris: Cerf, 1892. See review by X. Koenig, in Rev. de l'histoire des religions, 29 (1894), 340-44

Patterson, A. C., art., "Poor," EB, III, cols. 3808-11

Rahlfs, Alfred, עני und ענו in den Psalmen. Göttingen: Dieterich, 1892

Abrahams, Israel, Studies in Pharisaism and the Gospels. Cambridge: The University Press, First Series, 1917, Second Series, 1924

Katz, Mordecai, Protection of the Weak in the Talmud (Columbia University Oriental Studies, 24). New York: Columbia University Press, 1925

McCown, Chester C., "The Beatitudes in the Light of Ancient Ideals," JBL, 46 (1927), 50-61

Moore, George Foot, Judaism, see Bibliography, chap. III, sec. IV

CHAPTER X THE SON OF DAVID AND THE SON OF MAN

SECTIONS I TO III

Grant, Frederic Clifton, The Economic Background of the Gospels. London: Oxford University Press, 1926

Guthe, Hermann, Die griechisch-römischen Städte des Ostjordanlandes (Das Land der Bibel, II, 5.) Leipzig: Hinrichs, 1918

Jeremias, Joachim, Jerusalem zur Zeit Jesu (see General Bibliography)

Mahaffy, John Pentland, The Progress of Hellenism in Alexander's Empire. Chicago: The University of Chicago Press, 1905

——— ——— The Silver Age of the Greek World. Chicago: The University of Chicago Press, 1911

Mathews, Shailer, The History of New Testament Times in Palestine, 175 B.C.—70 A.D. Rev. ed. New York: Macmillan, 1910

Meyer, Eduard, Kleine Schriften zur Geschichtstheorie und zur wirtschaftlichen und politischen Geschichte des Altertums. Halle a. S.: Niemeyer, 1910; Kleine Schriften, II, 1924

Simkhovitch, Vladimir G., Toward the Understanding of Jesus and Other Historical Studies. New York: Macmillan, 1921

SECTION IV

See the Bibliography for chap. III, sec. III.

Herford, R. Travers, Pharisaism: its Aim and Method. New York: Putnam, 1912

——— ——— The Pharisees. London: Allen and Unwin, 1924

Leszynsky, Rudolf, Die Sadducäer. Berlin: Mayer und Müller, 1912

SECTION V

See the Bibliography for chap. VII, sec. IV

Bosworth, Edward Increase, The Life and Teachings of Jesus According to the First Three Gospels. New York: Macmillan, 1924

Case, Shirley Jackson, "The Rise of Christian Messianism," SEC, pp. 313-32

Fiebig, Paul, Das Vaterunser: Ursprung, Sinn and Bedeutung des christlichen Hauptgebetes. Gütersloh: Bertelsmann, 1927

Klausner, Joseph, Jesus of Nazareth. (See General Bibliography)

Patton, Carl S., "Did Jesus Call Himself the Son of Man," JR, II (1922), 501-11

Peake, Arthur S., "The Messiah and the Son of Man," in Bulletin of the John Rylands Library, VIII, 1 (Jan., 1924), also separate. Manchester: The University Press, 1924

"Symposium on Eschatology," JBL, 41 (1922), 1-204

Warschauer, Joseph, The Historical Life of Christ, with a Preface by F. C. Burkitt. London: Unwin, 1927

CHAPTER XI THE SHEPHERDS AND THE MAGI

See the Bibliography for the previous chapter

Abrahams, Israel, see the Bibliography for chap. IX, sec. V

Boehmer, Julius, "Die erste Seligpreisung," JBL, 45 (1926), 298-304. A convincing interpretation of "poor in spirit," which does not, however, prove that Matthew was right.

INDEX OF PASSAGES DISCUSSED OR QUOTED

INDEX OF PASSAGES DISCUSSED OR QUOTED

THE OLD TESTAMENT

APOCRYPHA AND PSEUDEPIGRAPHA

RABBINICAL WRITINGS

THE NEW TESTAMENT

GENERAL INDEX OF NAMES AND SUBJECTS

GENERAL INDEX OF NAMES AND SUBJECTS

Q

R

S

A NOTE ON THE TYPE IN
WHICH THIS BOOK IS SET

The type in which this book has been set (on the Linotype) is Old Style No. 1. In design, the face is of English origin, by MacKellar, Smith and Jordan, and bears the workmanlike quality and freedom from "frills" characteristic of English old styles in the period prior to the introduction of the "modern" letter. It gives an evenly textured page that may be read with a minimum of fatigue. Old Style No. 1 was one of the first faces designed and cut by the Linotype Company, and it is still one of the most popular.

SET UP AND ELECTROTYPED BY THE HADDON CRAFTSMEN, CAMDEN, N. J. · PRINTED AND BOUND BY H. WOLFF ESTATE, NEW YORK · PAPER MANUFACTURED BY S. D. WARREN CO., BOSTON ·